Developing Professional Practice 0–7

Sonia Blandford
Teach First, Institute of Education (London), Brunel University,
University of Oxford and University of Chichester

Catherine Knowles
Canterbury Christ Church University

Longman
is an imprint of

Harlow, England • London • New York • Boston • San Francisco • Toronto • Sydney • Singapore • Hong Kong
Tokyo • Seoul • Taipei • New Delhi • Cape Town • Madrid • Mexico City • Amsterdam • Munich • Paris • Milan

Pearson Education Limited
Edinburgh Gate
Harlow
Essex CM20 2JE
England

and Associated Companies throughout the world

Visit us on the World Wide Web at:
www.pearsoned.co.uk

First published 2009

ISBN: 978-1-4058-4114-6

British Library Cataloguing-in-Publication Data
A catalogue record for this book is available from the British Library

Library of Congress Cataloging-in-Publication Data
Blandford, Sonia.
   Developing professional practice, 0–7 / Sonia Blandford and Catherine Knowles.
     p. cm.
   ISBN 978-1-4058-4114-6 (pbk.)
   1. Early childhood education – Handbooks, manuals, etc.   2. Early childhood educators – Training of – Handbooks, manuals, etc.   I. Knowles, Catherine.   II. Title.
   LB1139.23.B58 2009
   372.21—dc22

                                                                        2009020713

10 9 8 7 6 5 4 3 2 1
13 12 11 10 09

Typeset in 9.75/12pt Giovanni Book by 35
Printed by Ashford Colour Press Ltd., Gosport

The publisher's policy is to use paper manufactured from sustainable forests.

£25·99

w/D

Developing Professional Practice 0–7

Visit the *Developing Professional Practice* Companion
Website at **www.pearsoned.co.uk/blandford** to find
valuable **student** learning material including:

- Podcasts featuring interviews with practitioners
- Videos with associated activities and questions
- Interactive tutorials for each chapter, including weblinks,
  questions and activities to take your thinking further
- Self-study questions to test and extend your knowledge
- A glossary of all the key terms in the book
- Extra cases studies.

The *Developing Professional Practice* series provides a thoroughly comprehensive and cutting edge guide to developing the necessary knowledge, skills and understanding for working within the 0–7, 7–14 or 14–19 age ranges. Each of the three titles offers a genuinely accessible and engaging introduction to supporting the education of babies to young adults. Discussion of current developments in theory, policy and research is combined with guidance on the practicalities of working with each age group. Numerous examples of real practice are included throughout each text.

The *Developing Professional Practice* titles each provide a complete resource for developing professional understanding and practice that will be invaluable for all those involved with the education of children from birth to 19 years.

Titles in the series:

Blandford & Knowles, *Developing Professional Practice 0–7*

Wilson & Kendall-Seatter, *Developing Professional Practice 7–14*

Armitage, Donovan, Flanagan & Poma, *Developing Professional Practice 14–19*

Brief Contents

Contents

This book is dedicated to Bethany, Mia, Elizabeth and Anna . . .

Preface

This book forms the first in a series aimed at developing professional understanding and practice for those involved with the education of children from birth to 19 years. The book focuses on practice and learning relating to the first seven years of a child's life, arguably the most important in setting the parameters for subsequent professional engagement with learners in all settings.

The book seeks to inform and develop a greater understanding of the early years context; written during a period of unprecedented change in the sector the challenge to the reader is how to interpret and apply the knowledge and experience conveyed in each section of the text. This will, in part, be determined by the setting in which you are employed and the age of the children with whom you enjoy working. The book embraces babies, toddlers and young children; technically this includes birth to five, Foundation Stage and Key Stage 1, though the text is not framed in this way.

The text speaks to those developing their professional practice whether as students or those employed in the early years sector in the broadest sense. This might include those of you who are developing your practice as childminders, nursery practitioners, foster parents, adopters, nannies, au pairs or teachers. Much of the guidance is applicable to the widest of age ranges practitioners will encounter in their professional lives, that of birth to seven years old. Such is the significance of this period in a child's life that the government has created a host of professional qualifications and standards related to every facet of professional life. This book relates to the Early Years Professional Standards (EYPS) and makes reference to the National Professional Qualification for Integrated Centre Leadership (NPQICL), essentially because these are the key qualifications needed for those working in more than one of the early years settings.

Readers are encouraged to reflect on their own experience as they consider each of the elements of practice which focus on learning in the early years sector. Part 1 presents the key influences on learning in the early years sector beginning with an introduction to the proliferation of policies emanating from government departments and agencies in recent years which has led to the legitimisation of practice and the raising of professional standards in the sector. Part 1 also considers communities of learners, values, development of learning and learners as individuals.

Part 2 sets learning practices within the framework of personalised learning. Founded on the effective collaboration of the practitioner, child and his/her parents/carers, where teaching is adapted to meet the learning needs of the individual child, it is strongly endorsed by the government, and many researchers and educationalists. Part 2 considers how personalised learning helps practitioners to support children in the development of the right behaviours/dispositions for learning and how Information Communication Technology and Assessment for Learning contribute to this process.

Part 3 focuses on enhancing learning practice primarily through the Continuing Professional Development of those involved in children's learning, development and well-being during the Early Years Foundation Stage and Key Stage 1. By considering the learning community, the collaboration of all those involved, including practitioners, children, parents, governors, professionals from the social and health services and those from the wider local community, Part 3 addresses the importance of practitioners' personal professional development for raising children's aspirations and achievements.

Part 4 considers key aspects of developing professional practice which will influence learning in the future. Effective leadership is fundamental to early years practice, raising standards and improving outcomes for all children. The collaborative approach which is beginning to emerge as the favoured model within the early years sector means that all members of the learning community share in the day-to-day leadership and management of the setting. In exploring the concept of 'distributed leadership', Part 4 shows how all those who work within the setting contribute to the development of its culture, the day-to-day and longer-term planning for children's learning and shape the partnerships which develop within the setting and beyond.

The book has many pedagogical features to help guide the reader, each element informed by research and practice. We invite you to use these in full; in this way you will extend your knowledge whilst developing as practitioners who will make a significant impact on all the children you meet. Focus on the chapter objectives presented as questions for you to consider and respond as you journey through the book. Utilise the pedagogic tools to encourage and develop learning in yourself and others. Engage with 'Connect and Extend' features and find out more from the texts suggested in each chapter. *Developing Professional Practice 0–7* aims to encourage you to experience and read more than we are able to present between the covers of this book. To this end a companion website has been developed **www.pearsoned.co.uk/blandford** which will be updated on a regular basis enabling you to engage further in developing your knowledge and understanding of the sector whilst encouraging you to create a community of practice for yourself and colleagues.

The book has been written in collaboration with Canterbury Christ Church University colleagues who have significant experience in the early years sector, developing professional practice and educational leadership; we are grateful to Professor Tricia David, Dr Sacha Powell, Kathy Goouch, Angela Nurse, Dr Viv Wilson and Peter Dorman for the significant contribution they have made to the creation of the text.

We are indebted to Rosemary Davis, Beth Buckley, Carolyn Silberfield, Sue Robson, Sally Palmer, Greg Parker and Mary Briggs who have given of their time freely, reflecting their commitment and enthusiasm for the sector in which they practise. A sector which is growing in the knowledge practitioners generate and share and the range of opportunities presented to practitioners as professionals responsible for the development of learning among the most precious in our community, children from birth to seven.

Acknowledgements

The authors would like to thank Sarah Battersby of Scarcroft Green Nursery, Mark Harrison of St Martin's Ampleforth, Fransis Rehal of Millmead Surestart Children's Centre and Brigitte Thibault of Lille Catholic University for their time and contribution in the course of writing this book.

The publishers would like to thank

Greg Parker, Edge Hill University
Sally Palmer, Head of Early Years, University of Gloucester
Mary Briggs, University of Warwick
Carolyn Silberfeld, Cass School of Education, University of East London
Sue Robson, Principal Lecturer and Head of Early Childhool Studies, Roehampton University
Beth Buckley, Senior Lecturer in Education, Liverpool John Moores University
Professor Emeritus Rosemary Davis, Visiting Professor, Oxford Brookes University, Westminster Institute of Ecucation

Publisher's acknowledgements

We are grateful to the following for permission to reproduce copyright material:

Figures

Figure 6.1 with kind permission from Springer Science+Business Media: *Education and Information Technologies*, ICT in the classroom: is doing more important than knowing? Vol. 9, No. 1, pp. 37–45 (Jadeskog, G. and Nissen, J. March 2004) © 2004 Kluwer Academic Publishers. Figures 11.1, 11.2, 11.3, 11.4, 16.1, 16.2, 18.2, 18.3, 18.4 and 18.5 from *Middle Leadership in Schools: Harmonising Leadership and Learning*, Pearson Education Ltd (Blandford, S. 2006); Figure 11.2 adapted from *Model for Self Evaluation*, Manchester LEA (1986); Figure 17.1 from *Championing Children*, 2nd ed., DfES Publications (DfES 2006) p. 4, Crown Copyright material is reproduced with permission under the terms of the Click-Use Licence; Figure 18.1 from *Managing International Schools*, Routledge (Blandford, S. and Shaw, M. (eds) 2001) p. 54; Figure 18.6 from *Middle Management in Schools: How to Harmonise Managing and Teaching for an Effective School*, Pearson Education Ltd (Blandford, S. 1997); Figure 19.2 from A Theory of Human Motivation, *Psychological Review*, 50(4), pp. 370–96 (Maslow, A.H. 1943), American Psychological Association.

Tables

Table 1.2 from *Every Child Matters: Change for Children*, DfES Publications (DfES 2004) p. 9, Crown Copyright material is reproduced with permission under the terms of the Click-Use Licence; Table 2.1 from *International Journal of Early Years Education*, by Keyes, C. Copyright 2002 by Taylor & Francis Informa UK Ltd – Journals. Reproduced with permission of Taylor & Francis Informa UK Ltd – Journals in the format Textbook via Copyright Clearance Center; Table 2.1 adapted from Contemporary perspectives on the roles of mothers and teachers, *More Talks with Teachers*, ERIC Clearinghouse on Elementary and Early Childhood Education (Katz, L.G. 1984), pp. 1–26; Table 8.1 from *Developing Thinking and Understanding in Young Children: An Introduction for Students*, Routledge (Robson, S. 2006) p. 95; Table on page 199 from *Observing and Assessing for the Foundation Stage Profile* Hodder and Stoughton (Hutchin, V. 2003). Reprinted by permission of John Murray (Publishers) Ltd; Table on page 362 from *Observing Children-Building the Profile* (2005) p. 30, Qualifications and Curriculum Authority (QCA); Tables 16.2 and 19.2 from *Middle Leadership in Schools: Harmonising Leadership and Learning*, Pearson Education Ltd (Blandford, S.

2006); Table 17.1 adapted from *Building Brighter Futures: Next Steps for the Children's Workforce*, DfES Publications (DfES 2008) p. 45, Crown Copyright material is reproduced with permission under the terms of the Click-Use Licence; Table 19.1 from Leading the team – managing staff development in the primary school by Knutton, S. and Ireson, G. in *Vision and Values in Managing Education*, p. 61 (Bell, J. and Harrison, B.T. (eds) 1995), David Fulton.

Text

Extract on page 32, Case Study on pages 204–5 and Examples on pages 272–3, pages 281–2, pages 308–9, and page 390 from *Case Studies for Early Years Professional Standards 2.1–2.7*, Canterbury Christ Church University (Goouch, K. and Powell, S. 2006); Activity on pages 149–51 from Using Texts to Ask Philosophical Questions (1) A P4C Strategy adapted by Jenny Morgan (Albuera Street School), http://wwwfp.education.tas.gov.au/english/philo1.htm, Government of Tasmania; Extract on page 240 from Pressure of Work that Travels Home, *Times Educational Supplement*, 16 February 1996 (Emma Burstall); Activity on pages 245–6 adapted from Don't worry, be happy, *Times Educational Supplement (TES)* (First Appointments), pp. 20–2 (Haigh, G.); Activity on pages 245–6 and Extract on pages 258–9 from *Professional Development Manual*, 3rd ed., Pearson Education Limited (Blandford, S. 2004); Extract on pages 300–1 from *Claiming Space: An In-depth Auto/biographical Study of a Local Sure Start Project, 2001–2006*, Centre for International Studies of Diversity and Participation (West, L. and Carlson, A. 2007) pp. 143–9; Extract on pages 422–3 from *Head of Department as a Leader and Manager*, West Sussex County Council (West Sussex Advisory and Inspection Service 1994) and *Middle Leadership in Schools: Harmonising Leadership and Learning*, Pearson Education Ltd. (Blandford, S. 2006) pp. 20–22.

In some instances we have been unable to trace the owners of copyright material, and we would appreciate any information that would enable us to do so.

Authors

Professor Sonia Blandford is currently Director of Leadership Development at Teach First, prior to which she was Pro-Vice Chancellor and Dean of Education at Canterbury Christ Church University. She has authored over 50 articles and books focusing on professional development, education leadership and management, special educational needs and music education.

As an adviser to the European Commission, Sonia was one of four Professors who produced the common principles that underpin Education Professional Development in Europe. Sonia has also contributed to the development of standards for the Early Years Professional Status and National Professional Qualification for Integrated Centre Leadership.

Sonia is a member of various European and national committees, has been a keynote speaker at education and early years conferences, and is a current contributor to Teachers TV.

Dr Catherine Knowles is a Senior Research Fellow at Canterbury Christ Church University. She has worked as a lecturer on the BA and PGCE primary education programmes and carried out research within the fields of primary modern foreign languages, peer-mentoring, citizenship education and character education within primary and secondary schools. Her work in education has contributed to the evidence base informing practice and policy and has been presented through a variety of conferences, seminars and publications. Her doctoral thesis explored moral education in secondary schools in France and England. Prior to this she taught religious education and science at secondary school level in England.

Contributors

Angela Nurse retired from Canterbury Christ Church University in 2007, where she had been Principal Lecturer in Early Years and Head of Department of Childhood Studies. During her long career at the University she was responsible for Early Childhood Studies degrees, the Foundation Degree in Early Years and a number of other programmes grounded in a multidisciplinary approach to working with very young children and their families. She is also currently deputy chair of the Early Childhood Studies Degrees Network and a committee member of OMEP. Much of her teaching career was with very young children with a variety of special needs, mainly in inner London and Kent. As well as running a specialised nursery for children with speech and language difficulties, she worked in an advisory capacity with teachers and colleagues in the other statutory services and within the private and voluntary sectors. She worked extensively with parents, often in their own homes. She has been a Registered Nursery Inspector and Chair of the governing body of her local school, which includes children with physical impairments. She has contributed to a number of publications, both in the UK and in France, including *Teaching Young Children* (1999), *Young Children Learning* (1999) and *Experiencing Reggio Emilia* (2001), as well as editing *The New Early Years Professional: Dilemmas and Debates* (2007). She now acts as a consultant in early years and writes on various aspects of early childhood.

Liz Hryniewicz is a Principal Lecturer in the Department of Childhood Studies at Canterbury Christ Church University. She is the Programme Director of the MA Early Years and was previously Programme Director for both Early Years Professional Status (EYPS) and National Professional Qualification for Integrated Centre Leadership (NPQICL). Her research interests include leadership, early literacy, multi-professional working and consultation with children. She is the author of *Teaching Assistants: The Complete Handbook*.

Guided tour

Each chapter begins with a list of **Learning objectives**, providing a quick overview of what will be covered and clearly setting out the key learning goals.

The relevant **Professional standards** are highlighted at the start of each chapter, drawing links between the chapter content and your professional development. A full list of the Early Years Professional Standards can be found in the appendix at the end of the book

In-margin **Connect & extend** boxes provide an excellent starting point for further research by creating links between the chapter content and external sources, including journals, policy documents and websites.

The **What happens in practice?** vignettes demonstrate how theory and policy impact on day-to-day practice.

Many are followed up with a **Reflect and relate to practice** feature, which provides an opportunity to stop and think about how this might influence your attitudes and potentially impact on your own practice. The triple star icon indicates extra questions that challenge you to take your thinking further.

The **Discussion point** feature highlights key controversies, presenting different perspectives on divisive issues and encouraging debate

'**Web' boxes** direct you to additional related resources that are available via the Developing Professional Practice companion website: www.pearsoned.co.uk/blandford

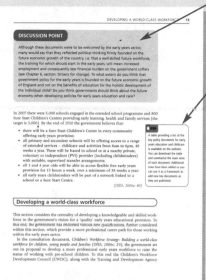

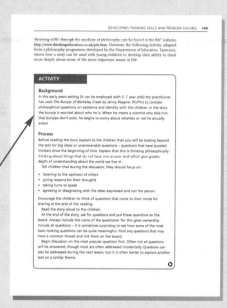

Activity boxes include tasks designed to help you to try out practical ideas and interrogate theories.

At the end of each chapter a **Glossary** is provided with clear definitions of all the key terms introduced in the chapter.

The **Find out more** feature provides guidance on how to take your reading further, suggesting a mixture of books, journals, policy documents and online resources that build on the material covered in the chapter.

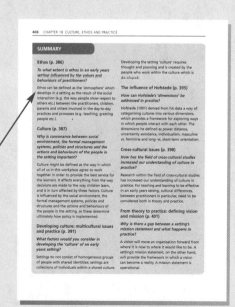

End of chapter **Summary** boxes bring together the key ideas covered in the chapter, to help consolidate what you've learned. They can also be a useful feature for revision.

Influences on Learning

- Chapter 1 – From Policy to Practice: Contexts of Learning
- Chapter 2 – Communities of Learners
- Chapter 3 – Values Promoting Learning
- Chapter 4 – Development and Learning
- Chapter 5 – Learners as Individuals

Part 1 presents the key influences on learning in the early years sector beginning with an introduction to the proliferation of policies emanating from government departments and agencies in recent years which has led to the legitimisation of practice and the raising of professional standards in the sector. Part 1 also considers communities of learners, values, development of learning and learners as individuals.

Pearson Education Ltd. Mike Bassett © Pearson Education Ltd. 2007

CHAPTER 1

From Policy to Practice: Contexts of Learning

By the end of this chapter you will be able to answer the following questions:

- What are the relevant government documents relating to early years education and childcare since 2005?
- What factors have influenced government policy?
- What factors can contribute to the creation of a learning context?
- Why should I study current research on early years learning contexts?

This chapter will support your understanding of the following Standards *(see Appendix 1)*: **Knowledge and understanding:** S03 and S06 ■ **Effective practice:** S08, S11 and S19 ■ **Relationships with children:** S25 and S28.

Introduction

> Every child deserves the best possible start in life and support to fulfil their potential. A child's experience in the early years has a major impact on their future life chances. A secure, safe and happy childhood is important in its own right, and it provides the foundation for children to make the most of their abilities and talents as they grow up.
>
> *(DfES, 2007: 7)*

In recent years, many developments have taken place in England, where government policy is embodied by the belief that every child deserves the best possible start in life as in the above quotation taken from the new *Statutory Framework for the Early Years Foundation Stage: Setting the Standards for Learning Development and Care for children from birth to five* (EYFS) (DfES, 2007). As a student embarking on the study of early years you are part of an exciting and challenging period in the history of childhood education and practice. The last decade has seen a domestic political shift in thinking on child development. There has been an increased emphasis placed on learning contexts, in terms of the **quality** (see Chapter 2) and place of early education and childcare; this has been at the forefront of research and government policy in many western European countries. Many policy organisations (e.g., Qualifications and Curriculum Authority (QCA), Sure Start, ContinYou, etc.), theorists and practitioners have contributed to the journey.

Quality: is the term used to describe the merits of teaching and learning within a setting.

We live in what is commonly termed a global world, made possible through advances in Information and Communication Technology (ICT) and a greater movement of people between countries. In practice, this means we cannot ignore the political, social, economic or educational systems of other countries; what happens elsewhere will have an impact on what happens in the UK. This has led to an increased interest in comparative international educational research, where the aim has often been that of 'borrowing' a particular policy or practice from a more effective educational system (Broadfoot, 2000). That said, the body of research studies documenting early years educational practice and policy in other countries has increased over the last few years and provides a valuable insight into how we approach early years practice in the UK. Consequently, you will find examples throughout this book, based on case studies and academic research studies, documenting early years international practice. In addition, the international Organisation for Economic Co-operation and Development (OECD) (2001), founded in Paris in 1961 to provide a forum for democratic governments to promote and support economic and social development, published *Starting Strong: Early Childhood Education and Care* in 2001. A comparative study of childcare and early years education in twelve countries, it highlighted a number of general issues, one being that of raising the quality of provision in early years (OECD, 2001: 8). This view is supported by the British government and reflected in their policies. Throughout this book you will be engaged, to varying degrees, with a range of documents, in particular government policy documents, and will consider how these are a necessary point of reference for both shaping and informing effective practice.

To begin, early years settings are loosely divided by age category: babies (0–3 years), Foundation Stage (3–5 years) and Key Stage 1 (5–7 years); there is, in practice, an over- lap both in provision and in children's development at each stage, an important point to remember throughout the book. Clearly there are significant differences between each age group; babies (0–3) are not toddlers and toddlers (3–6) are not young children (5–7 years). However, it is for you as practitioners to adapt your thinking as you read each policy and practice. Always be aware of the differences and overlaps; never assume that each sub-stage is the same as the next. Children are individuals who grow and develop at their own pace, guided by parents, carers and professionals. Consider your role in this relationship as you read through each chapter. Related gov- ernment policy, however, tends to be developed within the broader frame of early years. Increased provision requires increased capacity in the early years workforce, with a focus on quality childcare and early years education to compete with other European countries. The need and consequent provision of childcare has led to a raft of government reforms. By examining government policy on early years education and childcare, this chapter will consider the extent to which early years provision and the emerging learning context for babies, Foundation Stage and Key Stage 1 children has been shaped by national policy.

Context, when considered in association with learning, has a broader meaning than the rather simple definition offered by Chambers (1983: 271) dictionary, which defines it as *associated surroundings* or *setting*. Within an educational or learning frame- work, context encompasses the many factors which impact on a child's learning. This includes not only the created physical learning environment, the content of what is taught, models of teaching and learning, the social environment and the home envir- onment but also the interaction of these factors. By exploring 'context' within the broader meaning associated with learning, this chapter will also consider some of the factors which might influence the development of an effective learning context.

Creating policy: the national context

This section will provide a brief outline of the government policies which have influenced early years practice contemporarily. In examining chronologically the gov- ernment documents which have directly influenced the delivery of services within the early years, this section will provide some insight into national policy and in so doing will help you to consider which documents will be most helpful for informing prac- tice within a setting.

Given the centrality of government policy in providing the framework for the pro- vision and delivery of early years services, it is important to be able to understand and interpret what each document means for practice. As a practitioner you will have to decide, along with other team members, how you will implement a particular policy document. Some relate more directly to practice than others and you will refer to these on a regular basis, e.g. the *Statutory Framework for the Early Years Foundation Stage: Setting the Standards for Learning Development and Care for children from birth to five* (EYFS) (DfES, 2007) and the Key Stage 1 National Curriculum. To guide you through the documents which are examined in this section and as a reference point for your own use, Table 1.1 provides a chronological summary, outlining the principal aim of each document.

The present climate for change within early years, in England, began with the government's National Childcare Strategy, set out in their Green Paper, *Meeting the Childcare Challenge* (DfEE, 1998). By promoting the implementation and development of affordable, high quality education and care for 0–14 year olds, the strategy set childcare and education of the under fives more firmly within the political arena. This was followed by a number of policies and papers, intended to commit educators and other early years practitioners to improving outcomes for children.

In 1999, the government published *Early Learning Goals* (QCA) setting out attainment goals for 3–6 year olds. Although its treatment of play was supported by early years practitioners, its overemphasis on the achievement of certain standards in numeracy and literacy was heavily criticised; early years practitioners wanted a greater *focus on learning opportunities and experiences* (Soler and Miller, 2003). This was supplemented the following year by *Curriculum Guidance for the Foundation Stage* (QCA, 2000) which focuses on planning for the achievement of the early learning goals and provides examples of good practice. Although the less prescriptive tone of this document went some way in silencing the detractors, some remained critical of what was perceived to be an overemphasis on the development of skills and knowledge to meet National Curriculum requirements at the expense of the development of social and emotional skills. In the view of the critics, this tended to equate early years education with future economic growth (Soler and Miller, 2003), that is, with an emphasis on children who can reach knowledge and skills based targets to the detriment of those who cannot.

In 2001, the Department for Education and Employment (DfEE) (now the Department for Children, Schools and Families) published *Early Years Development and Childcare Planning Guidance 2001–2002* (DfEE, 2001a) to provide a framework for those working within the field. The idea of centres as integrated service providers (whereby health, education and social services are 'linked' together, either directly within the same location or indirectly through good channels of communication) as a means of responding to the social needs of a child or his/her family led to the development of the Early Excellence Centres programme in 1997. These aimed to offer education, childcare, health and social services to young children, parents and the wider community either directly or in partnership with other providers. This was the forerunner of the Sure Start children's centres programme, launched as a government initiative in 1998, with the aim of providing access to health, education and social services in one location to young children (0–5 years) and their parents living in deprived communities. To provide guidance for integrated service providers the government published *Early Excellence Centres: Developing High Quality Integrated Services* (DfEE, 2001b).

With an ever greater emphasis on raising standards in early years settings, the government commissioned a team from Manchester Metropolitan University to develop an effective framework for practice for those who work with children aged from birth to three years. The resulting framework, *Birth to Three Matters: The Next Steps* (DfES, 2002) was underpinned by three guiding principles widely recognised in the field of Early Years education and childcare:

Connect & Extend

Being familiar with the relevant policy documents is vital for early years educators and practitioners. Details can be accessed at **www.dcsf.gov.uk** and **www.teachernet.gov.uk**.

In addition this can be supplemented with related information from the Sure Start website, available at: **www.surestart.gov.uk** and the *Every Child Matters* website, available at: **www. everychildmatters.gov.uk**.

Research informs practice. It is worth being aware of recent research within the field of early years. If you have access to the journals listed in the references at the end of the chapter, it is a good idea to look them up on a regular basis.

Table 1.1 Government policy documents: informing early years practice

Document		Date	Aims
	Meeting the Childcare Challenge	1998	This green paper proposed the implementation and development of affordable, high quality education and care for 0–14 year olds; putting education and care for the under 5s more firmly on the government's education agenda – known as the National Childcare Strategy.
	Early Learning Goals	1999	This document set out attainment targets for 3–6 year olds.
	Curriculum guidance for the Foundation Stage	2000	The aim of this document is to provide guidance to practitioners on planning for learning, with a clear focus on the Early Learning Goals.
	Early Years Development and Childcare Planning guidance 2001–2002	2001	This provides a framework for those working within early years environments.
Early Excellence Centres: Developing High Quality Integrated Services		2001	Early Excellence Centres – providers of integrated services in one location (health, social and education) – were the forerunners of the Sure Start Children's Centres. This document provided guidance for professionals working within the centres.
National Standards for under 8s Day Care and Childminding		2001	This lists the standards for those working in early years settings.
Birth to Three Matters:		2002	Based on three guiding principles (which are documented within this chapter), this provided a framework for practice.
Every Child Matters		2003	Sets out a framework for improving the outcomes for all children.
Every Child Matters: Change for Children		2004	Provided a national framework for implementing change, particularly at the local level.
Children Act		2004	This gave legal force to the five outcomes of *Every Child Matters*.
Choice for Parents – the Best Start for Children: A ten-year strategy for childcare		2004	This document considers the government's plan to provide the best chances for every child. It considers childcare and family issues, particularly focusing on the work–family balance.

Green paper: in England, a green paper is the government's proposal of an action or plan of action. It provides opportunity for discussion and response.

Table 1.1 *Continued*

DOCUMENT	Date	Aims
The Common Assessment Framework (CAF)	2005	This assessment tool, which replaces all others, is used for children who need targeted support. By implementing the CAF, the additional needs of children can be met at an early stage by professionals from across the service providers.
Choice for Parents, the best start for children: making it happen – An action plan for the ten-year strategy: Sure Start Children's Centres, extended schools and childcare	2006	This document set out the government's plan for a more integrated service provision for young children, as well as childcare and family support services.
Childcare Act	2006	By conferring duties on Local Authorities to deliver the government's agenda for children and families, this Act provided the first legal framework for early years and childcare.
Children's Workforce Strategy: Building a world-class workforce for children, young people and families	2006	This document sets out the government's plan for a professional early years workforce.
Statutory Framework for the Early Years Foundation Stage: Setting the Standards for Learning Development and Care for children from birth to five (EYFS)	2007	This provides the framework for the delivery of services within early years settings. By clearly stating the early learning goals within six educational programmes it (officially) replaces *Birth to Three Matters, Curriculum guidance for the Foundation Stage* and *National Standards for under 8s Day Care and Childminding* (practitioners however, will still find elements of these documents useful to and relevant for practice).
The Children's Plan – Building brighter futures	2007	This document, by clearly stating the underlying principles (documented in this chapter), provides a clear view of the government's vision for all children in the UK – i.e. raise standards both in the provision of services and in children's aspirations and achievements.
Inclusion Development Programme Supporting children with speech, language and communication needs: Guidance for practitioners in the Early Years Foundation Stage	2008	The focus of this document is supporting children with language, speech and communication problems. It offers good advice for practice.

- Parents and families are central to the well-being of the child
- A relationship with a key person at home and in the setting is essential to young children's well-being
- Children learn by doing rather than being told.

(Abbott and Langston, 2005: 135)

Pre-prep: (short for pre-preparatory school) an independent school for children aged 3–8 years.

The sparcity of any previous government guidance and the production of materials (resources to use in the setting and advice relating to good practice) in conjunction with the framework, which could be used across early years settings, added to its general acceptability amongst practitioners. Furthermore the document was popular amongst early years practitioners in Australia, Ireland, Germany and China (Abbott and Langston, 2005). The following, taken from an interview with the head of a **pre-prep** school (an independent school for children aged 3–8 years), shows the extent to which government policy, as set out in their various documents, influences practice; it highlights the degree of autonomy practitioners have in adapting government policy:

WHAT HAPPENS IN PRACTICE?

Government guidance is crucial. It gives you the benchmark and you've got the experience to apply it to your situation. The government looks at the broad spectrum and you have to adapt it to your situation. It [government policy] helps us to confirm our principles. It's principles to context. So we [the team] all tend to agree on the principles but then we have to consider how we will adapt them to practice.

REFLECT AND RELATE TO PRACTICE

Some critics argue that the curriculum for the Foundation Stage is too 'target' focused and does not allow for the holistic development of all children (i.e. there is less opportunity for play and/or other activities which promote the emotional and social development of the child). Do you agree with the critics?

You should consider the above example of 'What Happens in Practice?' and also look up the early learning goals in the *Statutory Framework for the Early Years Foundation Stage: Setting the Standards for Learning Development and Care for children from birth to five* (EYFS) (DfES, 2007) – available at: **http://publications.teachernet.gov.uk**.

☆ ☆ ☆
Do you think that the *Statutory Framework for the Early Years Foundation Stage: Setting the Standards for Learning Development and Care for children from birth to five* (EYFS) (DfES, 2007) provides opportunity for the holistic development of the child? Considering the above example of 'What Happens in Practice?' and using the early learning goals within the six areas of learning in the EYFS – available at: **http://publications.teachernet.gov.uk** – how would you employ the EYFS to provide a curriculum which addresses the holistic development of the child? (You should consider this in a general sense.)

Multi-agency working

The government's vision in England is for a more integrated provision of education, health and social services. The aim is a 'seamless provision' with the 'joined-up' working of professionals. The result is a plethora of new terminology, which needs to be understood by practitioners – multi-professional teams, multi-agency working – without any real understanding of how these terms should be defined or what they mean in practice. This section will provide an insight into multi-agency working in practice and consider how, through the more integrated approach to the provision of services (health, social and education), practitioners can access extra support for targeted children.

Within the context of government policy, made known through their various documents, terms like 'integrated', 'seamless' and 'joined-up' define more precisely the type of service provision envisaged by the government. Through the sharing of information and the inherent avoidance of overlap, quick referral and the identification of gaps in provision, the government's vision is for a health, social and education service, where individuals and groups of individuals from the various service providers work more closely together to meet the needs of children, young people and families.

Professionals working together to support young people is not a new concept. Social services have worked with health and education services and the police since the 1970s providing support for vulnerable children and their families. However, the lack of information sharing between agents, the cumbersome system of child referral and the absence of lead professionals to co-ordinate the services provided to individuals have led to major changes in the way the system operates and is managed.

In 2003, the publication of *Every Child Matters* (HMG, 2003) set out the government's plan to maximise opportunities for all children and young people. This was set within the framework of five outcomes: be healthy, stay safe, enjoy and achieve, make a positive contribution and achieve economic well-being (see Table 1.2). The five outcomes or themes of *Every Child Matters* were given legal force by the 2004 Children Act and are the foundational block on which education, social and health services are provided. The government document, *Every Child Matters: Change for Children* (DfES, 2004b), sets out a national framework for implementing change, clarifying how this might be carried out at the local level.

Table 1.2 Five outcomes of *Every Child Matters*

Outcome	Statements
Be healthy	Physically, mentally and emotionally healthy Healthy lifestyles Parents promote healthy choices
Stay safe	Safe from maltreatment, neglect and violence Safe from accidental injury and death Safe from bullying and discrimination Safe from anti-social behaviour Parents provide safe homes and stability
Enjoy and achieve	Ready for school Attend and enjoy school Achieve stretching national education standards Enjoy recreation Parents support learning
Make a positive contribution	Engage and support the community and environment Engage in positive behaviour in and out of school Develop positive relationships Develop self-confidence and deal with life changes and challenges Parents promote positive behaviour
Achieve economic well-being	Engage in further education, employment or training after leaving school Ready for employment Parents are supported to be economically active

Source: Every Child Matters: Change for Children, Department for Education and Skills (DfES 2004a) p. 9

REFLECT AND RELATE TO PRACTICE

The five outcomes of *Every Child Matters* provide the framework for the delivery of early years services. Not all of the statements within the five outcomes will apply so directly within an early years setting. In your opinion, which of the statements need to be considered by an early years educator?

☆ ☆ ☆

Consider one of the five outcomes, appropriate to an early years setting. How, in practice, might you ensure that you are providing the opportunity for every child within a specific early years setting to achieve this outcome? For example, be healthy: physically, mentally and emotionally healthy – how would you ensure that each child has the opportunity to be physically, mentally and emotionally healthy?

Although the idea of 'joined-up' services aims to maximise the opportunities for all children, young people and families, Anning et al. suggest that it was a 'central tenet of New Labour policy for reducing poverty and social exclusion' (2006: 4). The Sure Start initiative of 1998 provides a good example of integrated services in practice. Usefully, Anning et al. suggest that integrated, **multi-professional working** in practice fits within the following hierarchical framework:

> **Level 1:** cooperation – services work together toward consistent goals and complementary services, while maintaining their independence;
> **Level 2:** collaboration – services plan together and address issues of overlap, duplication and gaps in service provision towards common outcomes;
> **Level 3:** coordination – services work together in a planned and systematic manner towards shared and agreed goals;
> **Level 4:** merger/integration – different services become one organisation in order to enhance service delivery.
>
> *(Anning et al., 2006: 6)*

Multi-professional working: professionals from different disciplines (e.g. health, social and education) working together, sharing expertise and opinions to agree an action in relation to a child and his/her family.

There is an integrated multi-agency prioritising service for those who may need targeted support. The one point of entry for the individual is through the Common Assessment Framework, which will initiate appropriate action from a multi-agency team if required. The *Common Assessment Framework* (CAF) (DfES, 2005) sets out details for 'a shared assessment tool' which can be 'used across agencies in England' (DfES, 2006b: 3). This is used for those who need targeted support; it aims to help practitioners assess the additional needs of a child or young person at an early stage so that they can work with families, agencies and other practitioners to meet those needs. From March 2008; the CAF replaced all previous assessment frameworks.

The five outcomes of *Every Child Matters* provide the standard by which the need for a CAF is measured. If a child is unable to reach one or more of the key outcomes without additional services, it is quite likely that a CAF will be required. *A Common Assessment Framework for children and young people: Pre-assessment check* is available online at **www.everychildmatters.gov.uk/caf**. It provides a framework for assessing if a child is going to achieve the five key themes of *Every Child Matters* and can be employed at any time to assess if a CAF is required. A CAF, however, would be needed in the following situations:

- You are concerned about how well a child is progressing. You might be concerned about their health, welfare, behaviour, progress in learning or any other aspect of their well-being. Or they or their parent may have raised a concern with you;
- The needs are unclear, or broader than your service can address;

- A common assessment would help identify the needs and/or get other services to help meet them.

(DfES, 2006b: 10)

REFLECT AND RELATE TO PRACTICE

What is the purpose of the Common Assessment Framework?

☆ ☆ ☆

In what situations would you envisage using the Common Assessment Framework?

Providing services for children

What principles underpin the Early Years Foundation Stage Curriculum?

The Childcare Act 2006 provided the first legal framework setting early years and childcare more firmly within the field of education. This section provides a résumé of the government documents related to the provision of early years education in practice; culminating in the *Statutory Framework for the Early Years Foundation Stage: Setting the Standards for Learning Development and Care for children from birth to five* (EYFS) (DfES, 2007), which provides the new framework for the delivery of services within all early years settings. Given legal force by the Childcare Act 2006 it now replaces the other frameworks on which it builds, *Birth to Three Matters* (DfES, 2002), *Curriculum Guidance for the Foundation Stage* (QCA, 2000) and *National Standards for under 8's Day Care and Childminding* (DfES, 2001).

Choice for Parents, the best start for children: making it happen – An action plan for the ten year strategy: Sure Start Children's Centres, extended schools and childcare (DfES, 2006a) set out the government's plan for the implementation of a more integrated service provision for young children, as well as childcare and family support services. The Childcare Act 2006 was at the foundation of the document and confers new duties on Local Authorities (LAs) to deliver the government's plan. By providing the first legal framework setting early years and childcare more firmly within the field of education, the Act confers the following responsibilities on LAs in delivering the government's plan:

- **Support parental choice**: new specific duties to seek parents' views and involvement; to secure sufficient childcare; to provide information and advice to parents; and to identify those who might not use early childhood services and encourage them to do so will help ensure parents can make the right choices for their children;

- **Focus on children's well-being and narrow gaps in achievement**: the new general duty on local authorities to improve the well-being of young children in their area, and to reduce inequalities, must drive all of their activities – including their efforts to increase parental involvement, choice and take-up of services;
- **Integrated services**: local authorities will be required to work with Secondary Heads Associations (SHAs) and Primary Care Trusts (PCTs) and the employment service in carrying out the duty to improve well-being and narrow gaps. They also have a duty to provide services in an integrated way, which makes them easier to access and of more use to parents and children. The key partners are under a reciprocal duty to work with the local authority and each other. Local authorities will in practice continue to work with a much wider range of public, private and voluntary sector partners.

(DfES, 2006a: 35)

Possible partners might include children's trusts, neighbourhood renewal, local businesses, charities (national or local) which work with schools, the library, local museums and art galleries, local sports teams. In addition, LAs not only provide valuable advice but actively broker links between schools and statutory and private sector providers of services, e.g. childcare advisers, literacy and numeracy advisers, speech therapists, providers of Continuing Professional Development (CPD) etc. They also provide information on government/LA initiatives, for example other youth service providers; all of which provide opportunities for identifying potential partners.

Foundation Stage: age 0–5

To meet the new challenges of delivering quality childcare and early years education, which will provide long-term benefits to children and families within the education market, the government proposed the following:

- setting clear expectations for children's development at age 5;
- learning from what works, especially on narrowing the gap in achievement and reaching particular groups;
- improving leadership and management of Sure Start Children's Centres and extended schools through better training, guidance and good practice; and
- using the Early Years Foundation Stage (EYFS) – a single framework for learning and development for children up to the age of 5 – to ensure consistently high standards and promote achievement.

(DfES, 2006a: 6)

The *Statutory Framework for the Early Years Foundation Stage* (EYFS) (DfES, 2007) provides greater guidance for practitioners across all early years settings (0–3, 3–5 years). Given legal force by the Childcare Act 2006 it now replaces the other frameworks on which it builds – *Birth to Three Matters* (DfES, 2002), *Curriculum Guidance for the Foundation Stage* (QCA, 2000) and *National Standards for under 8's Day Care and*

Childminding (DfES, 2001) – and provides the new framework for the delivery of services within all early years settings. The document clearly states the centrality of *Every Child Matters*, where early years educators must provide opportunity for all children to achieve the five outcomes by:

- setting the standards – providers should deliver individualised learning, development and care which enhances the development of all children in their care;
- providing for equality of opportunity – enable all children to experience a challenging and enjoyable programme of learning and development;
- creating a framework for partnership working – with parents, across settings, where children may attend more than one setting and with professionals from other relevant agencies;
- improving quality and consistency – providers must comply with the learning and development requirements (the early learning goals, the educational programmes and the assessment arrangements) and the welfare requirements (safeguarding and promoting children's welfare, suitable people, suitable premises, environment and equipment, organization and documentation);
- laying a secure foundation for future learning – through ongoing observational assessment which informs planning, a flexible approach which responds quickly to each child's needs and coherence and consistency across settings taking into consideration the child's home experiences.

(DfES, 2007: 9–10)

The standards document made clear the government's overarching aims for early years education: to raise standards and to narrow the gap between childcare and education. Underpinned by the idea of forging strong partnerships, creating an inclusive environment and personalising learning (see Chapter 10), the government's vision is for an early years education which provides opportunity for every child to achieve his/her potential. This was reinforced by the publication of *The Children's Plan – Building brighter futures* (DCSF, 2007) which focused on raising standards both in service provision and children's aspirations and achievements. With a view to making this country a better place in which to grow up, the document is underpinned by the following guiding principles:

- Government does not bring up children – parents do – so government needs to do more to back parents and families;
- All children have the potential to succeed and should go as far as their talents can take them;
- Children and young people need to enjoy their childhood as well as grow up prepared for adult life;
- Services need to be shaped by and be responsive to children, young people and families; not designed around professional boundaries; and
- It is always better to prevent failure than tackle a crisis later.

(DCSF, 2007: 4)

DISCUSSION POINT

Although these documents were to be welcomed by the early years sector, many would say that they reflected political thinking firmly founded on the future economic growth of the country, i.e. that a well-skilled future workforce, the training for which should start in the early years, will mean increased employment and consequently less financial burden on the government coffers (see Chapter 6, section: Drivers for change). To what extent do you think that government policy for the early years is founded on the future economic growth of England and not on the benefits of education for the holistic development of the individual child? Do you think governments should think about the future economy when developing policies for early years education and care?

In 2007 there were 5,000 schools engaged in the extended school programme and 800 Sure Start Children's Centres providing early learning, health and family services (the target is 3,000). By the end of 2010 the government believes that:

- there will be a Sure Start Children's Centre in every community offering early years provision;
- all primary and secondary schools will be offering access to a range of extended services – childcare and activities from 8am to 6pm, 48 weeks a year. These will be based in school or at a nearby private, voluntary or independent (PVI) provider (including childminders) with suitable, supervised transfer arrangements;
- all 3 and 4 year olds will be able to access flexible free early years provision for 15 hours a week, over a minimum of 38 weeks a year;
- all early years childminders will be part of a network linked to a school or a Sure Start Centre.

(DfES, 2006a: 80)

WEB

A table providing a list of the key policy documents for early years education and childcare is available on the website. You can download the table and summarise the main aims of each document. Additional rows have been added so you can use it as a framework to add new key documents as they are published.

Developing a world-class workforce

This section considers the centrality of developing a knowledgeable and skilled workforce in the government's vision for a 'quality' early years educational provision. To this end, the government has endorsed various new qualifications, further considered within this section, which provide a more professional career path for those working within the early years sector.

In the consultation document, *Children's Workforce Strategy: Building a world-class workforce for children, young people and families* (DfES, 2006c: 29), the government set out its proposal to develop a more professional early years workforce to raise the status of working with pre-school children. To this end the Children's Workforce Development Council (CWDC), along with the Training and Development Agency

(TDA), developed the *Early Years Professional National Standards* (CWDC, 2006). For those wishing to become an Early Years Professional (EYP) they would have to achieve Early Years Professional Status (EYPS) by demonstrating that they had met all the Standards covering the following six areas of competency:

- Knowledge and understanding
- Effective practice
- Relationships with children
- Communicating and working in partnership with families and carers
- Teamwork and collaboration
- Professional development.

(CWDC, 2006)

Attaining EYPS is seen as key to raising standards within early years settings, where those awarded EYPS will be expected to be proactive in improving practice in the settings in which they work (CWDC, 2006: 5), which does not include leading multi-agency children's centres. In early 2007, the CWDC issued guidance to the standards for the award of early years professional status (CWDC, 2007) and provides a list of approved EYPS trainers on its website. Details can be accessed at: **http://www. cwdcouncil.org.uk/projects/eypcandidates.htm**.

For those managing and leading children's centres, the National Professional Qualification in Integrated Centre Leadership (NPQICL) provides a more professional career path. The one year course, leading to the NPQICL, offers either a study based or research based route, entry to which is dependent on the candidate's previous experience and qualifications. National standards for leaders of integrated children's centres have been developed in parallel with the NPQICL award. This contrasts with France, where the majority of those engaged in childcare provision to the under threes have a healthcare training, while those who work in the *école maternelle* (part of the state funded educational system for three to six year olds) are graduates with a higher professional qualification in teaching (Baudelot et al., 2003: 109). It would be appropriate to consider other early years provision in Europe and the rest of the world.

Creating a learning context

Children do not learn in isolation. A number of factors, both inside and outside the setting, contribute to that experience. Through case studies, worked examples and the influence of established theorists and practitioners, this section will address the meaning of learning context and consider factors within a setting which enable children to develop as independent and competent learners.

Assimilation: taking in new knowledge to add to your existing knowledge or to change it.

Robson (2004: 207), subject leader for early childhood studies at Roehampton University, citing Gura (1996) refers to the 'two contexts of learning', which she defines as 'the inner, or individual context and the outer, or social context of learning'. This highlights the many factors under consideration when context is associated with learning. How a child learns may be an *inner* context (i.e. understanding and **assimilation** of knowledge, which can be dependent upon confidence and emotional well-being), whereas what a child learns, how the child is taught, what he/she is taught, who the child interacts with, the physical learning environment, the ethos of the environment might be considerations for the *outer* context. Learning, however, does not happen in isolation. All of these factors interact and contribute to the creation of a learning context. Jean Piaget, the Swiss developmental theorist, who developed his theories from observing his own children, highlighted the importance of providing a stimulating learning environment. Although he placed little emphasis on the important interactive role of educators in the learning process, his theory that babies and toddlers are actively involved in their own learning, i.e. cognitively engaged, eager to know about and understand what they are experiencing, has strongly influenced the way we view children's learning and development. The following two examples of 'What happens in practice?' highlight the importance of providing stimulating learning environments for babies and young children.

WHAT HAPPENS IN PRACTICE?

I have spent a great deal of time locating large, stable old-fashioned pushchairs for the nursery so that the babies can sleep outside and feel the air and the wind, watch the patterns that the leaves make or hear the noise of the wind as it rushes through the trees. We have large French windows in the 1–2 (year olds') room and they come and go as they please.

(Adapted from an interview with a leader practitioner at a nursery in Thanet)

WHAT HAPPENS IN PRACTICE?

In one day nursery babies and children were asleep under the vigilant observation of a practitioner (as required). Children were individually settled by their key person who stayed with them, which was usual practice. The sleep room had restful fresh lavender, delicate transparent material was draped from the ceiling, and soft lighting and soothing music added to the tranquil atmosphere. There was a choice of soft toys for children and books for those who wanted to rest and snuggle up for a story rather than sleep.

(Adapted from Ofsted, 2008: 23)

REFLECT AND RELATE TO PRACTICE

Why were these learning environments stimulating for the children? In what ways would they stimulate the children? You should consider all sensory stimulation – touch, sight, hearing, smell and taste.

☆ ☆ ☆

In what ways do these learning environments contribute to the children's cognitive engagement? Will they help the children to advance in their learning and development? In what areas and how?

You will find it helpful to look at the early learning goals and educational programmes in the EYFS (DFES, 2007: Section 2), available at: **www.teachernet.gov.uk/publications**.

What other issues might you consider when planning a classroom which is stimulating for children in year 1?

You will find the Key Stage 1 national curriculum helpful, available at: **www.curriculum.qca.org.uk**.

In addressing the holistic development of the child, Bronfenbrenner's (1979) ecological model of child development (i.e. the interrelationships of the child and his/her environment) provides a means of considering the multidimensional nature of context when associated with learning. By considering the interconnectedness of the different physical settings to which a child is exposed, it shows that a child's learning and development in an early years educational or childcare setting cannot be viewed in isolation from the home or broader social environment. Defining setting as 'a place where people can readily engage in face-to-face interaction' (Bronfenbrenner, 1979: 22), he underlines the importance of the 'connections between other persons present in the setting, the nature of these links, and those who deal with him [or her] at first hand, (1979: 7).

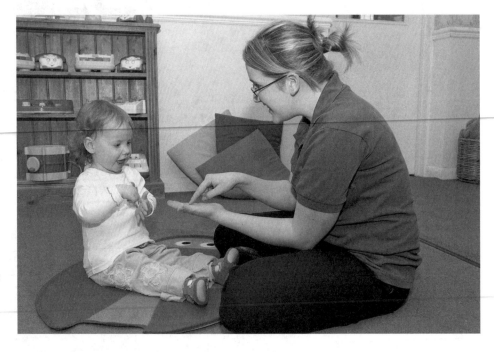

Photo 1.1
Through effective interactions with adults children can achieve their potential

Pearson Education Ltd. Jules Selmes © Pearson Education Ltd. 2004

The centrality of the social dimension of learning was given prominence by the Russian Psychologist Lev Vygotsky, who believed children learn first by experiencing social stimuli and can advance further in their learning if appropriately supported by a more able competent person (this might be another child or an adult where an adult might intervene with a relevant question or a comment, to help a child overcome a particular difficulty). This gap between what the child can achieve without help and what the child can achieve with appropriate support he called the **zone of proximal development**. In essence what these theorists highlight is that, through interactions with others, children are provided with greater opportunity to reach their potential; for practitioners this means recognising the learning needs of children and knowing how to respond to those needs.

Zone of proximal development: the gap between what the child can achieve without help and what the child can achieve with appropriate support.

Connect & Extend

Jean Piaget was not without critics, particularly in relation to his stage development theory (i.e. children go through identifiable stages of development in relation to their age – 0–2, 2–7 etc.). Look up his theory. Do you agree with it? Why/why not?

You will find the following books helpful: Piaget, J. (2001) *The Psychology of Intelligence*, London: Routledge, and Wadsworth, B.J. (1996) *Piaget's Theory of Cognitive and Affective Development: foundations of constructivism*, USA: Longman.

Connect & Extend

Although there were similarities in the work of Piaget and Vygotsky, the centrality of the social aspect of learning in Vygotsky's theory – i.e. a child experiences primarily through interaction with others and then internalises what he/she has experienced – brought a new dimension to child development theory. Compare their work. In what ways were they similar and different? Do you agree with Vygotsky's theory of child development? Why/why not?

You will find the following book helpful: Moony, C. (2000) *Theories of Childhood: an introduction to Dewey, Montessori, Erickson, Piaget and Vygotsky*, USA: Redleaf Press.

REFLECT AND RELATE TO PRACTICE

To what extent are early years practitioners responsible for both the 'inner' and 'outer' learning contexts (Gura, 1996) of the children in their setting?

You should consider this for 0–2 year olds and 3–5 year olds within the context of the EYFS, and for 5–7 year olds within the context of the Key Stage (KS) 1 National Curriculum. You should also consider this in relation to government policy and related criticism as outlined within the chapter.

 ☆ ☆ ☆

Select an area of the EYFS curriculum (for 3–5 year olds) and an area within the KS 1 National Curriculum (5–7 year olds) and consider how you would ensure that your teaching was addressing both the 'inner' and 'outer' learning contexts as discussed within this section. You will need to consider how you will plan for the activity – what early learning goals/learning objectives you will consider, the types of questions you might ask the children, how and when you might intervene to support them in their learning and what outcomes you expect. You will find Chapter 16, which addresses planning, useful.

Robson (2004: 207) suggests that in creating the 'right' learning context, practitioners need to *ensure that young children have opportunities to be physically and mentally active, in an environment which allows them to collaborate with others, both adults and children, as well as offering them opportunities to play and work alone.* Edwards (2006: 55), Professor of Primary Education at Leeds University, suggests that educators not only have to *consider how children learn, but need to attend to what children are learning, how they become people who are learners and . . . how that learning is supported.* In earlier research, Edwards (2004: 86), building on Burman's (2001) theory of child development, which suggested that *cultural context* provided a valuable *resource* for practitioners – something to be analysed to gain an insight into what the child is all about, highlighted the need for a greater comprehension of the role adults play in enabling and *encouraging* children to understand their *cultural world*.

DISCUSSION POINT

The following research briefing presents findings from a recent study of professional practices with under-ones in day care centres in Japan. It formed part of a larger comparative study carried out by Rayna (2004), with similar settings in France, where qualitative data was collected from six voluntary day care centres in Paris and Tokyo and their suburbs. The centres were asked to select the target children for observation – three boys and three girls in each setting of approximately 6, 18 and 30 months old. Discuss the following research briefing. What factors have influenced the creation of a stimulating learning context by these Japanese educators? In your opinion, what factors should be considered in creating an effective learning context for early years?

Play practices: babies under one year old at a Japanese day care centre

Observations confirm that play is a core activity and that children play all morning long. The educators maintain close physical proximity with the infants: holding them in their arms, sitting very near to them, and following them when they move around the room. They frequently stimulate the babies, offering various objects, initiating songs, and encouraging physical play. Toys and objects, mostly made of natural materials, are placed on low shelves at the disposal of the children and periodically brought out and put away. Play space is thus not cluttered with material. Infants are integrated into each other's play. The educators never leave infants alone to cry. Playing in the open air (in the garden or on the terrace) is very important. Educators consistently play with the babies and provide them with opportunities to interact with the older children and with the environment.

(Rayna, 2004: 40)

The following is a consideration of the views of the Japanese educators after watching a videotaping of the above observation.

Educators' views: play practices of babies under one year old at a Japanese day care centre

Japanese educators were generally pleased and proud of their practices. They see play as the best means to establish a secure relationship with the baby and a central activity for early socialisation. Concerned for the babies' happiness, the educators attempt to prevent them from crying and intervene immediately when crying occurs. They emphasise the importance of continuously encouraging the infant by reminding them of what they will soon be able to do later by themselves. Moreover they stress that it is not only important to play with infants, but also to find ways of helping infants enter into play with their peers. Staff collaboratively select the materials to be introduced to the babies. Part of the material is produced by themselves or by the older children of the centre (which admits children up to the age of 6). They stressed that play outside is very important for three reasons: improving health, developing social contacts with children of different ages, and discovering nature.

(Rayna, 2004: 40)

What type of learning context should be created?

In England, where there is the eventual expectation of responsible social interaction, the child is recognised as an individual within the wider community (Abbott and Langston, 2005: 132). **Affective development** (related to the emotions) is addressed alongside **cognitive development** (related to knowledge). Abbott and Langston (2005), early years specialists based at Manchester Metropolitan University who, within a team of colleagues, developed the framework for and co-wrote *Birth to Three Matters* (2002), suggest that social skills are developed through 'effective early relationships' and 'developing a sense of self . . . consistency of care' which 'involves positive feedback from those around the child' (2005: 132). The following What happens in practice? On page 22 is taken from an interview with the head of a pre-prep school, shows that certain factors (in terms of both the physical environment and the interaction of the educator with the child) are crucial in creating a learning environment for 3–5 year olds. It highlights how practitioners directly influence the type of learning context created.

Bridge (2001: 20), on the other hand, from the University of Birmingham and a proponent of the **High Scope curriculum** – a guided curriculum, characterised by **plan–do–review**, where educators support children in developing and carrying out plans and in choosing activities, but not in their actions – suggests that pre-school environments need to be more *home-like* and staff more *parent-like* to help children become social in what may seem like an alien environment. It would seem that this view contrasts with Finland, where Niikko (2004), an educationalist from the

Affective development: growth in emotional awareness, understanding and control.

Cognitive development: growth in understanding.

High Scope curriculum: a guided curriculum educators support children in developing and carrying out plans and in choosing activities, which enables them to carry out the activity themselves (Bridge, 2001).

Plan–do–review: children are appropriately supported in the selection and planning of an activity, which they carry out themselves and then review after thorough discussion with practitioners and other children.

WHAT HAPPENS IN PRACTICE?

It should be well planned, well structured and safe and secure in both senses of the word. By creating a safe and secure environment, I don't just mean in the traditional sense, although in that way as well. We talk a lot here about 'personal zones'. We mean that if children are walking down the corridor, for example, they can get to where they need to be going without anyone interfering with that. They feel safe. We also talk about 'depth of engagement'. So children should feel safe and secure in the sense that they can engage in what they are doing. So for example, no one is going to take their resources. That's facilitated by the adults there. It could be an adult-led activity or a child-initiated activity, but they need meaningful interaction with the adults to make the activity meaningful. So staff need to plan themselves into that activity. In addition our particular setting allows for a lot of play to take place outside. We have a courtyard and a mulberry tree – yes the aesthetic element is important.

University of Joensuu in Finland, suggests that questions like 'growing into a human being, care and introduction to social values as well as principles of morality are increasingly being overlooked [in early education] in favour of the needs of commerce and industry' (2004: 260). She further highlights the smaller gap which is now beginning to develop in Finland between schooling and early years education, a situation similar to that which is happening in England and reflected in government education policy.

DISCUSSION POINT

A narrowing in the gap between childcare and education should be hailed. However, some critics suggest that the move is closely aligned with national economic growth in that a well-skilled future workforce, the training for which should start in the early years, will mean increased employment (and a decrease in unemployment) and consequently less financial burden on the government coffers. They further suggest that in early years practice, this means an emphasis on skills and knowledge based targets at the expense of social and emotional skills.

What do you think about:

• The narrowing in the gap between childcare and education – should it be hailed?

- Early years education is driven by future economic growth – do you think training in social and moral values is/will be overlooked? Do you think training in social and moral values is important in the early years?

Pre-school provision

Rosenthal (2003), Professor of Social Work and Welfare at the Hebrew University of Jerusalem, suggests that 'quality' in early years education and childcare in 'a given society will reflect the valued educational goals and valued educational practice of the cultural communities constituting that society' (2003: 104). In essence, the 'quality' of teaching and learning in any given early years setting is influenced by the personal and educational values of its leaders and practitioners. Anning (2006b), in reviewing the results from the government funded Effective Provision of Pre-School Education Project (Sylva et al., 2003), a longitudinal study carried out from 1997 to 2003, with a sample of 3,000 children attending different types of pre-school, highlighted the following characteristics of high-quality **pre-school provision** (defined by Sylva et al., 2003 as education for 3–4 year olds):

Pre-school provision: education for 3–4 year olds in nurseries, children's centres (e.g. Sure Start) or playgroups.

- Adult–child interactions involving 'sustained shared thinking' (see Chapter 5) and open-ended questioning;
- Practitioners with a clear grasp of child development and good curriculum knowledge;
- Shared educational aims with parents;
- Formative feedback to children in learning episodes;
- Transparency in behaviour policies and practice.

(Anning, 2006b: 28)

Rosenthal (2003: 102), referring to the structural and process dimensions of quality, highlights the close relationship between the two in a child's developmental process. The structural dimensions she lists as group size, adult to child ratio, teacher education and training and the autonomy and support available to educators that encourage the provision of these experiences. The process dimensions, on the other hand, she refers to as children's social interactions and educational experiences. Citing results from the National Institute of Child Health and Human Development (NICHD) Early Child Care Research Network (1996, 1997, 1998, 1999 and 2000), she underlines the detrimental effect on child development of poor-quality pre-school settings, resulting in 'poor performance on cognitive and language tasks and more behavioural problems' (Rosenthal, 2003: 102). Guimaraes and McSherry (2002), in their study of curriculum approaches in pre-school centres in northern Ireland, highlighted a general division in the approach taken by most reception settings and that taken by nurseries, playgroups and private day nurseries. Their findings showed that while the majority of reception settings employed a predominantly adult-directed approach (e.g. adult reading a story, maths or spelling activities), nurseries, playgroups and private day nurseries devoted more time to a child-centred approach (e.g. free play). **Child-centred** – where children, undirected by the educator, select different activities

Child-centred: children select different activities for themselves from a range of resources on offer.

Photo 1.2 How do children's activities, appropriately supported by adults, help children to become independent learners?

Pearson Education Ltd. Jules Selmes © Pearson Education Ltd. 2004

Adult-directed: children's activities are led by the educator or practitioner (depending on the setting).

for themselves from a range of resources on offer and **adult-directed** – where children's activities are led by the educator. Supporting their findings with current research which tends to favour a more child-centred approach, giving children greater independence in learning, they were critical of a pre-school curriculum which adopted a predominantly adult-directed approach. This contrasts with the pre-school, infant and toddler centres in Reggio Emilia, Italy where small-group activities are often presented by the educators, but driven by the children. With the focus on the social aspects of learning (child–child and educator–child), there is a 'good balance of child-initiated and teacher-initiated activities' (Featherstone and Bayley, 2006).

Ethos and environment

It is self-evident that a stimulating learning environment will produce stimulating results. In helping children to develop as independent and confident learners, members of the learning community need to consider how to create a positive environment suitable for the age and needs of the children within the setting. Theorists and practitioners alike highlight the distinctive link between the ethos created in early years settings and their environment. In essence the 'atmosphere' which is developed within the setting, through the social interaction of those involved (practitioners, children, parents and others) and the day-to-day practices and processes (e.g. teaching), all contribute to the creation of the learning environment. This section will consider how, from a theoretical stance, practitioners can create a positive learning environment in practice.

Early years settings, like other communities, have their own characteristics and personalities. The culture of each setting is determined by individual and collective beliefs and values. A culture within a setting will manifest itself in many forms:

- practice: rites, rituals and ceremonies (e.g. how children are welcomed on a daily basis);
- communications: stories, legends, symbols and slogans (e.g. pictures and slogans on the walls showing that the setting is a place of learning for everyone);
- physical forms: location, style and condition of the school buildings, fixtures and fittings (e.g. are buildings clean and inviting places to be?);
- common language: phrases or jargon common to the school (e.g. are certain words employed to describe areas in the setting?; for example, 'cosy corner' for a reading area).

Differences between settings, related to the age of the children and community context, may be explained in terms of organisational and social structure, which are also reflected in the interpersonal relationships of those within the setting (e.g. adult–child interactions, adult–adult interactions and child–child interactions). These factors, which permeate the setting to such an extent that they drive the setting towards achieving goals, contribute to the development of an **ethos** (see Chapter 18). No single definition could adequately describe ethos, which is created through the values and behaviours of the participants in the early years community and reflected in the policies and practices.

> **Ethos:** the intangible 'atmosphere' within a setting, developed from and through the values, attitudes, culture and policies promoted.

There is a distinctive link between the ethos created in early years settings and their environment. Creating the right learning environment is at the heart of the British government's Building Schools for the Future project. Recognising the impact of physical environments on learning outcomes, the government set up the Building Futures Group in April 2002, a joint venture between the Commission for Architecture and Built Environment (CABE) and the Royal Institute of British Architects (RIBA), to address the future design of school buildings. Although this has not been extended to early years educational and childcare settings, the impact of inspirational learning spaces on 0–7 year olds is well documented in other countries and is considered below.

Featherstone and Bayley's (2006) consideration of the following physical features of the Reggio pre-school, infant and toddler centres in Italy highlights the emphasis on inspirational learning spaces:

- skillfully and thoughtfully adapted to the children
- spacious feel, plenty of light and muted colours on walls – colour is provided by the children and their work
- good storage
- clearly delineated areas
- well resourced with message boxes and displays of natural objects
- there is room for role play in the central piazza and areas for construction with bricks

- outside spaces are gardens, with trees, flowers, fruit, grass and hard surfaces, with provision for sand and water play.

(Featherstone and Bayley, 2006: 41)

In Denmark, Anning (2006a) underlines the availability and *quality* of childcare and early years education, where there is a greater emphasis on the physical learning environment than is at present the case in England. She highlights the 'extensive outdoor' play areas which surround 'purpose built-centres [with] high standards of resources and advantageous staffing ratios' (2006a: 4–5). The development and maintenance of the internal and external environment is a key activity.

It should consider the needs of the children. For example, a one-year-old child will be stimulated by eye contact and need help with eating, whereas a three year old will need direction and support in starting a pre-school curriculum which should be valued in its own right, not just as a precursor to school.

An uncared-for early years setting will reflect an uncaring community. Working in an environment that is in need of repair creates stress before any consideration of workload. As *Every Child Matters* recognised, working in an environment that is unhealthy (e.g. unclean, disorganised or unpleasantly decorated) is not conducive to healthy development. Members of the early years learning community need encouragement in order to fulfil the potential of each child and also themselves as practitioners.

SUMMARY

Creating policy: the national context (p. 4)

Why did the government create policies for the early years?

This section considers the shift in thinking on early childhood over the last decade. There has been an increased emphasis placed on learning contexts, in terms of the quality and place of early education and childcare; this has been at the forefront of research and government policy in many western European countries.

Multi-agency working (p. 9)

What are the aims of multi-agency working?

The government's vision in England is for a more integrated provision of education, health and social services. The aim is a 'seamless provision' with the 'joined-up' working of professionals, focusing on prevention and early intervention. For those who need targeted support the one point of entry is through the Common Assessment Framework (CAF).

Providing services for children (p. 12)

What principles underpin the early years foundation stage curriculum?

The Childcare Act 2006 provided the first legal framework setting early years and childcare more firmly within the field of education. The *Statutory Framework for the Early Years Foundation Stage: Setting the Standards for Learning Development and Care for children from birth to five* (EYFS) (DfES, 2007) provides the new framework for the delivery of services within all early years settings. Given legal force by the Childcare Act 2006 it now replaces the other frameworks on which it builds – *Birth to Three Matters* (DfES, 2002), *Curriculum Guidance for the Foundation Stage* (QCA, 2000) and *National Standards for under 8's Day Care and Childminding* (DfES, 2001).

Developing a world-class workforce (p. 15)

What is the role of new qualifications?

To this end the Children's Workforce Development Council (CWDC), along with the Teaching and Development Agency (TDA), developed the *Early Years Professional National Standards* (CWDC, 2006). Early Years Professional Status (EYPS) is achieved by demonstrating that all the Standards have been met. For those managing and leading children's centres, the National Professional Qualification in Integrated Centre Leadership (NPQICL) provides a more professional career path.

Creating a learning context (p. 16)

What factors contribute to creating the 'right' learning context?

In creating the right learning context, practitioners need to think not only how children learn, but also consider the physical learning environment.

Ethos and environment (p. 24)

What factors should be considered in creating a stimulating learning environment?

There is a distinctive link between the ethos created in early years settings and their environment. It is self-evident that a stimulating environment will produce stimulating results. Members of the learning community need to consider how to create a positive environment suitable for the age and needs of the children within the setting.

Glossary

Adult-directed: children's activities are led by the educator or practitioner (depending on the setting).

Affective development: growth in emotional awareness, understanding and control.

Assimilation: taking in new knowledge to add to your existing knowledge or to change it.

Child-centred: children are not directed by the educator, instead they select different activities for themselves from a range of resources on offer.

Cognitive development: growth in understanding.

Ethos: the intangible 'atmosphere' within a setting, developed from and through the values, attitudes, culture and policies promoted.

Green paper: in England, a green paper is the government's proposal of an action or plan of action. It provides the opportunity for discussion and response.

High Scope curriculum: a guided curriculum, which originated in America in the 1960s, whereby educators support children in developing and carrying out plans and in choosing activities which enables them to carry out the activity themselves (Bridge, 2001).

Multi-professional working: professionals from different disciplines (e.g. health, social and education) working together, sharing expertise and opinions to agree an action in relation to a child and his/her family.

Plan–do–review: a characteristic of the High Scope curriculum, whereby children are appropriately supported in the selection and planning of an activity, which they carry out themselves and then review after thorough discussion with practitioners and other children.

Pre-prep: (short for pre-preparatory school) an independent school for children aged 3–8 years.

Pre-school provision: education for 3–4 year olds in nurseries, children's centres (e.g. Sure Start) or playgroups.

Quality: is the term used to describe the merits of teaching and learning within a setting. It covers a broad area, encompassing teaching to the early learning goals to meet the individual needs (affective and cognitive) of each child and responding to learners as individuals. This is a contested area, particularly when determined by externally imposed standards. Quality should be internally driven.

Zone of proximal development: the gap between what the child can achieve without help and what the child can achieve with appropriate support. In essence, with appropriate, relevant and effective interactions with more able others, children are provided with greater opportunity to reach their potential.

Find out more

Anning, A. (2006) The integration of early childhood services, in Anning, A. and Edwards, A., *Promoting Children's Learning from Birth to Five: Developing the new early years professional***, 2nd edn, Maidenhead: Open University Press/McGraw-Hill, pp. 17–30.**
The government's vision for an integrated provision of children's services can seem like a difficult concept to comprehend. Given that it is still a relatively new concept, both in theory and practice, this is to be expected. In this chapter of the book she has edited with Anne Edwards, Anning provides a good outline of what integrated service provision means for early years practice.

David, T. (1990) *Under Five – Under-Educated***, Maidenhead: Open University Press.**

This book provides a good account of the historical, social and economic factors which have impacted upon early years provision within the UK. Although some of the national and international social statistics are a little dated, her reference throughout to international practice and in particular her examples of pre-school provision in other countries (Chapter 12) provides both interesting and informative insights into early years practice.

Evidence for Policy and Practice Information and Co-ordinating Centre (EPPI-centre), part of the Social Science Research Unit (SSRU) at the Institute of Education, London. The website can be accessed at: **http//eppi.ioe.ac.uk**. The website outlines the work of the Centre in education, including reviews of research evidence and the methods used to review public policy.

References

Abbott, L. and Langston, A. (2005) Birth to Three Matters: A Framework to Support Children in Their Earliest Years, *European Early Childhood Education Research Journal*, Vol. 13, No. 1: 129–143.

Anning, A. and Edwards, A. (2006) *Promoting Children's Learning from Birth to Five: Developing the new early years professional*, 2nd edn. Maidenhead: Open University Press/McGraw-Hill.

Anning, A. (2006a) Setting the national scene, in Anning, A. and Edwards, A., *Promoting Children's*

Learning from Birth to Five: Developing the new early years professional, 2nd edn. Maidenhead: Open University Press/McGraw-Hill: pp. 1–16.

Anning, A. (2006b) The integration of early childhood services, in Anning, A. and Edwards, A., *Promoting Children's Learning from Birth to Five: Developing the new early years professional*, 2nd edn. Maidenhead: Open University Press/McGraw-Hill: pp. 17–30.

Anning, A., Cottrell, D., Frost, N., Green, J. and Robinson, M. (2006) *Developing Multi professional*

Teamwork for Integrated children's Services. Maidenhead: Open University Press/McGraw Hill Education.

Baudelot, O., Rayna, S., Mayer, S. and Musatti, T. (2003) A Comparative Analysis of the Function of Coordination of Early Childhood Education and Care in France and Italy, *International Journal of Early Years Education*, Vol. 11, No. 2, June: pp. 105–116.

Bridge, H. (2001) Increasing parental involvement in the Preschool Curriculum: what an action research case study revealed, *International Journal of Early Years Education*, Vol. 9, No. 1: pp. 6–21.

Broadfoot, P. (2000) Comparative Education for the 21st Century: retrospect and prospect, *Comparative Education*, Vol. 36, No. 3: pp. 357–371.

Bronfenbrenner, U. (1979) *The Ecology of Human Development*. Cambridge, MA: Harvard University Press.

Burman, E. (2001) Beyond the baby and the bathwater: post-dualistic psychologies for diverse childhoods, *European Early Childhood Education Research Journal*, Vol. 9: pp. 5–22.

Chambers (1983) *Chambers 20th Century Dictionary*. Edinburgh: Chambers.

Children's Workforce Development Council (CWDC) (2006) *Early Years Professional National Standards*. Available at: **http://www.cwdcouncil.org.uk/projects/ eypcandidates.htm**.

Children's Workforce Development Council (CWDC) (2007) *Guidance to the standards for the award of early years professional status*. Available at: **http://www.cwdcouncil.org.uk/projects/ eypcandidates.htm**.

Department for Children, Schools and Families (DCSF) (2007) *The Children's Plan: Building brighter futures.* Norwich: The Stationery Office.

Department for Children, Schools and Families (DCSF) (2008) *Inclusion Development Programme: Supporting children with speech, language and communication needs: Guidance for practitioners in the Early Years Foundation Stage*. Nottingham: DCSF.

Department for Education and Employment (DfEE) (1998) *Meeting the Childcare Challenge*. London: HMSO.

Department for Education and Employment (2001a) *Early Years Development and Childcare Planning Guidance 2001–2002*. London: DfEE Publications.

Department for Education and Employment (2001b) *Early Excellence Centres: Developing High Quality Integrated Services*. London: DfEE Publications.

Department for Education and Skills (DfES) (2001) *National Standards for under 8's Day Care and Childminding*. Nottingham: DfES Publications.

Department for Education and Skills (DfES) (2002) *Birth to Three Matters*. Nottingham: DfES Publications.

Department for Education and Skills (DfES) (2003) *Every Child Matters: Summary*. Nottingham: DfES Publications, Ref: DfES/0672.

Department for Education and Skills (DfES) (2004a) *Every Child Matters: Change for Children in Schools*. Nottingham: DfES Publications, Ref: DfES/1089/2004.

Department for Education and Skills (DfES) (2004b) *Every Child Matters: Change for Children*. Nottingham: DfES Publications, Ref: DfES/1110/2004.

Department for Education and Skills (DfES) (2005) *The Common Assessment Framework*. Available at: **www.dfes.gov.uk**.

Department for Education and Skills (2006a) *Choice for Parents, the best start for children: making it happen – An action plan for the ten year strategy: Sure Start Children's Centres, extended schools and childcare*. Nottingham, DfES Publications, Ref: 0356-2006DOC-EN.

Department for Education and Skills (2006b) *The Common Assessment Framework for children and young people: practitioners guide*. Nottingham: DfES Publications. Available at: **www.everychildmatters.gov.uk/caf**.

Department for Education and Skills (2006c) *Children's Workforce Strategy, building a world-class workforce for children, young people and families*. Nottingham: DfES Publications.

Department for Education and Skills (2007) *Statutory Framework for the Early Years Foundation Stage: Setting the Standards for Learning Development and Care for children from birth to five* (EYFS). Nottingham: DfES Publications.

Edwards, A. (2004) Understanding Context, Understanding Practice in Early Education, *European Early Childhood Education Research Journal*, Vol. 12, No. 1: pp. 85–100.

Edwards, A. (2006) Young children as Learners, in Anning A. and Edwards, A., *Promoting Children's Learning from Birth to Five: Developing the new early years professional*, 2nd edn. Maidenhead: Open University Press/McGraw-Hill: pp. 54–75.

Featherstone, S. and Bayley, R. (2006) *Foundations for Independence: Developing Independence in the Foundation Stage*, 2nd edn. Lutterworth: Featherstone Education.

Guimaraes, S. and McSherry, K. (2002) The Curriculum Experiences of Pre-school children in Northern Ireland: classroom practices in terms of child-initiated play and adult-directed activities, *International Journal of Early Years Education*, Vol. 10, No. 2: pp. 85–94.

Gura, P. (1996) An entitlement curriculum for early childhood, in Robson, S. and Smedley, S. (eds) *Education in Early Childhood*. London: David Fulton Publishers in association with the Roehampton Institute.

HM Government (HMG) (2003) *Every Child Matters* (Green Paper). Norwich: The Stationery Office.

HM Treasury (2004) *Choice for Parents, The Best Start for Children: A 10 Year Strategy for Childcare*. Norwich: HMSO.

Miller, L. and Devereux, J. (2004) (eds) *Supporting Children's Learning in the Early Years*. London: David Fulton Publishers in association with The Open University.

Niikko, A. (2004) Education – a joint task for parents, kindergarten teachers and kindergarten student teachers, *International Journal of Early Years Education*, Vol. 12, No. 3: pp. 259–274.

Ofsted (2008) Early Years Leading to Excellence. London: Ofsted. Available at: **www.ofsted.gov.uk**.

Organisation for Economic Co-operation and Development (OECD) (2001) *Starting Strong. Early Childhood Education and Care*. Paris: OECD.

Qualifications and Curriculum Authority (QCA) (1999) *Early Leaning Goals*. London: QCA.

Qualifications and Curriculum Authority (QCA) (2000) *Curriculum Guidance for the Foundation Stage*. London: QCA.

Rayna, S. (2004) Professional practices with under-ones in French and Japanese day care centres, *Early Years*, Vol. 24, No. 1, March: pp. 35–47.

Robson, S. (2004) The Physical Environment, in Miller, L. and Devereux, J. (eds) *Supporting Children's Learning in the Early Years*. London: David Fulton Publishers in association with The Open University: pp. 205–216.

Rosenthal, M. (2003) Quality in Early childhood Education and Care: A Cultural Context, *European Early Childhood Education Research Journal*, Vol. 11, No. 2: pp. 101–116.

Soler, J. and Miller, L. (2003) The Struggle for Early Childhood Curricula: a comparison of the English Foundation Stage Curriculum, *Te Whariki* and Reggio Emilia, *International Journal of Early Years Education*, Vol. 11, No. 1: pp. 57–67.

Sylva, K., Melhuish, E., Sammons, P., Siraj-Blatchford, I., Tagget, B. and Elliott, K. (2003) *The Effective Provision of Pre-School Education Project: Findings from the Pre-School Period*. Research Brief No. RBX15-03. London: DfES Publications.

CHAPTER 2

Communities of Learners

By the end of this chapter you will be able to answer the following questions:

- What is a community of practice (Wenger, 1998)?
- How is a learning community influenced by and how does it impact on the local community within the framework of Sure Start programmes?
- How can early years practitioners involve parents as partners in their children's learning?

This chapter will support your understanding of the following Standards *(see Appendix 1)*:
Knowledge and understanding: S03 and S06 ■ **Effective practice:** S19 and S24 ■ **Relationships with children:** S26 and S27 ■ **Communicating and working in partnership with families and carers:** S29, S30, S31 and S32 ■ **Teamwork and collaboration:** S33 and S36.

Introduction

WHAT HAPPENS IN PRACTICE?

Older children (3–5 year olds)

Observation:

Outside, all staff and children participate in sitting or standing in a circle, surrounding and holding a large piece of fabric that they call 'the parachute'. They waft the parachute up and down. Some children go underneath and they call 'hello' to them. When sitting, they lift the parachute and staff look under and call hello to particular children on the opposite side to them. Later they place a teddy bear on top and bounce him by moving the parachute up and down either quickly or slowly. They make small movements, all whispering, to get him to go to sleep. Then, with excitement, they shout and use big movements to 'wake teddy up'. J talks to the children throughout the activity, encouraging, praising, enticing and instructing children as individuals and as a whole group. Occasionally a child breaks away and is gently encouraged to come back to the circle and rejoin the activities. The children all join in enthusiastically, singing, shouting, whispering, sitting, standing, turning, walking and running. The activity generates a sense of community, while individuals are sensitively acknowledged and encouraged.

(Goouch and Powell, 2006)

Independent (early years) school: an early years provider within the independent sector.

Private nursery: privately owned nurseries eligible to claim funding for the children who attend (within the allowance).

Voluntary (early years) setting: settings run by voluntary management committees.

Maintained early years setting: an early years setting which is maintained (funded) by the Local Authority.

Twenty-first century government policy has borne witness to a shift in thinking on education. It reflects a move away from education within the learning organisation to education within the 'community of practice' (Wenger, 1998). Etienne Wenger (1998: 5), the first to coin the phrase 'community of practice' and an internationally acknowledged expert on the subject and how institutions – schools, businesses etc. – can apply it, underlines the centrality of 'social participation' in a 'community of practice'. This concept, which is discussed in this chapter, is perhaps best understood in light of the above example of 'What happens in practice?', an observation in a nursery setting which, by showing the interaction of the various children and practitioners involved in carrying out the joint activity, perfectly embodies Wenger's idea of a 'community of practice'. By considering Wenger's idea, this chapter will address how early years settings (which include childminders, Local Authority nurseries, nurseries or early years centres, children's centres, playgroups, pre-schools or schools in the **independent**, **private** or **voluntary sector** and **maintained schools** (DfES, 2007a) can develop as communities of practice within the broader frame envisaged by the government.

Community of practice: underlying theory

In essence, **communities of practice** are characterised by social participation – the building of relationships (practitioner–child, child–child and parent–practitioner, etc.) through shared practice with common aims. This section will consider the idea of a community of practice, as outlined by Wenger (1998), and what this means for practitioners in early years settings.

Wenger (1998) delineates 'community of practice' within the wider concept of 'social learning theory', of which there are four parts: 'community (learning as belonging), practice (learning as doing), identity (learning as becoming) and meaning (learning as experience)' (1998: 5). In his theory, 'practice' binds the community together and is characterised by:

- mutual engagement
- a joint enterprise
- a shared repertoire.

He argues for 'identities and modes of belonging' as the primary focus of educational issues, with skills and knowledge as the secondary focus. In such a community, where identity is fully addressed, Wenger further suggests that 'education becomes a mutual developmental process between communities and individuals' (Wenger, 1998: 263). Before going any further it is a good idea to consider Wenger's ideas. Wenger defines identity as 'learning as belonging'. This means that the identity of the individual child is, for the time he/she is in a particular setting, shaped by the practice within (engaging in learning together) and interaction with others (through the process of learning together) in the setting. For Wenger, 'modes of belonging' is closely connected to and intertwined with identity. The child begins to belong to or have a sense of belonging to that setting in the process of engaging in the common practice of learning with the other children. In order to be able to engage in the process of learning they will interact with and form relationships with others (children and adults). For Wenger, the interaction with others through a shared practice (communicating with others enables a child to carry out the process of learning more effectively) places the emphasis on learning within a social context. This interaction with others is important. For Wenger, this will have a strong impact on a child's 'success' in learning.

Communities of practice: in essence, characterised by social participation – the building of relationships through shared practice with common aims.

DISCUSSION POINT

What do you understand by a 'community of practice'? Wenger was the first person to coin this phrase. Now there is a move to encourage all early years settings to be communities of practice. Consider what makes a setting a 'community of practice'. Would you argue for/against that all early years settings are already communities of practice? How do you think Wenger's view of settings ▶

as communities of practice will influence what happens, in relation to teaching and learning, on a day-to-day basis?

You will need to consider the concept of 'social participation' and what this means and what the community of learners would be like if learning took place in isolation.

The learning community

The framework proposed by the government for early years settings places a strong emphasis on the 'partnership working' of all those involved (practitioners, children, parents and other professionals) in the provision of what is commonly referred to as 'high quality' education and care. The idea of creating 'quality' settings, where children have 'quality' interactions with adults, is a common theme both in government policy and in the research literature. By showing how all members directly involved in the day-to-day practices of the early years setting can and should be encouraged to have an active part and shared commitment to the modelling of the community, this section will consider how the creation of 'quality' learning environments is internally driven.

It is self-evident that the early years are a crucial time in the learning and development of children. From birth to seven years, the pace of development is rapid (babies, toddlers, Foundation Stage and Key Stage 1). During this time, children begin to develop as **independent learners** (see Chapter 15). Anning and Edwards (2004: 221), who have written extensively on early years education, underline the centrality of 'quality interactions' with adults in the development of learning dispositions (this might include adults who engage with children in dialogue, show them respect, show them that they care for them and ask appropriate questions or make appropriate 'prompts' to support children's learning). By showing the impact on development of the different interactive environments to which a child is exposed, Bronfenbrenner's (1979) ecological model (i.e. the interrelationships of the child and his/her environment) highlights the impact of the community on learning and development.

Independent learner: a learner who has the belief in him/herself to think through learning activities, problems or challenges, make decisions about his/her learning and act upon those decisions.

Within the framework proposed by the government and legislated by the Childcare Act 2006, there is a greater emphasis on 'partnership working' within the immediate and wider local community. The integrated framework is founded on improved outcomes for all children and places greater responsibility on early years practitioners to understand that their setting is a community within a community. This can be defined as multidimensional with its:

- location – where it is, the influence of the environment and systems of control
- structure – the administrative elements and guidance that determine equality of provision
- process – the management of people and development of a shared understanding of beliefs and values (see Chapters 3 and 18)

- agencies – government, business, voluntary (i.e. non-profit-making companies, public trusts or voluntary societies, e.g. Barnado's Children's Society or Home-Start – a family support service offering informal support to parents and children in the local community), private, and sport and the arts.

All members of the early years setting, as participants, should be encouraged to have a shared commitment to the modelling of community (e.g. do all practitioners share in decision-making, the development of policies or are parents involved in their children's learning?). To be effective, early years settings need organisational structures (e.g. staffing structure – who is the leader and who reports to whom?), aims and guiding rules. As active players in the daily life of the setting, those involved, which might include, depending on the setting, children, parents, managers, educators (teachers/ nursery nurses), assistants, health workers (health visitors, school/setting nurses, child psychologists, pediatricians, children's allied health professionals, speech therapists, etc.), social workers (children and family social workers, **outreach** and family support workers and **portage workers**) and other support agencies (private, voluntary or Local Authority (LA) – LAs help settings to make the appropriate contact) work in partnership, sharing an understanding of the goals and targets that are to be achieved in a setting which makes provision for the delivery of high quality education and care. The determination of these goals is:

- reflective, in that the setting mirrors the local community involving its key players in determining values and practices
- individual, as all members will have their own identity with personal goals and objectives
- collective, in that a shared understanding of common beliefs and values will create a sense of community bound together by a recognisable identity and geographical location.

> **Outreach workers:** those who actively target those considered to be in need of and who otherwise would not know about the services provided through the centre.
>
> **Portage worker:** a person who provides a home early years educational programme to children in need of extra support.

DISCUSSION POINT

In what ways do you think practitioners contribute to the modelling of the learning community? You need to consider who decides setting policy, how personal values and beliefs will influence what happens in practice – i.e. the way practitioners relate to children and other members of staff – and whether they should influence practice.

Before continuing your journey through the communities of practice, it is worth reflecting on the idea of **'quality'**. The government's emphasis on 'quality' is reaffirmed by the Early Years Professional Standards, where settings are required to 'be accountable for the delivery of high quality provision' (CWDC, 2008: S24). Although it is a term used frequently in the context of early years provision, it still remains rather

> **Quality:** the term used to describe the merits of teaching and learning within a setting.

subjective. For example, that which is considered to be 'quality provision' in one set-ting/country may not be held in such high esteem in another setting/country. The idea that the 'quality' of the provision can be measured has been gaining momentum since 1996, when Ofsted extended their inspection process to cover state funded early years education within the voluntary, private and independent sectors. The Childcare Act 2006 brought further changes, legislating for the Early Years Foundation Stage (EYFS) across settings and detailing the registration process for providers of early years education and care. The result is a greater focus on 'quality'. Defining 'quality' within the context of the *Early Years Self Evaluation Form* (Ofsted, 2008a) (see Chapter 20), a requirement for inspections since September 2008, provides one way of addressing quality within the setting. Providers are asked to consider and provide evidence to show how well they are addressing and delivering the five outcomes of Every Child Matters through the themes of EYFS within the following areas:

- the learning and development of the children
- the welfare of the children
- the leadership and management
- the overall effectiveness of the early years provision.

(Ofsted, 2008a)

However, the idea of measuring 'quality' by the standards required by Ofsted is not without critics (Miller, 2000: 21). Miller, a senior lecturer in Early Years at the University of Hertfordshire, highlights the case of playgroups, where the traditional focus on children's learning and development is through play. Consequently, assess-ing the quality of numeracy or literacy according to Ofsted criteria is likely to lead to a poor outcome. However, quality remains a contested area, particularly when deter-mined by externally imposed standards and should be internally driven.

DISCUSSION POINT

How would you define 'quality' within the context of early years practice?

You will need to consider what is meant by quality and what aspects of practice need to be considered to provide high quality education and care within a setting. You will need to look up the *Statutory Framework for the Early Years Foundation Stage: Setting the Standards for Learning Development and Care for children from birth to five* (EYFS) (DfES, 2007a), Nottingham: DfES, available at: **www.everychildmatters.gov.uk**, along with the *Early Years Self Evaluation Form* (Ofsted, 2008a) and the *Early Years Self-Evaluation Form Guidance* (Ofsted, 2008b), both available at **www.ofsted.gov.uk**.

Do you think that defining 'quality' within the context of Ofsted requirements does justice to the concept of 'quality' provision in the early years? Why/why not?

Sure Start: a community within a community

The Sure Start programme, launched as a government initiative in 1998 with the aim of providing access to health, education and social services in one location to young children (0–5 years; initially it was for children 0–4 years) and their parents living in deprived communities, provides a good example of a community within a community. It was initiated as a means of helping children from deprived areas – providing health, education and social care under one roof – and supporting their parents. By addressing practice in one **Sure Start children's centre** and considering findings from the National Evaluation of Sure Start (NESS) project, this section examines the concept of a community of practice within the broader community, and considers the effeetivenss of the Sure Start programme to date.

Sure Start children's centres: aim to provide access to health, education and social services in one location to young children (0–5 years) and their families living in deprived communities.

The Sure Start programme was at the centre of the government's policy on childcare and early years learning, providing a framework and location for early years settings as communities within a community and how this can operate in practice. Initially hailed by many practitioners as an overdue initiative (Hannon and Fox, 2005: 3), the Sure Start programme aimed to give a 'better start in life' to young children living in deprived communities and provide their 'parents with greater resources of hope' (West and Carlson, 2007: 14). Although providers of services through Sure Start are given a relatively high level of 'autonomy' at the local level, the idea is that all projects build on the basic principles underpinning the initiative. The Sure Start philosophy is one of 'caring, learning and collaboration' (West and Carlson, 2007: 149). The following example of 'What happens in practice?' documents how this was put into practice at the outset of one Sure Start project, where systems developed in response to the needs of the local community.

WHAT HAPPENS IN PRACTICE?

The Sure Start Millmead project began in 2000, operating out of various small venues. In 2004 it became a Children's Centre, serving the needs of children from 0 to the extended age of 5 (0–4 years at the outset). Now housed in a new building, planned and developed in partnership with local parents, it became the first Community Mutual in 2006. 'A mutual society is defined as an organisation owned by its members and run, in theory, for their benefit. As a Community Mutual, parents buy £1 shares, making the programme, in theory, accountable to its shareholders – the parents' (West and Carlson, 2007: 25).

The new director of the project was appointed during an unsettled period within the local community. Parents were sceptical about the Sure Start project. Their concerns came from two angles. In the past they had been promised various local amenities which were never provided, e.g. a secondary school. In addition, they lacked a clear understanding of the Sure Start programme and

Mutual society: an organisation owned by its members and run, in theory, for their benefit.

although they recognised that children (0–4 years) had needs, they did not know what further provision was needed in the local community. The new director was well aware of the situation and moved swiftly to get the initiative established in partnership with parents. Her immediate priority was to establish 'small successful initiatives, which could be used as evidence of success and new possibility'. She believed strongly in providing support to and opportunities for families. Her underlying philosophy is what is commonly termed 'early intervention'; a system whereby she believed difficult situations could be avoided by enabling parents to understand their child's needs.

In forming the community, her priority was to identify a core group of parents who would represent the community as appointees to the board of management. In carrying out a needs audit, parents were consulted and services were provided in response to demand. The new director encouraged the proactive involvement of parents. Informal training days were organised and parents became involved in the interviews for new members of staff, the interior design of the building, publicising the project and running certain activities. Parents attending the centre liked the good 'interaction with staff and felt valued rather than judged'. Mandy, a single mother, who was initially sceptical about Sure Start, explained why it was different:

> because you are never used to people offering support for nothing. They always want something out of it or a result from it. Even health visitors when they come round to visit they always want the result of the children being healthy and happy so you are always under pressure to make sure that you are doing everything by the book, whereas Sure Start didn't judge.

(Based on West and Carlson, 2007)

DISCUSSION POINT

- In what ways did this Sure Start programme impact positively on the local community?
- How did the director become aware of the local needs?
- Do you think this type of practice is sustainable? Why/why not?
- Do you think this Sure Start Centre is effective? Why/why not?

In essence the Sure Start programme is underpinned by a philosophy focused on learning, development and achievement of potential through collaborative working (parents–children–practitioners and other support agents) and care. In practice, this means that Sure Start service provision will:

Photo 2.1 Does the involvement of parents in the design and organisation of programmes lead to better 'partnership working'?

Pearson Education Ltd. Mark Bassett © Pearson Education Ltd. 2007

- co-ordinate, streamline and add value to existing services in the Sure Start area;
- involve parents, grandparents and other carers in ways that build on existing strengths;
- avoid stigma by ensuring that all local families are able to use Sure Start services;
- ensure lasting support by linking Sure Start services for older children;
- be culturally appropriate and sensitive to particular needs;
- promote the participation of all local families in the design and working of the programme.

(Hannon and Fox, 2005: 6)

Although the example of 'What happens in practice?' highlights the very positive aspects of one Sure Start programme, early findings from the National Evaluation of Sure Start (NESS) project indicated minimal impact on children and families living in Sure Start local programme areas (SSLP) (HMSO, 2005). It was evident that, in areas where the key principles of the Sure Start initiative underpinned the provision and delivery of services, better outcomes for children and parents were to be found (HMSO, 2005: 29). Although the national evaluation calls into question the manner in which future Sure Start programmes might be implemented, the government document, *The Quality of Early Learning, Play and Childcare Services in Sure Start Local Programmes* (SSLP) (DfES: 2005b) reporting on the 'quality' aspect of SSLPs, is more positive. The findings, below, might provide a framework for future improvement:

- Services were being reshaped to promote good quality joint parent/child interactions, e.g. shared music activities.

- The quality of relationships between providers and users (parents and children) was seen as being central to effective provision (i.e. open channels of communication, involving parents in the running and organisation of the centre and activities).
- The nature of multi-agency working in SSLPs allowed services to be offered in good time to prevent difficulties developing, especially where children had additional needs – this was received positively by families.
- There were tensions between specialist practitioners. Early Years education practitioners prioritised preparation for school. Childcare practitioners prioritised language and social development.
- Some parents were reluctant to acknowledge that children learn through play (i.e. many parents support the teaching of literacy and numeracy in the earliest years of education at the expense of creative play which gives children the space and time to develop their imagination. Research findings suggest that allowing children time for creative play has greater benefits in both the short and long term on their learning and development. The government endorses the idea of a balanced curriculum with appropriate opportunity for play both indoor and outdoor.).
- Many parents preferred part-time daycare provision.

(DfES, 2005b: 3)

DISCUSSION POINT

What implications does the above list have for future practice?
  You need to consider what is working, what is not working and how it could be improved.

   In theory (and, for many, in practice), the Sure Start programme provides a practical means of delivering an integrated programme of services in one place. Although the National Audit Office has questioned the overall effectiveness of the Sure Start project (West and Carlson, 2007), it is underpinned by a strong political agenda focused on future economic growth and is likely to remain embedded in the political agenda for the foreseeable future.

Parents as partners

Government policy acknowledges that a child's environment and circumstances have a significant impact on his or her learning, attainment and future life chances, and that engaging parents and carers with learning will have a positive effect on children's achievement. By considering the centrality of parents in their children's learning, this section will address the factors which impact on parental involvement in early years settings and how these might be overcome. Those involved in the early years of a child's education recognise the need for:

- values shared by all
- children placed at the centre of all activity
- practice shared by all
- a venue shared by all.

Parental involvement in pre-school, nursery, childcare settings and school is vital for enhancing children's learning and development. It could also be the case that parents would benefit from involvement which would not only enable them to deepen their knowledge of their child's world, the teaching and learning methods employed and effective forms of negotiation with children, but could also provide opportunities for them to develop their personalities and further their own education. Carol Keyes (2002), Emeritus Professor of Pace University School of Education, New York and an early childhood consultant, suggests that 'unlike other kinds of relationships in people's lives, the parent/teacher pairing occurs by assignment rather than by choice', where 'the common interest is the schooling of the child' (2002: 17). That said, research has shown the positive effect of supportive parents who are both interested and involved in the education of their child. This is reflected in the Early Years Professional Standards: 'recognise and respect the influential and enduring contribution that families and parents/carers can make to children's development, well-being and learning' (CWDC, 2008: S29).

However, developing relationships with parents and enabling them to become partners in their children's learning can be undermined by difficulties. Parents may be too busy, they may have seen their own schooling in a negative light and feel intimidated by the educational environment or they may feel that they can entrust the education of their child to you and do not need to be involved. Or on the other hand, they may be eager and feel that the early years setting is not doing enough to involve them. Keyes (2002: 179) suggests that there are three basic factors which impact on the parent/teacher partnership:

- the degree of match between teachers and parents culture and values;
- societal forces at work on family and school; and
- how teachers and parents view their roles.

In essence, building effective child–parent–practitioner partnerships will mean overcoming these influencing factors. In practice it would be difficult to tackle each one individually – for example, culture may encompass a difference in opinion on how children should be disciplined. In other situations children may come from disadvantaged homes with low income, a single parent (often the mother) and an unsettled environment. These children can present with behavioural problems or other learning difficulties, commonly speech, language and communication problems. The effective practitioner will be appropriately sensitive to the child and his/her extra needs and home background. Equally the practitioner considers the mother. She may be struggling economically, socially and emotionally (she may feel isolated); the child may even be unkempt, but the bond between the mother and the child can be very strong. In practice, settings need to have a general policy for how they welcome and involve parents which can be adapted to meet individual needs as they arise (e.g. are the staff friendly towards the parents, does the setting have open channels of communication, does the setting keep parents informed of their child's progress – verbally, in writing, frequently, occasionally and are there open events such as Christmas concerts, etc.?).

One important aspect in the development of relationships with parents is that of the different roles of the parent and the practitioner/teacher in the life of the child. As Keyes (2002) points out, practitioners' roles are defined by their professional knowledge and understanding of children and their learning needs (holistic – cognitive, emotional and physical). On the other hand parents' roles are shaped by their children – the love, hopes and fears they have for them. She further suggests that knowing and 'understanding' the different roles can help both parents and practitioners to see how the roles can 'complement' each other, where appropriate and sensitive 'negotiations' and open channels of communication can help each 'point of view to enlighten' the other (Keyes, 2002: 184). Table 2.1, which Keyes adapted from Katz (1984), highlights the different roles of parents and teachers in relation to the child.

Considering each dimension in Table 2.1, what does this mean for practitioners?

- **Scope of function**: in essence the practitioner will have a specific educational remit, which, although it addresses the child's emotional, social and personal development along with the cognitive and physical dimensions, will be more limited than that of the parent and lasts for a specific period of time each day.
- **Intensity of affect**: the intensity of the emotional involvement of the practitioner with the child will be less than the child has with his/her parent.
- **Attachment**: although practitioners need to have meaningful interactions with the children within their setting, their 'attachment' to the children will be within the framework of acceptable professional conduct. On the other hand, the parents will have a deeper involvement with their children.

Table 2.1 Differences in the role of parents and practitioners

Role dimension	Parenting	Teaching
Scope of function	Diffuse and limitless	Specific and limited
Intensity of affect	High	Low
Attachment	Optimum attachment	Optimum detachment
Rationality	Optimum irrationality	Optimum rationality
Spontaneity	Optimum spontaneity	Optimum intentionality
Partiality	Partial	Impartial
Scope of responsibility	Individual	Whole group

Source: Keyes (2002), adapted from Katz (1984)

- **Rationality**: a practitioner's relationship with a child develops within a professional framework which is centred on the child and his/her learning and development. The need to plan for children's learning experiences tends to dictate a rational approach to children within the setting. The parents on the other hand can behave quite irrationally towards children, perhaps influenced by the closer emotional involvement.
- **Spontaneity**: the routine organisation of the day to day activities within the setting tends to limit opportunity for practitioner spontaneity. The focus, which is to be valued, tends to be on providing opportunity for children's spontaneity. Parents, however, can be very spontaneous in their love towards, interaction with and activities they do with their child.
- **Partiality**: a parent will be partial to his/her child. A practitioner on the other hand, although he/she is aware of the uniqueness of each child, will treat each child equally within the context of their particular learning needs. Practitioners do not show favouritism.
- **Scope of responsibility**: practitioners have responsibility for the group of children within their setting.

In essence, this involves finding appropriate and effective ways to involve and work in partnership with parents in a manner which complements their role. For practice, it means thinking of ways to involve parents in children's learning, showing that you care for their child and that you are interested in their child (e.g. this can be at the simple level of how you comfort and calm a child who on arrival at the setting is upset – you might take an 18 month old child into your arms and talk to them comfortingly, but this approach would not be appropriate for a 6 year old). In addition, it is

Photo 2.2
Involving and working with parents: how do practitioners complement their role?

Pearson Education Ltd. Jules Selmes © Pearson Education Ltd. 2004

showing parents that their child is part of the community. He/she is involved with the other children and is known by the practitioners.

Bridge (2001), an educationalist from the University of Birmingham, suggests that there is a gap between government policy and practice in childcare and early years settings in England. She attributed this to the rather nebulous meaning of 'parental involvement' and the lack of related research into the types of involvement which benefit children's learning (Bridge, 2001: 8). In pre-school settings she cites work demands, particularly on the mother, as the reason for less involvement, rather than parental lack of interest. In the following example of 'what happens in practice', she outlines an **action research** project developed, in a private pre-school in a relatively affluent area in England, to consider how the quality of parental involvement could be improved. It provides a good example of how the roles of parents and practitioners, as outlined by Keyes (2002), can complement each other.

Action Research: involves the identification of a practical problem/issue which is changed through individual or collaborative action, then researched.

High Scope curriculum: a guided curriculum, whereby educators support children in developing and carrying out plans and in choosing activities, which enables them to carry out the activity themselves.

Plan–do–review: children are appropriately supported in the selection and planning of an activity, which they carry out themselves and then review after thorough discussion with practitioners and other children.

WHAT HAPPENS IN PRACTICE?

Bell Nursery, located close to a new town in a rural area of England, offers 18 places to 3–5 year olds from 8.30am–5.30pm, Monday to Friday. In practice, the majority of children, from socially and economically middle class families, attend on a part-time basis, where the staff–child ratio is 1:6. Bell Nursery supports the High Scope curriculum. The nursery developed an unwritten policy of co-operation in the development of staff–parent relationships and although parents were supportive and responsive to the curriculum employed, active parental involvement was not a feature of Bell Nursery. In order to improve the quality of parental involvement, the Nursery developed an action research project employing the following strategies to both increase and evaluate parental involvement:

1   ask parents and children to plan together at home
2   observe children's play during 'Plan–do–review' time
3   ask parents about their involvement through planning.

The head teacher involved the staff at the outset, arranging a meeting to discuss their perceptions of parental involvement at Bell Nursery and what they wanted for the future. They decided that parents should be more involved in their children's learning. An informal approach (talking to parents as opposed to a letter) was chosen as the best means of involving parents in the planning activity. The following is a summary of the main findings:

• Children arrived at the pre-school sessions with clearer plans of their activity, knowing what they wanted to do and how to do it.
• 4 year olds often produced drawn and written plans, highlighting how parents and children had thought about problems which might arise in carrying out the activity.

- It provided an overlap between school and home, with children continuing plans at school.
- Planning the activity at home gave the children confidence, leading to improved socialisation (talking about their plan/activity) and competence in the pre-school setting.
- Children concentrated on the planned activities for longer periods of time and successfully completed more of their planned activity.
- Often increased the involvement of children's fathers.
- The curriculum became less staff-directed and more child- and parent-directed.
- Planning by parents and children produced many examples of high quality play.
- Staff spoke about having to hold back more and listen to children more carefully.
- Staff saw parent–child planning as the key to unlocking children's minds and enabled them to find out what children thought about and what was important and interesting to them.
- Staff found it easier to support children.
- Staff saw the importance of giving children time that extended day-to-day to allow their plans to develop.
- Planning at home resulted in play that was based upon children's own lives.
- Parent–child planning showed that children regularly learn through their real life relationships and experiences.
- Parents of 3 year olds were of the opinion that it helped them to form happy relationships with staff and other children, although they thought that they might be too young for planning activity in isolation from other activities.
- Parents of older children saw it as a valuable means of enabling children to develop self-discipline.
- Parents thought that it provided a self-imposed structure that helped children sort out how to go about things.
- Parents commented on the better channels of communication which were opened up with staff as a result.

The overall findings suggested that parents and the home culture are at the centre of children's lives and learning, putting parents in a strong position to influence much of the content and context of the curriculum.

(Bridge, 2001)

REFLECT AND RELATE TO PRACTICE

In what ways does this initiative at Bell Nursery, designed to involve parents in their children's learning and development, complement their role as outlined in Table 2.1? How important is the development of relationships in this example? You will need to give examples from the evidence provided.

☆ ☆ ☆

For each of the points addressed in the summary of the main findings, what do you think are the reason/reasons for the stated outcome?

For some of the points you are given a significant amount of information already to help you consider this.

In what other ways has this activity helped the children's learning and development?

You will find it helpful to look up the *Statutory Framework for the Early Years Foundation Stage: Setting the Standards for Learning Development and Care for children from birth to five* (EYFS) (DfES, 2007), available at: **www.everychildmatters.gov.uk** – and consider the educational programmes within each learning area.

Would you use this type of activity to involve parents in the learning and development of their children at Key Stage 1? Why/why not?

You also need to consider if it might be more appropriate to adapt it or employ a completely different method.

The following example of 'What happens in practice?' outlines the results from a relatively small-scale, qualitative study conducted in New Zealand by Duncan et al. (2006) which addressed parental involvement in early years settings. In contrast to Bridge (2001), Duncan et al. (2006) considered how three Early Childhood Centres helped families from disadvantaged communities. (The Early Childhood Centres of New Zealand shared a philosophy similar to the Early Excellence Centres of England, which were a forerunner of the Sure Start programme.)

WHAT HAPPENS IN PRACTICE?

Duncan et al. (2006 p. 2) underline 'positive, trusting, known stable relationships . . . as the basis for building strong links between the parents and others in the centre, where informal contact with staff was valued over and above formal contact'. They further suggested that informal involvement put less pressure on parents and provided a means of engaging parents whose own experience of school may have been negative or who have other work or family commitments. They highlighted the benefit of the following informal strategies as a means of building stable relationships with families:

create an environment where families feel welcome and comfortable . . . taking an interest in activities children do at home and linking these to their experiences in the Early Childhood Centre . . . assisting families on arrival and leaving to settle children, locate belongings etc.

The informal approach, they suggested, provided opportunity for 'information sharing' and 'making parents feel that they mattered'.

REFLECT AND RELATE TO PRACTICE

What strategies were used to involve parents? Do you think they are effective for this type of setting, where there are many disadvantaged families?

You need to consider how socio-economic factors influence parental involvement.

☆ ☆ ☆

Having read this example of 'What happens in practice?' how would you involve parents in an early years setting/school in a poor rural area in England?

You need to consider: if parents are not involved, why are they not involved, would they want to be involved, could you change their attitude if initially they had resisted involvement? In addition consider how you would involve parents who are keen to be partners in their children's learning. Consider children 0–2, 3–5 and 5–7 years.

Children's centres of the future

Although children's centres were initially developed in the poorest local government wards in England, they have been conceptualised as a universal service to support all children and their families. They are expected to provide:

- early years education
- high quality, flexible childcare
- opportunities for parents to be involved in their children's learning
- adult learning
- family support and outreach services
- child and family health services
- support for children and parents with special needs
- effective links with job centre plus local training providers, and further and higher education institutions.

This section will consider the purpose of children's centres in light of the services they provide.

Additionally, children's centres act as 'service hubs' within communities, offering a base for childminder networks with links to **neighbourhood nurseries**, out of school clubs and **extended schools**. Children's centres also have an instrumental role to play in training the childcare workforce and contributing to the childcare career development framework (see Chapter 11). The children's centre agenda mirrors the government's agenda for schools (i.e. the provision of extended schools) as set out in their *Five Year Strategy* (DfES, 2004). It is a challenging agenda, but offers real and exciting opportunities for schools and children's centres. The four main elements are:

Neighbourhood nursery: provides full-time, quality childcare, at a reasonable price, to the under 5s in the poorest areas of England.

Extended schools: a school providing services beyond the school day.

1 Extra flexibility in the system for schools to innovate
2 Collaboration between schools and other partners
3 An intelligent accountability framework
4 All schools will be encouraged to become extended schools.

We will now look at these in turn.

Extra flexibility in the system for schools to innovate

As guaranteed three-year budgets come on stream schools will be better placed to plan for their future. Every secondary school will not only be able to become a specialist school with a mission to build a centre of curriculum excellence but they can take on a second specialism to develop their mission further.

Collaboration between schools and other partners

This will include the private, voluntary and community sector providers, health and social care services etc., meeting the needs of children, the school and community.

An intelligent accountability framework

A new relationship with schools should enable school professionals to self-review and be accountable, with the inspection service confirming their position.

All schools will be encouraged to become extended schools

The collaboration of services and the specific outcomes for extended schools are closely aligned to children's centres. The provision outlined above is matched by the provision required of extended schools, as follows:

- childcare;
- adult education – adult learning and family Learning;
- parenting support programmes – information sessions, parenting programmes;
- community-based health and social care services – referral to a wide range of specialist services such as speech therapy, child and adolescent mental health services, family support services, intensive behaviour support, sexual health services for young people;
- **multi-agency** behaviour support teams;
- after-school activities – homework, study support, sport, music tuition, dance and drama, arts and crafts, special interest clubs, visits to museums and galleries, foreign language, volunteering, business and enterprise activities. This includes holiday activities.

Multi-agency: a group of professionals from the different disciplines – health, social and education – working together to support a child and his/her family.

This long term-investment by the government is about bringing together more opportunities and services into single settings (i.e. through children's centres and schools). Bringing services together makes it easier for the service providers (early years settings and schools) to work with the specialist or targeted service that some children need. This approach is very evident in many schools but the government is accelerating its programme to ensure the provision is in place by 2010. In view of this more integrated programme of working, it may be appropriate to consider a different word from 'school' to clarify what is intended; a more appropriate term might be 'Community Learning Centre'. The following 'What happens in practice?' is taken from an interview with the director of a Sure Start children's centre and provides a good example of this type of partnership working in practice.

WHAT HAPPENS IN PRACTICE?

At our centre, we have an organic model – it grows as parents and staff develop. It is different to what it was six years ago. For example, if a child spends two days a week here, we invite the parent to come in and spend a day with the child.

If there's a problem, for example financial, there's someone here to help them [the parents] sort it out. We also have, for example, ante-natal care and a peer breast feeding supporter. Parents can take a course on child speech and language development or a course on behaviour or they can join the netball team. We second staff into our programme. We work very closely with the health visitors, who are now in our building and they inform us of issues. [In addition] we have an adult speech and language therapy service and a paediatrician comes in every Thursday. They are all part of our team. We also have a community speech and language therapist and we have different courses which help the community.

REFLECT AND RELATE TO PRACTICE

To what extent does this Sure Start children's centre reflect the government's vision for children's centres and extended schools?

You will need to consider the bullet points listed on page 48.

 ☆ ☆ ☆

Consider the practices introduced into this Sure Start children's centre to increase 'partnership working' of all those involved. For each practice developed consider the reason/reasons why it was developed. For each practice introduced, can you think of an alternative?

You may consider that the one put in place by the centre was the best; in which case state that and justify why you think it is the best approach.

The benefits of children's centres

The vision for children's centres is to provide a central role in improving outcomes and well-being for all young children, and reduce inequalities in outcomes between the most disadvantaged children and the rest (DfES, 2005a). Through a case study, which highlights the advantages of the effective integrated working of service providers in reaching those 'most in need', this section will consider the benefits of children's centres on the lives of those whom they serve.

The impact of centres on children's lives cannot be overstated; for example, research has shown that pregnancy and the first year of a child's life are crucial to their future development, influencing such areas as their eating patterns, 'physical activity, well-being, cognitive development and emotional security' (Page, 2000, cited in DfES, 2007a: 8). Although children's centres can be a vital support to parents at this time, where the services of midwives, health visitors and other social service providers are freely available, many of the parents who are most in need do not know how to access the services provided; this has been addressed through outreach targeting. However, the following 'What happens in practice?' provides an example of how good communication between service providers, promoted through the integrated system of working, can provide help at a crucial time to 'most in need' parents.

WHAT HAPPENS IN PRACTICE?

Joanne, 24, was identified as being at risk of postnatal depression after a routine hospital visit when pregnant with her first child. She didn't have a family to support her, her circle of friends did not have children yet, and there was concern that she was going to be spending a lot of time alone at home with her baby. Joanne was assigned a befriender and it was through her befriender that she was introduced to the Newpin centre in Southwark when her daughter was 8 months old.

Joanne is now taking part in Newpin's play project (funded as an Early Learning Partnership project) with her second child, a two-year-old boy. In her group there are four parents and their children and two workers. Through play Joanne learns both how to relate better to her son and also how to help him developmentally.

Joanne says: 'He got this box and put it over his head – and instead of telling him it's naughty, I have to do it as well, to gain an understanding of why he is doing it. We copy them. It's fun to see the children responding to it.'

Joanne and her son paint and draw together and invent games with cardboard boxes. For Joanne it has been a lifeline and a chance to do things with her son she would never dream of doing at home, as well as to meet and talk with other people like her. The project co-ordinator Carolyn plans to take the project out to local disadvantaged families like refugees, asylum seekers and families identified by the Child and Adolescent Mental Health Service.

(DfES, 2007a: 12)

REFLECT AND RELATE TO PRACTICE

How has this mother been helped to support, interact with and stimulate her daughter and son?

Do you think this will be effective in the long term?

You need to consider this in relation to the children's learning, development and well-being.

As children progress through the early years of their life, a number of factors can have a strong impact on their future life chances – for example, the relationship they have with their parents, the extent to which they are stimulated and, as recent research has shown, the involvement of the father (DCSF, 2008: 10). These life chances are strongly related to poverty and deprivation, hence the location of the children's centres in the most disadvantaged areas in England.

Communities of learners: bringing it together

Local Authorities (LAs), as commissioners rather than providers of services, have been charged with offering high quality early years provision integrated with health and family support services (in essence they are there to support and guide the practices within the settings). There is a strong emphasis on parental involvement at all levels. Within children's centres this varies from governance and organisation through to parent education programmes and child–parent education and support programmes.

All early years settings are, or have the potential to be, communities of practice (Wenger, 1998) founded on the social participation of all those involved. Children's centres are a good example of a wider community of practice or a community within a community located within different buildings and areas – new builds in shopping precincts, within the most difficult housing estates, within the grounds of schools or local authority offices or in the premises of nursery establishments. Although the location of a number of children's centres within schools is not desirable, the integration of them within a school cluster supports the sharing of good practice and working together. The benefits of children's centres to the community are perhaps best summed up by the following comment made by the head teacher of a primary school in Kent: 'It is really clear in our reception class which children have been involved with Sure Start. They are generally happier children – and happy children make the best learners' (DCSF, 2008: 9).

SUMMARY

Community of practice: underlying theory (p. 33)

In essence, communities of practice are characterised by 'social participation' – the building of relationships (practitioner–child, child–child and parent–practitioner, etc.) through shared practice with common aims.

The learning community (p. 34)

How do practitioners contribute to creating the early years learning community?

All members of the early years setting, as participants, should be encouraged to have a shared commitment to the modelling of community. To be effective, early years educational settings need organisational structures, aims and guiding rules.

Sure Start: a community within a community (p. 37)

Building on a firm foundation: how would you improve practice in Sure Start centres?

The Sure Start programme was initiated as a means of helping children from deprived areas – providing health, education and social care under one roof – and supporting their families. By addressing practice in one Sure Start centre and considering findings from the National Evaluation of Sure Start (NESS) project, the benefits to the community of having services co-located in one setting are highlighted.

Parents as partners (p. 40)

Parents have a central role to play in the learning and development of their child/children. It is vital that they are involved from the earliest years. Although involving parents can be wrought with difficulties, practitioners should continue to work with parents finding effective ways to complement the parents' role.

Children's centres of the future (p. 47)

Although children's centres were developed to provide support to the most-in-need families and their children, they have now become a hub of activity providing services from early years education through to adult learning and family support.

The benefits of children's centres (p. 50)

Children's centres can provide valuable support to families and their children who might otherwise feel isolated (e.g. single mothers).

Glossary

Action Research: involves the identification of a practical problem/issue which is changed through individual or collaborative action, then researched. The problems may not be clearly defined and the change process may evolve through practice.

Communities of practice: in essence, communities of practice are characterised by social participation – the building of relationships (practitioner–child, child–child and parent–practitioner, etc.) through shared practice with common aims.

Extended schools: a school providing services (activities and further educational or health programmes for children, parents, families and the wider community) beyond the school day.

High Scope curriculum: a guided curriculum, which originated in America in the 1960s whereby educators support children in developing and carrying out plans and in choosing activities, which enables them to carry out the activity themselves.

Independent (early years) school: an early years provider within the independent sector, usually within an independent school.

Independent learner: a learner who has the belief in him/herself to think through learning activities, problems or challenges, make decisions about his/her learning and act upon those decisions.

Maintained early years setting: an early years setting which is maintained (funded) by the Local Authority (often located within a school).

Multi-agency: a group of professionals from the different disciplines – health, social and education – working together to support a child and his/her family.

Mutual society: an organisation owned by its members and run, in theory, for their benefit.

Neighbourhood nursery: a government initiative of 2001 to provide full-time, quality childcare, at a reasonable price, to the under 5s in the poorest areas of England.

Outreach workers: those who actively target (by visiting or making known in other ways) those considered to be in need of and who otherwise would not know about the services provided through the centre.

Plan–do–review: a characteristic of the High Scope curriculum, whereby children are appropriately supported in the selection and planning of an activity, which they carry out themselves and then review through discussion with practitioners and other children.

Portage worker: a person who provides a home early years educational programme to children in need of extra support. They work with and support the parents in the delivery of the programme and liaise with pre-schools/schools to help children make a successful transition into the educational setting.

Private nursery: nurseries which are privately owned by individuals or companies and are eligible to claim funding for the children who attend (within the allowance).

Quality: the term used to describe the merits of teaching and learning within a setting. It covers a broad area, encompassing teaching to the early learning goals to meet the individual needs (affective and cognitive) of each child and responding to learners as individuals. This is a contested area, particularly when determined by externally imposed standards. Quality should be internally driven.

Sure Start: see Sure Start children's centres.

Sure Start children's centres: launched as a government initiative in 1998, with the aim of providing access to health, education and social services in one location to young children (0–5 years) and their families living in deprived communities.

Voluntary (early years) setting: settings run by voluntary management committees of which some have charitable status. These settings often offer sessional care.

Find out more

Smidt, S. (1998) *A Guide to Early Years Practice*, **London: Routledge.**
Chapter 9: Partnerships with parents, considers practical ways of involving parents in children's learning. The chapter opens with a brief history of how parents came to be more involved in their children's education.

Wenger, E. (1998) *Communities of Practice: Learning, Meaning and Identity*, **Cambridge: Cambridge University Press.**
The idea of educational organisations as communities of practice is starting to shape classroom practice in schools and early years settings. Wenger (1998), the first to employ this phrase, gives a very detailed account of what this means in practice. It is worth reading his book and considering what this means for an early years setting and for an early years practitioner.

References

Anning, A. and Edwards, A. (2004) Young children as learners, in Miller, L. and Devereux, J. (eds) *Supporting Children's Learning in the Early Years*. London: David Fulton.

Bridge, H. (2001) Increasing parental involvement in the Preschool Curriculum: what an action research case study revealed, *International Journal of Early Years Education*, Vol. 9, No. 1.

Bronfenbrenner, U. (1979) *The Ecology of Human Development*. Cambridge, MA: Harvard University Press.

Children's Workforce Development Council (CWDC) (2008) *Guidance to the Standards for the award of Early Years Professional Status*: CWDC.

Department for Children, Schools and Families (DCSF) (2008) *Inclusion Development Programme: Supporting children with speech, language and communication needs: Guidance for practitioners in the Early Years Foundation Stage*. Nottingham: DCSF.

Department for Education and Skills (2004) *Five Year Strategy for Children and Learners*. Norwich: TSO.

Department for Education and Skills (DfES) (2005a) *Sure Start Children's Centres: Practice Guidance*. Nottingham: DfES Publications.

Department for Education and Skills (DfES) (2005b) *The Quality of Early Learning, Play and Childcare Services in Sure Start Local Programmes* (SSLP). Nottingham: DfES Publications.

Department for Education and Skills (DfES) (2007a) *Every Parent Matters*. Nottingham: DfES Publications.

Department for Education and Skills (DfES) (2007b) The *Statutory Framework for the Early Years Foundation Stage: Setting the Standards for Learning Development and Care for children from birth to five* (EYFS). Nottingham: DfES Publications.

Duncan, J., Bowden, C. and Smith, A. (2006) A gossip or a good yack? Reconceptualising parent support in New Zealand early childhood centre based programme, *International Journal of Early Years Education*, Vol. 14, No. 1: pp. 1–13.

Goouch, K. and Powell, S. (2006) Case Studies for Early Years Professional Standards 2.1–2.7. Canterbury: Canterbury Christ Church University.

Hannon, P. and Fox, L. (2005) Why should we learn from Sure Start, in Weinberger, J., Pickstone, C. and Hannon, P. (eds) *Learning from Sure Start: Working with Young Children and their Families*. Maidenhead: Open University Press.

HMSO (2005) National Evaluation of Sure Start (NESS) *Variation in Sure Start Local Programmes' Effectiveness: Early Preliminary Findings*; research report NESS/2005/FR/014. London: HMSO.

Katz, L.G. (1984) Contemporary Perspectives on the Roles of Mothers and Teachers. In *More Talks with Teachers*. Urbana, IL: ERIC Clearinghouse on Elementary and Early Childhood Education: pp. 1–26.

Keyes, C. (2002) A Way of Thinking about Parents/Teacher Partnerships for Teachers, *International Journal of Early Years Education*, Vol. 10, No. 3: pp. 177–191.

Miller, L. (2000) Play as a Foundation for Learning, in Drury, R., Miller, L. and Campbell, R. (eds) *Looking at Early Years Education and Care*. London: David Fulton: pp. 7–16.

Ofsted (2008a) *Early Years Self-Evaluation Form*. London: HMI Publications. Available at: **www.ofsted.gov.uk**.

Ofsted (2008b) *Early Years Self-Evaluation Form Guidance*. London: HMI Publications. Available at: **www.ofsted.gov.uk**.

Page, A. (2000) An International Symposium, London, No. 34, April 2000; cited in 'Changing Times: support for parents and families during pregnancy and the first twelve months'. Presentations to PC2000, National Family and Parenting Institute: available at http://www.ippr.org.uk/uploadedFiles/projects/Anne%20Page%20final%20draft.doc

Wenger, E. (1998) *Communities of Practice: Learning, Meaning and Identity*. Cambridge: Cambridge University Press.

West, L. and Carlson, A. (2007) *Claiming Space: An in-depth auto/biographical study of a local Sure Start project*. Centre for International Studies of Diversity and Participation, Department of Educational Research: Canterbury Christ Church University.

Values Promoting Learning

By the end of this chapter you will be able to answer the following questions:

- How would you define 'values' and other related terms?
- What are the influences and experiences which have impacted on the development of your individual values?
- How do these values relate to the principles and beliefs that contribute to the kind of provision you establish?
- How do you relate these to the way you respond to individual children and families?
- How do different value systems impact on the holistic learning environment that you provide?
- Can you identify some of the challenges you may face in responding to the needs of government and parental wishes which may conflict with personal viewpoints?
- Can you consider the issues from an international perspective and appreciate the variety and impact of different forms of childhood globally?

This chapter will support your understanding of the following Standards *(see Appendix 1)*:
Knowledge and understanding: S03 ■ **Effective practice:** S07, S08, S12, S13, S18 and S24
■ **Relationships with children:** S25, S27 and S28 ■ **Communicating and working in partnership with families and carers:** S30 ■ **Teamwork and collaboration:** S35 ■ **Professional development:** S39.

Introduction

It could be said that there are various kinds of confusion about human values
... There are many definitions and innumerable studies. No definition has
attracted widespread consensus ... One would be hard put to locate a useful
definition of values within the international community that is not
challenged by some alternative definition that is valued by others.

(Union of International Associations, Human Values Project; section 2.1)

This chapter focuses on an exploration of personal values and how these impact on
the quality of provision for young children and their families. Examples are given
from the UK and compared with approaches in a European and global context. Issues
to do with children's rights are raised, in reflection on the ability of adults to recognise
that children can have a voice in contributing to the society in which they live. A brief
exploration of the relationship between a child's individual development and learning and the expectations of the early years setting curriculum, in its widest sense, is
included. There are local or national requirements for practitioners to follow, inspected
by the Office for Standards in Education and similar agencies in the UK. Reference is
made to risk in relation to perceived dangers in the communities in which children
live and how young people can learn to safeguard themselves if they are not allowed
access to managed challenges.

   This chapter has been written at a time of rapid change for young children throughout the world, whether due to factors such as the AIDS (Acquired Immune Deficiency
Syndrome) pandemic or children's involvement in conflict, or because of a national
focus on the quality of early education and the foundation stage in school. Within the
UK as well as elsewhere, this has resulted in reconsideration, not only of the curriculum
but of the qualifications of those employed to care for and educate very young children. Traditionally the early years and foundation stage sectors have been viewed as
employment for females with low educational achievements, or who use it expedi-
ently while raising a family or prior to moving on to higher education. It has been
consequently poorly funded and wages have been low. This has been changing dramatically with large numbers of young people and experienced workers opting for
higher qualifications. It is now recognised that early years is a complex field in which
to work, where personal views and theory intermingle and often conflict. Not all of
those who currently work in the field will be traditional 'teachers', though many
others will have degrees and equivalent training. To cover all of those who work at a
professional level with young children the term 'early years practitioner' has been
selected.

Values to promote learning

Defining the word 'value' is hard. It is one of those words which is used frequently but
poorly defined. It includes notions of 'beliefs', 'attitudes' and principles' yet none of
these capture the essence of a 'value' being at the heart of an individual's existence.

Beliefs and attitudes are there to be changed as deeper knowledge and understanding are gained. Principles, now often formalised into 'sets' for different professions and institutions, govern people's behaviour as members of certain groups or form the basis of a theory or system of belief. This term, however, is often used interchangeably with values. Again, principles are liable to alter as different professional or political priorities come into play; they can be 'updated'. By exploring the meaning of values this section challenges the reader to consider the extent to which values are subject to situation and place.

'Values' are more deeply rooted than principles; they derive from an individual's earliest experiences of being part of a social group and are a reaction to how a child was treated and respected as he or she grew. They incorporate what is considered right or wrong, what is important in an individual's life and how other people are perceived and responded to. There is a strong 'ethical' dimension to the concept of 'values'. If they are to be interpreted in this way, then individuals need to be fully aware of the way they react to others; the regard in which they are held is governed by individual values and how the world is perceived.

In analysing the meaning of 'values' in the context of early childhood, a survey of recent, relevant, publications revealed few which indexed this term and entered into a debate on its meaning. One exception was Rinaldi (2006), known for her research on the **Reggio Emilia** approach to early years education in Italy, who returned numerous times to **values** in this collection of her speeches and writing. She suggests a possible definition:

> Values are the ideals that a person aspires to in his or her life which act as a point of reference to our judgments and conduct, and according to which we conform (or not) in our relations with the social group of reference (community, society, culture) . . . It is we, as people, who choose our values, confirm them and sustain them.

(Rinaldi, 2006: 138)

An exploration of 'values' in the early years needs not only to explore and define the concept of 'value' but also to place this exploration in all of its different contexts. Rinaldi prompts that values 'can only be defined in relation to the cultural, political and historical context' (2006: 138). There are personal (i.e. the derivation of the practitioner's personal beliefs, philosophies and values), individual (i.e. with reference to the child), community, national, European and global aspects to this analysis. These aspects are framed by the varying cultural and political perspectives which derive from the time, geographical location and economic circumstances which prevail at that instant.

Reggio Emilia: an approach to early education that originated in the small town of Reggio Emilia in Italy after the Second World War.

Values: 'the ideals that a person aspires to in his or her life' (Rinaldi, 2006).

DISCUSSION POINT

For example, children growing up in western industrialised states have an entitlement to and access to free healthcare, education and economic and social support, although the levels of these may vary in amount and quality. In contrast, the majority of the world's children from developing countries do not. Visitors from Beijing viewed an extract from a British television documentary which portrayed levels of poverty in the UK and commented that, in comparison with many children in China and elsewhere, these British children had a roof over their heads, clothes, food and other material goods, plus access to school (even if they chose not to attend) and adults in society who cared about their future. In many other countries, children are needed to add to the family and community economy as soon as they are able, either by actual physical work or by taking on household tasks, such as childminding, to release their mothers to work. In countries affected severely by AIDS, young children take responsibility for the well-being and survival of their whole family. Without the contribution from young children, families may not survive. Green (1998) offers a very different perspective from the mainstream view:

> aspects of the conventional view of Third World ('majority world' – does 'Third world' betray our values?) children also evaporate once children are handed the microphone. Many children see paid work very differently from officially sanctioned views of child labour as an evil which should be swiftly abolished. Children often *want* to work, valuing the confidence and self-esteem that their contribution brings to them, as well as the cash. They work in an astonishing range of jobs, usually for extremely little money, but their earnings often keep them and their families above the breadline.
>
> *(Green, 1998: 208)*

What do you think? Do you agree/disagree with this? Why/why not?

The United Nations Convention on the Rights of the Child 1989 (UNCRC)

Built on varied legal systems and cultural traditions, the Convention is a universally agreed set of non-negotiable standards and obligations. These basic standards – also called human rights – set minimum entitlements and freedoms that should be respected by governments. They are founded on respect for the dignity and worth of each individual, regardless of race, colour, gender, language, religion, opinions, origins, wealth, birth status or ability and therefore apply to every human being everywhere. With these rights comes the obligation on both governments and individuals not to infringe on the parallel rights of others. These standards are both

interdependent and indivisible; we cannot ensure some rights without – or at the expense of – other rights.

(UNICEF: www.unicef.org/crc)

The UNCRC applies to children from birth to eighteen. By briefly outlining the details of the countries which signed the UNCRC, the first legally binding document to include the complete range of human rights, this section considers what that means in practice.

In 2006, the UNCRC had been ratified by all but two of the world's nations. One of these was Somalia, a place which has been constantly at war since the convention was agreed; the other is the USA, partly because of the length of time it takes to obtain the agreement of individual states when there is new legislation, but also because it appears some sectors of American society object to handing over responsibility for their children to the state, especially in matters to do with corporal punishment. Once a nation has ratified the convention it is expected to incorporate it into its own legislation. In the UK, the convention's ideals were included in the Children Act 1989 and it was formally ratified in December 1991 (the UK did not ratify on everything though, e.g. children of refugees and asylum seekers). Progress towards complying with all the articles was monitored after two years, then every five years when each country must submit a report. UNICEF considers the most important of the 54 articles to be:

- All rights apply to all children without exception or discrimination of any kind (article 2).
- That the best interests of the child must be a primary consideration in all actions concerning children (article 3).
- That States have an obligation to ensure as much as possible every child's survival and development (article 6).
- Children's views must be taken into account in all matters affecting them (article 12).

It is the first legally binding international instrument to incorporate the full range of human rights – civil, cultural, economic, political and social rights (UNICEF: **www.unicef.org/crc**). The UNCRC is the background to the work undertaken with children. It should form part of a belief system at all levels and hopefully become part of the values which each individual holds personally.

REFLECT AND RELATE TO PRACTICE

Have you ever considered the lives of young children at other times or in other places? What do you really know about children's experiences beyond your own community? Explore your views, then share them with your learning community. Investigate other societies' expectations of their children through researching film, written sources and the internet. Revisit your values after this investigation. What has surprised you? What have you learnt?

Personal values

Defining, and therefore understanding, values leads to pinpointing what these mean personally for individuals. Reflecting on individual values, and the principles which derive from them, should enable one to see how children and adults are reacted to in different situations and the judgements that are made about them, resulting then in the decisions which are made in everyday professional lives. By considering the extent to which an individual's values affect the way he/she interacts with the children within the setting, this section challenges the reader to question his/her own values. Individual values, then, inform reactions and actions, quite often subconsciously unless practitioners are prepared to confront them openly and honestly. Responses to the families practitioners work with and their commitment to parental involvement often reflect their value systems very closely. If values are formed by the families and communities in which they grew up, then practitioners may act negatively towards the parents they encounter because they belong to a different class or cultural community. They may have different views on the way children should dress, speak and behave, on gender roles or the purpose and form of education that is offered in the nurseries and schools in the communities in which they now live. They may have views on physical punishment that are not shared, or may not understand 'play' and prefer to see a much more formal approach to young children's education and care.

Once practitioners are aware of the drivers which compel them to make sometimes simplistic and narrow judgements, then the impact these can have on children and families can be considered, hopefully creating an environment where all are valued for who they are and not what they are. If this is not done, then children's learning may

Photo 3.1
Do your values influence the way you relate to the children within your setting?

Pearson Education Ltd. Jules Selmes © Pearson Education Ltd. 2004

be restricted because their potential is not recognised when practitioners think it is limited by background.

DISCUSSION POINT

An example: an early years adviser was asked to visit a rural school nursery to offer advice on the development of a little boy which was causing concern to his teacher. The adviser was able to spend a couple of sessions in the nursery, working with the children and observing the child. At the end of her time there, the adviser could observe nothing about the child's behaviour that led her to conclude that his development was beyond the broad spectrum of what was expected for his age. In fact, he had blossomed in the small group she had engaged with and enjoyed talking with her and his peers. She discussed this with the nursery teacher, who was very caring and pleasant and committed to the children's welfare. The conversation was open and supportive and some suggestions were agreed, though the teacher really remained convinced that the child was developmentally delayed. 'After all', she said, 'I taught his parents and they were never very bright'.

Rosenthal and Jacobson (1968) identified in their research the concept of the 'self-fulfilling prophesy'. This means that children will quickly conform to the expectations teachers have of them, whether these expectations are positive or negative. In Iowa in 1970, Jane Elliott carried out an experiment (commonly referred to as 'Blue Eyes, Brown Eyes') with 8–9 year olds, depicted in the documentary *Eye of the Storm*. Although centred on the development of racism, it also demonstrates graphically how children's views of themselves can very rapidly be radically transformed according to the attitude towards them portrayed by a teacher.

Do you agree with this? Why/why not?

Professional identity, qualifications and pay

There may also be strong views on the worth of qualifications for those working in the early years. It may be considered that experience suffices and the necessity for higher qualifications at degree level and beyond may not be recognised. This has been a powerful response from those organising daycare in the private (for profit) and voluntary (not-for-profit) sectors, particularly in the UK, where financial viability is so important. If you are reading this, then you probably do view enhanced knowledge and understanding positively as a way of improving the quality of provision and practice in your work. By examining the notion of professional identity and status, which can lead, more often than not, to a hierarchical structure in the setting, this section explores the idea that these are closely linked to an individual's personal values and beliefs.

Theoretical perspectives, especially when based on first-hand experience, help to spread knowledge from generalisations about individuals to understanding far more about differences and the details of human development and learning. A commitment to improving qualifications – and so knowledge and understanding – may apply to an individual, through an enthusiasm for lifelong learning or by establishing learning communities which share a common passion for finding out all there is to know. Personal values could delineate how individuals engage in working with other professions, whether this is entered into wholeheartedly, sharing expertise, or whether practitioners retreat behind professional boundaries. In the UK, there has been *national* pressure towards 'working together' from the Children Act 1989 onwards through the Sure Start initiative to the development of children's centres where services, parents and representatives from local communities are located together. How this is done, however, has never really been opened up to greater debate. Jones et al. discuss:

> how constructions of professional identity and status can often lead to the development of hierarchies of service that may undermine democratic and shared communication. This point raises concerns . . . and suggests the need for a more deep-rooted examination of the ways that professional practitioners may relate to each other. A significant obstacle to service cooperation has been concerned with how practitioners appear to understand institutional and cultural dynamics required for improving communication and whether any barricades consisting of perceived difference and self-importance can be overcome.
>
> *(Jones et al., 2005: 209)*

All in all, personal values underpin how an individual views the people and the work in which he/she is involved and should ensure that he/she is confident in creating the best contexts for children's learning.

REFLECT AND RELATE TO PRACTICE

Have there been any incidents in your growing up where the response of an adult has had a negative effect on your self-esteem or your determination to follow a particular life pathway? Has this happened to other people in your family? Why did this occur? Was it due to prejudice (explore the different forms) or low expectations? How did you overcome this – have you? Explore these issues sensitively with members of your learning community.

ACTIVITY

1 What are your reflections on the status of children within our society and what have you read that supports your views? Note these down.

> 2 What do you consider are your personal values and where do you think they originate? Discuss this with others in your learning community.
> 3 How do you think your personal values are reflected in the work you do? Are there conflicts between what you are expected to do and what you would wish to do? Be critical. Prepare two lists to illustrate conflicts.

Individual values

At an individual level other people's value systems can be explored, as well as observing how children come to develop their own. The way in which children's development is supported will depend on a practitioner's own philosophies of 'childhood'. By considering the views of various renowned educationalists, this section explores the idea of childhood and shows how children's development of personal values is influenced by the way adults, in particular practitioners, relate to them and the extent to which they acknowledge that children have rights. Sociologists and historians have been debating 'childhood' for many years now, although this has centred predominantly on the experience of children in Europe and North America. This exploration of childhood intensified in 1962 when Philippe Aries' book *Centuries of Childhood* brought to an English-speaking audience the idea that childhood was a relatively new concept, starting to develop from the medieval period onwards. Before that, the separateness between children and adults was not so visible; Aries takes as his evidence, for example, paintings in which children are dressed as small versions of adults. Postman (1994 [1982]), an American Professor of Education who was renowned for his research and writings on media, postulated that it was the coming of the printing press in the fifteenth century which 'created a new definition of childhood *based on reading competence*, and, correspondingly, a new conception of childhood *based on reading incompetence*. Prior to the coming of that new environment, infancy ended at seven and adulthood began at once' (1994 [1982]: 18).

Postman considers 'children are the living messages to a time we will not see'. His classic book, *The Disappearance of Childhood*, was a forerunner of many similar publications which have debated the fate of children in the years since Postman's book was first published. Idealised versions of what childhood should be have been countered by other historians and sociologists since 1962, who, like de Mause (1974), point out that childhood for many was never freedom and sweetness, even if you survived the first few months. This must certainly be the experience of children born beyond the boundaries of the affluent 'first world', whose very existence demands that they work hard and are drawn into situations, such as famine and war, where the 'rights' enshrined by the UNCRC cannot support or protect them. These debates form the background to the development of attitudes towards the kind of provision created for children and the decisions made about their lives.

Do we believe, do our values promote, that childhood should be a time of freedom and discovery or do we consider that children need to be tamed and controlled by adults to ensure they *become* worthy workers and citizens?

Sometimes personal values may lead us to support the first ideal, but circumstances and practicalities conspire to lead to adopting the second. This has happened when national and local government policies and priorities, and sometimes parental views, have conflicted with deep-felt philosophies of how things should be for young children. In the UK, focus on early years from the mid-1990s onward has been welcomed by many, but not all. For example, to receive some additional funding, playgroups and pre-schools have felt it necessary to compromise their beliefs in play in order to match government requirements and reach its targets.

Lee's (2005) book, *Childhood and Human Value*, concentrates on these sorts of issues, but the focus shifts away from 'values' at an individual level towards an argument which explores 'the question of how children and childhood should be "valued" today and in the near future' (2005: 7). Here he equates 'value' with 'worth' and explores the relationships between adults and children which can often seem to be in conflict, particularly the tensions 'between loving and caring for children and valuing children as equals, between possessing them and seeing them as self-possessed' (ibid.). He identifies four ways in which children may be 'valued' in society:

- As innocents, 'whose innocence draws spontaneous love and reassurance from those more experienced than them'.
- As parental investments, 'who can be valued because of what they do for their parents' identities' or 'as a security against their parents' futures'.
- As bearers of cultural and familial heritage.
- As sites of state investment, which impacts upon the way children are educated 'as the future population of a state' thus giving 'policy-makers powerful justifications for shaping children's lives' (2005: 8–11).

Lee's argument develops the idea of 'separability', that children do not 'belong' to others but have rights to be themselves without eroding the relationships children have with their parents and communities. He observes:

> Children's apparent failure as individuals to be able to think and be responsible for themselves are principal reasons for their exclusion from decision-making processes. But if these qualities are, as I would argue, collective and institutional in origin, there is no reason why decision-making processes themselves should not be structured so as to assist children to be able to perform them. On this view, it is simply mistaken to reject children's rights to participation as based on a poor reflection of children's actual abilities.

(2005: 157)

Clark and Moss (2001) reported on research into listening to children which resulted in the Mosaic Approach. The research had been developed with children of three and four years old and later adapted to those who are under two and those who had English as an additional language. Clark and Moss discuss how they had generated a 'framework for listening to children'; this centres on:

- *Multi-method*: which recognises the different voices or languages of children;
- *Participatory*: where children are treated as experts and agents in their own lives;
- *Reflexive*: which includes children, practitioners and parents in reflecting on meanings and addresses the question of interpretation;
- *Adaptable*: so that it can be applied in a variety of early childhood institutions;
- *Focused on children's lived experiences*: so it can be used for a variety of purposes including looking at lives lived rather than knowledge gained or care received;
- *Embedded in practice*: a framework for listening which has the potential to be both used as an evaluative tool and to become embedded into early years practice (2001: 5).

Clark and Moss remind practitioners that young children communicate their views not only verbally but through 'their play, their actions and their reactions'. Listening to children requires that adults take these into account and begin to see the world from children's perspectives, 'acknowledging their rights to express their points of view or to remain silent' (2001: 7).

Clark and Moss pay tribute to work undertaken in the nurseries of northern Italy. A study of the Reggio Emilia approach to early education will reveal how children's participation is valued at all levels and how they co-construct their learning experiences, taking the lead in negotiating, with peers and others, in deciding what the focus of their learning should be.

REFLECT AND RELATE TO PRACTICE

This may be the time to start to think about the origins of your vision of childhood. You may like to reminisce about your own childhood or read the many biographies that have now been written where authors reflect on their experiences of growing up and how this has impacted on their adult lives. Childhood is also depicted in fiction and now in film and documentaries, increasingly available on the internet. You may be interested in paintings or photographs which are a rich source of images of childhood. Do not neglect the philosophers and educationalists who have influenced thinking of childhood. See who you can find. Assemble a portfolio or display of the most significant images for you with an analysis of why they are so powerful.

National values

The British government has, particularly since the mid-1990s, placed children at the centre of its policies. It is fair, however, to point out that the development of the national early years agenda has not always been straightforward nor clear-cut. By considering various views on approaches to early years teaching and learning, which are underpinned by and ultimately driven by values, this section challenges the reader to consider who is responsible for the children of a nation state.

UK residents are not confident in their national attitudes towards very young children and their values are sometimes unclear, whether in deciding the best form of provision for children, when formal schooling should start, whether children should be indulged or dealt with firmly and so on. The terminology used to describe adult relationships with children is in itself fraught with difficulties. Using the word 'belong', for example, raises the spectre of possession and control, when many would like to move away from these concepts towards a children's rights stance where children have more responsibility for themselves. There are few alternatives, however, which can be used to explore the child's relationship with his or her family and the state.

Ultimately, who is responsible for a nation's children? Lee (2005) highlighted one view of the 'worth' of children as being 'state investments' and this has been apparent in the struggle between an early years curriculum which is formal (i.e. introduces children early to a curriculum which is adult-selected and is 'taught') or a play-based curriculum when the children's developmental levels, abilities, interests and motivation are central to the content and essentially child-led. This would countermand the conviction that children need to be taught a limited selection of subjects (in the UK experience, Literacy, Numeracy, Science and ICT) which *may* be crucial in maintaining economic supremacy in years to come, rather than opting for developing children's sense of curiosity, love of learning and personal qualities such as confidence and esteem.

Despite the outcomes from a number of research studies (and growing knowledge of how the brain develops) there is still a reluctance to move away from learning objectives, outcomes and targets which leave adults in control. Even if play is a central tenet of a setting's philosophy, Hall (in Moyles, 1994), while supporting a more structured approach to adult involvement in play, warns against turning play into 'a mournful teacher-led experience', rather 'than a joyful children-initiated experience'; he states clearly that 'there are no penalties for ditching the teacher's ideas, if offered to the children creating a play scenario' (1994: 124).

This is a crucial area for debate as, depending on the outcome, it will form the foundation for the sort of childhood experience those concerned with the quality of young children's lives would wish to provide. There has never really been an open debate in the UK on early childhood where the central focus has been the child. The idea that children's needs should be at the forefront does not sit happily against a background where many adults still consider that children should be seen but not heard.

DISCUSSION POINT

Who should decide the nature of the provision in the early years? What needs to be included? Be visionary.

European values

In a European context, the development of a set of principles which relate to early childhood has been a late-comer in the European Union's deliberations. It was not until the end of the last century that the European community began to look more closely at the children who lived within its boundaries. This section addresses the progress made in Europe in developing a children's rights policy and considers the extent to which this would impact on other European countries. Ruxton (2001) points out that the Treaty of Amsterdam in 1997, which consolidated previous treaties, was the first to mention children specifically.

Euronet, the European children's network, co-ordinates the work of a number of organisations which are concerned with campaigning for the interests and rights of children. Its website publishes documents which refer to Europe's children. The EU which comprises twenty-seven countries now, contains approximately 94 million children and young people aged between 0 and 18. The report, *What About Us? Children's Rights in the European Union: next steps* (Ruxton, 2005) pays tribute to the UNCRC and recognises that any decisions the EU makes now will impact upon its children as they grow to adulthood. The report clearly states that:

> Children have their own specific rights as set out in the 1989 United Nations Convention on the Rights of the Child (UNCRC) and deserve attention as citizens of Europe today, not only as the workers of tomorrow . . . Yet too often children's interests are ignored, and their voices go unheard in the public arena. This is unsurprising, given that they cannot vote, they have little or no access to the media, and limited access to the courts. Nor are they members of powerful lobbying groups. Without access to these processes that are integral to the exercise of demographic rights, children and their opinions remain hidden from view and they are, in consequence, denied effective recognition as citizens.
>
> *(Ruxton, 2005: 8)*

The intentions set out in the report are to develop a children's rights policy, led by a commissioner supported by a Children's Rights Unit dedicated to developing and promoting children's rights across the EU. European intentions will impact upon national policies, as the results of any joint agreements will be written into individual state members' national legislation.

REFLECT AND RELATE TO PRACTICE

How will European policies impact on UK practice?

Global values

In the global context, it can be seen that children's childhoods can be very different and it is hard not to impose majority world values and conceptions of what childhood should be like on other communities, which is what has tended to happen until very recently. By outlining the different cultural values held by people of individual nation states, this section will consider the importance of having an openness to and knowledge of differences for effective and inclusive practice.

Access to the media has tended to mask the subtleties of life in different regions of the world, portraying all children and families in developing countries as a cause for concern, needing the financial support of affluent countries to ensure their survival. The personal values of practitioners working with young children lead them normally to be supportive and generous, but the situation is distorted by the need of those soliciting support to paint a picture which is as bleak as possible. Early years practitioners cannot ignore what happens elsewhere and raise up national drawbridges. There is a joint responsibility for *all* children, even if at a distance, and one never knows when a child may arrive in a setting who has had very different experiences from the majority of children who live in more privileged communities and may therefore have developed diverse sets of values. There are numerous examples which can all be drawn on when practitioners reflect on how they react to very young children and families whose cultural background is different from their own. Dwivedi, who works for the International Institute of Child and Adolescent Mental Health in the United Kingdom, highlights how important it is to 'be aware of the significance of different aspects of the communication process which relate to ethnicity and cultural values and identity and also to have an appreciation of the interplay of these factors with those of racism and cultural conflict' (1995: 153). He points out that it is not only words which take on different meanings according to the cultural background of the person speaking them, but also that body language and gesture do not have universal meanings. In Europe it is usually expected that children should look adults in the eye when they are addressed. It is rude not to do so. This is very different in other parts of the world where it is thought disrespectful for a child to make eye contact with an adult. An example of this relates to a nursery unit in East London; the teacher was very near to making a referral to the educational psychologist because a little boy from Somalia would not make eye contact with her. She had interpreted this as a sign that he was autistic and she was doing her best to find extra help for him. Some research and sympathetic support helped her to realise that all was as it should be with his development. Dwivedi also points to research which shows that:

> bilingual individuals have different values and even gender roles, depending on which language they use . . . When bilinguals speak in their second language their lack of proficiency affects their perception of themselves in relation to others; they may feel that they themselves are less intelligent, happy or confident and this can block and distort their affective communication.
>
> *(Dwivedi, 1995: 154)*

In a British context this is a very important point to make. As a nation, British citizens who are native English speakers have a reputation for being 'poor' at languages. This not only means that they are reluctant to learn new ones themselves (because doesn't everyone now speak English?) but bilingualism is also often viewed as a 'problem', even though speaking more than one language is the norm for most of the world's citizens and children can quite easily learn more than one in supportive circum-stances. Personal values should allow practitioners to see individual differences as strengths and meeting someone from elsewhere as part of their own development and lifelong learning.

The example in the following Discussion point reveals some of the inbuilt preju-dices people can hold, which can work against a child whose background is essentially different from the adults he meets outside the home.

DISCUSSION POINT

A little boy arrived in our nursery. He was four years old and had been to several nurseries in the area before coming to us. For the first week or so, he was quiet; though solitary, nothing led us to suspect he had particular difficulties. His parents were approachable and pleasant. Very quickly, however, his behaviour deteriorated and he became almost unmanageable in the group setting. Strategies were put into place to give him individual attention and support, but this was hard because he was aggressive towards children and verbally very manipulative with adults; he could quickly discover ways to 'wind them up'. As his behaviour deteriorated, so his parents withdrew from communicating with us. Through gathering his history from other settings and through Social Services, we were able to establish the family background and how the child had come to be as he was. His parents were from the Irish Republic; his father had left his wife and children when the boy's mother became pregnant and they had moved to London together. Unable to find steady employment, the family had no way to finance themselves and moved from one flat to another as rent became due. The boy himself told us that he had often had to leave his toys and, on one occasion his dog, when they flitted. He had also frequently to change his name. They were eventually housed in homeless families' accommodation in a neighbouring borough which, a few months later, was to become notorious when a newspaper exposed the conditions there. By the time he arrived in our nursery, he was angry and distrustful of adults and incapable of making relationships with other children because he feared that he would be moved on again. There were also child protection issues uncovered later.

How do we support a child like this? Some reactions were that he was not a British responsibility; that he was not the responsibility of our borough; that his parents had offended against their culture and religion, as well as abandoning the father's legitimate family and so on. At very few points in the interminable discussions about the child's future did the boy's needs seem to focus highly.

What is your view? Do you agree/disagree with the outcomes? Why/why not? Could this have been approached differently?

Green states very clearly that 'if lasting progress is to be achieved, children must be placed at the centre of the process, their hidden lives understood. Their voices must be listened to, their rights respected and their involvement sought' (1998: 208).

REFLECT AND RELATE TO PRACTICE

Review the Discussion point above. How would you honestly have responded to this situation? In the course of events the decision was made, because of the level of violence towards other children, that the child needed to move into special education. Was this fair? What other solutions could you suggest? Who should have been involved in the decision-making?

Learning

Learning (in the early years): is active and does not just apply to formal situations where a particular knowledge set, mostly selected by adults, is 'taught' to young children. Young children are learning to 'be'.

In promoting learning, practitioners need to define **'learning' in the early years** and establish what their own perspectives are on the nature of childhood. The environment created – physical, social and emotional – will depend very much on how children are valued and how prepared practitioners are to use their value systems to develop provisions which reflects these. Through the views of various established theorists and educationalists and a number of worked examples, this section will address the importance of establishing a perspective on the nature of childhood and consider the extent to which practitioners need to be prepared to change their own values.

Jerome Bruner (1915–), the constructivist, whose research has redefined children's thought, memory and learning processes posed the following question in 1960: 'What shall we teach and to what end?', adding later 'when and how?' (1977 [1960]). Perhaps now 'and who decides?' could be added?

Children's place in society and the relationship between family and state need to be openly explored. Dahlberg and Moss (2005) put forward an argument, set against the expansion of pre-school provision and the length of time children spend in institutions, which applies to everyone. They ask for an open debate which centres on how 'technology, science and management drive out ethics and politics' in pre-school ideology and practice, but it applies to other sectors of early years education and care. They deny that they hold:

> some nostalgic longing for days when children spent more time at home or were free to roam their immediate neighbourhoods; the institutionalisation of childhood is not necessarily a bad thing. But it does demand of us – as adults – to take responsibility for what we have set in motion, in particular to look critically at the conditions for childhood we are creating. Too often, however, this ethical and political subject – our responsibility for others – is replaced by a technical question: how effective are preschools/schools/school-age childcare in producing certain outcomes?
>
> *(Dahlberg and Moss, 2005: 3)*

Practitioners need to reflect upon the origins of their own values and be open to changing or expanding their views as they gain greater knowledge and experience. They need to be very clear about the nature of 'learning' in the early years and distinguish this precisely from 'teaching'. As Moss and Petrie (2002), who worked on the Early Years and Childcare International Evidence Project (2003, Institute of Education), alluded to above, there are often contradictions between personal philosophies and the policies and guidelines specified by governments and other bodies. Practitioners need to analyse what children's rights mean both in a personal response to children and how they work with them professionally. An empathetic knowledge and understanding of this phase of life is crucial to ensure that the centre of focus is always the child and that practitioners are able to be advocates on his/her behalf, even when the policies handed down seem to contradict this.

A child learns in all situations. 'Learning' is active and does not just apply to formal situations where a particular knowledge set, mostly selected by adults, is 'taught' to young children. Young children are learning to 'be'. The mantra for early childhood practitioners has been that there is no distinction for the child between 'work' and 'play'; this is a simplistic distinction about what actually goes on in the classroom or setting and needs to be further analysed. Bennett et al. (1997) in their research into play commented:

> The motivational force for playing is linked to learning, and *quality* learning is attributed more directly to play than to work. Accurate match is considered to be more likely through child-initiated activity, based on the theory that what they choose to do is what they need. In contrast, work may not be matched to their needs and interests, and therefore does not engage their attention or stimulate intrinsic motivation to the same extent . . . Play is seen as being fun and enjoyable, whereas work is serious and even onerous . . .
>
> *(1997: 51)*

Article 31 of the UNCRC states: 'All children have a right to relax and play, and to join a wide range of activities.'

In 2004 the UK Department for Culture, Media and Sport published its review of children's **play**, *Getting Serious About Play*. In this play was defined as 'what children and young people do when they follow their own ideas and interests, in their own way and for their own reasons' (2004: 6).

'Play', however, needs careful thought and definition. There is no real agreement as to what it is and a variety of terms are used in describing what it may be, such as exploration, free-flow, directed, repetitive and mastery. A number of theorists, including Piaget and Bruner, have explored its origins and purposes. Janet Moyles has written extensively about play and her book *Just Playing*, written in 1989, remains an accessible starting point to explore all aspects of play. In essence play offers to all an opportunity to:

Play: the activity children engage in when they follow their own ideas and use their imagination to invent and follow their own way in working out problems.

- develop physical skills and be aware of the capabilities of one's body
- come to terms with new information
- restructure previous knowledge according to new
- learn to make mistakes without discomfit
- be in control of one's own world without the oversight of an adult
- learn to take responsibility in a social context.

Photo 3.2
Do children make a distinction between work and play?

Pearson Education Ltd. Jules Selmes © Pearson Education Limited 2004

Worries and fears can be acted out and aspects of behaviour perhaps not allowed in the child's culture can be explored and pondered. This is not an exhaustive list but an indication of the opportunities play can offer. Practitioners, however, need to understand the process, be able to express and support its value and to understand when and how to add to children's scenarios to make it a richer, more challenging experience. The review cited above goes on to say:

> Different people have different definitions of play. From an early age, play is important to a child's development and learning. It isn't just physical. It can involve cognitive, imaginative, creative, emotional and social aspects. It is the main way most children express their impulses to explore, experiment and understand.

> *(Department for Culture, Media and Sport, 2004: 8)*

REFLECT AND RELATE TO PRACTICE

Think back to your own childhood. How much freedom did you have? What were your favourite activities? Who shared these with you? What did you feel like when you were experiencing these? What did you learn? Share your memories with others in your learning community. Are there differences because of the time and place in which the play occurred?

There are enormous challenges and many contradictions in approaching 'learning' in the early years. One of the conflicts arises because children's development is not always taken fully into account when their more formal education starts. In the UK reading and writing, especially, has been introduced very early in the belief that this will accelerate progress and give more time to learning these skills. The experience of continental neighbours has been, however, that by leaving this until children are developmentally ready (basic language development, for example, is not completed until five or six), these skills are far easier for children to achieve. Young children have been expected to sit and listen for far longer than they are generally ready to do; small boys in particular need to be active and many opportunities can be lost to explore and thus understand the world. As a result, one of the difficulties is that very young children have become disaffected from learning because of a much too early introduction to formal education which can cause many to feel failures; a cohort of children with 'special educational needs' has perhaps been created because of this. Many children have started primary school at four in the UK, although the Early Years Foundation Stage (DfES, 2007) in the UK now covers the age range from birth to six years of age (including the reception class). This was introduced from September 2008 and relates to all provision, whether private, voluntary or state. Its success in returning the UK's practice to principles based on the centrality of the child, child development and play opportunities will depend on the knowledge and understanding of the practitioners who must interpret it and put it into practice. Practice in some provision has been slow to follow the guidance, either because of a lack of experience in teaching staff or little belief in play based methods.

The statutory age for starting school in the UK remains the term after the child's fifth birthday, but few parents, and sometimes professionals, seem to be aware of this, though increasing numbers of UK parents are choosing to educate their children at home (see Education Otherwise website at: **www.education-otherwise.org**). In many other countries, formal schooling does not begin until six, even seven, and yet their children have tended to do as well as and even better than their British counterparts. In some learning communities, such as nurseries which follow the High Scope curriculum and particularly the group of nurseries in Reggio Emilia in northern Italy, learning very much follows the child's/children's own interests, with teachers and other adults used as resources to extend children's knowledge. Also, 'learning' takes place beyond the walls of the pre-school or school, in the family or in the social and cultural communities to which children belong. Here again the relationship between what the family considers is important for children to learn and what the state requires – which may be incompatible – are crucial questions on which to reflect. Children learn in different contexts according to their age, family situation and geographical location. For the 0–7 age group, this is very important as the home, the community, the pre-school and the school/extended school are all important contexts and the very young child needs to learn to adapt to and adopt the expectations of each, sometimes several in each day or week. Bronfenbrenner's theories (see Chapter 1) conceptualise this.

In other contexts, children's needs are rarely considered. In building new and in redeveloping towns and cities, housing complexes and shopping centres and the opportunities these should and could provide for 'learning' are mainly ignored. These issues have become even more important because of concerns about children's physical health, particularly obesity, because outdoor play is often feared and thus restricted. Moss and Petrie (2002) introduce their book by describing an adventure playground in North Wales which has become the 'children's own space which they gradually come to take responsibility for . . . they take part in staff selection, meeting candidates and giving their opinions' (2002: 1). Moss and Petrie go on to expand their concept of 'children's spaces' further:

[It] does not just imply a physical space, a setting for small groups of children. It also carries the meaning of being a *social* space . . . a *cultural space* where values, rights and cultures are created; and a *discursive* space for differing perspectives and forms of expression, where there is room for dialogue, confrontation (in the sense of exchanging differing experience and views), deliberation and critical thinking, where children and others can speak and be heard. In this sense, the concept of 'children's space' implies possibilities for children and adults to contest understandings, values, practices and knowledge.

(2002: 9)

Early years practitioners, in creating environments for children, need to consider their responses to issues of challenge and risk in society. Many parents, particularly in the UK, view life as very dangerous these days and strive to ensure their children are 'safe' at all times. Stringent health and safety legislation and the legal profession collude to remove 'challenge' from children's lives. Nurse (2007) explores how safeguarding children from abuse can often be to the detriment of allowing children to develop strategies to protect themselves. New et al. (2005) explore 'risk-taking' in this wider context:

Given the multiple challenges facing children, families, and teachers in an increasingly unpredictable global society, it may well be that the best way to keep children safe is to be willing, as adults, to take more risks on their behalf. Such a public embrace of negotiated risk taking makes explicit the moral dimensions of teaching – and invites parents and community members to join in the conversation.

They conclude:

In sharing stories of our own experiences with risk taking, we argue in favor of being less fearful and more open to an early childhood curriculum characterized by purposeful and collaborative risk taking. Such a 'risk-rich' early childhood curriculum

- acknowledges children as capable and desirous of testing their developing skills and understandings of and in the world,
- invites parents into collaborative relations that inform decision making about what and how children can learn, and
- encourages teachers to trust themselves and their children to learn together while exploring meaning making in the real world they inhabit.

(New et al., 2005: http://ecrp.uiuc.edu/v7n2/new.html)

REFLECT AND RELATE TO PRACTICE

Explore the issues to do with health and safety and protecting children. Are we, in making life 'safe' for children, actually addressing the realities of the twenty-first century? How can we ensure children can safeguard themselves? What about those children in the world whose lives are anything but safe? How should the global community support them?

DISCUSSION POINT

Being an early years practitioner, whether professionally as a teacher, a social worker, a health professional or within the private and voluntary sector, is a complex and demanding career if it is to be accomplished well. The child is at the centre of the practitioner's focus, but the child does not exist in isolation. The practitioner needs to know and respect other important actors in the child's life: parents, grandparents, siblings and the extended family as a starting point, then other professional agents who may impact upon the child's life. The practitioner's role is to have a deep understanding of the importance of these to the child and family, as well as the ability to know when to be honest about a lack of knowledge or inexperience and then to seek help whenever necessary.

Learning to respect families and children who have different backgrounds from the practitioner's own and to recognise the individuality of each child, family and community is a duty under national and international legislation, but is also a professional, personal and an ethical obligation. The people practitioners work with must be able to trust them. Practitioners in the early years must also be able to develop, and share, their understanding of the different professional backgrounds of all those who work within this area; professional philosophies, working practices and qualifications differ. 'Knowledge' is also constantly shifting, whether this is because the *interpretation* of certain facets changes or because new knowledge (e.g. brain development in the early years) comes into the public and professional domain. One of the overriding principles must be to analyse new knowledge in terms of early years practice and adjust accordingly.

Do you agree with this? Is there anything you would add or approach in a different manner? Why/why not?

SUMMARY

Values to promote learning (p. 56)

How do practitioners influence children's understanding of and values (personal) in the early years?

The development of personal values what you hold as right and wrong, what is important to you – will influence the way you relate to the children in your setting.

The United Nations Convention on the Rights of the Child 1989 (p. 58)

Why is the UNCRC important to practice in an early years setting?

The UNCRC applies to children from birth to eighteen. In the UK, the convention's ideals were included in the Children Act 1989 and it was formally ratified in December 1991.

Personal values (p. 60)

Why do practitioners need to understand the concept of personal values?

Individual values inform reactions and actions. Practitioners should question their values and consider the extent to which they value all children for who they are.

Professional identity, qualifications and pay (p. 61)

To what extent are professional identity, qualifications and pay limited to personal values?

Personal values underpin how an individual views the people and the work in which he/she is involved. Personal constructions of professional identity and status can undermine the development of shared values.

Individual values (p. 63)

How can an early years practitioner promote values for the learning and personal development of children within their setting?

Children's participation should be valued. They should be encouraged to voice their views.

National values (p. 65)

Who should decide the nature of early years provision in the UK?

The British government has, particularly since the mid-1990s, placed children at the centre of its policies. However, people in the UK are not confident in their national attitudes towards very young children and their values are sometimes unclear, whether in deciding the best form of provision for children, when formal schooling should start or whether children should be indulged or dealt with firmly and so on.

European values (p. 67)

How might the report, What About Us? Children's Rights in the European Union: next steps (Ruxton, 2005) *impact on the place of children in the European Union?*

The development of a set of principles which relate to early childhood has been a late-comer in the European Union's deliberations. The above mentioned report aims to develop a children's rights policy.

Global values (p. 67)

Do British cultural values impact on teaching and learning in early years settings?

In the global context, it can be seen that children's childhoods can be very different and it is hard not to impose majority world values and conceptions of what childhood should be like on other communities.

Learning (p. 70)

Why is establishing a perspective on the nature of childhood important?

In promoting learning, practitioners need to define 'learning' in the early years and establish what their own perspectives are on the nature of childhood. The environment created – physical, social and emotional – will depend very much on how children are valued and how prepared practitioners are to use their value systems to develop provisions which reflects these.

Glossary

Learning (in the early years): is active and does not just apply to formal situations where a particular knowledge set, mostly selected by adults, is 'taught' to young children. Young children are learning to 'be'.

Play: the activity children engage in when they follow their own ideas and use their imagination to invent and follow their own way in working out problems. It is solitary in babies and social in toddlers and older children, where learning to co-operate is an important aspect.

Reggio Emilia: an approach to early education that originated in the small town of Reggio Emilia in Italy after the Second World War. Children's participation is valued at all levels and how they co-construct their learning experiences, taking the lead in negotiating, with peers and others, in deciding what the focus of their learning should be.

Values: the ideals that a person aspires to in his or her life 'which act as a point of reference to our judgements and conduct, and according to which we conform (or not) in our relations with the social group of reference (community, society, culture) . . . It is we, as people, who choose our values, confirm them and sustain them' (Rinaldi, 2006).

Find out more

Alderson, P. (2008) *Young Children's Rights: Exploring Beliefs, Principles and Practice*, **2nd edn, London: Jessica Kingsley.**
This book addresses and debates children's rights and issues to do with citizenship, drawing on the United Nations Convention on the Rights of the Child. It adopts a clear child-centred approach starting with the very youngest children from birth onwards. It provokes readers to think about where power lies and who makes decisions, not necessarily expecting children to be able to do this all of the time. Case study material highlighting good practice supports her arguments.

Archard, D. (2004) *Rights and Childhood*, **2nd edn, Abingdon: Routledge.**
This book offers a clear introduction and analysis of children's rights, both from a philosophical and a legal perspective. Archard sets 'childhood' in a historical and a contemporary context and produces a balanced, but sometimes controversial, argument designed to make his reader think, whether a student or someone professionally involved.

Hallett, C. and Prout, A. (eds) (2003) *Hearing the Voices of Children: Social Policy for a new century*, **London: RoutledgeFalmer.**
This collection of chapters edited by Hallett and Prout reviews how conceptions of 'childhood' have altered in the last quarter of the twentieth century, not always to the benefit of the child. The authors of the various chapters reflect a global community as well as analysing and debating the status and participation of children in the UK in issues to do with policy, the law, welfare and poverty.

Moyles, J. (ed.) (2007) *Early Years Foundations: Meeting the Challenge*, **Maidenhead: Open University.**
This book is very much centred on early years professionals working within the Early Years Foundation Stage. Starting from the principles of the EYFS, its authors offer support to practitioners 'in dealing with a range of issues and challenges in a sensitive and professional manner'. In highlighting the principles which guide the implementation of the EYFS, the reader is exhorted to abide by his or her own knowledge of 'what is right' for young children, rather than 'conforming to the demands made by government and policy makers'. The book covers issues to do with culture, diversity and identity, as well as play and curriculum areas.

References

Aries, P. (1962) *Centuries of Childhood*. New York: Vintage Books.

Bennett, N., Wood, L. and Rogers, S. (1997) *Teaching Through Play*. Buckingham: Open University Press.

Bruner, J. (1977) *The Process of Education* (originally published in 1960). Cambridge, MA: Harvard University Press.

Clark, A. and Moss, P. (2001) *Listening to Children: The Mosaic Approach*. London: National Children's Bureau.

Dahlberg, G. and Moss, P. (2005) *Ethics and Politics in Early Childhood Education*. Abingdon: Routledge and Falmer.

De Mause, L. (1974) *The History of Childhood*. New York: Psychology Press.

Department of Culture, Media and Sport (2004) *Getting Serious about Play: A Review of Children's Play*. Available at **www.culture.gov.uk**.

Department for Education and Skills (DfES) (2007) *The Early Years Foundation Stage*. Nottinham: DfES Publications.

Dwivedi, K.N. (1995) *Race and the Child's Perspective*, in Davie, R., Upton, G. and Varma, V. (eds) *The Voice of the Child: A Handbook for Professionals*. London: RoutledgeFalmer.

Green, D. (1998) *Hidden Lives: Voices of Children in Latin America and the Caribbean*. London: Cassell.

Hall, N. (1994) *Play, Literacy and the Role of the Teacher*, in Moyles, J.R. (1994) *The Excellence of Play*. Buckingham: OU.

Hallett, C. and Prout, A. (2003) *Hearing the Voices of Children: Social Policy for a New Century*. London: RoutledgeFalmer.

Jones, L., Holmes, R. and Powell, J. (2005) *Early Childhood Studies: A Multiprofessional Perspective*. Maidenhead: Open University.

Lee, N. (2005) *Childhood and Human Value*. Maidenhead: Open University.

Moss, P. and Petrie, P. (2002) *From Children's Service to Children's Spaces*. London: Routledge.

Moyles, J.R. (1989) *Just Playing: The Role and Status of Play in Early Childhood Education*. Buckingham: Open University Press.

Moyles, J.R. (1994) *The Excellence of Play*. Maidenhead, Berkshire: Open University Press.

New, R.S., Mardell, B. and Robinson, D. (2005) *Early Childhood Education as Risky Business: Going Beyond What's 'Safe' to Discovering What's Possible*. ECRP: Fall, Vol. 7, No. 2: Urbana-Champaign, University of Illinois.

Nurse, A.D. (2007) Safeguarding Children, in Nurse, A.D. (ed.) *The New Early Years Professional: Dilemmas and Debates*. London: David Fulton.

Postman, N. (1994) *The Disappearance of Childhood* (first published 1982). New York: Vintage.

Rosenthal, R. and Jacobson, L. (1968) Pygmalion in the classroom: *Teacher Expectations and Pupils' Intellectual Development*. Austin Tx: Holt, Rinehart and Winston.

Rinaldi, C. (2006) *In Dialogue with Reggio Emilia: Listening, Researching and Learning*. Abingdon: Routledge.

Ruxton, S. (2001) Towards a Children's policy for the European Union? in Foley, P., Roche, J. and Tucker, S. (eds) *Children in Society: Contemporary Theory, Policy and Practice*. Basingstoke: Palgrave/Open University.

Ruxton, S. (2005) *What About Us? Children's Rights in the European Union: next steps*. Brussels: Euronet.

Union of International Associations (UIA) *Human Values Project*. Available at **www.uia.org/values**.

United Nations (1989) *United Nations Convention on the Rights of the Child*. Geneva: UN.

CHAPTER 4

Development and Learning

By the end of this chapter you will be able to answer the following questions:

- What is the importance of child development in determining the way provision is organised for young children?
- Define 'child development' and other related terms.
- How is the model used in the UK and elsewhere not a 'universal' model and what are the other perspectives that are just as relevant to optimal development?
- How resilient are children and how can they overcome a number of setbacks?
- What is the relationship between how a child develops individually and how is more formal learning influenced by this development?
- How can knowledge of child development improve and heighten children's learning experiences?
- How can we understand that knowledge in this field is not absolute and that new research findings are adding to our understanding constantly?
- What are the consequences of adopting a viewpoint that is too simplistic in judging a child's progress?

This chapter will support your understanding of the following Standards *(see Appendix 1)*:
Knowledge and understanding: S01, S02 and S06 ■ **Effective practice:** S09, S10, S12, S14, S15, S16, S17, S21 and S23 ■ **Relationships with children:** S25 and S28 ■ **Communicating and working in partnership with families and carers:** S29.

Introduction

Understanding a person's behaviour is less like understanding a physical event than it is like understanding a work of art: individual actions, like musical phrases, are not made sense of by showing them to be instances of general laws, but by indicating their relationship to the whole of which they form a part.

(White, 1985: 71)

This chapter explores the importance of knowledge of how children develop in the early years with the proviso that this is a complex area to study, highlighted by the above quote, where many of the presumptions that have been accepted easily over a number of decades are now being challenged. This is a result of new knowledge from research, such as in brain development, or because the resilience of young children has now been recognised. Many concepts to do with the development of children have been based on a small number of children (e.g. Piaget studied his own children), particularly those from European or north American backgrounds. Little so far has entered mainstream thinking about children who have grown up in other areas of the world. It is recognised now that children's development is not simply linear; rather, children's development plateaus, accelerates and deviates according to the environment and context of their lives.

Child development knowledge is deemed essential for all those working with children from 0–7 years, in whatever location. Yet, the study of child development has not been prioritised, particularly in initial teacher education, since the reforms during Margaret Thatcher's government when a study of child development was excluded alongside sociology, psychology and philosophy which were not then deemed essential to the practical craft of the classroom. Dame Gillian Pugh (2001), who has written widely on early years education and is currently on the board of the Children's Workforce Development Council, highlights '[the] inappropriateness of the content of teaching training for nursery and infant teachers, with a curriculum that neglects child development' (2001: 22).

Currently there is a general demand in support of reintroducing the study of child development into professional programmes and continuing professional development. What we have always to be mindful of, however, is that this is a complex area of study where superficial knowledge, which may lead us to make pat judgements, can possibly do more harm than good. Abbott and Langston (2005) caution against a simplistic view of the study of child development:

> One problem with this approach is that, traditionally, childcare courses have presented the study of child development in a simplistic way, detailing milestones which are easily understood and set out the child's expected development in vision, motor movement, language, communication, cognition and social and emotional areas. However, the analysis of the child into such units obscures from view the sentient child who is active in their own development and who is a person in their own right.

(2005: 9)

In the example later in the chapter, decisions were to be made about Toby without listening to the views of his mother and other relatives and without understanding the family history. His grandfather had not spoken until he was three and his aunt's silence in class always annoyed teachers!

Development as a complex process

An ability to know and understand children's stages of development – where they are at – is essential in establishing where practitioners would wish them to progress and the opportunities they need to provide to match interests and to supply sufficient 'challenge' (in Vygotsky's educationalist terms) to enable a child to achieve. By examining the origins of our knowledge on child development and considering the extent to which practitioners should be influenced by developmental charts, this section highlights the centrality for practitioners in acknowledging that each child is unique in terms of learning and development.

Much of the prior knowledge on how children develop has been gained from people like Piaget or Gordon Wells who watched their own children and recorded their development in minute detail. Darwin was also probably influenced in developing his theories, not just through his journeys but by observing his own children. It could be said that the detailed knowledge of how children develop is based on a handful of northern European children! If medical research was based on so few subjects, there could be little confidence in the results. Hindley (1979) in his inaugural lecture reflected on the sources of knowledge of child development and commented:

> I have come to what, to me at any rate, is a rather interesting conclusion,
> namely, that much of the pioneering work in the study of human development
> and human psychology, has, in fact, been based on a mere handful of
> subjects – sometimes one, sometimes two, sometimes even three or four.

(1979: 27–28)

Hindley added Freud and Watson to those named above, as well as reflecting on the use of statistics which so easily wash out or conceal individual differences. He states: 'In developmental research, and in much educational research, the use of group averages may be helpful in gaining some idea of general trends, but gives little idea of process' (1979: 29). Morgan (1994), renowned for her work in the field of anthropology, also made the point that, in the study of evolution, *the archetypal human being was a male*, sometimes female, very rarely a child.

Other sources of knowledge about how children develop originated with research and experimentation. The growth in psychology as a major field of academic interest and study, particularly after the Second World War, saw the development of various 'schools' of thought, such as behaviourism. For a long time the way that child development has been viewed has been from a northern hemisphere/'western' perspective, where researchers and practitioners from all professional backgrounds have tended to look at the PILES (Physical, Intellectual, Linguistic, Emotional and Social) aspects of development separately and in a linear way. Sometimes they have concentrated on trying to understand and chart specific aspects, like memory or moral development.

Quite rigid timeframes were originally established for developmental milestones, often following a health model, and certain authors have been influential in this approach (e.g. Mary Sheridan's *The Developmental Progress of Infants and Young Children*, updated frequently from the 1960s onwards). These checklists were used by paediatricians and health visitors, amongst others, to chart children's progress and, sometimes, before the Warnock Report 1978 and the Education Act 1981 (which introduced the idea of a spectrum of special educational needs), to decide which school a child would attend, whether mainstream or special.

Although these developmental charts have a part to play, this approach does not always take into account the considerable individual differences nor the context in which babies and children grow. Of course, parents have always compared the age at which their babies achieved one of the major milestones, though interpretation of these (especially in first words or toilet-training) is somewhat hard.

The ability to understand child development comes from more than a familiarity with charts and checklists, however. It depends on experience, openness to watching children in a variety of contexts over long periods of time and a willingness to debate what is observed with others who know the child. If, though, practitioners are going to be able to 'understand the work of art' they need not only the knowledge and understanding of how children grow biologically, but also need to experience a fascination in the wide variety of developmental characteristics that young children exhibit. Then they need the curiosity to explore and dwell on those differences, to work out what they mean for working relationships with the child. They also need to be very much aware of the *context* of what they are observing. How well a child is progressing is judged by the norms of the time and place in which he/she is living.

DISCUSSION POINT

Many women in the UK were enlisted into traditionally male jobs during the Second World War when the men were fighting overseas. Day nurseries were established to care for their young children. After the war the government was concerned to get men back into jobs and therefore nurseries were closed and women were mainly returned to their traditional roles within the home. The government appropriated John Bowlby's developing theories of maternal deprivation and attachment to underpin their policy, yet only understood what he was saying in part, as much of what he had researched at that point had been based on children who had experienced being taken into care.

REFLECT AND RELATE TO PRACTICE

What is your opinion of mothers working outside the home when their children are very small? Consider both the negative and positive issues. Explore Bowlby's theories in more depth. What was he really saying about very young children's needs and experience?

It is essential to recognise the interplay between different developmental aspects and the varying development timeframes adopted by individual children. Keenan (2002) proposes:

> Development is also *multidimensional* and *multidirectional*.
> Multidimensionality refers to the fact that development cannot be described by a single criterion such as increases or decreases in a behaviour. The principle of multidirectionality maintains that there is no single, normal path that development must or should take. In other words, healthy developmental outcomes are achieved in a wide variety of ways.
>
> *(2002: 3)*

The idea of gains and losses is further explored by Keenan who gives the example of how formal schooling can expand a child's knowledge base and develop his or her intellectual skills, at the same time as restricting 'their creativity as they learn to follow rules defined by others' (ibid.).

What is not always recognised is the *plasticity* of human development; that is to say, that infants and young children who experience very traumatic events in their young lives can, in many ways, recover completely or partially some of the development or functioning lost if supported to do this. This moves away from the idea of *critical periods*, introduced by Konrad Lorenz, after which children cannot compensate in this way. It may be harder to recoup, but at least until five years of age there is a good chance that developmental losses may be made up. Some aspects of development, however, may not be so easily compensated for; a number of 'wild children' have caught the imagination of doctors, psychologists and writers over time. These are chil dren who are thought to have been raised by animals or who have managed to survive on their own after abandonment. Their stories are recounted in Newton (2003). What cannot usually be established, however, is why these children were abandoned in the first place. Was there already an underlying problem like autism or profound deafness? From studies of these children it seems that though certain functions can be achieved, others are difficult to progress, particularly language and social skills. The well-known study of Genie is outlined later in the chapter to illustrate this point.

Yet children's brains can reorganise if there has been traumatic injury. Infants who have had to have brain surgery where part of the brain is removed can recover completely. This is in contrast to adults, such as Luria described in his work with *The Man with a Shattered World* (Luria and Solotaroff, 1975), who never fully recovered from his wartime brain injury but was still ably to express lucidly what abilities he had lost. Much of the early 'mapping of the brain' from the early twentieth century on has come about through studies of people who have received such injuries during wartime. The study of the development of the brain in infants and young children has accelerated as the technologies for investigating brain function have improved dramatically. Through scans, what parts of the brain are activated when a baby or child is given a stimulus can be clearly seen. It is obvious how the brain dramatically increases in size in the early years. It is now generally accepted that a baby is born with a far larger number of synapses than he or she requires and it is interaction with the environment which will decide which connections between neurons are made and which will die away. The assumption is made that the richer the environment the more connections are made, on the basis of 'use it or lose it' (Eliot, 1999). What it is not yet possible to do is pinpoint the minutiae of what happens in the brain in response to every stimulus given. The reason the brain contains so many 'extra' neurons when a baby is born seems to be that it allows for the infant to adapt and develop to match the requirements of the environment in which he or she is born. If brain development was fixed before birth then this could not happen. It therefore allows for the plasticity highlighted above.

> ### REFLECT AND RELATE TO PRACTICE
>
> How does an understanding of a child's development impact on what happens in teaching and learning?

Nature versus nurture

Nurture:
development is environmentally determined.

Nature:
development is genetically determined.

The 1960s and 1970s saw the culmination of a great debate centred in the field of intelligence. This was termed the **nurture–nature** debate; how much did we inherit and how much was due to the context in which we grew? By examining the historical context of this debate, this section challenges the reader to consider the extent to which intelligence is determined by genes. This was centred on intelligence quotients (IQ) and led by Eysenck and Jensen, two eminent American researchers, and very much became involved in racist issues. The central question was whether black Americans were genetically less intelligent than whites, or whether perceived differences were due to the circumstances in which they grew and the low expectations of the more powerful white majority. Not so much was known then about genetics but what was important was the interplay between genetics (what is inherited from parents) and the environment in which children grow. When expectations are high, children's performance increases to reach those expectations. This was important in helping to recognise the impact of adult opinions on children's self-esteem and learning. There was also an important side issue. Many children were subjected to intelligence tests, both here and in the USA. Many of these were culture-specific and depended on an understanding of the language and social situations experienced by children in a particular social and cultural group.

Decisions were being made until the late 1970s about children's levels of intelligence, and thus the form of schooling the children were entitled to (special or mainstream), at very young ages, based on the outcomes of these intelligence tests. In the UK it resulted in much larger numbers of boys, especially, who attended special schools than the percentage population warranted. Examples of questions in one of these tests included recognising a saucer (when most children's experience by then was of mugs or beakers, including the author's own daughter who promptly said 'plate' when she was asked!). Other outdated language included 'nightgown'. It also became apparent that children's performance was not fixed. The example in the following Discussion point, though it occurred a while ago, is salutary in providing a lesson to all practitioners who are involved on a daily basis in making decisions about children on limited information.

DISCUSSION POINT

Carrie, one of twins, was in a bad mood on the day she saw the educational psychologist (EP) just before she was due to leave the nursery for primary school. Both twins had had some 'developmental delay' but had made good progress at the nursery. Carrie had objected to leaving her play in the nursery to be tested by the EP in the medical room. We protested too as it seemed unfair that she had to do this in unfamiliar surroundings with a person she did not know well and who would not let one of us go with her. Her mum had not been able to attend because of work commitments and trusted us to ensure all went well. Just as we expected, her end result indicated that she would be better placed in a school for children, in the language of the time, with moderate learning difficulties. We protested again. Her sister was to go to her local primary school, having tested 'within normal limits'. We did not want to see the two separated and knew their mum would be distraught. We also knew that Carrie's abilities probably surpassed her sister's but she had a stronger, less malleable personality! Under the onslaught, the EP agreed to return the following week to undertake a parallel form of the test. We quite honestly discussed the outcomes with Carrie, who quite easily at five understood the consequences of not complying. We bribed her too. If she behaved herself she could go to the shops and choose sweets for the whole nursery. The EP was amazed and said she had never seen this happen before – Carrie's IQ score had risen by ten points and she could go to school with her sister. Years later a colleague met the family and shared her delight with the mum that both had done very well.

Activity

This applied to an IQ test not so often used these days. There are, however, many other ways in which children's abilities and progress are determined. What does this case study demonstrate that could apply to current day practice? How can you ensure that children in your care are not disadvantaged because of systems and expectations which are not to their benefit? What is your role? These children were from an Afro-Caribbean background. What are the implications of the systems in the UK for testing children fairly?

The 'nature–nurture' debate is still with us but it has now come to include a much more focused argument because of the work in genetics and in mapping the human genome (the complete set of genetic materials). As scientists identify genes which seem to carry the pattern for human characteristics – moving beyond markers for particular diseases into those which may carry, for example, personality traits, physical characteristics or predispositions to particular interests and achievements – then the danger is that once again judgements will be based on limited information, genes instead of IQ. What needs to be taken into account, again, is the interaction between an individual's genetic makeup and the environment in which he/she grows. For a long time, researchers have studied identical twins, particularly those separated at birth. Many did not know of each other's existence but similarities in the choices they made and their life paths have fascinated the researchers and others. These similarities *could* be explained by the genetic duplication, but it could also be possible that the researchers were finding what they were looking for and publicising it was popular and captured the public's imagination. As Brookes (1999) points out, finding enough separated twins of the same age to compare is difficult, then adds that we could not clone a new, identical, person from a set of genes: 'This is because memory and experience are not preserved in DNA' (1999: 177).

Rutter (2006) reviewed the nature–nurture controversy and the interplay between genes and behaviour, regretting that those promoting behavioural genetics and socialisation theory have for so long been in two opposing camps, 'leading to much fruitless dispute and serious misunderstandings' (2006: vi). He concludes:

> It is of little value to attempt to quantify the relative influence of the two in any precise way, because it will vary by population and over time. Moreover the precise estimates for the strength of genetic and of environmental influences have few policy or practice implications.

(2006: 221)

Photo 4.1 To what extent do genes determine ability?

Pearson Education Ltd. Jules Selmes © Pearson Education Ltd. 2004

One caution in the new understanding of the role our genes play in our development is against 'reductionism', that is, exaggerating their impact and so reducing the huge number of possibilities each child has to achieve in life.

The great thinkers in child development theory

In a study of child development, as in any other discipline, there will be those whose theories and practices will have added greatly to the body of knowledge we have today. In identifying some of these thinkers, others are necessarily left out and any such list inevitably depends on the interests of the person who compiles it. This section will provide a brief overview of the great thinkers who have influenced child development theory over the last century and a half.

When it comes to the 'greats', everyone will have his or her favourites, whether it is because there is wholehearted agreement with them or because they have made readers rethink beliefs or even provoked anger. Sometimes revisiting a theorist after a number of years, and a lot more experience, can clarify and confirm what he or she was saying. There is also, perhaps, a difficulty in translation, not just of individual words but of ideas from one context to another. The group of thinkers identified here can be criticised easily because they come from a European or American tradition, rather than from the wider world, and the majority are male. This can only be a brief overview. A much fuller selection can be found on the UNESCO website (**www.ibe.unesco.org/publications/thinkers**) where detailed biographies of one hundred thinkers on education can be found, spanning over two thousand years. Original publications and later biographies will also guide readers in their quest to understand more. Those mentioned below do, however, represent a number of the viewpoints raised in the rest of this section and many have a continuing impact on how young children are viewed today. The selection covers not only great teachers but also psychologists, biologists, doctors, linguists, writers and philanthropists who have worked to expand knowledge and in the interests of children and so demonstrates how diverse those interested in this whole area are. The trick will be to ensure that the massive field of expanding knowledge is integrated and the lessons for practice recognised.

DISCUSSION POINT

Starting with the Unesco website select a variety of thinkers who interest you and explore their ideas. Relate this to the context in which they were writing and try to see connections between their ideas and their lives. What do you think is the continuing impact of their views on the way we educate and care for young children now?

Those highlighted below exemplify thinkers whose views relate very clearly to the early childhood field. Skinner, an English graduate who later became a psychologist, is renowned as a leader in the development of 'behaviourism' which, simply, looked at how much was learnt through imitation and how learning was progressed by reinforcing good responses and ignoring the poor. Piaget, a biologist, introduced a more 'constructivist' approach, in which earlier experience was built on to construct new knowledge or understanding, in relation to the environment. He developed a 'stage' theory but has been criticised, by Donaldson (1978) and others, for not recognising the specifically cultural aspects (mountains in Switzerland) and the rigidity of the language he used in developing these theories. His theories, however, have been the starting point for critical analysis of the way children learn, and, in many ways, in the way schools are organised today. Vygotsky, and later Bruner, developed the stage theory ideas but set the child very much at the centre of his or her social world. Ideas

Spiral curriculum: learning is revisited at increasingly more complex levels.

such as the zone of proximal development which encouraged adults to challenge children's thinking and of the **spiral curriculum**, where learning is revisited at increasingly more complex levels, developed from their ideas. Bronfenbrenner's theories have already been discussed in Chapter 1; he is a good example of a theorist who places the child in the centre of the social milieu in which he or she grows. In the realm of language development, Chomsky introduced the idea that language acquisition could not be explained by pure imitation, rather that children were born with an innate capacity to learn language (the LAD/Language Acquisition Device). This is termed the **nativist** approach, but has been counteracted by the **interactionist** view, by Gordon Wells in the UK amongst others, where the social relationship between adult and child is seen to be crucial to good language skills.

Nativist: (approach to language acquisition) assumes that children are born with an innate capacity to learn language.

Interactionist: (view to language acquisition) assumes that the social relationship between the adult and the child is crucial to good language skills.

A further selection would highlight those more involved perhaps in practice than theory. One of these, Comenius, has been rather lost to the west in the past fifty years but this Czech educationalist from the seventeenth century supported early education for both boys and girls which was based on play and first-hand experience and moved away from being solely religious in nature. Rousseau brought a refreshing viewpoint to the state of childhood, arguing that a child is born 'perfect' but is later corrupted by the ills of society (though this did not prevent him from placing his own children 'in care'). Robert Owen at the beginning of the nineteenth century not only built and developed a school which was truly enlightened for the period (with first-hand experience, dance, music and geography as well as literacy and numeracy) but also established the Co-operative Movement to give families a much better standard of living than was normal in mills and factories at the time. The Macmillan sisters, later in that century and into the twentieth, were also concerned very much with children's health and quality of life and worked in deprived areas of Britain to improve these. Deptford in London was to be the focus of much of their work, where the training college for nursery teachers opened in 1930. Froebel, Steiner, Montessori and Malaguzzi (Reggio Emilia) are also renowned for their continuing contribution to the education of young children in the particular kinds of educational provision they established. Before going any further it is worth considering what this is:

- Friedrich Froebel (1782–1852): founded the 'kindergarten' in Germany. Strongly influenced by the natural world, Froebel proposed a system based on play where teachers were directors and guides of children's learning. His theory was that by allowing children to play freely with different materials, their interest would be aroused and sustained.

- Rudolf Steiner: Austrian by birth, established the first Waldorf school in Germany in 1919, in response to the destruction of the First World War. His educational system is based on the holistic development of the child through unification of body, mind and spirit.
- Maria Montessori: born in Italy in 1870, opened her first 'house' in Rome in 1907 for children from poor families. Her philosophy, based on the idea of 'freedom with limits', encourages children to engage in 'spontaneous activities within a carefully prepared environment with structured materials' (Follari, 2007: 222).
- Loris Malaguzzi: established the Reggio Emilia pre-school system in Reggio Emilia in Italy (see Chapter 10).

Current status of child development

What is the status of child development now, both in the sense of its functional use for practitioners and the research that is undertaken? By considering current research within the field of child development, this section encourages the reader to consider the extent to which research studies should influence practice within early years settings.

In the field of research, a number of longitudinal studies are being undertaken in the UK, which leads the field in this type of research. Significant amongst these are the National Child Development Survey, commenced in 1958, which involves a cohort of babies born in one week in March (about 17,000 individuals). This cohort has now been followed up six times. In 1970 another cohort was selected and this has now been followed up five times. These two cohorts offer an opportunity for comparison between the two groups. A further study is reviewing children who were born in 2000 and 2001 (the Millennium Cohort Study). Additionally there are local studies, such as the Avon Longitudinal Study of Parents and Children (ALSPAC), also known as 'Children of the 90s', which aims to identify:

> ways in which to optimise the health and development of children. Our main goal is to understand the ways in which the physical and social environment interact, over time, with the genetic inheritance to affect the child's health, behaviour and development.
>
> *(www.ich.bris.ac.uk/welcome)*

In Europe, the World Health Organisation (WHO) in June 1985 initiated the European Longitudinal Study of Pregnancy and Childhood (ELSPAC) which is also co-ordinated by the University of Bristol. In other countries similar surveys are being undertaken. In the USA, for instance, the National Institute of Child Health and Human Development (NICHD) in 1987 decided to instigate a national study into the effects of child care on the development of infants and toddlers. This was later extended to pre-school years and further. The results of this research study have been published and are available in a book from the NICHD Early Child Care Research Network (2005).

DISCUSSION POINT

Look at the above mentioned longitudinal studies in more detail. Each has a specific focus. What is this? What has already been learnt from the follow-up surveys? Create a chart to document what you find in your research. Choose one each in your group and present your findings to each other.

In addition to these, there are now far more students enrolled both at undergraduate and postgraduate levels who are studying children's development, as well as teachers and others who undertake research within their classrooms in order to find out more about children. Despite the pressures to assess and prepare targets for ever younger children, one consequence of increased national interest in small children's progress has been greater interest in and acceptance of observation (rather than checklists) of young children as a method of assessment. Though this is not a skill that people are at ease with immediately, it does offer the opportunity to see more naturally and exactly how children are engaged in their setting, rather than limiting what is recorded about their behaviour to a restricted set of criteria which have been pre-selected by adults. Knowledge gained from these observations, as well as outcomes from more formal studies, is valuable but cannot remain locked in a classroom or in the realm of academia; its implications for practice must be recognised and brought into the public domain. This is the opinion that those quoted below are voicing.

A letter published in *The Daily Telegraph* in September 2006 highlighted concerns over the perceived increase in childhood depression and the conditions in which many children now grow up. The letter, signed by over a hundred professionals and academics working in this field, stated:

> we are deeply concerned at the escalating incidence of childhood depression and children's behavioural and developmental conditions. We believe this is largely due to a lack of understanding, on the part of both politicians and the general public, of the realities and subtleties of child development.

This echoes one of the most often voiced concerns now within the early years field, along with the paucity of young children's physical play. After being neglected for a while, particularly in the school setting, children's emotional development must become a central focus for practitioners and government. Legislation which has led people away from physical contact with young children must be revisited, to ensure that we are comfortable with offering children the reassurance they need. There may also be more clinical reasons why this is so important, not solely in developing good self-esteem and emotional well-being. Gerhardt (2004) draws on her experience as a psychotherapist working with mothers and their babies and her knowledge of brain development to postulate how important affection is in shaping babies' brains. She writes: 'The baby is an interactive project not a self-powered one. The baby human has various systems ready to go, but many more that are incomplete and will only develop in response to other human input' (2004: 18).

A number of researchers have pointed out, using graphic evidence from brain scans of small infants, how rapidly the brain develops and organises itself in the first five years of life. Eliot (1999) points out that the brain trebles in size in the first year of life and is 'virtually fully grown' by the time the child enters school. She comments: 'Experience of course, accrues through life, but it is infinitely more potent in the earliest years and months when the synapses are still forming and the brain is at the height of its plasticity' (1999: 392).

There are some areas where this 'compensation' does not happen so easily and practitioners must then be aware when the environment does not support a child so well and think of ways to ensure that any difficulties do not become deep-set and long lasting. Perhaps it is valid then to return to the concept of **critical** (or sensitive) **periods** in reflecting on particular aspects of development. Two aspects highlighted are normally the development of vision and the acquisition of language.

Critical period: (also referred to as key or sensitive period) periods, especially in young children, when the brain is 'trained' to make certain developmental jumps.

One of the illustrations used to demonstrate how important it is to ensure that the conditions are right to acquire language is the story of Genie, a girl who had been completely isolated from social contact with her family for twelve years. Although she recovered certain aspects of functioning, her language has never really developed beyond the level of a two-year-old (Eliot, 1999) and she continues to have some emotional and social problems. This pattern of development has also been recognised in the reports of wild children, discussed earlier in this chapter. Expanding on this is consideration of *resilience*. How is it that some children seem to survive appalling backgrounds and experiences and then succeed in life? In the past decade, many autobiographies have been written that tell people's stories. These have been christened 'misery memoirs' by the media but the best of them acknowledge the individual circumstances that have enabled them to succeed. Often natural ability is there, but a common theme is the presence of a person who cares about the child, not necessarily

Photo 4.2
Appropriate support and care can have a strong impact on a child's development

Pearson Education Ltd. Jules Selmes © Pearson Education Ltd. 2004

a parent or other relative. There have also been some strong rebuttals to the idea of preciousness of the first few years of life in ensuring future success; these include the work of Clarke and Clarke (1976, 2000) and Bruer (1999).

The early years is a more complex area to chart for the many professionals who work with young children. Not only do they have to consider how to observe and record more formal achievements (a debate in itself) but they also have to take into account the developmental pathways each individual child is following and how this impacts on a practitioner's judgement about his or her accomplishments. Children do not develop and learn in a standardised, linear fashion. They may concentrate on particular developmental areas or reach a plateau in certain skills, then suddenly make a great leap forward. The 'What happens in practice?' below illustrates how learning is holistic, meaning that you cannot separate one area of development from the others in a young child's pattern of development.

WHAT HAPPENS IN PRACTICE?

Like his mother and his aunt, Toby was very quick to develop physically. He crawled at five months, went up the stairs at six, then stood independently at nine months and walked a month later. His finer motor skills were also well developed and at eight months he could build a tower of six or more bricks and at fifteen could thread wooden beads onto a string. He achieved these without ever being shown. His speech, however, did not conform to this precocious pattern. Although he could understand at an age appropriate level and there were no concerns within the family over this, the health visitor was very concerned that no sentences were forthcoming as he approached his third birthday. Just as she was preparing a referral for a speech therapy assessment, Toby celebrated his third birthday. Within a week of this, Toby asked his first question, and then never stopped talking:

Toby: 'Why did the man get the cake?' (watching a cartoon)
Grandfather: 'You tell me why!'
Toby: 'Cos he was bigger.'

REFLECT AND RELATE TO PRACTICE

What are the implications of the above example for those who work in the field, in making judgements and thus decisions about children's needs based on limited knowledge? What concerns does it raise in the way children are viewed by practitioners and specialised professionals? How far can published developmental norms (based on research on groups of children) help you to identify individual children's learning needs? In terms of communicating with parents and other relatives, what does this example have to tell you?

A world view

By considering various studies which have influenced the way we view child development and the impact of the World Health Organisation on that, this section questions the extent to which these studies provide a global perspective of the related field.

The approach and expectations of those who work with or who are interested in child development are changing. The need to explore other theories of child development, which have not emerged from an essentially northern European experience, is increasingly being recognised. Gielen in his foreword to Saraswathi's (2003) publication writes: 'In practice, the study of human development meant the study of American and European children, adolescents and some adults' (2003: 13).

There has been a tradition of studying the origins of human societies and cultures in anthropology. A classic study was undertaken by anthropologist Margaret Mead (published in 1928), who was the first in her field to research childrearing practices in Samoa. A more recent addition to the academic disciplines, ethnography, attempts to capture the social lives of people going about their ordinary, everyday, activities without researchers judging or placing *social meaning* on what they are seeing (Brewer, 2000). Blurton Jones (1993), for example, has explored the lives of children in hunter-gather communities in Africa and compared different childrearing practices in two communities in Botswana and their impact on later development.

These sorts of studies, however, have relied on western academic researchers investigating societies from the outside in. What needs to happen now is that what occurs in other countries and cultures needs to be made more visible, so that we can reflect on the lessons they have for us in a world that is becoming smaller. For example, the work of educators in New Zealand is now well known and its implications for other communities is being explored. Their work has centred on the coming together of two independent traditions (Maori and white) into one interwoven approach to the early years, Te Whariki (OECD, 2004).

Recently the World Health Organisation (WHO) has taken the lead, via the University of British Columbia in Canada, in bringing together the different strands of thinking on child development globally. This has been entitled the WHO Hub for Early Child Development (ECD). It recognises that:

> Different cultural views of ECD exist in the world and indicate that early childhood development is conceived of differently in cultural context within and across nations. These cultural understandings encompass a wide range of intersecting ideas about such things as what constitutes personhood, childhood, development health, illness, well-being and their determinants, as well as interactions between them. Not all of these understandings are compatible with each other nor are they always compatible with global perspectives such as UN declarations . . . Due to the range and diversity of cultural understanding of ECD, the aforementioned developmental domains used to study ECD in developed countries (physical, social, emotional, cognitive and communication) should not be considered exhaustive. Others would recognize different domains, such as spiritual, moral, or personal

development . . . Further work is needed to create a more holistic view of child development that is inclusive of multiple cultural perspectives.

(www.earlylearning.ubc.ca/WHO/)

In October 2006 the WHO published a draft version of its *Organizational Hub for Early Childhood Development*. This sets out its intentions, including an aim to 'investigate the contribution to children's success in school' as well as pulling together the international perspectives on child development. For example, the WHO's Multicentre Growth Reference Study Group has now published new development milestones, based on looking at different international cohorts. It has organised the results of this research into 'windows of achievement', rather than fixed milestones (WHO, 2006).

DISCUSSION POINT

Thinking about child development in the UK and similar more affluent societies has tended to concentrate on a defined set of developmental and academic norms. Reflect on these and their impact on the way provision for young children has been organised in the last twenty years or so. What has been the impact of using these expectations of how children develop on the kinds of 'curricula', in the broadest sense, that have been created? Looking at the work already done in Canada and by the WHO, what would be the impact of following different perspectives of development? For example, if a child's emotional development were seen to have the highest priority, how would provision be organised in your community?

Development and learning: bringing it together

As the national focus has turned again towards early years, there has been a resurrection of interest in child development as a valuable field of research, as well as being extremely important in a practical sense. Secure knowledge is essential but those involved have to analyse more clearly what they think they know. There cannot be experiments on children which are to their detriment. The interplay between the various aspects of development, as well as the social and cultural contexts in which children grow, is a further area to consider. There needs to be a review of the existing knowledge of how children grow and learn with an evaluation of how this impacts on those who practise as teachers and early years professionals.

Child development has tended to focus on cognitive aspects, and overlook the interdependency of emotional and physical development. Despite the work of Vygotsky, Bruner and Bronfenbrenner, social aspects of development are not always considered when formal curricula are put into place. Research into how the brain develops and functions has reawakened to some degree the debate over the importance of first-hand experience and play and this has now been written into guidelines targeted at early years practitioners, particularly the Early Years Foundation Stage in the UK. This, however, is tempered by the requirement to observe, plan and reach targets which may actually reduce the amount of learning if it detracts from the adult's knowledge of the child's own level of development and interests. Increasingly the importance of emotional development (the interplay between parents and other close family members) has started to emerge as a cause for concern, as well as a topic for research. There is now considerable concern about childhood depression and its origins. More is now understood about the impact of poor emotional nurturing in the early years on subsequent brain development. Experience of, and research in, children's homes and orphanages, like those in Romania where children were frequently not picked up or cuddled, has resulted in a greater understanding of the importance of physical interaction with young children to ensure that holistic development is optimal. There is a warning here; knowledge of brain development and of genetics cannot ever be used to restrict a child's potential.

Although there is a general developmental framework onto which we can map the major attributes of a child's individual development, the interest is in the detail and the difference, in recognising what interests and motivates a child. Then we can start to see ways in which we can work together with the child and his or her family to capture this and expand knowledge. This link with theory and practice is a good point to end this section and to consider future priorities.

WHAT HAPPENS IN PRACTICE?

A little boy, four years old, in a nursery school in an urban area was fascinated by the body and how it was put together. The staff quickly picked up on his interest and contacted the local hospital which was happy to offer a model skeleton to the school which it no longer required. Along with this, books and other resources were gathered together to support the child's interest. A strong torch enabled him, for instance, to contemplate the circulation of the blood by shining it through his own hand. Any questions he asked were answered honestly and often staff and child explored together to discover knowledge that neither knew. Experiments were devised to solve a number of problems. Other children became interested in this project and joined in, adding to the original child's self-esteem and sense of achievement as he explained quite difficult concepts to his peers. The whole project lasted well over a term and was opened-ended. As new thoughts and facts were uncovered the children returned to the topic. This had not been planned, but erupted from an individual child's passion. Instead of thinking up sterile activities to ensure that all developmental aspects had been covered, the staff were able to see not only cognitive and language development but also physical (how long does it take to run up that hill?), and social and emotional aspects were clearly covered in a natural, holistic way.

REFLECT AND RELATE TO PRACTICE

Compare the above example with any examples of practice from the provision you have visited or in which you work. Have you experienced similar scenarios where the learning has been so child-initiated, collaborative and so rich? If not, why do you think this is? Share your experiences and think of ways in which ideas that children have put forward to you could have been developed. How do your reflections take child development into consideration?

ACTIVITY

1 What do you know already about child development? Write this down. How does your current knowledge impact upon your practice?
2 How do you think your upbringing within your family or community has been critical in your response to how you support young children's growth and learning?
3 Having read the materials in this section, how do you think your ideas and philosophy about young children learning have altered? Write a time plan which indicates how you intend to redesign your professional practice.
4 If you accept that child development is complex both as a field of study and in a practical sense, how can we establish common baselines? Should we?
5 Moves are currently afoot in the UK to plan more for the individual through learning plans but how can we achieve this, if the more we observe development and learning the more complex it becomes?
6 There is increasing concern about children's emotional development. Is this a legitimate worry? How can we ensure that children's emotional needs are met? What constrains us and how can we overcome our own anxieties?

SUMMARY

Development as a complex process (p. 81)

How should we interpret learning in light of child development theories?

Developmental charts are helpful, but do not consider individual differences. Practitioners need experience, time to observe children, and time to discuss their progress in order to help them advance in their learning.

Nature versus nurture (p. 84)

To what extent is a child's learning and achievement determined by nature?

Practitioners should not exaggerate the genetic impact on children's learning, but should consider the huge number of possibilities each child has to achieve in life.

The great thinkers in child development theory (p. 87)

What do you think is the continuing impact of 'The Greats' on the way we educate and care for young children now?

The philosophies developed by the great thinkers of the past few centuries have had an impact on early years education contemporarily.

Current status of child development (p. 89)

What is the status of child development now, both in the sense of its functional use for practitioners and the research that is undertaken?

Practitioners should reflect on the extent to which research studies should influence accepted practice in early years settings.

A world view (p. 93)

Why do you think educationalists have traditionally considered child development theories from a north European or north American perspective?

We live in a global world, where international educational practices vary. Practitioners should reflect on the extent to which child development should be considered from a global perspective.

Development and learning: bringing it together (p. 94)

What is the current situation with research into development and learning?

As the national focus has turned again towards early years, there has been a revival of interest in child development as a valuable field of research.

Why is emotional nurturing important in a child's development?

The relevance of emotional interaction with children in helping them to become motivated learners has come to the forefront of research over the last few years.

Glossary

Critical period: (also referred to as key or sensitive period) periods, especially in young children, when the brain is 'trained' to make certain developmental jumps.

Interactionist: (view to language acquisition) assumes that the social relationship between the adult and the child is crucial to good language skills.

Nature: development is genetically determined.

Nativist: (approach to language acquisition) assumes that children are born with an innate capacity to learn language.

Nurture: development is environmentally determined.

Spiral curriculum: learning is revisited at increasingly more complex levels.

Find out more

Blakemore, S.-J. and Frith, U. (2005) *The Learning Brain: lessons for education*, **Oxford: Blackwell.**
This is an easily accessible text which explains clearly the links between the science of the brain, learning and education. It, however, recognises that neuroscience will not be the answer to all the issues in the classroom, but considers carefully the relevance of brain research to, for example, hot-housing and learning difficulties such as dyslexia and autism. It takes a measured approach, with well thought through possibilities and practical applications.

Gopnik, A., Kuhl, P.K. and Meltzoff, A. (2000) *How Babies Think*, **London: Weidenfeld & Nicolson.**
The authors draw on many years of research experience in a number of related fields to explain clearly how much babies already know about the world when they are first born and how quickly they learn more. They explore, for example, language acquisition and brain research. It is well written in an accessible style but this belies the complexity of the knowledge and research on which the book draws to present to its reader a full picture of a baby's true competence.

Keenan, T. and Evans, S. (2009) *An Introduction to Child Development*, **2nd edn, London: Sage.**
This is a comprehensive text which covers not only classic research into child development but incorporates issues, such as risk and resilience, as well as bringing readers up to date with new developments. This publication bridges the gap between basic child development texts and research publications and papers. It offers challenge to those who wish and need to know more.

Pound, L. (2005) *How Children Learn: from Montessori to Vygotsky – Educational Theories Made Easy*, **Leamington Spa: Step Forward.**
The author links theory to practice, while asking the question 'How do children learn?'. It introduces well-known educational theorists such as Montessori, Piaget and Vygotsky as well as others such as Dewey and Donaldson who have played major parts in constructing current approaches to early years learning and teaching. It is a very good starting point for those new to expanding their knowledge about the 'great educators', with good links to other, more specific, texts.

References

Abbott, L. and Langston, A. (2005) *Birth to Three Matters: Supporting the Framework of Effective Practice*. Maidenhead: Open University.

Blurton Jones, N.G. (1993) The Lives of Hunter-Gatherer Children: Effects of Parental Behaviour and Parental Strategy, in Pereira, M.E. and Fairbanks, L.A. (eds) *Juvenile Primates*. New York: Oxford University Press: pp. 309–326.

Bowlby, J. (1953) *Child Care and the Growth of Love*. London: Pelican.

Brewer, J.D. (2000) *Ethnology*. Buckingham: Open University Press.

Brookes, M. (1999) *Get a Grip on Genetics*. London: Weidenfeld & Nicolson.

Bruer, J.T. (1999) *The Myth of the First Three Years: A New Understanding of Brain Development and Lifelong Learning*. New York: The Free Press.

Clarke, A.M. and Clarke, A.D.B. (1976) *Early Experience: Myth and Evidence*. London: Open Books.

Clarke, A. and Clarke, A. (2000) *Early Experience and the Life Path*. London: Jessica Kinsley.

Daily Telegraph (2006) Modern life leads to more depression among children (Filed: 12/09/2006). London: Telegraph Group Ltd.

Department for Culture Media and Sport (2004) *Getting Serious About Play – A Review of Children's Play*. London: DCMS.

Department for Education and Skills (DfES) (2007) *The Early Years Foundation Stage*. Nottingham: DfES Publications.

Donaldson, M. (1978) *Children's Minds*. London: Fontana.

Eliot, L. (1999) *Early Intelligence: How the Brain and Mind Develop in the First Five Years of Life*. London: Penguin.

Follari, L.M. (2007) *Foundations and Best Practices in Early Childhood Education: Histories, Theories and Approaches to Learning*. Columbus, OH: Pearson/Merrill Prentice Hall.

Gerhardt, S. (2004) *Why Love Matters: how affection shapes a baby's brain*. London: Routledge.

Hindley, C.B. (1979) *Conceptual and Methodological Issues in the Study of Child Development: An Inaugural Lecture*. London: University of London Institute of Education.

Keenan, T. (2002) *An Introduction to Child evelopment*. London: Sage.

Luria, A.R. and Solotaroff, L. (1975) *The Man with a Shattered World: A History of a Brain Wound*. London: Penguin.

Morgan, E. (1994) *The Descent of the Child*. London: Penguin.

Newton, M. (2003) *Savage Girls and Wild Boys: A History of Feral Children*. London: Faber & Faber.

NICHD Early Child Care Research Network (2005) *Child Care and Child Development*. New York: The Guilford Press.

OECD, Directorate for Education (2004, March) Five Curriculum Outlines: online at **www.oecd.org/dataoecd/23/36/31672150.pdf**

Pugh, G. (2001) *Contemporary Issues in the Early Years: Working Collaboratively for Children*. London: Sage.

Rutter, M. (2006) *Genes and Behaviour: Nature–Nurture Interplay Explained*. Oxford: Blackwell.

Saraswathi, T.S. (ed.) (2003) *Cross-cultural Perspectives in Human Development*. London: Sage.

Sheridan, M.D., Frost, M. and Sharma, A. (1997) *From Birth to Five Years: Children's Developmental Progress*. London: Routledge.

Schoon, I. (2006) *Risk and Resilience: Adaptations in Changing Times*. Cambridge: Cambridge University Press.

Wells, G. (1986) *The Meaning Makers*. London: Heinemann.

White, J. (1985) The Importance of Educational Psychology, in Claxton, G., Swan, W., Salmon, P., Walkerdine, V., Jacobsen, J. and White, J. (1985) *Psychology and Schooling: What's the Matter?* Bedford Way Papers 25. London: Institute of Education.

World Health Organisation (WHO) *WHO Hub for Early Child Development*. Available at: **www.earlylearning.ubc.ca/WHO/**.

WHO Multicentre Growth Reference Study Group (2006) WHO Motor Development Study: Windows of achievement for six gross motor development milestones, *Acta Paediatrica*, Supplement, 450: 86–95.

CHAPTER **5**   Learners as Individuals

By the end of this chapter you will be able to answer the following questions:

- Why is the framework within which you view diversity and difference amongst children important to their learning?
- Why is the development of positive relationships (child–child, child–practitioner, parent–child and practitioner–parent) so important in helping children to become independent learners?
- How can practitioners create an enabling learning environment?
- Why are good communication skills important to the concept of independent learning?

This chapter will support your understanding of the following Standards *(see Appendix 1):*
■ **Knowledge and understanding:** S02, S03 and S06 ■ **Effective practice:** S07, S08, S10, S11, S12, S13, S14, S15, S17, S18 and S22 ■ **Relationships with children:** S25, S26, S27 and S28.

Introduction

Supporting Learning: Warm, trusting relationships with knowledgeable adults support children's learning more effectively than any amount of material resources.

(DCSF, 2008: 23)

Treating children as individuals and helping them to progress as confident and competent **independent learners** is most succinctly delineated within the context of this quote from government policy on early years. It is at the very foundation of effective teaching and learning from the earliest years of education. This chapter will consider how children's learning can be developed and enhanced through the creation of the right sort of learning environment, where they are appropriately supported by practitioners.

Learning styles vary from individual to individual; the Learning and Skills Research Centre (a government sponsored organisation which supports evidence-based policy development and research for post-16 learning) identifies 71 different approaches to learning (Robson, 2006: 3). Effective early years practitioners will consider how children learn, what motivates children and the extent to which they should be supported and guided and develop teaching repertoires accordingly. The *Statutory Framework for the Early Years Foundation Stage: Setting the Standards for Learning Development and Care for children from birth to five* (EYFS) (DfES, 2007) advocates 'ongoing observational assessment to inform planning for each child's continuing development through play based activities with a flexible approach that responds quickly to children's learning and development needs'.

The development of both a positive image of self (a belief in one's personal competency) and high self-esteem (defined by Brooker and Broadbent (2003: 33) as 'the value a child assigns him or herself') is strongly associated with educational achievement (Dowling, 2000) and developing as an effective learner (Whitebread, 2003). Whitebread (2003: 6), a psychologist and early years specialist at Cambridge University, takes this further, by suggesting that children's emotional and intellectual development is enhanced by three factors: a feeling of 'love and self-worth', a feeling of emotional security and feeling 'in control'. For the early years practitioner this means acknowledging each child as an individual and creating a learning environment where they feel valued.

Employing the following four guiding principles underpinning the Early Years Foundation Stage as a framework, which are applicable to babies, toddlers and young children, this chapter will consider how children's learning and development can be enhanced when they are acknowledged as individuals:

- Each child is unique: recognises that every child is a competent learner from birth who can be resilient, capable, confident and self-assured.
- Develop positive relationships: the commitments are focused around respect; partnership with parents; supporting learning and the role of the *key person*.

Independent learner: a learner who has the belief in him/herself to think through learning activities, problems or challenges, make decisions about his/her learning and act upon those decisions.

- Create enabling environments: the commitments are focused around observing, assessment and planning; support for every child; the learning environment; and the wider context – transitions, continuity, and multi-agency working.
- Learning and development: recognises that children develop and learn in different ways and at different rates, and that all areas of learning and development are equally important and interconnected.

(DfES, 2007: 9)

DISCUSSION POINT

Reflect on these four principles within the context of 'each child is an individual learner'. Do you think that your personal values and beliefs would/could influence the extent to which these principles underpin your day-to-day practice in an early years setting?

You should consider their influence on your teaching and the children's learning, the way you relate to children and the way you plan for learning. You can revisit your ideas at the end of the chapter.

You will find a table on our **website** of useful and relevant government documents for considering independent learning in practice. By completing the two columns Aims of document and Relevant points for your own notes (e.g. if it, or parts of it, are useful for your own practice and why) you can use the table for practice, updating as necessary.

Each child is unique

This section considers practical ways of acknowledging that each child is unique. By providing an overview of the government's view on inclusive practice, it prompts the reader to consider how he/she would address diversity and difference in the setting.

Educational practice is underpinned by a political agenda which accepts and celebrates diversity and difference. The government's aim is quite clear: an inclusive education across all educational settings in England. The EYFS is founded on 'equality of opportunity, where practice is anti-discriminatory, ensuring that every child is included and not disadvantaged because of ethnicity, culture or religion, home language, family background, learning difficulties or disabilities, gender or ability' (DfES, 2007: 7).

Croll and Moses (1998), and Rosenthal (2001), known for their research in the field of Special Educational Needs, consider that developing inclusive educational settings demands practitioners, researchers and academics to critically engage with what constitutes effective education for all. This requires the individual to determine their views, values and attitudes towards those perceived to be different, as Rosenthal states:

> [to] address discrimination and education for all we have to move towards more fully promoting the inclusion agenda, we have to provide regular meaningful dialogues between [children and practitioners] and we have to individually examine and adjust our own less-social perceptions, values and actions. All of us need to experience and hear each other's point of view; and the differences between us have to be acknowledged and explored, rather than ignored and denied.

(2001: 385)

Inclusion seeks to facilitate diversity, variety and to celebrate difference as a spectrum upon which all children are viewed equitably. For early years settings this means having an environment and policy which fits the children's needs. It is the responsibility of the setting to assess, provide for and evaluate the needs of their learners. Settings need to listen to the voices, experiences and views of their parents. Practitioners need to listen to the voices, experiences and views of the children. This is as important for babies and toddlers as it is for 3–5 or 5–7 year olds. Nutbrown and Clough, highly regarded for their work on inclusion in the early years, suggest that 'including babies means finding ways to listen to them and becoming sensitized to their needs and wants' (2006: 74). The following 'What happens in practice?' provides an example of what this means for practitioners:

Photo 5.1 Do you listen to the voice of the children?

Pearson Education Ltd. Jules Selmes © Pearson Education Ltd. 2004

WHAT HAPPENS IN PRACTICE?

A childminder took 13 month old Demetrius to watch the trains. She held his hands and patiently supported him as he walked up the steps of the footbridge and bent beside him – her arms around his tummy – as he looked through the railings on the top of the footbridge. In the distance a train was approaching – Demetrius loved the trains and this little outing to watch them go under the bridge was one of his favourite events of the day. As the train came nearer, two strangers walked over the footbridge – Demetrius took his eyes off the train and his gaze fixed on the strangers as they approached him, smiled at him and continued past. Demetrius' childminder gently turned his head – returning his eyes to the train which was about to pass under the bridge. Demetrius struggled slightly in an attempt to continue watching the new people he was so fascinated by, but his childminder had brought him to see the trains and, from her point of view, he was missing the event he usually enjoyed.

(Nutbrown and Clough, 2006: 74–75)

REFLECT AND RELATE TO PRACTICE

What were the learning needs of this 13 month old boy? How did the childminder respond to his learning needs?

☆ ☆ ☆

How did the childminder support the child's learning? Would you have acted in the same way? Why/why not?

Learning in a setting which accepts, adapts and promotes diversity and difference is a positive social and cognitive experience for the child. The following, adapted from an interview with a nursery manager who works with blind and visually impaired children, provides an example of how a practitioner's sensitivity to the needs of all children can enhance their learning experience.

Big Mack switch: a technological device, with built-in memory and an on/off button, which allows messages to be recorded and played back when the switch is pressed.

WHAT HAPPENS IN PRACTICE?

The children are highly motivated by music. They (often) say hello and share their news through a hello and drum song. Recently we have started using a **Big Mack switch** (a device, with an on/off button, which allows messages to be recorded and played back when the switch is pressed). Staff share the responsibility of recording an appropriate word or phrase on the Big Mack and children are given as much support as necessary to operate the switch to reply. It is lovely to see their expression and the growing understanding of cause and effect. We are currently looking to extend the type of switches we offer by enabling children with less refined physical movement to operate them, for example by squeezing or breaking a sound beam.

REFLECT AND RELATE TO PRACTICE

What do you think the practitioners in this nursery setting were hoping to achieve (with the children) in employing a Big Mack switch? In what ways will the activity have achieved its aims? (you need to consider if the children will have advanced in their learning)

☆ ☆ ☆

Do you think this was an appropriate way of responding to the learning needs of the children within this setting? Why/why not? Consider what outcomes the practitioners had in mind when planning for and implementing this activity. Would you have employed the same activity to help these children to advance in their learning?

It is, however, of equal importance to enable all children to develop an openness to and respect for difference and diversity. The following 'What happens in practice?', adapted from an interview with a senior lecturer in education at a university in northern France, considers how to encourage children to develop an openness to and respect for cultural differences. She describes the type of approach practitioners take in France when teaching English/German as a foreign language in an early years setting (4–7 year olds). Many of the suggestions are generic and can be applied to a number of different activities.

WHAT HAPPENS IN PRACTICE?

First of all it would be wrong to show only the differences in the other culture. Secondly one has to be careful not to stereotype the other culture. This is difficult to do.

Every time we want to show some aspect of the other culture, it is important to make children express how they do it themselves. For example, breakfast.

[By] asking everyone [what they have for breakfast], the teacher can show that in the classroom there are quite a lot of differences though all are French or English or . . . etc.

This is the same in the other country, what they are going to see/hear is an example that tries to show what many people do in this part of the world, but not all and that there is nothing like *the* French or *the* Germans.

Before showing interest for the other one over 'there', it is important to show interest for the children 'here' and the great variation between us. Otherwise, children won't be able to concentrate. They will want to make the comparison 'and we at home . . . .', 'And I do this', etc.

For me it is important to make children understand that difference is the norm, that difference is not better or worse or unequal. Differences are often a question of code. For example, people shake hands or nod or kiss or bow to greet each other. This is just what culture has taught people to do – a code that functions in this part but nothing more.

Children are quite interested by food. It is important to make them understand the difference between saying 'I don't like this' or 'yuck, disgusting' by showing, explaining or even letting them try some food. A birthday party may be different in this or that country but even if the satisfaction at receiving presents is expressed differently, the emotion inside is the same.

Differences are easy to handle with animal shouts. For example, the French rooster says 'cocorico', the German one says 'kikerikiki' and your rooster says 'cockedoo'. Which rooster is right? None of them are. The noise is interpreted by a group of people, this interpretation is, valid for this group of people. It's just a code that children learn in their family, at school . . . If one wants to be able to travel, to communicate with this other group of people, one has to learn their code. It's not dangerous, it's fun to understand different codes. In children's literature, there are plenty of stories with 'cultural' noises.

The intercultural aspect of learning languages is, for me, the essential part. If you don't teach the intercultural aspects as well as the language there is a risk of developing prejudice. I meet so many world travellers, language experts, who come back home with as many prejudiced ideas as they had before their travels.

For me there is this fundamental ethical aim in teaching foreign languages. I always try to work for more understanding, for more peace.

REFLECT AND RELATE TO PRACTICE

Do you think these are good examples of how cultural differences can be addressed in practice? Why/why not? How would you address cultural difference in an early years, multicultural setting?

Barriers to a child's progress exist due to a complex interplay of factors: attitudes, values, experiences and practices existing at the child's social, biological and educational level. In order to effectively understand and meet the needs of some learners, practitioners need to employ an **interactionist** approach to assessing and understanding the child's learning needs (i.e. they need to actively interact with the child as opposed to passive observation). Practitioners need to acknowledge their own learning needs and develop reflective skills in order to respond effectively to the needs of all children. Although there are certain recommendations for accommodating the social, environmental and learning needs of children with specific pedagogical needs, there is no 'blueprint' for all children. Each case is as individual as is each practitioner and setting and needs to be assessed, understood and provided for in context.

Interactionist: (view to language acquisition) assumes that the social relationship between the adult and the child is crucial to good language skills.

Develop positive relationships

The close connection between the development of **self-esteem** and social interaction is generally acknowledged. By considering how children develop as and become 'masters' of their own learning, this section will address how the development of positive practitioner–child relationships, both in a social capacity and through specific teaching practices, such as **sustained shared thinking**, a method for working collaboratively with children, can enhance children's learning and help them to develop as competent, independent learners.

Self-esteem: the extent to which a person values him/herself.

Brooker and Broadbent (2003: 33) define self-esteem as 'the value a child assigns him or herself', where an arbitrary measure of such is described as 'the disparity between what a child would like to be like and that child's view of how he or she actually is'. They further suggest that for the child, this is reflected in the perceived value he/she has in the opinion of the practitioners, i.e. practitioners should approach teaching and learning with a positive attitude to children's potential, communicating to them a firm belief in their competency as learners. This is exemplified in the Reggio Emilia system, where relationships with others are seen as being central to learning and development (see Chapter 10).

Enabling children to develop emotional security is dependent on enabling them to have trust in the wider environment (Whitebread, 2003: 7). This largely depends on the child's ability to develop positive relationships with peers and with 'significant' adults; where 'significant' adults will probably be those with whom the child has most contact, e.g. parents, practitioners or key persons. Robson (2006: 47–48), an early years educational specialist at Roehampton University, highlights the importance of 'pretend shared play'. She underlines the value of 'shared experiences' with peers for helping children to develop as 'thinkers'. This view is supported by Hendy and Toon (2001), educational specialists who have considered early years drama in some depth; they define 'pretend play as children engaging with a series of different behaviours and events. It is about trying out ideas, motivations and reactions to events in make-believe situations' (2001: 22). Wood and Attfield (2005), known for their research on play in the early years, suggest that 'play enables children to create their own rules, determine appropriate behaviours, define roles and test their own boundaries as well as those imposed by adults' (2005: 82). They further suggest that 'the wide repertoire of social skills and emotional literacy' demanded by play contexts can contribute to children's ability to 'become successful players'.

In helping children to develop the necessary skills for independent learning, practitioners need to be able to identify, not only the needs of the child, but also know when to intervene with a comment or a question and when to allow the child the time and space to think through the problem him/herself. The government, supported by recent research findings, is keen to promote **'sustained shared thinking'**. Siraj-Blatchford et al. (2002) define this as 'an episode in which two or more individuals "work together" in an intellectual way to solve a problem, clarify a concept, evaluate activities, extend a narrative etc. Both parties must contribute to the thinking and it must develop and extend' (2002: 8). For sustained shared thinking to be effective in practice, practitioners need to have developed relationships of trust with the children within their setting and know them well – what they can do, what they can achieve with appropriate support from the practitioner, what their interests are – this enables activities which help the child to develop a skill or advance in knowledge to be planned. The planning needs to consider the type of questions you will ask the child, when and how you will structure the questions, for example, build on the child's achievements – 'You've thought a lot about where to paint the sun, but where will you paint the trees?' In this way practitioners become involved in the thinking with the child.

Developing positive dispositions to learning is closely related to a child's level of confidence, which in turn can impact on motivation. Psychologists suggest this is related to children's own theories about learning which produce certain recognised patterns of behaviour in approaching new learning challenges (Brooker and Broadbent, 2003: 51). Dweck (2000) refers to these as **'mastery-oriented'** and **'helpless-oriented'** behaviour. Children who display a *mastery* orientation towards a difficult task remain confident in attitude and approach, whereas those who display a helpless-orientation lose focus and concentration and adopt an attitude of failure. Brooker and Broadbent (2003: 54), citing Carr (2001), suggest that children can develop *mastery* by being 'ready, willing and able to learn'. Dweck (2000: Cited in Robson 2006: 52–53) highlighted the following characteristics of mastery-oriented children and helpless-oriented children.

Mastery-oriented children tended to:

- not see themselves as failing
- engage in self-motivating strategies
- engage in self-instruction or self-monitoring
- remain confident that they would succeed
- have an attitude that they could learn from their failures
- did not see failure as an indictment of themselves as people.

The helpless-oriented children tended to:

- quickly denigrate their abilities
- lose faith in their ability to succeed
- focus on their failures rather than their successes
- lose focus on the task
- abandon strategies they had previously used successfully
- give up trying more quickly than the mastery-oriented children.

Sustained shared thinking: an episode where individuals work together in an intellectual way to solve a problem, clarify a concept, etc. All parties must contribute to the thinking and it must develop and extend (Siraj-Blatchford et al., DfES, 2002).

Mastery-oriented: children who remain confident in attitude and approach towards a difficult task. They believe in their own ability as learners and want to succeed.

Helpless-oriented: children who lose focus and concentration, adopting an attitude of failure, when faced by a difficult task.

By citing the example of a multicultural early years classroom, where teaching repertoires failed to value cultural differences, Brooker (2005: 127) highlights the difficulty for practitioners in helping children to develop mastery skills. She calls for 'a range of learning styles', rather than 'a one size fits all'. Whitebread (2003) highlights the centrality of adults in enabling young children to feel empowered. Children who feel in control of a task, he further suggests, 'respond positively to failure, and try harder the next time, believing all the time in their own ability to be successful in the task' (2003: 8–9). He cites democratic parenting styles as a good example of how adults enable children to develop mastery behaviour. In such a style 'there are rules to which a child is expected to conform, they are applied consistently and they are discussed and negotiated with the child' (ibid.). The centrality of relationships to a child's development is self-evident.

Broadhead (2004: 123), an early years specialist at Leeds Metropolitan University, connects learning dispositions with **emotional intelligence**, which she defines as our ability to 'actively manage our interactions with others'. Goleman (1999), however, offers a more comprehensive definition within the following context: 'the capacity for recognising our own feelings and those of others, for motivating ourselves, and for managing emotions well in ourselves and in our relationships'.

Emotional intelligence: the ability to manage one's emotions when alone or when interacting with others.

Broadhead (2004: 123) suggests that when children are able to operate within the 'cooperative domain', for example, 'when they play with others who manage this domain effectively', even though the individual may not be able to do this, she suggests, they are acting within a phase or stage of coping with their interaction with others. She cites play as an excellent means of supporting and promoting emotional intelligence. She suggests that when play is collaborative, by fixing upon and engaging with the knowledge of other children, those with a less developed emotional intelligence can engage more meaningfully with 'the world around them'.

Photo 5.2 Are these children developing their emotional intelligence?

Pearson Education Ltd. Lord and Leverett © Pearson Education Ltd. 2008

In practice, Brooker and Broadbent (2003) suggest that personal, social and emotional development are addressed both spontaneously and in planned activity, where the 'role of the skilled practitioner is to be alert to the multiple meanings of children's everyday experiences in and out of the classroom' (2003: 30). That is, is their interpretation the same as yours or what you would expect? Do you need to clarify the point through carefully thought out and appropriate questioning? Should you use this point as a means of further developing their learning? This demands a focused approach on the part of the early years practitioner. Whitebread (2003: 9) provides the following framework of practice for developing an integrated approach to personal, emotional and social education which can be used effectively within an early years setting:

- create an atmosphere of emotional warmth, within which each child feels individually valued
- communicate high expectations to all children
- praise and recognise children's achievements, particularly when they are the result of a special effort
- run an orderly classroom that has regular classroom routines
- always explain to the children the programme of events for the day and prepare them for transitions
- put children in control of their own learning; allow them to make choices
- exercise democratic control; involve children in decisions about classroom rules and procedures and enforce rules fairly
- criticise a child's actions, but never the child.

DISCUSSION POINT

What type of learner do you want to develop in your early years setting?
   Identify the main characteristics of a mastery-oriented child. Make a list of the strategies you could use to help children develop mastery-oriented characteristics.

Create enabling environments

In creating enabling educational environments for children (i.e. settings in which all children can develop confidence in their ability as learners and competency in learning), government policy is unequivocal. They should be developed in response to the cognitive, affective and physical learning needs of the child. In practice, this means developing a cycle for learning, which, in essence, is based on the cyclical nature of observing, assessing and planning (see Chapter 16). The more effectively this is carried out by the practitioner, the more enabling the learning environment for the child. This section considers how practitioners can create such environments for the children in their setting and challenges the reader to consider the key factors in the creation of an effective learning environment.

The development of an effective cycle for learning is enhanced by pleasant physical surroundings and good interactions within the community (child–child and adult–child). The following, adapted from an interview with the manager of a private nursery in York, lists factors (non-hierachical) fundamental to the creation of an enabling learning environment:

- resources (paint, toys etc.)
- trained members of staff
- quality genuine interactions with children – actually listening to what children are saying and being genuinely interested
- the environment – keeping it clean and making it pleasant
- replenishing resources
- making sure (resources) are accessible to the children
- having lots of pictures of children doing normal things – put them at the children's height and frequently draw the children's attention to them.

At the centre of any community of practice is respect – respect for each other, for property, space and learning. Children need to know from a young age that they matter. A child cannot respect others if he/she has very little self-respect. Bertram and Pascal (2002: 97), education specialists at the University of Birmingham, citing the seminal work of Lipman (1989) – an American professor of philosophy who founded philosophy for children (P4C) – which explored respect in six year olds, suggest that when a child's self-respect and respect for others is developed, their educational progress is enhanced. Although it is widely acknowledged that parents are the primary educators of their children, it is important to teach and reinforce what respect means in practice. Some children may come from families where they are either not shown respect or are not made to feel that they matter. Michele Borba (2001: 131), an educational consultant and former teacher in America, has written a number of books on parenting. The following, adapted from her list of 'what respectful people do', provides a framework for helping older children to develop respect in early years settings:

- Encourage children to wait until someone has finished speaking before they speak.
- Do not allow children to answer back.
- Encourage children to respect their immediate environment.
- Enable children to listen to the views of others, without interrupting them.
- Teach children to listen to the opinion of others.
- Teach children to respect each other's privacy.
- Children should respect each other's belongings.
- Teach them to obey their educators even when they do not feel like it.
- Do not allow children to use 'bad' language.

The use of the word 'obey' in the above example is worthy of consideration. It might be more appropriate to promote self-learning and self-development in partnership with educators, practitioners and parents through negotiation rather than 'obedience'.

One possible way of encouraging respect, which is more appropriate for older children, is to allow them to keep records in a personal notebook relating to something that has meaning for them (e.g. they could draw a picture or choose an object); practitioners should make time to discuss with the children why their chosen picture or object is of importance to them. This can both encourage and promote respect for personal views and opinions. However, the idea of treating babies and toddlers with respect and showing that respect are of equal importance. Practitioners need to consider how they can provide opportunities for this age group to both initiate and choose their own activities, how they respond to them and how they can 'reach' them at their level. Allowing them to sleep when they are tired rather than at a defined sleep time, engaging with them rather than talking to an adult over them and comforting them if they are upset provide opportunities for making that respect known.

DISCUSSION POINT

Reflect on what you have read in the chapter up to this point. What factors do you think are fundamental in creating an effective learning environment?

You should also consider such factors as your values – will they influence what happens in practice, your attitude to children's learning, the techniques you would employ to help children develop as independent learners and differing strategies for implementing these techniques depending on the child's competency as a learner?

Establishing basic factors, as part of the daily life of the early years setting, will make the cycle for learning more manageable. The question for practitioners is that of how to initiate the process. The starting point is seeking and interpreting evidence. However, the Qualifications and Curriculum Authority highlights the importance of knowledge and understanding of children's learning and development in planning appropriate and challenging activities:

> Practitioners' values and beliefs will affect their teaching and how children learn. Motivating children to concentrate, to persevere and to try several ways to make something work rather than giving up requires practitioners to use encouraging, friendly, optimistic and lively approaches to support children. Enabling children to learn should be based on knowing when it is timely to intervene and when to hold back.

(QCA: 2000: 43)

Knowledge and understanding of children's learning and development will enhance analysis of observational evidence and enable practitioners to take effective steps to plan for the child's learning. Assessment (Chapter 9) and planning (Chapter 16) are discussed in more detail in other chapters and will not be further discussed here.

However, it is important to remember that the learning cycle is a continuous process, which will be fundamental to daily practice. The question for practitioners is how to make education more responsive to an individual child and how to deliver personalised learning. The answer is having high expectations of all children (i.e. you believe all children are competent learners who can do good work and you let them know this by giving encouraging positive feedback) so that staff can build on the knowledge, interests and aptitudes of every child while involving children in their own learning through shared objectives and feedback. This process helps children to become confident learners and enables children to develop the skills they will need beyond institutionalised learning situations.

Learning and development

This section considers the idea that children learn in different ways and consequently need to be provided with different learning experiences during the early years of their education. The way practitioners view intelligence can influence how this is implemented in practice. At this stage in their development, however, children may not have developed a particular talent and although it is important to be aware of the different ways children learn, they need to be continually provided with different learning experiences. The development of children's intelligence is closely connected with their personal well-being and the extent to which they are enabled to develop as independent learners. This concept is given further consideration within the context of teaching for the development of good 'communication skills'.

Practitioners acknowledge that each child is unique in the way he/she both learns and develops. They also recognise that both learning and development are interconnected and should be treated as such across all areas of the curriculum. In practice this means providing opportunity for each child to experience different types of learning and giving consideration to the different ways children learn. This can be influenced by the way we view intelligence. John West-Burnham and Max Coates (2005: 44), known for their work within the field of educational leadership, are critical of the assumption, which they believe still dominates many learning institutions, that intelligence is predominantly a genetic attribute and is 'expressed through logical and reasoning abilities'. Holding such a view suppresses the idea that intelligence can be developed and enhanced through teaching. Howard Gardner of Harvard University, with his renowned theory of multiple intelligences (1983), brought a broader perspective to the way we view intelligence. Although he is not without critics most notably White (2002), Gardner put the idea of intelligence as a multidimensional concept on the educational map. In Gardner's theory we develop intelligence by responding to and assimilating information in different ways, e.g. through social contact, movement, emotions and through our senses, etc. Some children are born with natural talent in a particular area, but effective practitioners and good pedagogy help children to develop their intelligence, or more aptly, as Gardner would suggest, their intelligences. Gardner suggests that children are born with the following 'combination of eight intelligences and learn best when they are using their strongest intelligences' (Borba, 2001: 264–265):

1 **Linguistic learners** like to read, write and tell stories.
2 **Bodily/kinesthetic learners** like to do sports and are good at artistic expression. They are skilled in fine motor tasks.
3 **Intrapersonal learners** have strong self-understanding, are original, enjoy working alone to pursue their own interests and goals, and have a strong sense of right and wrong.
4 **Interpersonal learners** understand people, lead and organise others, have lots of friends, are looked to by others to make decisions and mediate conflict and enjoy joining groups.
5 **Musical learners** appreciate rhythm, pitch and melody, and they respond to music.
6 **Logical/mathematical learners** understand numbers, patterns and relationships, and enjoy science and maths. They categorise, ask questions, do experiments, and figure things out.
7 **Spatial learners** like to draw, design and create things, and imagine things and daydream. They remember what they see, read maps and charts, and work well with colours and pictures.
8 **Naturalists** like the out-of-doors, are curious, and classify the features of the environment.

DISCUSSION POINT

In the 'nature–nurture' debate (see Chapter 4), that is, there are some who argue that if a child is not born with a particular talent (e.g. music) this area of intelligence cannot be developed. However, government policy, supported by research, tends to reject this view, suggesting that enabling children to experience and actively participate in learning, where they are appropriately supported by practitioners, helps them to develop, to a lesser or greater degree, as competent learners in all intelligences. What is your view of intelligence? Do you think the idea that intelligence is a natural attribute would influence the way you approach teaching and learning in practice? Why/why not?

On the surface, the above list of intelligences can seem quite challenging for practitioners. In practice, however, they can be introduced and developed as part of the cyclical teaching process (observe, assess, plan). It means providing the opportunity for each child to have the related type of learning experience on a number of occasions, observing in which areas the child's talents lie and considering how these can be enhanced or how a weaker intelligence could be further developed.

What is your view on the idea of multiple intelligences as proposed by Gardner (1983)? You might find White, 2002, helpful (see references). Do you agree with the idea that practitioners should teach to the strongest intelligences?

You should consider such issues as a broad and balanced curriculum, the young age of the children within the context of life-long learning, the idea of developing both strengths and weaknesses, the extent to which you would continue to teach for a particular intelligence when a child's strengths may lie in another area and other issues you consider to be relevant.

Effective teaching for both learning and development will depend, to a large degree, on helping children to become independent learners. In practice, this means addressing the cognitive, affective and behavioural dimensions of learning, which, with careful planning, can be effectively addressed through the learning goals (see EYFS). Ferre Laevers (1994: 161) of Leuven University sees 'emotional well-being and involvement' as being central to quality learning in the early years. Laevers suggests that emotional well-being is dependent on the extent to which children 'feel at ease, find an atmosphere in which they can be spontaneous and are satisfied in their basic needs such as the need for attention and affection, the need for social recognition, the feeling of competence' (ibid.). This calls for appropriate 'pedagogical intervention' and in the case of helping children to both feel and be involved he calls for practitioners to set up 'challenging' environments 'favouring involvement' (e.g. appropriate posters on the walls reinforcing activities/issues raised in practice, opportunity for collaborative work, appropriate and relevant questioning, etc.). The idea of emotional well-being is becoming an increasingly popular issue in educational circles in terms of how it relates to independent learning. This view is supported by Bertram and Pascal (2002: 93) who identify it as a core consideration for independent learning, along with 'dispositions to learn and social competence and self-concept'.

> **Connect & Extend**
>
> The idea of multiple intelligences is coming more to the fore in the field of education. You should familiarise yourself with Gardner's work by reading the following two books:
>
> Gardner, H. (1983) *Frames of Mind: The Theory of Multiple Intelligence*. London: Fontana Press.
>
> Gardner, H. (1999) *Intelligence Reframed, Multiple Intelligences for the 21st Century*. Circles, New York: Basic Books.
>
> When you have read them you should be able to critique his work. Do you agree with Gardner? Why/why not? What is your opinion?

DISCUSSION POINT

Look up the document the *Statutory Framework for the Early Years Foundation Stage: Setting the Standards for Learning Development and Care for children from birth to five* (EYFS) (DfES, 2007), available at: **www.dcsf.gov.uk**. Consider Appendix 1 – Assessment Scales. Identify which of the scales relate to the core areas outlined by Bertram and Pascal (2002: 93).

In practice the core areas outlined by Bertram and Pascal (2002) are integrated and should be addressed alongside the cognitive dimension of learning and development.

The extent to which children develop these skills, with appropriate support from educators, hinges on their self-confidence. This is both enhanced through and to a large degree founded on effective communication, an idea strongly endorsed by the government and reflected in their policy documents:

> The development and use of speech, language and communication are at the heart of young children's learning. Much teaching is delivered verbally; and children require good communication skills to make friends, to participate in group activities and to develop higher-level thinking skills. Children's later achievements are dependent on their ability to communicate effectively. It is vitally important to ensure that we do everything that we can to help all children to become skilful and confident communicators.
>
> *(DCSF, 2008: 8)*

The EYFS (DfES, 2007) places a strong emphasis on the development of language for communicating, thinking, the linkage of sounds and letters, reading and writing. Language development is a gradual process in children, which begins in the home and continues to develop through early years education, school and into adulthood. Babies' language development is very important (Karmiloff and Karmiloff-Smith, 2001). They start to learn language by listening to other people talking. By the time they are 20 months they will have developed a small vocabulary of everyday words which they will have heard repeatedly; their pronunciation may still be unclear. Although their cognitive development of language will be increasing, much of their communication at this stage will be non-verbal – smiling, looking, making sounds and responding to adult language. It is not until 30 months that they start to use simple sentences and with support from practitioners can advance quite quickly in their acquisition of language.

Language is a powerful medium for developing – expressing needs, emotions, thoughts and ideas. Whitehead describes language as being 'something to do with the complex business of getting two minds in contact, because the exchange of meanings is at the centre of human communication' (1997: 4). Riley and Reedy (2003), from the University of London and known for their work on children's thinking and language development, suggest that 'thinking is developed through the child's growing control of spoken language'. Using language more 'precisely', they suggest, enables children 'to generalise, categorise, to manipulate ideas and to explore ideas of cause and effect' (2003: 63). This builds on the seminal work of Jerome Bruner, an eminent psychologist renowned for his work on cognitive learning and development, who described language as a 'tool of thought, by demonstrating the ways in which language enables children to develop their thinking and perform tasks which would otherwise be impossible' (Whitebread, 2003: 4). Bruner's studies of children and language have led to the idea that age is no barrier to teaching, when the matter is presented in an accessible form. This idea is at the root of effective learning and is encompassed by Bruner's phrase, the **spiral curriculum**, which refers to the repeated 'revisiting' of the curriculum, or necessary parts of the curriculum in different ways.

Spiral curriculum: learning is revisited at increasingly more complex levels.

Riley and Reedy (2003) refer to the Bristol Study (Wells, 1987) which explored the development of language with a sample of 128 children from the age of 13 months through to school age. The results highlighted the importance of adults in children's language development. The findings suggested that 'children learn language best . . . when adults attend to, and are interested in what children are saying and enter with them in real conversations' (Riley and Reedy, 2003: 64). This type of interaction needs to be encouraged in early years settings. Effective communication through language helps children to develop as competent learners.

Whitebread advocates that early years educators 'provide opportunities for meaningful conversations between groups of children, and between children and adults' (2003: 17). A more traditional approach is found in the work of Jean Piaget, the developmental psychologist, whose pioneering work with children has had a strong influence on educational thought. He developed the idea that children are active participants in the construction of their own meanings, i.e. through learning experiences – either individually or collaboratively – children construct their own understandings. However, he has been highly criticised for underestimating the role of adults in children's language development (Whitebread, 2003: 3). Piaget saw adult intervention as negative. Intervention was seen as depriving the child of the opportunity to discover language for him/herself. Vygotsky, on the other hand, famous for his **zone of proximal development** – whereby children can learn when they are supported in activities which would otherwise be beyond their own ability – saw adult intervention within the context of social learning. He underlined the importance of adults both supporting children, through appropriate intervention and modelling good practice, in enabling children to develop social and cognitive skills.

Zone of proximal development: the gap between what the child can achieve without help and what they can achieve with appropriate support.

DISCUSSION POINT

The *Statutory Framework for the Early Years Foundation Stage: Setting the Standards for Learning Development and Care for children from birth to five* (EYFS) (DfES, 2007) places a strong emphasis on the development of language for communicating, thinking, the linkage of sounds and letters, reading and writing. It states that:

Children's learning and competence in communicating, speaking and listening, being read to and beginning to read and write must be supported and extended. They must be provided with opportunity and encouragement to use their skills in a range of situations and for a range of purposes, and be supported in developing the confidence and disposition to do so.

(DfES, 2007: 13)

Look up this document, which is available at: **www.dcsf.gov.uk**. Consider the early learning goals for communication, language and literacy (DfES, 2007: 13). To what extent does the development of effective communication skills impact on a child's ability to develop as an independent learner?

SUMMARY

This chapter has highlighted the importance of acknowledging each child as an individual in helping him/her to develop as an independent learner. The way practitioners interact with children, how they interact and their views towards intelligence all contribute to the development of an enabling learning environment where children are provided with the opportunity and appropriately supported to reach their full potential.

Each child is unique (p. 102)

How would you address diversity and difference in practice?

This section considers practical ways of acknowledging that each child is unique. The government's aim is quite clear: inclusive practice across all educational settings in England. This requires practitioners to determine their views, values and attitudes towards those perceived to be different.

Develop positive relationships (p. 107)

How would you help children in your setting to become independent learners?

The close connection between the development of self-esteem and social interaction is generally acknowledged. Developing positive dispositions to learning is closely related to a child's level of confidence, which in turn can impact on motivation. This section considers how, through the development of positive relationships,

practitioners in all early years settings can help children to become independent learners.

Create enabling environments (p. 110)

In your opinion, what are the key factors in creating an enabling environment?

This section considers how practitioners can create enabling environments for the children in their setting. Government policy within this area is unequivocal; environments should be developed in response to the cognitive, affective and physical learning needs of the child. In practice, this means developing a cycle for learning, which is based on observing, assessing and planning. The more effectively this is carried out by the practitioner, the more enabling the learning environment for the child.

Learning and development (p. 113)

To what extent do communication skills impact on a child's ability to develop as an independent learner?

This section considers the idea that the way practitioners view intelligence may influence the way and extent to which they provide children with the opportunity to experience different types of learning. It further suggests that intelligence, children's well-being and independent learning are closely connected and can be developed and enhanced through the development of 'good communication' skills.

Glossary

Big Mack switch: a technological device, with built-in memory and an on/off button, which allows messages to be recorded and played back when the switch is ressed.

Emotional Intelligence: the ability to manage one's emotions when alone or when interacting with others.

Helpless-orientation: children who lose focus and concentration, adopting an attitude of failure, when faced by a difficult task.

Independent learner: a learner who has the belief in him/herself to think through learning activities, problems or challenges, making decisions about his/her learning and acting upon those decisions.

Interactionist: to actively interact with the child, where the social relationship between the adult and the child is crucial.

Mastery-oriented: children who remain confident in attitude and approach towards a difficult task. They believe in their own ability as learners and want to succeed.

Spiral curriculum: learning is revisited at increasingly more complex levels.

Sustained shared thinking: an episode in which two or more individuals 'work together' in an intellectual way to solve a problem, clarify a concept, evaluate activities, extend a narrative, etc. Both parties must contribute to the thinking and it must develop and extend (Siraj-Blatchford et al., DfES, 2002).

Zone of proximal development: this is the gap between what the child can achieve without help and what the child can achieve with appropriate support. In essence, with appropriate, relevant and effective interactions with more able others, children are provided with greater opportunity to reach their potential.

Find out more

Department for Children, Schools and Families (DCSF) (2008) *Inclusion Development Programme. Supporting children with speech, language and communication needs: Guidance for practitioners in the Early Years Foundation Stage,* **Nottingham: DCSF Publications.**
This document provides a good theoretical background, including a definition of the relevant terms, to speech, language and communication skills. The manner in which it deals with this important aspect of the curriculum provides thought-provoking material for developing the related skills with children in an early years setting.

Holland, R. (1997) 'What's it all about?' – how introducing heuristic play has affected provision for the under-threes in one day nursery, in Abbott, L. and Moylett, H. (eds) *Working with the under-3s:* *responding to children's needs,* **Buckingham: Open University Press: pp. 116–129.**
Ruth Holland gives good coverage to heuristic play in practice. By looking at the role of adults and how heuristic play can be employed effectively across the appropriate age range, she offers valuable ideas for its practical implementation.

Dean, J. (2006) *Meeting the Learning Needs of all Children,* **Abingdon: Routledge.**
This book considers personalised learning in the primary school, but its particular focus means it is applicable in early years settings. Joan Dean has a particularly good section on considering the differences in learning approach between boys and girls, which is worth reflecting upon – how do you try to meet the learning needs of boys and girls? (Chapter 5).

References

Bertram, T. and Pascal, C. (2002) Assessing what matters in the early years, in Fisher, J. (ed.) *The Foundations of Learning*. Buckingham: Open University Press.

Borba, M. (2001) *Raising Moral Kids*. San Francisco, CA: Jossey-Bass.

Broadhead, P. (2004) *Early Years Play and Learning: Developing Social Skills and Cooperation*. Abingdon: RoutledgeFalmer.

Brooker, L. (2005) 'Learning to be a Child: Cultural Diversity and Early Years Ideology', in Yelland, N. (ed.) *Critical Issues in Early Childhood Education*. Maidenhead, Berkshire: Open University Press, pp. 115–131.

Brooker, L. and Broadbent, L. (2003) Personal, social and emotional development: the child makes meaning in a social world, in Riley, J. (ed.) *Learning in the Early Years: A Guide for Teachers of Children 3–7*. London: Paul Chapman: pp. 29–61.

Carr, M. (2001) *Assessment in Early Childhood Settings: Learning Stories*. London: Paul Chapman.

Croll, P. and Moses, D. (1998) Pragmatism, ideology and educational change: the case of special educational needs, *British Journal of Educational Studies*, Vol. 46: pp. 11–25.

Department for Children, Schools and Families (DCSF) (2008) *Inclusion Development Programme. Supporting Children with Speech, Language and Communication Needs: Guidance for Practitioners in the Early Years Foundation Stage*. Nottingham: DCSF Publications.

Department for Education and Skills (DfES) (2007) *Statutory Framework for the Early Years Foundation Stage: Setting the Standards for Learning Development and Care for Children from Birth to Five* (EYFS). Nottingham: DfES Publications.

Dowling, M. (2000) *Young Children's Personal, Social and Emotional Development*. London: Paul Chapman.

Dweck, C. (2000) *Self-Theories: Their Role in Motivation, Personality and Development*. Hove: Psychology Press.

Gardner, H. (1983) *Frames of Mind: The Theory of Multiple Intelligence*. London: Fontana Press.

Goleman, D. (1999) *Working with Emotional Intelligence*. London: Bloomsbury.

Hendy, L. and Toon, L. (2001) *Supporting Drama and Imagination Play in the Early Years*. Buckingham: Open University Press.

Karmiloff, K. and Karmiloff-Smith, A. (2001) *Pathways to Language: From fetus to adolescent*. Cambridge, MA: Harvard University Press.

Laevers, F. (ed.) (1994) *Defining and Assessing Quality in Early Childhood Education*. Leuven, Belgium: Leuven University Press.

Lipman, M. (1989) *Philosophy Goes to School*. New Jersey, New York: Temple University Press.

Nutbrown, C. and Clough, P. (2006) *Inclusion in the Early Years*. London: Sage.

Qualifications and Curriculum Authority (2003) *Foundation Stage Profile Handbook*. London: QCA.

Riley, J. and Reedy, D. (2003) Communication, Language and Literacy: learning through speaking and listening and reading and writing, in Riley, J. (ed.) *Learning in the Early Years: A Guide for Teachers of Children 3–7*. London: Paul Chapman.

Robson, S. (2006) *Developing Thinking and Understanding in Young Children: An Introduction for Students*. Abingdon: Routledge.

Rosenthal, H. (2001) Discussion paper: Working towards inclusion: I am another other, *Educational Psychology in Practice*, Vol. 17, No. 4: pp. 306–392.

Siraj-Blatchford, I., Sylva, K., Muttock, S., Gilden, R. and Bell, D. (2002) *Researching Effective Pedagogy in the Early Years* (REPEY), Research Report No. 356. Nottingham: DfES Publications.

Wells, C. (1987) *The Meaning Makers: Children Learning Language and Using Language to Learn*. London: Hodder and Stoughton.

White, J. (2001) *The Child's Mind*. London: Routledge Falmer.

West-Burnham, J. and Coates, M. (2005) *Personalising Learning: Transforming Education for Every Child*. London: Continuum.

White, J. (2001) *The Child's Mind*. London: Routledge Falmer.

Whitebread, D. (ed.) (2003) *Teaching and Learning in the Early Years*. London: RoutledgeFalmer.

Whitehead, M. (1997) *Language and Literacy in the Early Years*, 2nd Edn. London: Paul Chapman.

Wood, E. and Attfield, J. (2005) *Play, Learning and the Early Childhood Curriculum*. London: Paul Chapman.

Framing Learning Practice

Part 2 sets learning practices within the framework of personalised learning. Founded on the effective collaboration of the practitioner, child and his/her parents/carers, where teaching is adapted to meet the learning needs of the individual child, it is strongly endorsed by the government and many researchers and educationalists. Part 2 considers how personalised learning helps practitioners to support children in the development of the right behaviours/dispositions for learning and how Information Communication Technology and Assessment for Learning contribute to this process.

Pearson Education Ltd.© Pearson Education Ltd. 2004

CHAPTER 6

Computer Technologies and Environments for Learning 0–7

By the end of this chapter you will be able to answer the following questions:

- What is the rationale for the deployment of technology in education?
- What are the competing pedagogies which underpin the software design?
- How has the developing nature of technology impacted on education?
- Should/could technology enable or transform educational practice?

This chapter will support your understanding of the following Standards *(see Appendix 1)*:
■ **Knowledge and understanding:** S02 ■ **Effective Practice:** S12 and S15 ■ **Relationships with children:** S26 ■ **Communicating and working in partnership with families and carers:** S29 and S31 ■ **Professional development:** S37, S38 and S39.

Introduction

A particular difficulty in education is that of 'historical amnesia'. It is easy to assume that the way early years settings are at any point of time is how they have always been and how they are likely to remain. This is a particular issue in the area of technology, an area which has seen and continues to see immense change both in context and in application in early years settings. Not convinced about how rapid the technological changes have been? John Maddison, writing in 1983 and one of the earliest to address the relationship between technology and education, described a range of computer systems suitable for school use. Among these was the BBC model B machine; this system had 64K of internal memory (today, the minimum is 1GB), ran in up to 16 colours and cost around £800 plus an additional £32 for the optional disk drive. In the space of 25 years there has been a rapid increase in processing power coupled with an equally rapid relative decrease in price, together with a miniaturisation of the technology. Hence in 2008 you can drive a car with far more computer power than was available to the first astronauts on their trip to the Moon. It is these changes in digital technology which make them so ubiquitous and have allowed them to become so embedded in our society. This chapter will consider both how the developing nature of technology and its increasing use in society has impacted on education and the extent to which it can transform education.

Connect & Extend

A 22-year-old starting to work in early years settings in 2010 could work until retirement in 2055. The last babies, toddlers and young children in early years settings that he/she would encounter are likely to live on to the age of 80, that is until 2135 or beyond.

Try to imagine the world that will exist at these points of time and remember, your job is to prepare the learners and citizens of tomorrow not yesterday.

Changing society – changing educational demands?

In the run-up to the 1997 election, Tony Blair's 'New Labour' committed themselves to an extensive programme of educational reform; central to this was the use of ICTs. This section challenges the reader to consider the extent to which ICT in schools settings has changed children's learning.

While many developments in the use of **Information Communication Technology (ICT)**; any technology which is used for the communication of information, from personal computers to DVDs) in education occurred through the 1980s and 1990s the most significant macro-level initiative was to begin with the change of the political players in 1997. In the run-up to the election 'New Labour' stated that:

- All schools and most early years settings will be connected to the **superhighway** free of charge (a communication system, connected through a fibre-optics network, for the fast transfer of information, e.g. the internet)
- Half a million teachers will be trained
- Our children will be leaving school IT-literate
- Schools will be able to exploit the best that technology has to offer.

(Source: Connecting the Learning Society, 1997)

Once elected these manifesto pledges were rapidly enacted: a rapid increase in computer hardware and software provision in schools, an equally rapid development of

Information Communication Technology (ICT): any technology used for the communication of information.

Superhighway: a communication system (connected through a fibre-optics network) for the fast transfer of information, e.g. the internet.

broadband technology and a programme of training for all teachers. Charles Clarke, Home Secretary from 2004 to 2006, was to admit later that this had been a 'leap of faith' (DfES, 2003a: 5), but it is clear that such massive investment in finance and training had a positive impact on ICT provision in schools; demonstrably they are more technologically-rich environments. The extent to which actual learning activities in schools have changed to any radical degree does, however, remain in question. A particular difficulty, though, was that it was grounded in a technologically romantic view of change, that simply by providing the hardware and infrastructure base and coupling this with basic training in the use of the hardware, change in educational practice would simply happen. Clarke's view may be preferable to that reported by John Maddison a generation earlier, when it was suggested by a chair of education in one of the shire counties that teachers who had been involved in the development of educational film and television should get themselves back into the classroom to do the job that they were paid for – 'to teach'. In early years settings this has also been an issue with private and mainstream nurseries adopting technology for learning.

Contrary to this view, the following, taken from an interview with a leader of practice in a nursery in Thanet, provides a good example of technology use with babies and toddlers.

WHAT HAPPENS IN PRACTICE?

Toddlers can play with microphones and sounds by recording their own voices. Babies and toddlers really enjoy hearing themselves and others responding to the sound. We also use light boxes to explore colours or natural objects, like leaves and projectors, to enable them to play with shadows. Any programmable musical toys that move are really stimulating and exciting for babies.

Light and sound stimulation is particularly effective with babies and toddlers, and such technology can be found in nurseries and Foundation Stage settings. Do you think that the technology has been used effectively in early years settings? Why/ why not? Will it stimulate learning?

Imagine you have planned for this activity and are now observing children 0–3 years carrying out these activities. What thoughts would you be having? How could you further develop this activity to help these children progress in their learning? Remember, the children will be of differing abilities.

The drivers for change

By providing a brief outline of the government driven change in schools to meet the needs of an increasingly competitive global marketplace, this section encourages the reader to consider why ICT was considered to be so central to this process.

During the early years of the twenty-first century a number of briefings by government representatives made their position clear. They argued that society was changing and would continue to do so and that such changes required a rapid change in education; the UK had to compete in an increasingly competitive global marketplace. There were fewer opportunities for unskilled, unproductive members of society; a society in which skills rapidly became obsolescent and the living wage increasingly difficult to attain. People were living longer and the change in demographics would have important effects on society. As the balance between young workers and older retired members of society changed it would become increasingly difficult to maintain an adequate pension provision and health services. As a result of these demands a small nation such as ours had to make the most efficient use of its human capital. Our society had to move rapidly to a position in which the traditional boundaries between school, work and retirement would meld into a continuous process of life-long learning.

REFLECT AND RELATE TO PRACTICE

What role do you think technology had to play in this view of a 'changing society'?

Why do you think the New Labour government wanted to invest so heavily in ICTs?

ICT in learning settings

Children presented with 'new' technologies are able to access them with the guidance of practitioners. By addressing, the albeit short, historical context of ICT in education, this section encourages the reader to consider the place of the early years practitioner in the deployment of ICT with children and the extent to which ICT can be used to extend children's learning.

Terry Mayes (2002), from the Research Centre for Lifelong Learning at Glasgow Caledonian Universities, places our present discussions regarding the use of ICTs in education within a wider historical framework. He highlights the fact that the historical introduction of what appeared to be powerful new media – radio, film, video, television – were each confidently predicted to herald a period of new and more effective educational methods. That such movements, including eTelevision, failed to make the predicted impact, he argues, is based upon a fundamental 'pedagogical heresy', that is, the material was badly presented to practitioners/teachers, many of whom elected, for whatever reason, not to deploy the new technology in their classrooms/ early years settings.

We have seen that much of this early thinking was driven by a simplistic view of the use of ICT in learning. There was talk at the time of connecting all schools via the internet to a central hub of high-quality resources. At its most extreme, it was believed, by some, that children would then be able to access these through application or experience, perhaps with the support of teaching assistants, and thus overcome the need for teachers. Such a view was not new and is based on the assumption that the central purpose of education is the simple transmission of a body of knowledge. It was suggested that teachers' workload could be eased by using the internet to readily download teaching materials and lesson plans and make use of a range of recommended software packages. Another alternative was that of the sharing of materials across schools, which many argue lessens the pressure on practitioners. The downside of this type of practice, however, is that teachers and practitioners may not use technology effectively and may lose ownership of both the lesson content and pedagogical design which underpins the classroom activity. In spite of the various criticisms surrounding the use of technology in educational settings, its wider deployment is seen as being pivotal in the changing global world of the future. This is reflected in the following words of Lynton (1989), from the National Center on Education and the Economy – a non-profit-making organisation established in Washington in 1989 to raise standards in education and employment:

> Education is receiving increasing pressure from changing global economic circumstances and complex social needs . . . simply knowing how to use tools and knowledge in a single domain is not sufficient to remain competitive as either individuals or companies. People must learn to apply tools and knowledge in new domains and different situations.

DISCUSSION POINT

Early thinking on the use of ICT in learning, at its most extreme, tended to overlook the role of the teacher. There was talk at the time of connecting all schools via the internet to a central hub of high-quality resources. It was believed, by some, that children would then be able to access these, perhaps with the support of teaching assistants, and thus overcome the need for teachers. Such a view was not new and is based on the assumption that the central purpose of education is the simple transmission of a body of knowledge.

What do you think? Does the Foundation Stage teacher have a role in learning through ICT?

Why use technologies in education?

Behaviourist/ instructional: this approach to learning assumes a step-by-step approach to knowledge accumulation, based on a system of rewards.

By considering the rationale for using ICT in educational settings and a **behaviourist/ instructional** approach to learning, largely abandoned by the 1970s but often resurrected in the form of assessment packages, this section encourages the reader to consider the implications for children's learning in using ICT in educational settings.

Peter Twining (2007), a senior lecturer at the Centre for Curriculum and Teaching Studies (CATS) at the Open University, has written widely on ICT and education and has provided a very useful synthesis which identifies the following rationales most frequently given for the use of ICT in education:

- in order to learn IT skills
- as a tool to achieve traditional teaching and learning goals across the curriculum
- in order to achieve traditional teaching and learning goals across the curriculum
- in order to extend and enrich learning across the curriculum

- in order to motivate learners
- as a catalyst for educational change
- because of the impact of ICT on the nature of knowledge
- as a tool to support learners in thinking about their own learning
- in order to support access to the curriculum for those who might otherwise be excluded from it
- in order to increase productivity in education
- in order to reduce the cost of education
- in order to make education more efficient
- as a substitute for teachers
- in order to reward learners
- as a preparation for living in a society that is permeated with technology
- as a preparation for employment
- in order to support and stimulate the country's economic development
- in order to impress stakeholders (e.g. inspectors, funders, prospective parents/students/pupils)
- in order to reduce inequalities between students/pupils with differential access to ICT outside formal education.

DISCUSSION POINT

Look at the 'rationales' and consider how these fit with your earlier thinking.
Which, for you, are the most important elements? Can you rank them in order?
Do you and your work/study colleagues share the same ranking?

If we look back to initial government thinking on the use of ICT in learning, we see that it was somewhat contradictory. On the one hand ICT is presented as an enabling tool, that is, as a more efficient means of meeting traditional educational ends.

WHAT HAPPENS IN PRACTICE?

(3–5 year olds)

Children are given disposable cameras to record their play activities. The subsequent pictures are then displayed around the setting or sent home to the children's parents to show what they have been doing. Children use simple paint programs to design pictures and make their own name tags using simple word processing. They use software to compose pictures by selecting and moving objects around the screen and can use simple software to listen and respond to stories.

Do you think that the use of technology at this nursery will enhance the children's learning? Why/why not?

Attempts to structure learning through the use of technology were first seen in the use of 'Skinner's' teaching machines. These were the forerunner of computer-assisted programmes for step-by-step teaching of school subjects. Designed in 1954 by Burrhus Frederick Skinner, an American psychologist, the frame presents information and leads the learner, through a branching system, to the next learning step depending on the response given. They could be completed on paper or computer and offered a behaviourist/instructional approach to learning which assumes a step-by-step approach to knowledge accumulation, based on rewards (see Table 6.1). Whilst such training systems had been largely abandoned by the 1970s, attempts to resurrect learning packages based upon behaviourist/instructional approaches to learning, now often linked to assessment and progress-tracking, remain a recurring feature of the technology landscape.

Table 6.1 Behaviourist approaches to learning through ICT: key features

The learner has little or no control and is seen by the software designer as a passive recipient.

With packages of this type the designer assumes that the function of the package is to transfer a complex body of content to the learner in an unchanged manner.

A highly complex body of knowledge is presented in a series of small steps or independent chunks of information.

The programme makes use of constant positive feedback in the form of unrelated, artificial and contrived rewards.

It is assumed that learning is easily transferred from one context to another.

Photo 6.1 Does technology extend children's learning?

Pearson Education Ltd. Jules Selmes © Pearson Education Ltd. 2008

Technology: is this a solution?

By questioning the use of downloadable materials, which can inadvertently change the power-relationship between teacher and the provider, rendering the practitioner/teacher a mere supervisor of ready-made solutions, and how the use of some software types can reduce the learner to a passive responder, this section considers, through the views of other researchers, the effective use of ICT in educational settings.

> ### REFLECT AND RELATE TO PRACTICE
>
> An issue for critical consideration of such pre-packaged technology systems is that of power, particularly where the power lies in the teaching–learning enterprise. We have already seen that the use of downloadable materials changes the power-relationship between practitioner/teacher and authority, providing the possibility for the practitioner/teacher to become a mere supervisor of ready-made solutions. Similarly the use of some software types can reduce the learner to a passive responder.
>
> What is your view? How can technology stimulate learning?

Building upon Twining's rationales for ICT outlined earlier, he developed what he terms the 'Computer Practice Framework' (CPF) (see Table 6.2). The CPF pulls together three earlier models of technology usage in education – Heppell's '4 Stage Model' (1993), Chandler's 'Locus of Control' and Taylor's 'Tutor, Tool, Tutee' (1980) – all of which provide frameworks for teaching and learning using ICT in education. (Details of each of these models are found on our **website**.) Twining's model has three core dimensions: Quantity, Focus and Mode, outlined in Table 6.2.

Twining's model is useful as it places the use of technology in the wider context of classroom environments. The view is of course not new, but echoes the comment made by Allan Ellis (Associate Professor and Director of Research and Research Training in the School of Social Science, Southern Cross University, Australia and with interests in educational technology) more than thirty years ago, that 'thinking about computers in education does not mean thinking about computers, it means thinking about education'.

Practitioners and technology

While practitioners may feel that they have complete autonomy within their early years setting/classroom, they actually work within a carefully regulated system. Constraints may be explicit or implicit. They may be at the national level, through legislation or current government initiatives; they may be at the local level of the individual setting/school and how it operates. Within these overlapping cultures, individual practitioners/teachers bring their own view of the purpose of education and how their setting/classroom should function to achieve this. This section considers both the implicit and explicit constraints which can impact on practice.

Table 6.2 The Computer Practice Framework – its three core dimensions

Quantity: relates both to the amount of available resources in the school and also to the amount of time when they are actually being used.

Focus: the objectives being supported by the technology use. This is subdivided into three further elements:

- IT – that is, using the technology to meet IT-specific goals (rather than as a medium for learning a different subject).
- Other – a catch-all which relates to using the computer as a reward, as a presentation tool, as a means of carrying out administrative and teaching functions.
- Learning tool – which is in turn divided into three further elements relating to:
  - curriculum tool, to support learning in curriculum areas other than specifically in IT;
  - **mathetic tool**, used to enhance learning through active participation and exploration, using Papert's (1993) term to represent the use of technologies to support wider **metacognitive development** (development of knowledge through self-relfection);
  - affective tool, where technology is used to support the **affective** aspects of children's development (i.e. self-esteem and confidence).

Mode: this final dimension (relating specifically to Stage 4 of Heppell's model) relates to the impact which the use of technology has on the curriculum to support, extend and transform the non-IT aspects of the curriculum.

Source: Twining (2007)

Mathetic tool: used to enhance learning through active participation and exploration.

Metacognitive development: development of knowledge through self-reflection.

Affective development: growth in emotional awareness, understanding and control.

The selection and deployment of any technology, whether that technology be video, CD, light and sound sensor boxes, camera or computer, operates within these overlapping and often competing views. However, newly developing technologies have a particular capacity to impact directly on the roles, responsibilities and power-relationships within individual settings/classrooms. Consider the following examples of technology use in early years settings.

WHAT HAPPENS IN PRACTICE?

In the setting

January–February 2007

A practitioner was working with a group of early years children. They were producing a puppet play to be shown to the rest of the school. Unfortunately the play theatre was rather small and couldn't be seen at the back of the hall. A number of the children were also rather intimidated by performing to so many other children.

The teacher discussed the problem with a colleague. They arranged for a number of the older pupils to work with the younger ones. One of the older children had experience of using 'Moviemaker' at home, so together they planned, shot and edited a video version of the play. After adding an audio track the video was ready for showing to the school.

A copy was cut to CD for children and parents who had missed the original showing.

What do you think?

To what extent has ICT been effectively used to extend the children's learning?

WHAT HAPPENS IN PRACTICE?

A private nursery in the west of England has installed a light and sound sensor room. The room utilises pre-programmed patterns to stimulate children's language and imagination. The room is also used to calm children who find self-control difficult. The success of the room has been commented on by practitioners and parents in the setting. Babies and toddlers enjoy and engage with the lights and sounds leading to effective language, colour and sound recognition and calm behaviour.

WHAT HAPPENS IN PRACTICE?

A childminder has installed a computer in her living room/play area. Toddlers have been encouraged to play on the computer using BBC learning programs. These are supported by children's television.

The childminder develops numeracy and literacy through play and stimulates discussion on the use of the computer.

REFLECT AND RELATE TO PRACTICE

In the above two examples, how have the babies and toddlers been helped to develop? What could be added to the learning environments?

☆ ☆ ☆

How could practitioners further develop the children's learning?

Figure 6.1
Technology
activities:
the twin
dimensions

Source: Jedeskog
and Nissen (2004)

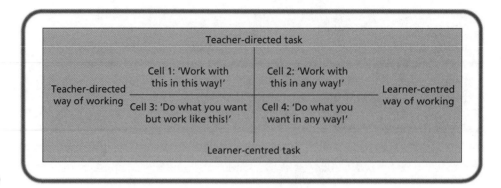

For young children in schools there is a wealth of literature relating to ICT pedagogy. Outside the UK context Jedeskog and Nissen (2004: 37) investigated features of technology practice in Swedish schools, particularly how these impact on the declared national aims of creating a good learning environment and helping children move from passively receiving information to actively seeking it. Their research examined what they suggest are the growing moves in education, from content to form and the dissolution of educational boundaries in terms of room, time and activity (i.e. a form of learning which uses face-to-face teaching and e-learning (often referred to as 'blended learning', thus dispensing with the need for a fixed room, time and activity). Their observations were analysed using a framework (see Figure 6.1) which places technology activities in relation to the twin dimensions of 'task objective' and 'methods of doing the task'.

Jedeskog and Nissen suggest that activities in Cell 1 reflect a 'behaviourist' approach to learning which they rarely observed and therefore did not consider further in their research. Also they found that Cells 2 and 4 could be combined as they seldom saw pupils carrying out tasks totally at their own discretion. The conclusions to the research are clear in the question which forms the title of the paper, 'Is doing more important than knowing?'. They suggest that the shift in many Swedish classrooms to placing greater emphasis on the development of pupil autonomy carries with it an inherent danger, i.e. pupil understanding fails to develop:

> that using ICT-based learning may make it too easy to hand over much responsibility to the pupils themselves where the process of transferring responsibility seems to end up in a situation where 'to do' receives more attention than 'to understand' with the hope that as long as the pupils are occupied in front of the computer there is always the chance that they might manage their own learning process
>
> *(Jedeskog and Nissen, 2004: 44)*

Didactic teaching:
a form of teaching whereby the 'active' practitioner presents information to the 'passive' child.

Such a conclusion may seem like a call to those who wish for a return to **didactic teaching** methods (a form of teaching whereby the 'active' practitioner presents information to the 'passive' child). However, it seems to highlight the need to ensure that practioners/teachers plan carefully to support children's growing autonomy, by placing greater emphasis on both the deployment of cognitive knowledge (understanding) and metacognitive skills (i.e. understanding through self-reflection and understanding the 'how' of learning). Consider the following Case study.

CASE STUDY

The need to raise standards in core subjects, particularly in literacy and numeracy, has been a key driver in the rapid government investment in the deployment of technologies in schools. Becta, the government organisation responsible for developing technology in education, has carried out a series of studies which investigate the possible correlation between schools' use of ICT (measured by the Ofsted grade given for 'ICT learning opportunities') and their pupils' achievement in national tests. The studies were carried out at whole school level and employed tests of statistical significance to consider associations/relationships between variables. Thus, the 2003 report (Becta, 2003) analysed the Ofsted findings of the 2,582 schools inspected in 2000/01 and related their use of ICT to pupil achievement as measured by end of key stage tests. They reported the following continuing trends found in earlier reports:

- high ICT schools outperformed low ICT schools in the same socio-economic group;
- improved standards are more closely linked to effective use of ICT than to the quality of school leadership per se;

- the effective use of ICT in subjects was linked to an increased performance in subject standards;
- the presence of ICT resources alone is less important than the combination of good resources and effective ICT teaching.

The report challenges the simple assertion that schools in less favourable socio-economic circumstances or pupil's prior attainment are bound to achieve less well; a finding which closely matches that of the Primary National Strategy (a government initiative to raise standards in Primary schools) (DfES, 2003b: 21).

Rather than simply providing an analysis of the data, the report authors identify what they consider to be the key factors or 'ICT enablers' which taken together are crucial in the development of good learning opportunities in ICT. These they state as ICT resourcing, ICT leadership and ICT teaching, together with general school leadership and general teaching standards. The report points to a linear relationship between the number of factors in place and the provision of good ICT learning opportunities; the more factors in place the better the provision was found to be (Becta, 2003: 28, 29).

DISCUSSION POINT

With reference to the above Case study consider your own classroom/ school/setting:

- What features support or inhibit your effective use of ICT?
- Do these factors match those found in the report?
- How is the effective use of ICT measured in the report?
- Do you think that other aspects need to be considered?
- Which of the drivers for change are measured here? Which are not?

Photo 6.2
Do practitioners have a role in the deployment of ICT with children?

Connect & Extend

Marc Prensky (2001) in his book *Digital Game-Based Learning* developed the concept of digital natives and digital immigrants. One possible way of using this in an early years setting is to consider one age group (3–5 year olds) as digital immigrants and babies and toddlers as digital natives. Look up his work and consider how this and his other ideas could be developed within an early years setting.

Though the report acknowledges that the effective use of ICT in schools is a 'developing model' (Becta, 2003: 9) as only between 15 percent and 20 percent of schools have all ICT enablers in place, the report presents clear evidence of the positive impact of ICT on pupil attainment. The case is further strengthened by the fact that the evidence base for the report is actually stronger than first appears; 821 schools which were given a short inspection due to their success in the previous inspection-round are missing from the data. It might be thought that such a positive picture should form the conclusion of this chapter. Hence, whilst the research briefing presents a positive view of the use of ICT, it highlights a fundamental problem. We are seemingly left with attempting to measure **constructivist activity** (**qualitative/descriptive**) with **objectivist measures**.

Environments and technologies for learning: bringing it together

Constructivist activity: children construct their own meaning or understanding through personal experience.

Today, in industrialised countries, most people are doing jobs that did not exist when they were born . . . the competitive ability is the ability to learn.

(Papert, 1993)

When asked once if he thought that technology would be the Trojan horse for educational change, Papert replied that it wasn't the horse which was effective, it was the soldiers inside the horse (see the **website** for an explanation of the 'Trojan horse'). If technology is going to be effective, it is going to be the people (practitioners/teachers) inside the technology which will make the change.

REFLECT AND RELATE TO PRACTICE

These are some opinions on the use of ICT – do you agree/disagree? Why/why not?

- Learners are not viewed as passive receivers of knowledge whether that source be human or electronic.
- Learning is complex and multi-dimensional.
- Learning has both affective and cognitive elements.
- Knowledge understanding and skills are most effectively acquired within meaningful contexts.
- Learning takes place in social interactions.
- ICTs should support the development of collaborative self-monitoring, problem-solving skills.
- The effective use of ICTs should form part of a rich multi-sensory environment, should support learner autonomy and scaffold learning.
- Learning is often full of false starts, misdirection and requires persistence.
- The use of ICTs should support reflection and the development of deep problem-solving strategies.
- Technology can provide further stimulation beyond the use of computers through the keyboard.

Qualitative/ descriptive: evaluation based on the quality of the observation; it is not measured objectively, but is subject to the observer's view.

Objectivist measures: based on an acknowledged standard extrinsic to the person measuring, i.e. it does not depend on the person's personal views.

SUMMARY

Changing society; changing educational demands? (p. 123)

Do you think ICT is effectively used in early years settings/schools?

In the run-up to the 1997 election, Tony Blair's 'New Labour' committed themselves to an extensive programme of educational reform; central to this was the use of ICTs. This section questions the extent to which ICT in schools settings has changed children's learning.

The drivers for change (p. 124)

Why was ICT so central to the government's drive for change in schools?

This section considers the need for a rapid change in education in the UK to meet the needs of an increasingly competitive global market place.

ICT in learning settings (p. 125)

How can technology be used to develop and extend children's learning?

Children presented with 'new' technologies are able to access them with the guidance of practitioners. They use them to learn and develop.

Why use technologies in education? (p. 126)

What are the implications for children's learning?

This section considers the implications for practice in the deployment of various technologies in educational settings and how the views of practitioners, both on the rationale for the deployment of ICT resources in schools settings and their use, can impact greatly on classroom practice.

Technology: is this a solution? (p. 129)

How can technology be used to improve children's outcomes?

This section considers, through the views of other researchers, the effective use of ICT in educational settings. It questions the use of downloadable materials, which can inadvertently change the power-relationship between teacher and provider, rendering the practitioner/teacher a mere supervisor of ready-made solutions. Similarly the use of some software types can reduce the learner to a passive responder.

Practitioners and technology (p. 129)

What is role of the practitioner in the effective deployment of ICT in school settings?

While practitioners may feel that they have complete autonomy within their setting/ classrooms, they actually work within a carefully regulated system. This section considers both the implicit and explicit constraints which can impact on practice.

Glossary

Affective development: growth in emotional awareness, understanding and control.

Behaviourist/instructional: this approach to learning assumes a step-by-step approach to knowledge accumulation, based on a system of rewards.

Constructivist activity: children construct their own meaning or understanding through personal experience.

Didactic teaching: a form of teaching whereby the 'active' practitioner presents information to the 'passive' child.

Information Communication Technology (ICT): any technology which is used for the communication of information, from personal computers to DVDs.

Mathetic tool: used to enhance learning through active participation and exploration.

Metacognitive development: development of knowledge through self-reflection.

Objectivist measures: based on an acknowledged standard extrinsic to the person measuring, i.e. it does not depend on the person's personal views.

Qualitative/descriptive: evaluation based on the quality of the observation; it is not measured objectively, but is subject to the observer's view.

Superhighway: a communication system (connected through a fibre-optics network) for the fast transfer of information, e.g. the internet.

Find out more

Poulter, T. and Basford, J. (2003) *Using ICT in Foundation Stage Teaching*, **Exeter: Learning Matters.**
This book has been written for those undertaking both undergraduate and postgraduate initial teacher training courses. Consequently it offers a step-by-step approach to implementing ICT in settings, detailing how to carry out a needs audit, and addresses practical ways of developing ICT across the six learning areas of the EYFS.

Becta (2008) *Next Generation Learning Right Now: Recognising ICT excellence in schools.*
By providing a brief summary of how 27 award winning schools and other organisations have implemented ICT, this document provides some ideas for practice and inspiration for developing ICT within the setting. It is recommended that you look up the school's website, provided with each summary, which in most cases gives details of how they are implementing and deploying ICT

in practice. (Becta is the government agency responsible for developing ICT across educational settings.)

Becta (2008) *Harnessing Technology Review 2008: The role of technology and its impact on education.*
In 2005 the government published *Harnessing Technology* which set out its plans for developing ICT across educational settings. This document examines what has happened in practice since that time and makes recommendations for the further development of ICT in educational settings. It is important to be up to date with what is happening in relation to ICT and to think about how you can improve your own practice. This document will give you a clearer picture of how educational settings across the UK are deploying ICT. It is available, along with a summary (*Harnessing Technology: Next Generation Learning*), at **http://publications.becta.org.uk**.

References

Becta (2003) Primary School – ICT and Standards: an analysis of national test data from Ofsted by Becta. Available online at **http://www.becta.org.uk/research/** [last accessed 06/07].

DfEE (1997) *Connecting the Learning Society: National grid for learning*. The government's consultation paper. Summary, London: DfEE Publications.

DfES (2003a) *Fulfilling the Potential: Transforming Teaching and Learning Through ICT in Schools*. Nottingham: DfES Publications.

DfES (2003b) *Excellence and Enjoyment: A Strategy for Primary Schools*. Nottingham: DfES Publications.

Jedeskog, G. (2007) *ICT in Swedish Schools 1984–2004: how computers work in the teacher's world*. Seminar.net – International journal of media, technology and life long learning Vol. 3, No. 1, 2007.

Jedeskog, G. and Nissen, J. (2004) Is doing more important than knowing?, *Education and Information Technologies*, Vol. 9, No. 1: pp. 37–45.

Lynton, E. (1989) *Higher Education and American Competitiveness*. Washington, DC: National Center on Education and Economy.

Maddison, J. (1983) *Education in the Microelectronics Era*. Milton Keynes: Open University/McGraw-Hill Education.

Mayes, T. (2000) *Pedagogy, Lifelong learning and ICT: A Discussion Paper for the IBM Chair presentation*. Research Centre for Lifelong Learning, Glasgow Caledonian Universities.

Papert, S.A. (1993) *Mindstorms: Children, Computers and Powerful Ideas*. New York: Basic Books.

Prensky, M. (2001) *Digital Game-Based Learning*. New York: McGraw-Hill.

Twining, P. (2007) dictated: Discussing ICT, Aspirations and Targets for Education: a synthesis of the rationales for the use of ICT. Available online at: **http://www.med8.info/dictated/rationales.htm** [last accessed 07/07].

By the end of this chapter you will be able to answer the following questions:

- What does personalised learning mean for the early years of education?
- What is the government's view on personalised learning?
- How do the principles underpinning the *Statutory Framework for the Early Years Foundation Stage: Setting the Standards for Learning Development and Care for children from birth to five* (EYFS) (DfES, 2007) provide a framework for implementing personalised learning programmes within early years settings?
- What factors contribute to effective personalised learning in the early years?

This chapter will support your understanding of the following Standards *(see Appendix 1)*:
■ **Knowledge and understanding:** S03 ■ **Effective practice:** S07, S08, S10, S13, S14 and S22
■ **Relationships with children:** S25, S26, S27 and S28 ■ **Teamwork and collaboration:** S33.

Introduction

WHAT HAPPENS IN PRACTICE?

Toddlers

I use mind mapping as a really effective way of extending toddlers' thinking. For example, we might put a bucket of water in the middle of the floor and mind map that. You are looking for connections that are already made and looking to extend and develop children's thinking.

(Interview with an early years leader of practice in a nursery in Thanet)

Mind mapping: a non-linear diagram, based on a central idea, used to clarify ideas for decision-making or further action.

The publication, in early 2007, of the *Statutory Framework for the Early Years Foundation Stage: Setting the Standards for Learning Development and Care for children from birth to five* (EYFS) (DfES, 2007) provided a framework for early years practitioners and reflected the government's vision of teaching for learning through the development of **personalised learning** programmes, beginning in the earliest years of education. In their document, *2020 Vision: Report of the Teaching and Learning in 2020 Review Group*, published a year earlier, the government clearly stated what this meant for practice:

Personalised learning: the adaptation of teaching and curriculum to meet the learning needs of the individual child.

> put simply personalising learning and teaching means taking a highly
> structured approach to each child's and young person's learning, in order
> that all are able to progress, achieve and participate. It means strengthening
> the link between learning and teaching by engaging *children* – and their
> parents – as partners in learning.

(DfES, 2006: 6)

In essence, personalising learning means developing teaching strategies and practices in response to the individual learning needs of the child. It is characterised by positive child–practitioner relationships and will be most effective when that relationship is good, i.e. the practitioner appropriately supports the child in his/her learning and through the collaborative process which develops thus empowers the child to feel confident in approaching his/her learning experiences. By considering teaching and learning within the new framework for the early years foundation stage and government thinking on education for the twenty-first century, this chapter will address what personalised learning means in practice for educators (practitioners and teachers) and learners (0–7 years). A table of government documents which will be useful for this chapter is available on our **website**.

Expectations

In developing personalised learning programmes to meet individual needs, the government proposes a holistic approach (i.e. where the development of personal, social and emotional skills in particular are developed across the curriculum) to the delivery of six key areas (personal, social and emotional development; communication, language and literacy; problem-solving, reasoning and numeracy; knowledge and understanding of the world; physical development; and creative development) (DfES, 2007: 11). For practitioners this means having high expectations of all children, building on the knowledge, interests and aptitudes of every child, involving children in their own learning, helping children to become confident learners and enabling children to develop the skills they will need beyond school. By outlining the framework for personalised learning envisaged by the government and offering opportunities for discussion and reflection this section challenges the reader to consider the centrality of having high expectations of all children in helping them to develop as confident learners.

The government's delineation of personalised learning as a 'learner-centred . . . knowledge-centred . . . assessment-centred' programme is not a new statement (DfES, 2006: 6). Since the 1960s, classroom practice has been influenced by the **child-centred** theories of Piaget (see Chapter 1), Montessori (see Chapter 15) and Frobel (founder of the kindergarten). These theorists emphasised the need for practitioners to reflect on classroom organisation and approaches to learning and teaching. For practitioners the initial question is how to make education more responsive to the individual learning needs of each child. This is discussed within the chapter, but it is worth reflecting at this stage on what this means in practice:

Child-centred: children undirected by the educator select different activities for themselves from a range of resources on offer.

- Connecting learning to what children already know, including from outside the classroom.
- Enthusing children through teaching and engaging their interest in learning.
- Identifying, exploring and correcting misconceptions.
- Enabling learners to be active and curious.
- Providing work which is sufficiently varied and challenging to maintain their engagement, but not so difficult as to discourage them (DfES, 2006: 6).

REFLECT AND RELATE TO PRACTICE

For each of the points listed above, relating to how practitioners and teachers can make teaching more responsive to the learning needs of the individual child, can you give one example of how you would do this in practice or what approach you would take?

You can choose any age group (babies, toddlers, 3–5 year olds or 5–7 year olds) for each of the points. You will find the EYFS (DfES, 2007) helpful – available at: **www.everychildmatters.gov.uk**, and the Key Stage 1 National Curriculum – available at: **http://curriculum.qca.org.uk**.

In order to develop positive dispositions to learning, children need to believe that they are capable of learning (Dowling, 2000: 12). This places responsibility on early years educators to consider their attitude to each learner, how they encourage achievement and its success, how they correct children's errors and how they discipline children, etc. Robson (2006), a principal lecturer at Roehampton University, who has written widely on early childhood education, suggests that 'the ways in which children see themselves as thinkers and learners is dependent upon their self-image, **self-esteem** and view of themselves as part of their surrounding social world' (2006: 39). The close connection between children's intellectual and emotional development is widely acknowledged. This is supported by the EYFS (DfES, 2007) which acknowledges personal, social and emotional development alongside the development of skills and knowledge.

Self-esteem: the extent to which a person values him/herself.

DISCUSSION POINT

To what extent do you think that children's personal, social and emotional development impacts on their ability to achieve?

How would you ensure your teaching was addressing personal, social and emotional development as a cross-curricular element?

Consider babies, toddlers, 3–5 year olds and 5–7 year olds. You will need to look up the relevant learning area within the EYFS (DfES, 2007) and the Key Stage 1 National Curriculum. The first step is to define personal, social and emotional development, i.e. in terms of what skills, attitudes and understandings the children need to develop, and the second step is to consider how you will help them to do this.

You can review this at the end of the chapter.

Developing knowledge, understanding and skills

The knowledge, understanding and skills needed in order to develop good learning relationships are fundamental to effective teaching. Moreover, learning behaviours are integrated components of the classroom rather than fragmented attributes of the child (Cornwall and Tod, 1998). Practitioners need to encourage learners and provide responsive instruction. This section will consider how the social dimensions of the setting (practitioner–child interaction and child–child interaction), practitioner knowledge, understanding and skills and other related factors, particularly the manner in which learning goals are communicated, all impact on children's learning and achievement.

The social context of the classroom has long been researched and the importance of wider influences on learners' behaviour should not be ignored (e.g. a child's interaction with his/her peers, the extent to which practitioners communicate meaningfully with the child). Case study research suggests that the quality of the relationship between the educator and learner is very significant (Cline, 1992). Stoll et al. (2003: 137) advocate 'positive relationships as a secure basis for learning'. Earlier research (Serow and Solomon, 1979; Prawat and Nickerson, 1985) suggests that children are more likely to develop positive attitudes and behaviours when they experience positive relationships with their educators. In addition, children's emotional development is influenced by the example of positive role models (e.g. do you show respect to all children, do you value their work and show them that you do, do you get on well with other members of staff, etc.?). MacNaughton (2003: 33) highlights the underlying principle of 'social roles and behaviour being caught not taught'. Within the early years setting, the positive role model of the practitioner can help children to become effective learners.

Practitioners' self-perception of their skills and confidence is an important consideration for the management of relationships in the educational setting. Practitioners who feel confident and competent have a more positive approach to teaching and learning. They tend to be self-motivated decision-makers who do not give up when faced with new challenges. This in itself provides an example to the children. In addition, it is particularly relevant in light of the government's call for personalised learning and teaching against the backdrop of a workforce relatively inexperienced in the competencies of personalising learning. Although personalised learning is to be embedded in all initial teacher training programmes in England, educational settings are presently developing continuing professional development courses to build staff competency in the necessary requirements. The government document *2020 Vision: Report of the Teaching and Learning in 2020 Review Group* (DfES, 2006: 31) outlines these as:

Assessment for learning: practitioners use the information from setting/ classroom observation to involve the children in deciding their learning objectives and how best they can meet them.

- analysing and using data, with a specific focus on **assessment for learning**
- understanding how children learn and develop
- working with other adults (including parents and other children's services professionals)
- engaging children as active participants in learning.

DISCUSSION POINT

Consider the above staff competencies outlined by the government as basic requirements for the personalisation of learning. How will a children's workforce which lacks experience in these areas negatively impact on teaching and learning in the classroom and other settings?

You should consider this in the context of the management of relationships in the classroom. You will also need to look up these competencies in the above mentioned government document and consider what more the government has to say on this topic – available at: **http://www.teachernet.gov.uk/_doc/10783/ 6856_DfES_Teaching_and_Learning.pdf**.

Active learning of this kind is to be encouraged if learners are to be motivated and take responsibility for their own achievements. Learners need to be self-motivated and collaborate with others to construct their knowledge. The recent study of Sylva et al. (2007) which addressed curricular quality and day-to-day learning activities in pre-school, drawing on data from the Effective Provision of Pre-school Education and the Researching Effective Pedagogy in the Early Years studies, suggested that high quality (see Chapter 2) early years settings more frequently employed child initiated activities

> This enabled children to spend more time in cognitively enriching activities such as creative play, language or science activities. In addition, they were more engaged with their peers and spent more time in one-to-one interactions with their teachers.
>
> *(Sylva et al., 2007: 63)*

Moll and Whitmore (1998) describe the educator's role as guide and supporter, active participant in learning, evaluator and facilitator.

All of these activities are part of the relationship between practitioner and learner but there are many less definable or measurable facets to the relationship, such as the ability to encourage the learner or providing responsive instruction. Castelikns (1996) states responsive instruction is typified by educators showing that they:

- are available for support and instruction
- are willing to take the learner's perspective on work problems
- are willing to support the learner's competencies
- will challenge the child to be active and responsible in choosing, planning, executing and evaluating the activity and its outcomes.

Involving learners in the planning of their study or learning objectives is not a new strategy and was reaffirmed in the revised Code of Practice (DfES, 2001) for children with SEN. The benefits to learners range from ownership of targets to more accurate judgements, and hence assessment, of their own performance (Munby, 1994). For very young children, learning objectives need to be communicated in a less formal manner. Young children need to have some concept of why they are carrying out an activity or what they might achieve by doing so; otherwise learning is happening in a vacuum for them. However, they will have no conception of learning objectives, if they are formally stated at the beginning of an activity by the educator. Careful consideration needs to be given to why children are carrying out an exercise and how you will communicate the aims of that exercise. One possible way might include the use of a flip chart to communicate the objectives through a pictorial representation. To achieve this kind of learner involvement presupposes an encouraging relationship between educator and learner. The following, taken from an interview with the head of a **pre-prep** school, shows how learning goals can be communicated (meaningfully) to young children (3–5 year olds).

Pre-prep: (short for pre-preparatory school) an independent school for children aged 3–8 years.

WHAT HAPPENS IN PRACTICE?

When you are initiating a new area of activity it will be more adult directed. Adults will be saying such things as could we try this or that? Or could we use that there? So the adults will be engaging with the children at the start (of the activity) to give it a focus and to get the children on board. [In essence] to let them know that we need to engage in this activity because it is worthwhile. You must communicate learning goals so that they can get something out of it. I don't propose sitting and reading the learning objectives aloud, but it [the activity] needs to be carefully planned and structured so that they [the children] get something out of it. Children might be more directed in the use of for example [specific] equipment. Children could use equipment incorrectly and then that would detract in some way from the activity [from the learning value of the activity].

REFLECT AND RELATE TO PRACTICE

What general strategies have been employed to help these children learn?

Consider the learning strategies employed to help these children learn. To what extent is their learning personalised?

To what extent do you think that children need to know the learning objectives to be successful in an activity?

List the ways you could initiate an activity with children between 3 and 5 years old to help them to engage in learning.

Relationships with peers are also considered to be important factors in learning. Research indicates that adult-directed, large group activities in early years settings offer little opportunity for child-initiated activities and peer interaction (Sylva et al., 2007). Vygostsky (1962) (see Chapter 1) emphasised the pivotal contribution of social interaction to **cognitive development** and the view that cognitive development is a process of continuous interplay between the individual and the environment. It follows that classroom groupings for teaching and peer relationships could have a significant impact on learning. The lack of appropriate social and interpersonal skills and competencies can result from any home background so it is important that a holistic approach to teaching enhances positive learning behaviours by encouraging:

Cognitive development: growth in understanding.

- high feelings of self-worth
- a robust sense of self
- self-reliance
- autonomy

- a positive view of the world
- a sense of personal power.

These are significant in relation to babies, toddlers and young children; personalised learning applies to children of all ages.

DISCUSSION POINT

Consider Vygotsky's view that cognitive development is a process of continuous interplay between the individual and the environment. Consider ways you could help the children in an early years setting (consider 0–2 year olds and 6 year olds) to develop each of the characteristics mentioned in the above list.

Creating enabling environments

The child-centred focus promoted through the development of personalised learning programmes requires practitioners to reflect on classroom organisation and approaches to learning and teaching. By considering the views of established researchers/practitioners, this section asks the reader to reflect on factors which contribute to the creation of an enabling learning environment in practice.

Personalised learning embraces every aspect of early learning, including Information Communications Technology (ICT), curriculum choice, organisation and timetabling, assessment arrangements and relationships with the local community. The child-centred focus promoted through the development of personalised learning programmes requires educators to reflect on the organisation of the learning environment and approaches to learning and teaching. This is to be hailed as a means of raising standards and promoting improved outcomes for all children. Solity (1992) provides a useful summary of what this means in school practice which is applicable to other settings:

> The classroom is then geared to stimulate children, to encourage interest and of their learning to be based on their experiences. The teacher is a facilitator, promoting learning and acting as the child's guide in the learning process.
>
> *(Solity, 1992: p. 9)*

For the practitioner this means having an organised and systematic approach to individual learning needs. Rita Cheminais (2004), a School Improvement Adviser for Inclusive Education, provides a framework for practice within the context of an inclusive teaching and learning environment; the following has been adapted from her framework for an early years setting and primary school:

1 A welcoming, friendly and supportive climate is of prime importance; where children and staff feel secure, are able to share feelings and ask questions; where misunderstandings are dealt with sensitively, and used as positive teaching points and where put-downs are not permitted.

Photo 7.1
How do you help children to develop confidence in their ability as learners?

Pearson Education Ltd. Jules Selmes © Pearson Education Ltd. 2004

Multi-sensory teaching: means using separately or at the same time a visual (seeing), auditory (hearing) or kinesthetic-tactile (feeling) approach to help children's learning.

VAK learning strategies: *Visual* (what is learnt through seeing); *Auditory* (what is learnt through hearing); *Kinaesthetic* (what is learnt through touch/feeling).

2 Practitioners who have high expectations and make this clear to children, and incorporate the learning cycle structure (plan, assess, plan – informed by assessment, etc.). This entails establishing a positive mindset and readiness for learning; connecting children's previous learning to new learning; giving children the big picture, sharing the lesson objectives and expected outcomes with children where appropriate; breaking learning down into achievable steps, as well as providing extension activities, utilising **multi-sensory teaching** and learning approaches; ensuring children are active participants throughout the learning experience; providing opportunities for children to demonstrate their knowledge and understanding (e.g. through questioning or presenting their work to the group – with support), and to review and reflect upon their learning at the end of the learning activity, in order to ensure new knowledge is not lost.

3 Providing opportunities for children to talk about their learning, e.g. describing the different ways they talked through a problem; asking open questions to prompt alternative solutions and approaches; and ensuring that children work in a variety of ways – in pairs and small groups, as a whole group or independently – during the learning activity.

4 Practitioners commenting on children's work, indicating clearly what each child needs to do in order to improve, or make their next piece of work of 'premier league' quality.

5 Practitioners being empowered to utilise their strengths; being clear about their role in relation to the effectiveness of their Visual (what is learnt through seeing), Auditory (what is learnt through hearing), Kinaesthetic (what is learnt through touch/feeling) (**VAK**) support strategies, in consolidating and extending children's' learning.

REFLECT AND RELATE TO PRACTICE

Summarise the strategies suggested by Cheminais (2004) to meet a child's individual learning needs.

☆ ☆ ☆

Consider each point suggested by Cheminais – how it is implemented, if it will work in practice, if there is a different/better approach and how Cheminais's suggestions can be enhanced in practice.

Developing thinking skills and problem-solving

Having a feeling of independence and autonomy enhances a child's desire and ability to be self-motivated. One way to enable children to develop a sense of independence is to help them to think for themselves and enable them to work through problems. By examining a number of ways that practitioners can help children to develop thinking skills, particularly through philosophy which is beginning to gain popularity amongst practitioners and teachers of younger children and through a case study which examines practitioners' perceptions of children's thinking, this section challenges the reader to consider innovative and effective ways of helping children to develop thinking skills in the setting.

Enabling children to become independent learners for life is one of the greatest gifts an educator can give a child. Having a feeling of independence and autonomy enhances a child's desire and ability to be self-motivated. Enabling children to develop a sense of independence and helping them to think for themselves and work through problems needs to start at the earliest opportunity to enable children to become familiar with this type of thinking and reflection. In an early years setting, it will start in a simple way, for example asking a child their opinion on a particular situation, activity or issue and getting them to think how it could have been done differently or perhaps improved upon. Consider 'What happens in practice?' on p. 148, developed from an interview with a practice leader in a Thanet nursery. It provides an example of how practitioners can find out what children already know, how they think, etc., and how practitioners can use this information to help the children develop.

The government document, *2020 Vision: Report of the Teaching and Learning in 2020 Review Group*, in the context of personalised teaching and learning clearly states that:

> Learners are active and curious: they create their own hypotheses, ask their own questions, coach one another, set goals for themselves, monitor their progress and experiment with ideas for taking risks, knowing that mistakes and 'being stuck' are part of learning.

(DfES, 2006: 6)

WHAT HAPPENS IN PRACTICE?

3–4 year olds

I have mind-mapped with this age group before going to the beach. You cannot make assumptions about what they already know and it is a good opportunity to discover their thinking and the connections that are already made. Mind-mapping after the visit enables you to see those new connections – it could be about the smells of the seaside or what they saw or heard. They could have misconceptions that you can explore. It is a really good way for a practitioner to see the patterns in children's thoughts.

DISCUSSION POINT

Would you use mind-mapping as a tool to help you know how well a child is thinking and making connections? Why/why not?

Robson and Hargreaves (2005), however, highlight the difficulty in defining thinking or the development of thinking skills within an educational context. They offer the following definition:

> Thinking clearly involves much more than the acquisition of knowledge. Critical judgement, creativity, decision-making, and the ability to act independently and to reflect on one's own thinking (metacognition) are all involved.

(2005: 82)

More recently Philosophy 4 Children (P4C) has developed as a valuable and effective way of promoting and supporting children's thinking (Whitebread, 2003; Robson, 2006). Philosophy as a medium for enhancing thinking skills in children was developed in America in response to the lack of thinking skills amongst university students. Initiated by Lipman (1991), P4C aims to 'encourage children to think critically, caringly, creatively and collaboratively' (P4C, 2007). Teaching for thinking through philosophy enables practitioners to 'build a community of enquiry, where participants create and enquire into their own questions and learn how to learn in the process' (P4C, 2007). Robson (2006) draws attention to the current debate relating to the teaching of philosophy to young children. Whilst children's questioning is to be valued, White (2002) notes that not all questions are philosophical. Others argue against philosophy for young children on the grounds that they do not have the cognitive ability to differentiate between **philosophical questions** and those which are not. A greater insight into what constitutes a philosophical question and teaching

Philosophical questions: those which do not have a close-response answer and tend to relate to deeper, life issues (e.g. what makes people happy?).

'thinking skills' through the medium of philosophy can be found at the P4C website: **http://www.thinkingeducation.co.uk/p4c.htm**. However, the following Activity, adapted from a philosophy programme developed by the Department of Education, Tasmania, shows how a story can be used with young children to develop their ability to think more deeply about some of the more important issues in life:

ACTIVITY

Background

In this early years setting (it can be employed with 5–7 year olds) the practitioner has used *The Bunyip of Berkeley Creek* by Jenny Wagner (Puffin) to consider philosophical questions on existence and identity with the children. In the story the bunyip is worried about who he is. When he meets a scientist who tells him that bunyips don't exist, he begins to worry about whether or not he actually exists!

Process

Before reading the story explain to the children that you will be looking beyond the text for big ideas or unanswerable questions – questions that have puzzled thinkers since the beginning of time. Explain that this is thinking philosophically: thinking about things that do not have one answer and which give greater depth of understanding about the world we live in.

Tell children that during the discussion, they should focus on:

- listening to the opinions of others
- giving reasons for their thoughts
- taking turns to speak
- agreeing or disagreeing with the *ideas* expressed and not the person.

Encourage the children to think of questions that come to their minds for sharing at the end of the reading.

Read the story aloud to the children.

At the end of the story, ask for questions and put these questions on the board. Always include the name of the questioner for this gives ownership. Include all questions – it is sometimes surprising to see how some of the most basic-looking questions can be quite meaningful. Find any questions that may have a common thread and link them on the board.

Begin discussion on the most popular question first. Often not all questions will be answered, though most are often addressed incidentally. Questions can also be addressed during the next lesson, but it is often better to explore another text on a similar theme.

▶

If questions are slow to come or discussion doesn't fire, the following is a guaranteed discussion starter:

If something exists it . . .

Children usually begin with 'some thing that exists . . . moves, eats, talks, has a heart, can be seen . . .' and the conclusion is that people, animals, rocks, the sky, the world, the Universe all exist because they meet one of the criteria. Usually, the children will raise the issue of Santa Claus or ghosts or bunyips. Do they exist? Now there develops a broadening of thinking and often the conclusion will be: 'if you believe in something, it exists'. When this happens, thinking has gone from the concrete to the abstract.

Types of questions children ask

- How come the bunyip didn't look at himself in the mirror to see what he looked like?
- Why did the bunyip want to know what the others saw?
- Why does the man talk to something that doesn't exist?
- Did the bunyip look horrible?
- Who am I?
- How come the animals talk?

Other questions the practitioner can ask
(In the unlikely event the children don't have any!)

- Do we need to know what we are to know who we are? (The bunyip was asking, 'what am I?')
- Does what we look like affect who we are?
- Does what we look like affect our behaviour?
- What is it that makes something handsome?
- Do we depend on the opinions of others to know who we are?
- Do we have friends who are like us?
- Do we have friends who are not like us?
- Do we celebrate differences?
- Do we try to be like others or do we try to be different from others?
- How different can we be from each other?

Now there is potential to discuss racism, multiculturalism, stereotyping, behaviour, bullying – almost anything – depending on which way you lead it. You should, however, keep your opinion out of the discussion.

Follow-up activity

Children write down their name and age and list their favourite things: toys, books, television programmes, activities, friends, thoughts.

Ask children to identify which things tell most about them and who they are.

(Adapted from *Books into Ideas*, Tim Sprod, Hawker Brownlow (1993), page 85.)

Other texts on theme of existence

There's a Sea in my Bedroom, by Margaret Wild.

The Dream Dragon, by Y. Winer.

Stickybeak, by Maurice Gleitzman.

(http://wwwfp.education.tas.gov.au/english/philo1.htm)

DISCUSSION POINT

Would you use this activity as a means of helping children to develop their thinking skills? Why/why not? What aspects are good? What aspects do you consider not to be so good in practice?

The development of thinking skills in the early years encompasses a relatively broad area and in a more detailed analysis has been given further consideration through the research briefing in the following Case study. Although it forms part of a larger study, funded by the Froebel Research Fellowship; which investigates 'Ownership and Autonomy in Early Learning', the Case study has been adapted from a report of a related pilot study which addressed practitioner perceptions and practices in relation to the development of thinking in children aged 3–5 years (Robson and Hargreaves, 2005). The Case study summarises the views of five early years practitioners working in a state nursery or reception class in England, where data was collected by interview and addressed the following research questions:

- What are practitioners' working definitions of 'thinking'?
- What are practitioners' perceptions about their roles in supporting and extending children's thinking?
- Do practitioners believe that the Curriculum Guidance for the Foundation Stage has had an impact on their practice in relation to supporting and extending children's thinking?

CASE STUDY

The results highlighted the difficulty in defining thinking skills. Although the majority gave the most common definition of thinking as problem-solving, a number offered alternative definitions. All of the practitioners interviewed, however, agreed that it was important to help children to develop their thinking skills. The majority of practitioners saw this within the context of problem-solving and its relevance as a life skill. The strongest reason for developing children's thinking skills was offered by one early years educator who said: 'It's the way they are going to learn. It's like the way I learn. I do something and think about it.' Another highlighted the importance for children of being able to 'relate it to things they already know.'

Although there is a view amongst educators that thinking skills underpin all learning, the practitioners interviewed for the study held differing views as to where it occurred in the curriculum. One practitioner supported the view that it would 'come through every curriculum area', while others were divided between communication, language and literacy and knowledge and understanding of the world. A number of practitioners valued 'outdoor activities for supporting children's thinking' in that it gave the children 'time, space' and 'the opportunity just to "be"'.

The practitioners interviewed were asked to consider other activities which helped children to develop thinking skills. Interestingly, they did not support Robson and Hargreave's (2005) view that **pretend play** was an important activity for developing thinking skills. A number, however, saw the value of role play in enabling children to think.

Pretend play: make-believe activities developed by children.

When asked to respond to the widely held view and supported by the more recent work of Siraj-Blatchford et al. that 'freely chosen play activities often provide the best opportunities to extend children's thinking' (2002: 12), the majority of practitioners agreed with the statement. One practitioner said in relation to adult-led or child-initiated activity: 'If the child feels they have made the choice, then the outcome is always going to be better. Self-selected activities are much more inspiring for the children.'

In relation to size of group, some proposed pair work, while other practitioners proposed small groups of three or four children. This supports research which highlights the benefits of small group work for promoting children's thinking. The practitioners were generally divided over the extent to which adults should interact with the children in helping them to develop their thinking skills. One practitioner was concerned 'about the potential danger of adults leading the conversation too much in a very small group, or one-to-one with a child, since a child's own ideas may be restricted'. Another practitioner was of the opinion that it was the 'quality of interaction between adult and child'. Their differing views support the general debate concerning the extent to which activities should be adult-led or child-initiated. However, the recent study of Sylva et al. (2007: 63) which addressed curricular quality and day-to-day learning activities in pre-school, drawing on data from the Effective Provision of Pre-school Education and the Researching Effective Pedagogy in the Early Years studies, suggested that high quality early years settings more frequently employed child-initiated activities:

'This enabled children to spend more time in cognitively enriching activities such as creative play, language or science activities.' In addition, 'they were more engaged with their peers' and spent more time in 'one-to-one interactions with their teachers'.

In the present study of Robson and Hargreaves (2005) one practitioner highlighted the difficulties for practitioners in knowing when to intervene: 'finding the right point to become involved and the right way to extend someone's thinking . . . it's about extending rather than redirecting . . . and the moment you have that as the aim . . . you are always extending children's thinking.' In relation to allowing children time for thinking, the results tended to be unanimous – children needed to be given time to develop their thinking.

In practice, many of those interviewed employed similar teaching stategies to help children to develop their thinking skills. Many modelled speculative talk for example, 'imagine if' or 'I wonder what will happen?'. One practitioner said that when children were asked to discuss something in pairs she would ask them questions like, 'What did you think? Or what did you talk about? Or what did you think might happen?'

However, overall practitioners commented on time as an issue in helping children develop thinking skills. Educators in nursery settings had more time to facilitate children's thinking skills than those teaching in reception classes, where the demands of the early years foundation stage curriculum put constraints on the amount of time available to spend on teaching thinking skills.

(Based on Robson and Hargreaves, 2005)

REFLECT AND RELATE TO PRACTICE

Identify practitioners' perceptions about their roles in supporting and extending children's thinking.

☆ ☆ ☆
Do you agree with the strategies they have employed to help children develop their thinking skills?

Make a list of all the strategies you would use in an early years setting to develop children's thinking (consider 3–5 year olds and 5–7 year olds). You will need to look up the relevant learning area in the EYFS (DfES, 2007) and the Key Stage 1 National Curriculum.

Problem-solving and reasoning

Enabling children to develop confidence in their ability as learners depends on having meaningful, interactive relationships with practitioners. Problem-solving covers a broad area from thinking about how to develop a play activity or what activity to play to working out how to solve a mathematical problem. This section will address the role of practitioners in helping children to develop their reasoning skills and ability to solve problems.

Robson (2006: 177) suggests that problem-solving is a 'goal-directed activity', which is at the foundation of 'human intellectual functioning' (Whitebread, 2003: 15). MacNaughton and Williams suggest that for the educator, 'problem-solving involves helping children learn how to find answers to puzzles, questions, dilemmas, issues, predicaments and quandaries they face in their daily world' (2004: 306). This will range from a simple problem to a complex issue. In the context of independent learning, the practitioner's role is that of enabler. The question being, how can I help this child to be one step closer to the process of finding a solution to this problem him/herself?

Research underlines the centrality of play in developing children's ability to problem-solve (MacNaughton, 2003; Whitebread, 2003; Robson and Hargreaves, 2005; Robson 2006; Sylva et al., 2007). Whitebread suggests that play offers a valuable means of enabling children to 'make sense of their world in a way that is unique and individual to them, of which they are in control' (2003: 17). He further emphasises the bene-fits of play as a tool for enabling children to problem-solve, investigate or engage in 'various forms of self-expression'. For many children, he notes, play helps them to 'place new information in meaningful contexts'. In practice, making time for problem-solving activities should be written into planning. Whitebread (2003: 17) advocates

Photo 7.2
How do practitioners help children to become competent problem-solvers?

Pearson Education Ltd Garetti Boden © Pearson Education Ltd 2006 an integrated approach, where tasks are organised to 'stimulate mental activity and educators employ problem-solving and investigational approaches wherever possible' (e.g. ask the children appropriate questions, etc.). This can be done mainly through **scaffolding** the children's learning (i.e. by supporting them primarily through asking them appropriate questions they can advance further in the learning activity than would have been the case if they had worked without your appropriate interventions).

This is supported by MacNaughton and Williams (2004: 307) who advocate the following as a means of addressing problem-solving in the early years setting:

- facilitate a problem-solving climate
- create time to problem-solve
- create space to problem-solve
- use materials to encourage problem-solving
- show familiarity with how to problem-solve
- choose appropriate problems to solve.

Scaffolding learning: the educator supports the learner, to help them to build on their previous knowledge and learn new information.

Creativity

Ofsted defines **creativity** according to the National Advisory Committee on Creativity, Culture and Education (NACCE) report as: 'Imaginative activity fashioned so as to produce outcomes that are both original and of value' (HMI, 2003: 4). The emphasis is on teaching for creativity – i.e. enabling children to be creative as opposed to creative teaching. For early years practitioners this means knowing when and how to make provision for this type of creativity. By considering what it means in practice and looking at some of the ways it can be developed in practice, this section provides opportunity for the reader to further reflect on ways to help children to become more creative.

In a global market, where intellectual property (creative ideas) is a significant and growing part of the economy, it is important for educators to encourage creativity from a young age. In essence it means helping children to have ideas about how to develop or carry out something new.

Creativity: teaching which focuses on outcomes, to enable children to think and/or act imaginatively, to generate a new idea.

The EYFS delineates creative development within the following context:

Children's creativity must be extended by the provision of support for their curiosity, exploration and play. They must be provided with opportunities to explore and share their thoughts, ideas and feelings, for example through a variety of art, music, movement, dance, imaginative and role play activities, mathematics and design and technology.

(DfES, 2007: 15)

Although teaching for creative development within this context covers a relatively broad area of arts based subjects, educators should consider a child's natural aptitude for a specific subject within this field; not every child will be a gifted musician.

Creativity, in an educational setting, is developed when children are 'actively involved in their own learning' (Prentice et al., 2003: 189). Being in *control* or feeling empowered, as discussed by Whitebread (2003: 6), is a prerequisite for creativity. In relation to enhancing creativity, Prentice et al. (2003: 189–190) advocate guiding, supporting and encouraging children, as they 'explore the potential of ideas'. They further suggest that allowing time for this 'exploratory stage, enables children to develop confidence in their own abilities to direct the course of their activities and further refine and share their ideas with adults and their peers'. However, they underline the importance of enabling children to develop a firm knowledge and skills base.

Scaffolding learning can provide a valuable tool for enabling children to develop creative thinking. Employing this technique, the educator supports the learner to help him/her build on previous knowledge and learn new information, in order to achieve the intended outcome of the activity (based on the Vygotskian concept of the **zone of proximal development**. The general techniques associated with scaffolding – 'questioning, prompting, praising, confirming, pointing things out to children and modeling' (MacNaughton and Williams, 2004: 333) – can all be used effectively by educators to develop children's creativity. Through experience and training educators will know when and which technique to employ when working on a one-to-one basis with a child or during small group work with children.

Robson (2006: 172) suggests that creativity depends upon the development of certain 'emotional qualities' in the learner, namely 'self-esteem and **mastery**'. She further suggests that the type of thinking required for the development of creativity – '**hypothesising** and imagination' – demands a certain level of confidence on the learner's part and a 'willingness to take risks'.

Zone of proximal development: the gap between what the child can achieve without help and what the child can achieve with appropriate support.

Mastery oriented: children who remain confident in attitude and approach to a difficult task. They believe in their own ability as learners and want to succeed.

Hypothesising: a theory/provisional explanation of something which can be proved/disproved by fact.

REFLECT AND RELATE TO PRACTICE

Creative development is a key area within the EYFS curriculum. Look up the educational programme and early learning goals (Creative development) in the *Statutory Framework for the Early Years Foundation Stage: Setting the Standards for Learning Development and Care for children from birth to five* (EYFS) (DfES, 2007). How could you help children (3–5 year olds) to develop in this area of learning (consider general strategies)?

Bringing it together: observation

Observing children is key to effective practice in settings and can be both planned and unplanned. Effective implementation of personalised learning programmes in early years settings and schools depends on practitioners knowing their learners. This is achieved informally through the daily adult–child interaction within the setting, which can provide a useful insight into a child's level of ability. Observation is more formal when practitioners take a highly structured approach to children's learning by carrying out planned observations of individuals or groups of children. Observation, however, is only useful when practitioners know what they are looking for (Broadhead, 2004: 57). This needs to be carefully considered. What do you want to know about the child? Why do you want to know this? How will it affect the way you plan for the child's learning and development? (see Chapter 16).

Observation enables the practitioner to develop repertoires to develop and address the learning needs of babies, toddlers and young children. In order to give each child the best possible chance of developing as a competent and confident life-long learner, ongoing observational assessment is vital for early years practitioners. This type of approach enables educators to make work varied, challenging and engaging, which enthuses, encourages and motivates learners (an observation schedule is available on our **website**).

SUMMARY

Expectations (p. 140)

Why is it important to have 'high expectations' for children's learning?

To deliver the curriculum in a setting or school practitioners/teachers need to have high expectations of all children, build on the knowledge, interests and aptitudes of every child, involve children in their own learning, help children to become confident learners and enable children to develop the skills they will need for school and beyond.

Developing knowledge, understanding and skills (p. 141)

How does the practitioner impact on a child's development of knowledge, understanding and skills?

Practitioners need to encourage learners and provide responsive instruction.

Creating enabling environments (p. 145)

What factors contribute to the creation of an enabling environment?

The child-centred focus promoted through the development of personalised learning programmes requires practitioners to reflect on classroom organisation and approaches to learning and teaching.

Developing thinking skills and problem-solving (p. 147)

What is the role of the educator in helping children to develop thinking skills and problem-solving?

Having a feeling of independence and autonomy enhances a child's desire and ability to be self-motivated. One way to enable children to develop a sense of independence is to help them to think for themselves and enable them to work through problems.

Problem-solving and reasoning (p. 153)

How would you help a child in an early years setting to develop his/her reasoning skills and ability to solve problems?

Research underlines the centrality of play in developing children's ability to problem-solve. Play gives the children the freedom to be creative and think through problems as they arise.

Creativity (p. 155)

What factors need to be considered to help children become creative thinkers?

Practitioners need to help children develop a creative way of thinking where the emphasis is on teaching for creativity, i.e. enabling children to be creative as opposed to creative teaching.

Bringing it together: observation (p. 157)

What is the role of observation in developing children's learning styles?

Effective implementation of personalised learning programmes in early years settings depends on practitioners knowing their learners. This is achieved informally through the daily adult–child interaction within the setting, which can provide as useful an insight into a child's level of ability as a planned observation.

Glossary

Assessment for learning: practitioners use the information from setting/classroom observation to involve the children in deciding their learning objectives and how best they can meet them.

Child-centred: children are not directed by the educator; instead they select different activities for themselves from a range of resources on offer.

Cognitive development: growth in understanding.

Creativity: teaching which focuses on outcomes, to enable children to think and/or act imaginatively, to generate a new idea.

Hypothesising: a theory/provisional explanation of something which can be proved/disproved by fact.

Mastery oriented: children both believe in their own ability as learners and want to achieve success in learning.

Mind mapping: a non-linear diagram, based on a central idea, used to clarify ideas for decision-making or further action.

Multi-sensory teaching: means using separately or at the same time a visual (seeing), auditory (hearing) or kinesthetic-tactile (feeling) approach to help children's learning.

Personalised learning: the adaptation of teaching and curriculum to meet the learning needs of the individual child. It is based on the collaborative approach of the practitioner, child and his/her parents/carers where practitioners are continuously collecting and evaluating evidence of learning, with a view, through discussion with the child, of engaging him/her in his/her learning to achieve the best possible outcomes for the child both emotionally and academically.

Philosophical questions: those which do not have a close-response answer and tend to relate to deeper, life issues (e.g. what makes people happy?).

Pre-prep: (short for pre-preparatory school) an independent school for children aged 3–8 years.

Pretend play: make-believe activities developed by children.

Scaffolding learning: the educator supports the learner, to help them to build on their previous knowledge and learn new information, in order to achieve the intended outcome of the activity (based on the Vygotskian concept of the zone of proximal development).

Self-esteem: the extent to which a person values him/herself.

VAK learning strategies: *Visual* (what is learnt through seeing); *Auditory* (what is learnt through hearing); *Kinaesthetic* (what is learnt through touch/feeling).

Zone of proximal development: this is the gap between what the child can achieve without help and what the child can achieve with appropriate support. In essence, with appropriate, relevant and effective interactions with more able others, children are provided with greater opportunity to reach their potential; i.e. practitioners and teachers who recognise the learning needs of children and know how to respond to those needs.

Find out more

West-Burnham, J. and Coates, M. (2005) *Personalising Learning: Transforming education for every child*, **London: Continuum.**
Chapter 11, Creating a learning-centred school, considers through a case study in a primary school the different aspects of the school, learning and teaching etc. which need to be addressed to develop an educational setting where the focus is on personalised learning. For each area it provides an outline of what it is in theory, considers the policies which will need to be developed in the school/setting and considers how it is developed in practice. This chapter provides a good insight into personalised learning in practice.

Philosophy for Children:
http://www.thinkingeducation.co.uk/p4c.htm
This website provides a good background to philosophy in practice. Reflect on the following: should philosophy be addressed in the early years of education?

Learning and Teaching Scotland, a leading curriculum development organisation for Scotland, provides good advice – theoretical and practical – on creativity in education. It is available at: **www.ltscotland.org.uk/ creativity/aboutcreativity/index.asp.**

Duffy, B. (2006) *Supporting Creativity and Imagination in the Early Years*, **Maidenhead: Open University.**
This book provides both a theoretical insight into and ideas for creativity in practice: music, drama, pretend play, etc.

References

Broadhead, P. (2004) *Early Years Play and Learning: Developing Social Skills and Cooperation*. Abingdon: RoutledgeFalmer.

Castelikns, J. (1996) Responsive instruction for young children: a study of how teachers can help easily distracted children become more attentive, *Emotional and Behavioural Difficulties*, Vol. 1, No. 1, Spring, pp. 22–33.

Cheminais, R. (2004) Inclusive schools and classrooms, SENCO Update, May, pp. 6–7, London: Optimus.

Cline, T. (1992) Assessment of special educational needs: meeting reasonable expectation?, in Cline, T. (ed.) *The Assessment of Special Educational Needs*. London: Paul Chapman Publishing.

Cornwall, J. and Tod, J. (1998) *IEPS: Emotional and Behavioural Difficulties*. London: David Fulton.

Department for Education and Skills (DfES) (2001) *Code of Practice for Special Educational Needs*. London: HMSO.

Department for Education and Skills (DfES) (2006) *2020 Vision: Report of the Teaching and Learning in 2020 Review Group*. Nottingham: DfES Publications.

Department for Education and Skills (DfES) (2007) *Statutory Framework for the Early Years Foundation Stage: Setting the Standards for Learning Development and Care for children from birth to five* (EYFS). Nottingham: DfES Publications.

Dowling, M. (2000) *Young Children's Personal, Social and Emotional Development*. London: Paul Chapman.

HMI (2003) *Expecting the Unexpected: Developing Creativity in Primary and Secondary Schools*. Ofsted, E-publication.

Lipman, M. (1991) Philosophy for Children, in Costa, A.L. (ed.) *Developing Minds*. Alexandria, VA: Association for Supervision and Curriculum Development: pp. 35–38.

MacNaughton, G. (2003) *Shaping Early Childhood: Learners, Curriculum and Contexts*. Maidenhead: Open University Press.

MacNaughton, G. and Williams, G. (2004) *Teaching Young Children: Choices in Theory and Practice*. Maidenhead: Open University Press.

Moll, L.C. and Whitmore, K.F. (1998) Vygotsky in classroom practice: moving from individual transmission to social transaction, in Faulkner, D., Littleton, K. and Woodhead, M. (eds) *Learning Relationships in the Classroom*. London: Routledge.

Munby, S. (1994) Assessment and Pastoral Care: sense, sensitivity and standards, in Best, R., Lang, P., Lodge, C. and Watkins, C. (eds) *Pastoral Care and Personal–Social Education: Entitlement and Provision*. London: Cassell.

Philosophy for Children (P4C) (2007) Available at: **http://www.thinkingeducation.co.uk/p4c.htm**.

Prawat, R.S. and Nickerson, J.R. (1985) The relationship between teacher thought and action and student affective outcomes, *The Elementary School Journal*, Vol. 85: pp. 529–540.

Prentice, R., Matthews, J. and Taylor, H. (2003) Creative Development: learning and the arts, in Riley, J. (ed.) *Learning in the Early Years: A Guide for Teachers of Children 3–7*. London: Paul Chapman.

Robson, S. (2006) *Developing Thinking and Understanding in Young Children: An Introduction for Students*. Abingdon, Oxon: Routledge.

Robson, S. and Hargreaves, J. (2005) What do early childhood practitioners think about young children's thinking? *European Early Childhood Education Research Journal*, Vol. 13, No. 1: pp. 81–96.

Serow, R.C. and Solomon, D. (1979) Classroom climates and students' inter group behaviour, *Journal of Educational Psychology*, Vol. 71: pp. 669–676.

Siraj-Blatchford, I., Sylva, K., Muttock, S., Gilden, R. and Bell, D. (2002) *Researching Effective Pedagogy in the Early Years* (REPEY), Research Report No. 356. Nottingham: DfES Publications.

Solity, J. (1992) *Special Education*. London: Cassell.

Stoll, L., Fink, D. and Earl, L. (2003) *It's About Learning (and it's About Time): What's In It For Schools?* London: RoutledgeFalmer.

Sylva, K., Taggart, B., Siraj-Blatchford, I., Totsika, V., Ereky-Stevens, K., Gilden, R. and Bell, D. (2007) Curricular quality and day-to-day learning activities in pre-school, *International Journal of Early Years Education*, Vol. 15, No. 1, March: pp. 49–65.

Vygotsky, L.S. (1962) *Thought and Language*, edited and translated by Hanfmann, E. and Vakar, G. Cambridge, MA and New York: MIT Press.

White, J. (2002) *The Child's Mind*. London: RoutledgeFalmer.

Whitebread, D. (ed.) (2003) *Teaching and Learning in the Early Years*. London: RoutledgeFalmer.

By the end of this chapter you will be able to answer the following questions:

- How do I identify the most important dispositions for learning?
- What factors contribute to self-motivation?
- What is the role of in-house continuing professional development in meeting the demands of personalised learning?

This chapter will support your understanding of the following Standards *(see Appendix 1)*:
■ **Knowledge and understanding:** S02 and S03 ■ **Effective practice:** S07, S08, S10, S11, S14, S19 and S22
■ **Relationships with children:** S26 ■ **Professional development:** S38.

Introduction

WHAT HAPPENS IN PRACTICE?

The atmosphere in the setting has to be relaxed and concentrated. Mocking or laughing at someone has to be clearly and strongly forbidden and every effort (a child makes) has to be encouraged. Praise is very important. Before a child dares to speak, he/she needs to be confident in his/her ability to produce the right sound, word, sentence . . . One useful means is to encourage repetition collectively and often. If the practitioner hears a good 'production' (sound, word or sentence), he/she can ask a particular child, with praise, to say it to the others; but he/she should not ask a child to repeat, individually, something new if he/she does not volunteer to do it.

On the same principle, listening tasks or others are given to teams of children and the tasks have to be feasible for the team. It's not important that each child succeeds but that the team succeeds. So in the group, children are more confident to try. Nobody is forced to do or say something in front of the entire group if he/she does not feel ready. Stress lowers the chances of success.

Also, the 'status' of error is important. Errors are part of the learning (and children should be made aware of that). Practitioners can't expect children to produce/reproduce without error the first time. Some children are quicker than others. That is natural. Some can do it the first time, others have to listen more often before they can reproduce it. Practitioners have to respect the quiet ones. Of course they have to stimulate and invite them too; but some children have to listen a long time before they can produce a sound. This is the same in the mother tongue.

Again singing is very useful. It's impossible to put the tonic accent in the wrong place in a song, so singing together is a very interesting means of training pronunciation. Another means of training speech is to give tasks where speech is needed in pair work. Here children can train without fear of exposing the 'imperfections' in their production to the whole group.

One necessity is also to give speaking tasks that make sense for the child. A question should always be a real question, i.e., if you ask, it means that you don't know the answer. Can it be fun to ask an old pal 'what's your name?' so the teacher has to give new secret names for example if they want to train this question. The question must be real. It could easily be done in a guessing game where the object is really hidden.

(Interview with a senior lecturer in education at a university in the north of France. Although she describes the type of approach practitioners take when teaching English/German as a foreign language in a primary school, many of the suggestions are generic and can be applied to different activities.)

You will have understood from your work thus far that the foundations for learning are laid down in the early years of a child's life irrespective of the setting, from home to classroom. Enabling children to become confident, independent learners, curious for knowledge and eager to understand, needs to start at the earliest possible moment. For practitioners, this means enabling children to have the motivation to learn alongside the skills, knowledge and understanding needed to develop. As the above 'What happens in practice?' shows, certain strategies can be used to create an enabling learning environment, which in turn help to promote independent learning. Anning and Edwards suggest that in practice, children need help 'to become learners, to enjoy learning and to feel that they are people who are able to learn' (1999: 59). By addressing the idea of **learning dispositions**, this chapter will consider those which contribute most in enabling children to make sustained progress and achieve their full potential. Furthermore, it will consider how the development of these dispositions is part of the holistic development of the child. Before reading this chapter, reflect on the following, considering what each statement might mean for practice (you can review your thoughts when you have read the chapter):

1 Learning behaviour is influenced by individual characteristics.
2 Learning behaviours are influenced by learning, teaching styles and curriculum.
3 Learning behaviours are linked to social factors.

Learning dispositions: an inner attitude, which can be developed in a setting and predisposes a child to want to and to be able to advance in learning.

Dispositions for learning

Robson (2006: 94) defines learning dispositions as a 'combination' of motivation and strategies to develop learning known as 'situated learning strategies'. Citing Carr (2001: 19), she clarifies 'situated learning strategies [within the context of] knowledge and skills that are being used with a particular purpose in mind, linked to social partners and practices, and tools'. Dowling (2000) on the other hand, makes a stronger connection between dispositions for learning and attitudes. By referring to Lillian Katz, she states: 'attitudes consist of a set of beliefs, a disposition demonstrates those beliefs in behaviour' (2000: 67). In essence, a disposition for learning can be described as an inner attitude, which can be developed in a setting and predisposes a child to want to and to be able to advance in learning. Although learning behaviours are influenced by an individual's characteristics, children need the knowledge, understanding and skills to choose to behave in certain ways. In the setting practitioners have a central role in nurturing those dispositions for learning in children. By considering through examples of practice, current thinking on attitudes children need to develop to be motivated and advance in their learning, this section challenges the

Photo 8.1 How does this activity help the child to develop positive dispositions for learning?

Pearson Education Ltd. Jules Selmes © Pearson Education Ltd. 2004

reader to consider how he/she can effectively help children to develop positive dispositions for learning.

Educators and researchers acknowledge the importance of developing children's dispositions for learning alongside the development of their skills and knowledge; a view supported by the government. A child who is a gifted mathematician can only 'become' a mathematician if he/she is willing to do so.

Thody et al. (2000) advise that children need knowledge, understanding and skills to be able to choose to behave in certain ways. As practitioners we need to develop each child's ability to:

- have positive self-awareness, self-confidence and self-esteem
- understand the links between their feelings and their actions
- have ways to express their feelings
- understand that there are choices
- develop effective communication skills
- develop decision-making skills.

Dowling (2000: 67), a strong proponent of teaching for the development of learning dispositions, highlights the centrality of the early years practitioner in enabling children's positive *predispositions* to flourish. Failure to nurture positive characteristics in children tends to weaken their natural talent in that particular area. Dowling (2000: 68) suggests that dispositions for learning are those which help children to 'progress and achieve'. These she cites as 'motivation, perseverance, curiosity, creativity, problem-solving and reflection' (see Photo 8.1). Consider the following two examples of 'What happens in practice?'. The first is taken from an interview with the manager of a nursery in York and addresses the strategies used in practice to help children develop the right dispositions for learning.

WHAT HAPPENS IN PRACTICE?

We encourage them and promote independent activities. We always have a construction area with sand and water. The children can go and play there when they want to. Children develop the right dispositions for learning by being with adults who are enthusiastic and praise the children.

This second example is taken from an interview with the head of a pre-prep school in Yorkshire and shows a positive approach to engaging children in learning.

WHAT HAPPENS IN PRACTICE?

We try to give children responsibility throughout the school. This is tied up with motivation – if children are taking responsibility then they are more likely to be motivated (self). Here, the ethos of 'community and shared responsibility' is fostered throughout the school. And we also involve parents. Children love talking about what they are doing or have been doing. So we have meetings with parents and children talking about what they've been doing. We'd like to have more regular meetings like this which include the children.

REFLECT AND RELATE TO PRACTICE

Compare and contrast the strategies employed in these settings to encourage children to learn and to want to learn. Do you think they are effective? Why/why not?

☆ ☆ ☆
Consider the strategies employed in these settings to encourage children to learn and to want to learn. What strategies would you use in practice to help children develop positive dispositions for learning? (babies and toddlers; 3–5 year olds and 5–7 year olds)

In practice the compartmentalisation of specific dispositions for learning is a contested area (Dowling, 2000: 68). To further expand on this view, Robson (2006: 95), for example, supports the learning dispositions advocated by Carr (1998, 2001) and drawn from *Te Whariki*, the New Zealand early years curriculum (Ministry of

Table 8.1 Learning dispositions developed from the strands of the New Zealand Curriculum

The Strands of the New Zealand Curriculum *Te Whariki*	The domains of learning disposition ('The behaviour we look for')
Belonging	Taking an interest
Well-being	Being involved
Exploration	Persisting with difficulty, challenge and uncertainty
Communication	Expressing a point of view or feeling, communicating with others
Contribution	Taking responsibility

Source: Robson (2006) p. 95

Education, New Zealand, 1996). Carr (cited in Robson, 2006: 95) sets dispositions within *Learning Stories*, a framework for observation developed in New Zealand. Table 8.1 sets learning dispositions within this framework and provides a useful tool for planning teaching strategies in response to developing learning dispositions in children.

DISCUSSION POINT

Consider the six areas covered by the early learning goals and educational programme in England (Personal, social and emotional development; Communication, language and literacy; Problem-solving, reasoning and numeracy; Knowledge and understanding of the world; Physical development; and Creative development).

In your opinion what are the learning dispositions needed for each of the areas, which you would look for in a child. A table which you can complete is available on our **website**.

Affective development: growth in emotional awareness, understanding and control.

For practitioners, developing children's dispositions for learning can be a harder task than developing their skills and knowledge base. From a practical stance this, in part, is due to the **affective** nature of 'dispositions', i.e. they relate to the emotional dimension of the child. In addition, the lack of consensus amongst practitioners and researchers over the constituent behaviours which come under the umbrella of dispositions for learning reflects the difficulties in practice. Dowling (2000: 78) calls for 'agreed understandings about the behaviours that constitute positive dispositions for learning' in the development of common assessment procedures.

The development of a Child Involvement Scale by Ferre Laevers (1994) and employed in the Effective Early Learning (EEL) and Accounting for Life-Long Learning (AcE) projects, which addressed children's behaviour in the early years, has provided practitioners with the means to measure dispositions for learning, irrespective of their constituent elements. Laevers focused on involvement as an overall indicator of the development of related positive dispositions for learning. For Laevers (2000: 25), child involvement is an indicator of learning at a deeper level, an area which broadly covers all learning dispositions. Laevers equates satisfaction with involvement, which he suggests stems from the child's desire to find out. Motivation, he further suggests, comes from a natural drive to explore, to investigate situations, things and people.

Laevers' holistic definition of involvement, which tends to be founded on what Broadhead (2004) refers to as 'curiosity', has strong implications for practice and goes a long way in helping practitioners arrive at an understanding of dispositions for learning in practical terms.

However, helping children to develop positive behaviours for learning is dependent upon planning for each child's needs, informed by knowledge of the child, through ongoing observational assessment. For practitioners, it also means considering questions within the realms of philosophy – for example, what is the foundation of self-motivation, what makes children happy in their learning or how can I help children to enjoy learning? The Child Involvement Scale (Ferre Laevers, 1994), can be used in early years settings to observe the extent to which a child is involved in a specific activity according to the following scale:

- Concentration
- Energy
- Creativity
- Facial expression and posture
- Persistence
- Precision
- Reaction time
- Language
- Satisfaction.

(Dowling, 2000: 79)

Connect & Extend

Developing a scale to measure aptitude towards learning of individuals is an excellent exercise for enhancing teaching. It enables the practitioner to focus on the area and to reflect on practice. Try to develop your own reference points based on this chapter for measuring children's development of positive learning dispositions.

REFLECT AND RELATE TO PRACTICE

What dispositions do you think that a child should develop to be an effective learner?

Look up the six areas covered by the early learning goals and educational programmes. Select an area and plan an activity using the above scale to observe how involved the child is in the activity. You need to consider how you will plan for this – e.g. what will you look for in practice?

Interactive learning/interactive behaviour

Dowling (2000: 80) suggests that dispositions for learning are 'caught not taught'. She suggests, that although children's learning traits are developed through an interesting curriculum, the behaviour and activities of educators have central importance in the development of positive learning behaviours. By considering principles developed by the government in conjunction with the TDA for managing behaviour in educational settings this section will consider how helping children to develop positive learning dispositions is closely connected with how practitioners manage children's learning and their approach to and management of their behaviour.

Although there is the expectation that practitioners will create an enabling learning environment, their principal role is that of educator, where the environment created provides the foundation for and not the focus of effective teaching and learning. This is highlighted by the following Discussion point.

DISCUSSION POINT

Dowling (2000: 82) underlines the negative impact on the development of independent learners when such a disordering of educational priorities exists. 'How will children learn?' she asks, 'if everything they do is always regarded as intrinsically clever.' In such a 'benign environment', she suggests, there is nothing to 'challenge' the child's 'intellectual development'.

What is your view?

Managing a child's learning is closely connected with managing their behaviour and helping them to manage their behaviour for learning. For this to be effective in practice, you have to find strategies that *you* feel comfortable working with. The following core principles from the government (DfES/TTA, 2002) for application in schools might be considered for all early years settings:

- plan for right behaviour (e.g. are the necessary resources accessible to the child? will the child know how to use the resources?)
- work within the 4Rs (Rights, Rules, Routines, Responsibilites) framework
- separate the (inappropriate) behaviour from the child, i.e. separate the action from the person
- use the language of choice (e.g. How could you do that?)
- keep the focus on primary behaviours
- actively build trust and rapport
- model the behaviour you want to see
- always follow up on issues that count
- work to repair and restore relationships.

Physical development

Physical activity has a central role to play in the development of behaviour for learning and thinking in young children. Bailey et al. (2003: 157) suggest that 'through movement, children learn about their bodies, their physical and social environments, they try out different roles and rules and they test themselves'. The *Statutory Framework for the Early Years Foundation Stage: Setting the Standards for Learning Development and Care for children from birth to five* (EYFS) (DfES, 2007) acknowledges the close connection between physical and intellectual development. Physical development is considered alongside the development of skills and knowledge in the delivery of the six areas covered by the early learning goals and educational programmes within the new statutory framework. By outlining the views of various established researchers in the field of sports science and early years physical education and through a research briefing charting the approach to physical development in various countries, this section examines the relevance of physical activity in helping children to develop positive dispositions to learning.

Physical activity has an important role to play in the holistic approach to child development envisaged by the government for the educational settings of the twenty-first century. As with the other areas of the framework, physical development should be addressed through 'planned purposeful play with a balance of adult-led and child-initiated activities' (DfES, 2007: 11). The document clearly states that through the educational programme:

> **The physical development of babies and young children must be encouraged
> through the provision of opportunities for them to be active and interactive
> and to improve their skills of coordination, control, manipulation and
> movement. They must be supported in using all of their senses to learn about
> the world around them and to make connections between new information
> and what they already know. They must be supported in developing an
> understanding of the importance of physical activity and making healthy
> choices in relation to food.**
>
> *(DfES, 2007: 15)*

How physical development can be central to early years learning and practice can vary. Maude (2003: 218) proposes 'building on play' in developing a 'movement curriculum for young children'. She underlines the relevance of this for both their intellectual and physical development. Not only do children bring a 'rich movement vocabulary' to play, she suggests, but play involves both '**gross and fine motor skills**' – skills central to 'children's movement development'.

Bailey et al. (2003: 157–158) propose dance, games, gymnastics, swimming and outdoor play as effective activities to address physical development in young children. In addition they highlight the importance of movement 'experiences such as physical education lessons, playground games and informal physical activities' for giving children 'experiences of delight which may be missing from other parts of their daily lives'. This is to be hailed by educators.

Every Child Matters extols the centrality of enjoyment in enabling children to achieve. This further highlights the important role of games for the holistic development of

Gross motor skills: the ability to use the bigger muscles in the body (i.e. those needed for crawling, walking and running, etc.).

Fine motor skills: the ability to use small muscles in the hand which are also connected with eye movements. These are particularly important for writing.

Cognitive development: growth in understanding.

Psychomotor: physical co-ordination.

the child. Citing Wuest and Bucher (1995) they suggest that games provide opportunities for **cognitive** (intelligence), affective and **psychomotor** (physical coordination) **development**. In addition they highlight the importance of games as a medium for problem-solving and decision-making; an area addressed in more depth in Chapter 7. They call for a child-initiated approach to planning games, either individually or in small groups, which they suggest encourages creative thinking skills. In Bailey's (2000) earlier work, which addressed the relationship between values and physical education, he highlighted the relevance of games in the 'development of values, where co-operating with others, establishing team work, trust and leadership skills are all developed through playing games'. Each element resonates with behaviour for learning.

The following Discussion point compares and contrasts the approach to physical development in early years settings in a number of countries throughout the world. It has been adapted from work by Helen Penn (2005: 163–166), Professor of Early Childhood at the University of East London. This excerpt charts her experiences of early childhood education and care in developing and other countries. She starts with *Canada – the land of the great outdoors.*

DISCUSSION POINT

What struck me was the immobility of the children in most education and day care environments. They seemed to be encouraged not to move about too much for fear of endangering themselves or other children. A similar situation was witnessed in Australia. Penn comments on her lack of surprise, in a country where the emphasis is on removing all conceivable hazards, rather than enabling children to deal with them.

In one day care nursery in the UK, the only exercise children had was to go to a carpeted exercise room, where they were allowed to walk on a beam 6 inches off the floor, provided they held the hand of a childcare worker. Staff were so concerned about risk. This is only part of the problem; physical activity is not conceived of as exercise but as a means to an end – learning. Penn contrasts this with the Nordic countries, where the view is that children must learn to adapt to their environment. In Denmark, children may build huts, light camp fires, or swim in the sea in their forest kindergartens. In these countries the outdoor life is valued for itself and not as a means to improved intellectual performance.

In the Soviet system a great deal of attention is paid to physical fitness. Soviet kindergartens were routinely supplied with dance/gym space, and many had swimming pools. The kindergartens offer programmes for various kinds of highly specific physical exercises, including foot strengthening exercises (for children with flat feet).

In Africa . . . dancing and singing in many nurseries is second nature. Dance has a particular status in society, as a collective expression of emotion.

What do you think?

The writer implies that the place of physical education on the curricula of early years educational settings is driven by political or cultural norms. To what extent do you agree with this view for each of the countries discussed in the discussion point?

Motivation to learn

One of the most important dimensions of behaviour for learning is the ability of practitioners to both recognise motivating factors in children and to motivate them, which might be considered more a parental role, but is clearly linked to developing learning in all early years settings. By addressing how motivation is closely linked to the affective dimensions of learning, this section examines the place of the practitioner as both educator and role model in enabling children to be self-motivated learners. Various worked examples will help you to consider how this can be effectively developed in practice.

Broadhead (2004: 123) suggests that children's motivation is closely connected with emotional well-being. She uses the analogy of a thirsty child not being in a *learning state*. When the child is given water he/she is able to return to the task in hand with greater concentration and motivation. This, she suggests, is the same for emotional well-being. When a child's emotional well-being is satisfied, motivation is enhanced.

Photo 8.2 How frequently should children be praised?

Pearson Education Ltd. Tudor Photography © Pearson Education Ltd. 2004

The following provides an example of how, through informal observation, practitioners can assess what factors motivate individual children. It is taken from an interview with an early years leader of practice in a nursery in Thanet:

WHAT HAPPENS IN PRACTICE?

A 2 year old in the nursery loved to go outside and whenever he did he was never just interested in the bikes or the cars. He was always looking up at the sky or the trees. It was easy to talk to him about what he saw; the birds or insects or plants. Some practitioners and parents think that outside is for play or running around and letting off steam. Often children learn even more outside because they are more motivated.

REFLECT AND RELATE TO PRACTICE

Do you think this activity will help the 2 year old to become more motivated? Why/why not?

 ☆ ☆ ☆

How would you follow up this activity to help this child become a more self-motivated learner?

How do we know whether a child is motivated? Ongoing formal and informal observational assessment enables practitioners to know children as individuals, through determining what works as an effective means of motivating them. Nutbrown (1999: 35) citing Bruce (1987: 26) suggests that this provides a means for practitioners to 'work with the child rather than against what is natural'. Nutbrown (1999: 35) further suggests that with subsequent interventions, children are more likely to 'sustain their effort, to struggle and persevere', when faced with a difficult task. Wood and Attfield (2005: 94–95) advocate scaffolding, when focused on 'joint problem solving' (adult–child). In essence this would mean building on a child's aptitudes. Robson (2006: 185) suggests that motivation is a significant component of problem-solving, where good adult–child and child–child relationships are a major contributory factor to success.

DISCUSSION POINT

In your opinion, what are the contributory factors to motivating a child?

How would you motivate children in an early years setting? Consider 1–2 year olds, 3–5 year olds and 5–7 year olds. You should also consider how you would develop a motivating environment.

Practitioners who are motivated and committed to educational excellence will create an environment which motivates children. Early years educators who know and understand how to motivate children will enable children to achieve their full potential and lay a strong foundation for future learning. All practitioners are able to create conditions which focus on achieving excellence. They should encourage participation and facilitate peer work. As an educator, an early years practitioner will serve as a role model to the children he/she teaches. Stoll et al. (2003: 122), a University of London Professor, suggests that 'one of the most powerful ways leaders can lead others' learning is through modeling'. Practitioners who inspire and motivate children to achieve high standards and to work towards fulfilment of their aims will model these attributes themselves. In practice this will require early years practitioners to:

- provide children with challenges and intellectual stimulation
- celebrate children's success
- enable children to participate
- encourage pair and small group work
- develop positive assessment systems
- enhance children's self-esteem
- have high expectations for all children and articulate this
- be aware of and use the rewards that children value
- be aware of and use various and appropriate means of feedback to children.

Clearly motivation is more than satisfaction; it also requires knowledge and understanding of what is expected and the outcome of the activity or the confidence to develop and practise without predetermined expectations.

WHAT HAPPENS IN PRACTICE?

Daniel, aged five, planned to make a table from a large construction kit. He selected the correct pieces and assembled them in the right order. He became frustrated when the final product would not stand up. Daniel did not know how to interlock the tubes into the joints and asked his teacher for help. He had created a meaningful problem but lacked the requisite problem-solving strategies: she intervened sensitively to discuss the problem with Daniel and identify possible solutions. She modelled the task using the correct language to describe her actions. She demonstrated how to line up the lugs on the poles with the hole in the joint and twist it to lock it firmly in place. Daniel watched intently, repeating some of the words and phrases used. The teacher asked him to show her how to interlock the tubes to check his understanding, offering further support by revising the task and praising his new skills. Her interactions were contingent on Daniel's motivations and goals so that the episode involved mutual contributions to teaching and learning. Daniel showed determination, concentration and perseverence and was pleased to be able to show a successfully completed table to his peers at review time. He was observed later that week demonstrating this process to another child using similar techniques to those modelled by the teacher.

(Wood and Attfield, 2005: 95)

REFLECT AND RELATE TO PRACTICE

What or who motivated Daniel at each point in the task? At which points could he have become demotivated? Identify, at each relevant point in the task, how the teacher helped Daniel to become motivated/prevented demotivation.

Developing practice

In practice, it is important for practitioners to consider how they can be more 'in tune' with the child and their learning. This means having a greater understanding, from both a theoretical and practical stance, of the factors which impact on children's motivation for learning. In considering the importance of in-house Continuing Professional Development (CPD) in enabling practitioners to become more aware of the ways children develop as self-motivated learners, the section opens with an outline of the Adult Engagement Scale, developed as part of the Effective Early Learning (EEL) project. Presented as a simple framework, it encourages readers to consider how it could be used as a tool for both individual improvement (generally) and for specific areas of practice. The section closes with a summary, developed by the government in conjunction with the TDA, of how CPD can be initiated within the setting to help practitioners develop and improve their approach to personalised learning.

In terms of developing practice, Dowling (2000: 82–83) endorses the Adult Engagement Scale, developed for the EEL project. Through the following core areas, practitioners can assess their effectiveness as leaders of learning within their early years setting:

- **Sensitivity**: how well the adult is tuned in and the degree of response to the feelings and well-being of the child.
- **Stimulation**: how effective the adult is when taking part in the child's learning
- **Autonomy**: the degree of freedom which the adult provides to allow the child to experiment, make judgements, choose activities and express ideas. It also includes the boundaries established to deal with conflict and behaviour.

This type of activity reflects the government's vision for ongoing practitioner CPD to meet the demands of personalising learning. The vision, as outlined in the government's document, *2020 Vision: Report of the Teaching and Learning in 2020 Review Group* (DfES, 2006: 31), encourages in-house CPD to build practitioner 'capacity for self-development' in the following ways:

- much of the activity should be setting based, with a focus on teaching and learning
- much of the activity should be closely integrated with, and run parallel to, the daily practices of the practitioner, since it is here where change is most difficult, but most needed

- much of the activity should involve practitioners working together in small groups
- knowledge and skills transfer is slow and usually takes time to embed – make small incremental changes
- educators need to be able to choose the practices they change and the techniques they use
- educators need to see unfamiliar new practices being used in practice
- educators need to be coached and supported as they wrestle with the transfer of knowledge and skills.

(DfES, 2006: 31)

ACTIVITY

Imagine you are responsible for developing an in-house CPD activity in an early years setting of your choice. How could you use the above mentioned approaches (see DfES, 2006: 31) as a starting point for the activity? You should refer to the 'What happens in practice?' research briefings in this chapter and the various scales employed for measuring educator/child effectiveness to help you. Outline your plans for the proposed CPD activity.

Behaviour for learning: bringing it together

Having read the chapter, to what extent do you now agree/disagree with the following statements?

- Learning behaviour is influenced by individual characteristics.
- Learning behaviours are influenced by learning, teaching styles and curriculum.
- Learning behaviours are linked to social factors.

SUMMARY

Dispositions for learning (p. 163)

Which dispositions for learning do you think need to be developed?

Practitioners agree that motivation is central to learning. In practice, however, the compartmentalisation of specific dispositions for learning is a contested area.

Interactive learning/interactive behaviour (p. 168)

Does constant praise detract from independent learning?

Practitioners need to consider when to positively reinforce children's learning and when to correct. The way practitioners manage children

SUMMARY *CONTINUED*

in their setting is central to effective teaching and learning.

Physical development (p. 169)

To what extent is physical activity connected to and intertwined with intellectual development?

Physical activity is a valuable and necessary means of helping children's cognitive, affective and physical development.

Motivation to learn (p. 171)

What motivates children to learn?

The ability of practitioners to both recognise motivating factors in children and motivate them is vital if children are to become independent learners.

Developing practice (p. 174)

Could the Adult Engagement Scale help you to become an effective leader of learning?

The Adult Engagement Scale, developed for the EEL project, can be used by practitioners to assess their effectiveness as leaders of learning within their early years setting.

Glossary

Affective development: growth in emotional awareness, understanding and control.

Cognitive development: growth in understanding.

Fine motor skills: the ability to use small muscles in the hand which are also connected with eye movements. These are particularly important for writing.

Gross motor skills: the ability to use the bigger muscles in the body (i.e. those needed for crawling, walking and running, etc.).

Learning dispositions: an inner attitude, which can be developed in a setting and predisposes a child to want to and to be able to advance in learning.

Psychomotor: physical co-ordination.

Find out more

Doherty, J. and Bailey, R. (2002) *Supporting Physical Development and Physical Education in the Early Years*, Maidenhead: Open University.
Richard Bailey is well known in the field of Sports Science. This book provides good practical ideas for physical education and development in practice, from babies and toddlers to young children.

Hutchinson, N. and Smith, H. (2004) *Intervening Early: Promoting Positive Behaviour in Young Children*, London: David Fulton.

Practically based, this book has a good chapter on developing effective relationships with children, which will complement what you have read in this chapter.

Curtis, A. and O'Hagan, M. (2003) *Care and Education in Early Childhood*, London: RoutledgeFalmer.
Audrey Curtis and Maureen O'Hagan have written a good chapter on How Children Learn (Chapter 3). It provides an insight into the issues/areas underlying the development of appropriate learning behaviours).

References

Anning, A. and Edwards, A. (1999) *Promoting Children's Learning from Birth to Five: Developing the New Early Years Professional*. Buckingham: Open University Press.

Bailey, R. (2000) The value and values of physical education and sport, In Bailey, R. (ed.) *Teaching Values and Citizenship across the Curriculum*. London: Kogan Page.

Bailey, R., Doherty, J. and Jago, R. (2003) Physical development and physical education, in Riley, J. (ed.) *Learning in the Early Years: A Guide for Teachers of Children 3–7*. London: Paul Chapman.

Broadhead, P. (2004) *Early Years Play and Learning: Developing Social Skills and Cooperation*. Abingdon: RoutledgeFalmer.

Bruce, T. (1987) *Early Childhood Education*. London: Hodder and Stoughton.

Carr, M. (1998) *Assessing Children's Learning in Early Childhood Settings*. Wellington, New Zealand: New Zealand Council for Educational Research.

Carr, M. (2001) *Assessment in Early Childhood Settings*. London: Paul Chapman.

Department for Education and Skills (DfES) (2006) *2020 vision: Report of the Teaching and Learning in 2020 Review Group*. Nottingham: DfES Publications.

Department for Education and Skills (DfES) (2007) *Statutory Framework for the Early Years Foundation Stage: Setting the Standards for Learning Development and Care for children from birth to five* (EYFS). Nottingham: DfES Publications.

Department for Education 2nd Skills/Teacher Training Agency (2002) *Qualifying to Teach–Professional Standards for QTS and Requirements for ITT*. London: HMSO.

Dowling, M. (2000) *Young Children's Personal, Social and Emotional Development*. London: Paul Chapman.

Goleman, D. (1999) *Working with Emotional Intelligence*. London: Bloomsbury.

Laevers, F. (ed.) (1994) The Leuven Involvement Scale for Young Children (manual and video) Experiential education series, No. 1. Leuven: Centre for Experiential Education.

Laevers, F. (2000) 'Forward to Basics! Deep-level-learning and the Experiential Approach', *Early Years*, Vol. 20, No. 2: pp. 20–29.

Maude, P. (2003) 'How do I do this better?' From movement development into physical literacy, in Whitebread, D. (ed.) *Teaching and Learning in the Early Years*. London: RoutledgeFalmer.

Ministry of Education, New Zealand (1996) *Te Whariki: Early Childhood Curriculum*. Auckland: New Zealand Learning Media.

Nutbrown, C. (1999) *Threads of Thinking*. London: Paul Chapman.

Penn, H. (2005) *Understanding Early Childhood: Issues and Controversies*. Maidenhead: Open University Press/ McGraw-Hill Education.

Riley, J. (ed.) (2003) *Learning in the Early Years: A Guide for Teachers of Children 3–7*. London: Paul Chapman.

Robson, S. (2006) *Developing Thinking and Understanding in Young Children: An Introduction for Students*. Abingdon: Routeledge.

Stoll, L., Fink, D. and Earl, L. (2003) *It's About Learning (and it's About Time): what's in it for schools?* London: RoutledgeFalmer.

Thody, A., Gray, B. and Bowden, D. with Welch, G. (2000) *The Teacher's Survival Guide*. London: Continuum.

Tod, J., Powell, S. and Cornwall, J. (2003) *A Systematic Review of How Theories Explain Learning Behaviour in School Contexts*. London: Teacher Training Agency.

Whitebread, D. (ed.) (2003) *Teaching and Learning in the Early Years*. London: RoutledgeFalmer.

Whitehead, M. (1994) *The Development of Language and Literacy*. London: Hodder and Stoughton.

Wood, E. and Attfield, J. (2005) *Play, Learning and the Early Childhood Curriculum*. London: Paul Chapman.

Wuest, D. and Bucher, C. (1995) *Foundations of Physical Education in Sport*. St Louis, MI: Mosby.

By the end of this chapter you will be able to answer the following questions:

- Why is observation central to assessment for learning?
- How can I provide constructive feedback to children about their learning?
- Why is assessment for learning central to planning?
- How do I make assessment for learning part of daily classroom practice?

This chapter will support your understanding of the following Standards *(see Appendix 1)*:
■ **Knowledge and understanding:** S01 and S02 ■ **Effective practice:** S07, S10, S11, S12, S13, S14, S21, S22 and S24 ■ **Relationships with children:** S26 and S27 ■ **Professional development:** S39.

Introduction

DISCUSSION POINT

Enabling babies, toddlers and young children to develop a positive self-image and positive feelings for or dispositions to learning calls for constructive sensitivity to assessment on the part of the early years practitioner. The Assessment Reform Group (ARG) (2002) suggest that comments which 'focus on the work rather than the person are more constructive for both learning and motivation'. To consider how this can be put into practice the following case study has been adapted from a training course provided for early years practitioners by Mary Jane Drummond (2003: 59–161), a Lecturer at the University of Cambridge Faculty of Education. She employed an activity called 'Judge and Jury' from *Making Assessment Work*, a set of activities developed by Drummond, Rouse and Pugh (1992).

In the following activity, early years educators: explored the distance in terms of power between the assessor and the assessed, and the rights and responsibilities associated with this relationship. The crude analogy, suggested by the title of the activity . . . can be justified as a reminder of the relative powerlessness both of the prisoner in the dock and of children in schools and classrooms.

Judge and Jury
 1 When I am assessing a child's learning, I feel . . .
 2 When I write something down about a child, I feel . . .
 3 When I think my judgements can help a child, I feel . . .
 4 If I thought my judgements could harm a child, I would feel . . .
 5 The word 'power' makes me think of . . .
 6 As an early years educator/as a teacher, I have a responsibility to . . .
 7 This responsibility makes me feel . . .
 8 As an early years educator/as a teacher, I have the right to . . .
 9 This right makes me feel . . .
10 I do not have the right to . . .
11 Children are powerful when . . .
12 Children have the right to . . .
13 If I knew what a difference my assessments might make in 20 years' time, I . . .
14 The best way to describe my relationship with the young children I work with is . . .

In the analysis of over 150 responses: a number . . . clustered around the idea of a benevolent, enabling teacher, for example responses referred to the responsibility to reassure, nurture, encourage, care, provide for, reinforce, support and enable children. A smaller number of more emphatic replies refer to the responsibility to empower, enhance, stimulate, stretch and 'open doors'.

Activity

How would you respond to each of these statements? If you have not had experience of practice, there may be some questions that you will want to leave out.

Assessment for learning: practitioners involve children in deciding their learning objectives.

Observational assessment: practitioners observing and evaluating children's learning either planned or as incidental observation.

Summative assessment: a summary of a learner's achievements at a given moment in time.

Formative assessment: practitioners evaluate children's learning and using this information involve children in deciding their learning objectives.

As with all government initiatives, the focus is clear; assessment should be central to improving standards and raising achievement. In practice, this means, as far as is possible, children and practitioners working together to decide 'where the learners are in their learning, where they need to go and how best to get there' (ARG, 2002). This process is known as assessment for learning (AfL) and should be central to day-to-day practice in the setting and the school. This chapter will consider how the process of assessment for learning can and should be at the centre of day-to-day practice in early years settings. Although the particular focus of this chapter is on **AFl** in the Early Years Foundation Stage, the underlying principles of the AfL process make it equally applicable to Key Stage 1.

It is now widely acknowledged and strongly endorsed by the government that the early years of education are critical for the development of life-long learning skills. In practice, this means 'learning and development that is planned around the individual needs and interests of the child and informed by the use of ongoing **observational assessment**' (DfES, 2007). The introduction of the Foundation Stage Profile (QCA, 2003) – the statutory **summative assessment** for all children at the end of the Foundation Stage (at the end of the reception class year), in response to the increased number of children already in education on entry to primary school, has brought greater focus to assessment in the early years. A positive initiative has been how the Profile has necessitated closer working between primary schools and providers for the under fives. Based on a number of **formative assessments**, in the six key areas of Learning and Development (personal, social and emotional development; communication, language and literacy; mathematical development; knowledge and understanding of the world; physical development; and creative development) throughout the Early Years Foundation Stage, it is crucial that a record of children's achievements is made available to the primary schools. Assessment is clearly set out in the *Statutory Framework for the Early Years Foundation Stage: Setting the Standards for Learning Development and Care for children from birth to five* (EYFS) (DfES, 2007: Appendix 1) and discussed in more detail in the *Foundation Stage Profile Handbook* (QCA, 2003). The nine-point scale is also available on our **website**.

Policy to practice

Assessment for Learning (AfL) underpins the government's plan to raise children's achievement. This section will consider the policy documents which directly inform practice in the setting and address the ways in which AfL differs in the early years of education.

The government's commitment to raising standards in the early years through effective assessment is supported by the documents detailed in Table 9.1, all of which provide valuable guidance for practitioners (many are supported by a CD-Rom). Educational policy and practice have advanced at a fast pace over the last decade and this summary will need to be kept up to date.

Before going any further it is worth considering the different types of assessment that have been mentioned thus far and how, in practice, they are interconnected:

- Formative assessment: assessment which informs future planning for children's learning. The final summative judgements made for the Profile are based entirely on ongoing formative assessment made throughout the child's time in the foundation stage (QCA, 2005b: 5).
- Assessment for learning: this is formative assessment which fully involves children and practitioners together in deciding where the learners are in their learning, where they need to go and how best to get there (QCA, 2005b: 6).
- Summative assessment: any assessment which summarises where learners are at a given point in time (DfES, 2004) – e.g. the result of a written test or a mark for a particular piece of work.

DISCUSSION POINT

With three or four other members of your group discuss what you understand by 'Assessment for Learning'. List the ways you might implement it into your daily setting/classroom practice. You can review this at the end of the chapter.

Connect & Extend

The Assessment Reform Group, originally funded by the British Educational Research Association (BERA) and presently by The Nuffield Foundation, was set up as a Policy Task Group on Assessment. The group commissioned Professors Paul Black and Dylan Wiliam when they were employed by Kings College, London, to carry out a review of classroom assessment and its effect. Their findings were published in *Inside the Black Box* (Black and Wiliam, 1998). Look up this book. What were the main findings? What implications do these have for practice?

Assessment for Learning underpins the government's vision for a national programme of personalised learning and the move towards teaching for independent learning (see Chapter 15). Related policy documents reflect the influence of the Assessment Reform Group's (ARG) review of practice in the classroom, the findings of which were summarised in *Inside the Black Box* (Black and Wiliam, 1998) which highlighted the benefits of assessment for learning as a valuable means of raising children's achievement.

Assessment for learning with young children however, is different from assessment for learning with older children. The nature of teaching and learning in early years settings, with its focus on play and open ended tasks, means that it is not always possible or appropriate to make children aware of learning objectives prior to an activity. However, acknowledging the

Table 9.1 Government policy documents informing Assessment for Learning

Document	Summary
Statutory Framework for the Early Years Foundation Stage: Setting the Standards for Learning Development and Care for children from birth to five (EYFS) (DfES, 2007).	Appendix 1 clearly sets out the 13 assessment scales each with 9 points, based on the early learning goals. It further considers how the 9 points can be used/applied in assessing a child.
Foundation Stage Profile Handbook (QCA, 2003)	Considers assessment in practice, detailing, through case studies, both how to make judgements on children's achievements and how to standardise assessment in the setting.
Seeing Steps in Children's Learning (QCA, 2005a)	By focusing on continuity and progression, this document considers how to analyse and evaluate formal observations of children within a setting. It can be used in conjunction with the *Foundation Stage Profile Handbook*.
Observing Children: Building the Profile (QCA, 2005b)	This document considers the centrality of observation in enabling practitioners to know children well, with the aim of adapting teaching to meet individual learner needs.
Improving Outcomes for Children in the Foundation Stage in Maintained Schools (DfES, 2006)	This document focuses on effective target setting in the early years.
Assessment and Reporting Arrangements: Key Stage 1: Foundation Stage, years 1 and 2 (QCA, 2007)	The QCA, responsible for publishing the *Assessment and Reporting Arrangements* (available at: www.qca.org.uk), update this document regularly and also provide further practical guidance on the Foundation Stage Profile within it.
Building a Picture of What a Child Can Do (QCA, 2004)	Provides information on making a final judgement on a child's achievement at the end of the Foundation Stage with a particular focus on standardising assessment.

importance of providing children with a focus to learning the Qualifications and Curriculum Authority clearly states: 'Practitioners should discuss their learning with the children, giving feedback when appropriate without interrupting their play and identifying next steps with them'(QCA, 2005b: 6).

In practice, assessment for learning in the Foundation Stage includes:

- Formative assessment based on observations and other evidence of learning [see p. 181].
- Discussions with children about their learning whenever possible and involving them in self-assessment.
- Assessment used to inform planning.
- Involving children in planning their next steps.

(QCA, 2005b: 11)

Formative assessment based on observations and other evidence of learning

Through ongoing, formal and informal observation, practitioners will get to know the needs of the children within their setting. This is the key to ensuring that teaching is focused on individual learning needs. In essence formative assessment is a cyclical process involving the gathering, analysis and evaluation of evidence of a child's/ children's learning, where the practitioner reflects upon the best way to move the child's/children's learning forward. By considering formative assessment in practice, this section considers how practitioners can effectively integrate the process into teaching and learning.

Assessment for learning is based on the continual process of 'seeking and interpreting evidence' (ARG, 2002) about children's learning and development. Such assessment becomes formative assessment (informs planning) 'when the evidence is actually used to adapt the teaching work to meet the needs' (Black and Wiliam, 1998: 2). Hutchin (2003), Regional Adviser for the Foundation Stage in the DCSF **National Strategies** (a government driven programme to raise standards across the field of education by providing support to settings and schools) cited by the QCA (2005b: 15), highlights the following, as ways that practitioners will gather evidence of children's learning during the foundation stage:

National Strategies: government-driven programme to raise standards across the field of education by providing support to settings and schools.

- observations
- conversations with the children
- information from parents
- samples, e.g. drawings
- from others involved with the child, e.g. bilingual assistants
- collected from other settings that the child has attended.

When considering assessment it is important to remember that each child is unique and through the ongoing process of collecting evidence of learning, both formally and informally, a practitioner will get to know the children in his/her setting well. This is the key to ensuring that teaching is focused on individual learning needs.

Photo 9.1 How will this drawing show you the child has progressed in his/her learning?

Pearson Education Ltd. Tudor Photography © Pearson Education Ltd. 2004

For the practitioner, knowing where to start can be challenging. Fisher (2002a: 55), an early years adviser in Oxfordshire, in her work of the same name, proposes 'starting from the child'. She suggests that assessing what children already know when they arrive in the setting can initiate planning. She further suggests that a certain level of flexibility is needed and the opportunity for children to carry out a number of open-ended tasks should be provided. These may be initiated by the practitioner, but should be open by outcome to allow the children to think through problems. Through this process, practitioners will come to know the child and gain a greater insight into his/her skills, knowledge, understanding, character and potential. The following 'What happens in practice?', adapted from an interview with a leader of practice in a nursery in Thanet, shows how observation of 0–3 year olds can be used to inform teaching.

WHAT HAPPENS IN PRACTICE?

I recommend that you don't go in with set outcomes in your head. The baby or young child may take you on a different path and you have to really focus on what the child is doing and what they are getting out of it. It is important not to always focus on an activity which is laid out or organised by adults. For example I was watching a two year old who noticed that light was coming through the stained glass window in the nursery and falling on his hand. I watched him as he was putting his hand in and out of the beam of coloured light. As I watched he went to get a bucket so that he could catch the light in his bucket. These are 'awe and wonder' moments that are not planned for but provide a rich source of discussion and interaction.

This is where the role of a key person is so important. If you are tuned into the individual children that you are key worker for you get to know what makes them tick and what interests them. You are genuinely interested in their next step whatever it is. You look for where they are and where they are going.

REFLECT AND RELATE TO PRACTICE

What does this tell you about where this two year old boy is in his learning?
What would you do next to help him progress in his learning?

Overall and Sangster (2006: 75), senior lecturers in education who have written widely on primary education, suggest that 'for formative assessment to be successful it is about creating a classroom in which children become engaged in learning which is meaningful to them and you and they have strategies to respond to their learning needs'. In practice this means considering how to engage children in learning which is meaningful to them, the stategies you need to develop to help you to respond to their learning needs and the strategies you need to help them develop in response to their learning (you need to keep strategies for independent learning at the forefront of your planning). To do this effectively, practitioners need to know how young children learn and develop.

Smidt (2005: 43), an education consultant, suggests this enables 'us to recognise significant moments in learning'. The nurture–nature debate, relating to children's intellectual abilities, has been discussed in Chapter 4 and is only briefly mentioned here. One school of thought promotes the idea that unless a child has natural talent in a particular area, it cannot be developed through learning experiences. Those, on the other hand, who support the idea of 'nurture' through learning experiences, offer a more hopeful and positive view for educators. They suggest that, through meaningful educational opportunities, children can develop in all areas of learning. To understand, however, both how children learn and manage formative assessment in practice, Black and Wiliam (1998: 14) underline the importance of steering a middle path between the two extremes (nurture–nature). They refer to this as the 'untapped potential' view, which assumes that 'so-called ability is a complex of skills which can be learnt' (i.e. children can develop in all areas of learning with appropriate support and relevant activities with which they can engage). Although the relevance of genetically determined intelligence cannot be overlooked, assuming that all children have potential will enhance your interaction with the children and, as evidence suggests, help them to learn (Black and Wiliam, 1998). Once you have made the assumption that every child can learn and every child can achieve, you will have a firm foundation on which to build effective formative assessment.

In order to plan, implement, assess appropriate tasks and move children forward in their learning you need to consider how to engage each child with the activity. The following 'What happens in practice?' has been adapted from an interview with a senior lecturer in education at a University in the north of France and considers the importance of understanding how children learn in order to engage them in the learning process. She describes the type of approach practitioners take when teaching English/German as a foreign language in a primary school. However, many of the suggestions are generic and can be applied to a number of different activities.

WHAT HAPPENS IN PRACTICE?

How do you make learning a foreign language pleasure or fun for that age group?

The teacher has to know what makes fun or pleasure for that age. I always tell my students to observe and listen to the children on the playground during breaks. You have to know their needs.

Teachers have to try to remember themselves as children – what did they like? What made them proud? What made them laugh?

When I had (taught) this age group I always planned a surprise in the lesson, without telling them. They had quickly understood that there would be something strange, funny [or] good during the course [of the lesson] but they did not know when to expect it. So they concentrated to be sure not to miss the fun.

During my planning I always thought carefully about something that would make the whole lesson fun – nice. Something I always tell my trainees, don't ever do an activity that bores you.

The teacher has to carefully choose the activities – too difficult, too easy, too long (will not be enjoyable for the children). This means that for a period of 45 minutes I planned at least five or six different activities. Each new learning [exercise] was presented in a different way or as a different activity [in order to] feed different learning styles, visual, listening, handling, moving.

REFLECT AND RELATE TO PRACTICE

Consider the interview you have just read.

What strategies are used to engage children in learning which is meaningful to them?
What strategies are used to respond to their learning needs?
Have the children been helped to develop learning strategies?
How does this relate to formative assessment?

Being aware of how children learn and more importantly the learning needs of the individual children within your setting will enable you to effectively integrate and manage the formative assessment process. In practice, assessment will be a cyclical process, which informs long-, medium- and short-term planning (medium-term planning is not always used in early years settings – see Chapter 16). It involves gathering evidence of children's learning, analysing and evaluating the evidence and allowing time to reflect on how you will 'develop learning priorities or targets for the children across the breadth of the curriculum as appropriate' (QCA, 2005b. 16). On a daily basis this cycle will include:

- Incidental observations, when the practitioner notices something significant he or she is not involved in.
- Participant observations, where the practitioner is fully involved with the children.
- Carrying out one planned focused observation for each child (3–5 minutes) where the practitioner stands back to watch a child in a play based or independent self-chosen activity inside or outside.
- Informal discussions with parents.
- Informal discussions with the child.

(QCA, 2005b: 16)

Observing children first hand is central to good teaching and learning. This means developing the necessary skills to ensure that 'observations' are being effectively used to inform teaching and develop the children's learning. In practice, there are a number of different ways of observing children: participant observation, incidental observation and planned 'focused' observation. The following framework, developed as a set of questions, will help you to do this; consider:

1 What aspect of learning do I want to assess?
2 What is the best way of collecting this data? (What type of observation?)
3 What am I looking for? (Consider the assessment scales.)
4 What does it tell me about the child?
5 What aspects do I need to consider to help this child develop/progress more autonomously? (Be flexible – later in the day, you might see another dimension of the child which will alter your plan.)
6 How much time do I need to give this child to develop this skill/progress in this area?

Developing observation as part of effective teaching and learning will come with the continuous practice necessitated by day-to-day life in an early years setting. However, the QCA (2005b: 18–19) make the following suggestions, which help you to integrate observation into daily practice:

- Participant and incidental observation: make notes to add to the children's records later. You can use self-adhesive notes or have a page in your daily planning schedule with the children's names and a space to record 'significant' learning/event.
- A **planned 'focused' observation**: this should be written into planning. You will probably do one per term. Observe a child for a minimum of 5–6 minutes, engaged in either 'an independent self-chosen activity or play-based learning'.

Planned 'focused' observation: 'when a practitioner stands back to observe children in independent, child-initiated, play-based activities' (QCA, 2005b: 15).

These are the most useful (see **Appendix 1** to this chapter for an observation schedule).

The Assessment Reform Group (2002) emphasise the need for the understanding of learning to be a two-way process, whereby learners are made aware of how they are learning. This is supported by Overall and Sangster (2006: 66) who refer to the centrality of the internal dialogue – which they define as 'talking within the head' – in the learning process. They propose pair or small group work as a natural means of enabling children to become aware of the 'how' of learning. They further suggest that the interaction of the practitioner with the young learner in explaining how to carry out a particular task or getting them to talk about what they know or how they know if they have completed a task well or badly provides a natural means of enabling the child to become aware of the learning process. In addition, it provides a means of integrating children's self-assessment into practice. There is also much to be gained by thinking out aloud and planning this with the children in your care.

DISCUSSION POINT

What does the phrase 'knowing the how of learning' mean to you?
Why do children need to know about how they learn?

Learning styles have been discussed at some length in Chapter 7, but it is worth reflecting on the following summary adapted from Smidt (2005: 36–42):

- *Children search for meaning* – it seems as though they ask themselves questions.
- They learn through *social interaction*.
- *Scaffolding*, as developed by Vygotsky, can help a child to fulfil his/her potential (i.e. within an appropriately supportive framework – a child can do what they would not be able to do without help).
- *Play* is an important vehicle for learning.
- *Talk and language* have an important role in the learning process – through practitioner/learner talk/questioning.
- Children learn through *exploration*.
- *Children will learn best when they can see the point of what they are being asked to do.*
- Learning is enhanced when learners *feel positive* about themselves and about what they are learning.

REFLECT AND RELATE TO PRACTICE

Each point can be used to make learning more meaningful to young learners by helping them to become aware of how they are learning. For each one consider with one or two examples, either through an activity, question or reflection, how you could do this in practice. Remember, focus on teaching for independent learning.

Involving children in self-assessment and discussion of their learning

Providing children with the opportunity to discuss their work provides a means of appropriately rechannelling their thinking. To be of benefit, discussion needs to be given careful thought. This section examines possible ways of discussing children's work with them, in a manner which enhances their learning.

Black and Wiliam (1998: 11) highlighted the benefits for children, in terms of improved knowledge and understanding, when they have the opportunity to discuss their work with practitioners. This can be done both formally and informally and provides a means of appropriately rechannelling children's thinking. Often, this will be questioning children about their work. To be of benefit, it needs to be given careful thought. The following has been adapted from Black and Wiliam (1998: 11–12) and provides a good framework for considering how to use questioning effectively:

- Give children *time to respond to questions* (reflection time).
- Let children *discuss their thinking in pairs* before one of the 'pair' reports back. This tends to work better with older children.
- Give children a choice of answers and let them *vote* on the correct response.
- *Good questions are hard to generate and practitioners should collaborate, and draw – critically – on outside sources, to collect such questions.* It is good to write possible ways of both asking children questions and answering children's questions into short-term plans.

Photo 9.2 How would you ensure that these children are discussing their work?

Pearson Education Ltd. Jules Selmes © Pearson Education Ltd. 2008

Good questioning is founded on the idea of teaching for independent learning. Practitioner questions should challenge children in their learning. They should provide opportunity for the children to start taking responsibility for their own learning, opening channels for thinking, creativity, problem-solving and decision-making. Black and Wiliam (1998) in their study of assessment highlighted the following:

> there are clearly-recorded examples of such discussions (teacher–child) where teachers have, quite unconsciously, responded in ways that would inhibit the future learning of a pupil. What the examples have in common is that the practitioner is looking for a particular response and lacks the flexibility or the confidence to deal with the unexpected.
>
> *(1998: 11)*

DISCUSSION POINT

Consider as many ways as possible of asking children questions or providing direction which both promotes and enhances independent learning.

The routine, daily interaction of the early years practitioner with the child provides many opportunities for questioning in class room practice. For example, during the course of carrying out a particular activity a child may ask a question, directing it at one of his/her peers or at the educator. The educator may respond directly, if this is appropriate, or respond with another question to illicit a deeper thought process in the child. Alternatively the child's question may initiate a related discussion between children. In both cases the child will be demonstrating his/her knowledge, skills or understanding.

Effective Formative Assessment needs to be constructive. It should motivate children, moving them towards self-mastery. It is important to remember that children's confidence develops step by step and is fuelled by their successes – recall the adage *success breeds success.* This is best achieved by focusing on the individual; their achievements and their continuing progress. By focusing on the child during discussion time, practitioners also provide opportunity for child self-assessment. Although Formative Assessment needs to be corrective, failure should not be the focus of feedback, nor should practitioners compare the seemingly better achievements of other peers.

In essence, motivational feedback (focuses on progress and success) is central to effective Formative Assessment and is closely linked to enabling children to be ready, willing and able to learn. Margaret Carr (2001), who has considered assessment in the early years through stories and is also a writer of fiction, delineates these dispositions within the following context: 'being ready is about seeing the self as a participating learner, being willing is recognising that this place is (or is not) a place for learning, and being able is having the abilities and funds of knowledge that will contribute to being ready and being willing' (2001: 23). The ARG (2002) proposes AfL approaches which 'protect the learner's autonomy, provide some choice and constructive feedback, and create opportunities for self-direction' as a means of preserving and enhancing motivation.

REFLECT AND RELATE TO PRACTICE

Having read this section, make a list (for practice) of the ways you could help a three year old child who has just started following the Foundation Stage curriculum to be *ready, willing and able* to learn.

At Key Stage 1, constructive marking and feedback, if used appropriately by teachers, are powerful tools for enabling children to take ownership of their work and move towards self-motivated improvement. This has three core elements:

1 The child is fully aware of the learning objectives.
2 The child is made aware of the extent to which the learning objectives have been achieved.
3 The child knows how to go about achieving the shortfall in the learning objectives.

For young children, however, feedback is usually given by practitioners on a moment-to-moment basis – orally or by the use of coloured stickers, which young children can stick on their clothes or hands. Written feedback is less likely to be employed. For children at Key Stage 1, teachers will probably give feedback both orally and through written comment, with oral feedback providing greater opportunity for child self-assessment. Written comments can be time consuming for the teacher and careful thought needs to be given to the purpose. Feedback is only constructive when children are enabled to act upon it. Shirley Clarke (1998: 70), lecturer in assessment and curriculum at the Institute of Education, University of London, suggests that effective feedback (at Key Stage 1 and beyond) needs:

• to be based on clear learning intentions
• to take account of pupil self-evaluation
• to highlight where success occurred and where improvement could take place
• to be in a form which is accessible to the learner
• to give strategies for improvement
• allocated time in which to take place or be read
• some focused improvement, based on the feedback to take place.

Assessment used to inform planning

Good planning is the key to making children's learning effective, exciting, varied and progressive. Good planning enables practitioners to build up knowledge about how individual children learn and make progress. It also provides opportunities for practitioners to think and talk about how to sustain a successful learning environment.

(QCA, 2001: 2)

Assessment for learning should be part of daily practice within the setting and consequently is central to the planning process. This section considers how, through effective planning, short-, long- and medium-term (when it is employed within the setting), practitioners can incorporate AfL into their teaching and make it a part of their day-to-day practice.

Effective planning, with its focus on the child, teaches the learning goals in all six areas of learning and development (personal, social and emotional development; communication, language and literacy; problem-solving, reasoning and numeracy; knowledge and understanding of the world; physical development; and creative development) with a clear view of where the child should be in terms of knowledge, understanding and skills. For this process the following documents provide valuable guidance: *Foundation Stage Profile Handbook* (QCA, 2003: ch. 2) and *Seeing Steps in Children's Learning* (QCA, 2005a). However, planning in the early years is usually informed by observation. (See Appendix 2 for planning schedule.) Although planning is addressed in Chapter 15, the place of assessment for learning in the planning process is considered here. Assessment for learning should be written into long-, medium- and short-term plans. By incorporating it into planning, it will become part of daily practice, be a more manageable process and reduce practitioners' workload. The following, adapted from an interview with the head of a pre-prep school, reflects the centrality of assessment for learning in the planning process:

> [Assessment for learning is] absolutely fundamental (to planning). It is fundamental that you respond to children's learning needs. They will be diverse. The important thing is staff who know the children well and carefully plan for those needs. I let staff do their own planning; they are very capable. We have weekly and end-of-term meetings [related to planning]. Staff also meet in between to do planning. There is an overview and then they plan individually.

In practice, long- and medium-term plans will include a number of formative assessments (approximately one per term) which can be used as evidence for the Foundation Stage Profile. Plans may not include much more detail than a brief statement reminding the practitioner to carry out a formal observation of certain children, focusing on their level or achievements in a particular area of the curriculum. Plans would indicate that this would be carried out over a period of time to include all children. Short-term plans, however, are different in that, drawn from the long-term plan, they are based on ongoing observational assessment of the children on a day-to-day basis and focus more directly on where the children are in their learning and what you will do to help them progress. On a daily basis you will be collecting evidence of children's learning through both formal and informal interaction with them. Short-term plans, usually developed on a weekly basis, should be flexible enough to take into account daily impromptu happenings which provide new insights into a child's learning. Short-term plans, however, will include prompts indicating to you when to collect evidence about a child's learning, what you are looking for, what questions you might ask the child, how you will ask the question, when you might intervene with a question or a comment, if you will scaffold learning or what you will do to move that child forward in his/her learning. They will also include notes to indicate how you are going to alter your teaching to take into account any new evidence of learning. The following 'What happens in practice?' has been adapted from an interview with the manager of a nursery in York and provides a good example of how assessment for learning can be incorporated into planning for young children (0–2 year olds).

WHAT HAPPENS IN PRACTICE?

Long-term planning is done a year in advance and then broken down by months. Everyone brings their views and observations on a particular topic and we consider if the children have enjoyed it. We are very free in our planning [for this age group]. For example if a child had picked up leaves on their walk to nursery in the morning, and hadn't done that before, we can use that throughout the day.

At the moment we are using *Birth to Three Matters* [with this age group], where assessment is based around observation. Every child has a key person who is responsible for observing him/her. However, we all make observations and once a day, when the babies and young children are having their sleep, we will discuss our observations and consider their progress and what we will do [in relation to their future progress]. In addition we have [related] staff meetings once a month.

REFLECT AND RELATE TO PRACTICE

With the increasing focus on teaching for independent learning, how will this influence the way you address assessment for learning in your short-term planning?

You will need to consider such issues as how you might phrase questions or prompts and your interaction with the child to give more responsibility to the individual child.

Involving children in planning their next steps

This section considers how children can be appropriately involved in planning their learning. It addresses why the curriculum needs to be balanced to cover the teaching and application of skills, concepts and knowledge and why learning objectives should be shared with the children to the extent that they have an awareness, where appropriate, of the goals on which they need to focus.

The last few years have witnessed a shift in classroom practice, particularly in the way children have become involved in their own learning. There is the expectation that practitioners, by making children fully aware of the learning objectives and outcomes of a particular activity/lesson and involving them in planning their next steps, will enhance their learning. In practice how is this achieved? Clarke (2002) suggests that 'balancing the curriculum' to cover both the teaching of skills, concepts and knowledge and their application, 'sharing unit coverage throughout lessons and separating learning objectives from the context of learning' will help children to be more aware of the goals on which they need to focus. Each child is unique and the extent to which an individual has achieved the expected outcomes will determine the next steps in his/her learning. For younger children, the following, adapted from an interview with the head of a pre-prep school, highlights how feedback to children (3–5 year olds) can be used to involve children in this process:

WHAT HAPPENS IN PRACTICE?

A lot [of feedback] is immediate. This age group needs immediate feedback – so for example we might say such things as – is that what you expected? Or could that have been done differently? etc. Feedback needs to happen there and then.

So it's making use of opportunities as they arise. It's facilitating children to make choices and give reasons why. Staff planning is responding to children's needs as they see them.

REFLECT AND RELATE TO PRACTICE

Do you think this is a good example of effective feedback to children? Why/why not? Make a list of all the ways you could give constructive feedback to children (consider 3–5 year olds).

In essence, involving children in planning their learning helps them to take ownership of the work. For the practitioner, this involves guiding the children in their decision-making. It is a time for guided choice, not free choice. Child-initiated activities will lend themselves more easily to this type of child involvement than adult-led activities. That said, there are always opportunities to involve children in 'what next?' The responsibility is with the practitioner to consider how this can be effectively implemented (e.g. constructive questioning). For child-initiated activities, allowing time for the children to plan and discuss their activity in advance will bring greater clarity to their thought process and will provide further opportunity for stimulating ideas. There will be children who do not want to plan; they should be allowed to get on with the task in hand. The High Scope curriculum is founded on this type of activity and is discussed in more detail in Chapter 2.

The following 'What happens in practice?' provides two examples of how practitioners continued to make children aware of the learning objectives during the lesson. In these examples the children generate the ideas.

WHAT HAPPENS IN PRACTICE?

Foundation Stage

[The practitioner] tended to use a flip chart, often producing spider diagrams or clear visual images, and asked questions like what do you know about . . . ?, what would you like to know about . . . ?, how could we find out about . . . ? The main impact was that children's enthusiasm and confidence about the topic was increased.

One reception teacher got the children to make a poster for the coverage for reading and the same for writing for the half-term, asking them what she should draw or write on the poster. She reported that the children often referred to the posters, pointing at them at relevant times and sometimes getting up to look more closely at one of the elements.

(Clarke, 2002: 18)

REFLECT AND RELATE TO PRACTICE

To what extent have these practitioners involved children in planning their next steps?

☆ ☆ ☆

Having read this section, how would you involve children (3–5 year olds and 5–7 year olds) in planning their next steps in learning?

Assessment for learning: bringing it together

Assessment for learning should be central to day-to-day practice. The routine, daily interaction of the early years practitioner with the child provides many opportunities for embedding formative assessment in class room practice. The introduction of the *Statutory Framework for the Early Years Foundation Stage: Setting the Standards for Learning Development and Care for children from birth to five* (EYFS) (DfES, 2007) has put a greater emphasis on outcomes and accountability in educational improvement. Although this is highly positive in many respects, it can be a cause for divided priorities amongst early years practitioners. Many may feel that with a strong focus on the development of the necessary skills – knowledge and understanding to meet educational targets – children's achievement, in what are often referred to as the 'soft skills' (DfES, 2006: 10) – self confidence, self-esteem and other social and emotional skills, is not fully acknowledged. Although recent government educational policy is underpinned by the themes of personalised learning and teaching for independent learning, on the surface it might seem that there is a gap between policy and practice (i.e. the government uses the rhetoric of or associated with the 'softer skills', but in practice promotes a skills and knowledge based, target-driven curriculum). Bertram and Pascal (2002: 88), education specialists at the University of Birmingham, suggest that 'what is easily measurable cannot reflect the immense complexity of early learning'. However, the breadth of the learning goals and educational programmes in the EYFS provide, with effective planning for assessment for learning, the flexibility to address and acknowledge the holistic development of the child.

Connect & Extend

Reflect again on the definition of AfL: 'Assessment for Learning is the process of seeking and interpreting evidence for use by learners and their teachers to decide where the learners are in their learning, where they need to go and how best to get there' (ARG, 2002).

To what extent is AfL a partnership between the learner and the teacher? How should this be managed in practice? You will find the following documents useful: Qualifications and Curriculum Authority (2003) *Foundation Stage Profile Handbook*, London: QCA (available at: **www.qca.org.uk**) and Assessment Reform Group (ARG) (2002), *Assessment for Learning: 10 principles*: ARG (available at: **www.assessment-reform-group.org.uk**).

SUMMARY

Policy to practice (p. 181)

How does Assessment for Learning differ in the early years?

Assessment for Learning (AfL) underpins the government's plan to raise children's achievement. Although AfL is increasingly employed in the early years, it is different from assessment for learning with older children; it is not always possible or appropriate to make children aware of learning objectives prior to an activity in the early years.

Formative assessment based on observations and other evidence of learning (p. 183)

Why is observation central to good classroom/setting practice?

Through ongoing, formal and informal observation, practitioners will get to know the needs of the children within their setting. This is the key to ensuring that teaching is focused on individual learning needs. By considering formative assessment in practice, this section considers how practitioners can effectively integrate the process into teaching and learning.

Involving children in self-assessment and discussion of their learning (p. 189)

Why is it important that practitioners give careful consideration to how they discuss children's work with them?

Providing children with the opportunity to discuss their work provides a means of appropriately rechannelling their thinking. To be of benefit, discussion needs to be given careful thought. This section examines possible ways of discussing children's work with them, in a manner which enhances their learning.

SUMMARY *CONTINUED*

Assessment used to inform planning (p. 191)

Why should assessment for learning be central to the planning process?

Effective planning teaches to the learning goals in all six areas of learning and development, in the light of where each child is – in terms of knowledge, understanding and skills – and where each child should be according to their own developmental needs within the broader external objectives which can be changed, developed or ignored, but will be useful to both the learner and practitioner. Assessment for learning should be written into long-, medium- and short-term plans. By incorporating it into planning, it will become part of daily practice,

be a more manageable process and reduce practitioners' workload.

Involving children in planning their next steps (p. 193)

How do you involve children in planning their learning?

This section considers how children can be appropriately involved in planning their learning. The curriculum should be balanced to cover the teaching and application of skills, concepts and knowledge. Learning objectives should be shared with the children to the extent that they have an awareness, where appropriate, of the goals on which they need to focus.

Glossary

Assessment for Learning: practitioners use the information from setting/classroom observation to involve the children in deciding their learning objectives for all activities and how best they can meet them.

Formative assessment: informs practice, in that practitioners, through observation and other means, find evidence for and evaluate children's learning, using this information to involve the children in deciding their learning objectives and how best they can meet them.

National Strategies: government-driven programme to raise standards across the field of education by providing support to settings and schools.

Observational assessment: practitioners observing and evaluating children's learning, either as a planned observation or as an incidental observation.

Planned 'focused' observation: 'when a practitioner stands back to observe children in independent, child-initiated, play-based activities' (QCA, 2005b: 15).

Summative assessment: a summary of a learner's achievements at a given moment in time (e.g. the result from a written test).

Find out more

Gardner, J. (ed.) (2006) *Assessment and Learning.* **London: Sage Publications.**
Through the contribution of various authors this book addresses assessment across the field of education.

Hutchin, V. (1999) *Right from the start: Effective Planning and Assessment in the Early Years.* **Abingdon: Hodder and Stoughton.**
Provides good guidance to effective assessment in the early years and how this can become part of planning.

Wiliam, D. (2008) *Assessment for Learning: Why, what and how?*
By focusing in particular on the need for the continuing training of teachers/practitioners in the area of effective assessment for learning, this book provides a good insight into assessment for learning, complementing what you have read within this chapter.

References

Assessment Reform Group (ARG) (2002) *Assessment for Learning: 10 Principles*: ARG.

Bertram, T. and Pascal, C. (2002) Assessing what matters in the early years, in Fisher, J. (ed.) *The Foundations of Learning.* Buckingham: Open University Press: pp. 87–101.

Black, P. and Wiliam, D. (1998) *Inside the Black Box: Raising Standards Through Classroom Assessment.* London: nferNelson.

Carr, M. (2001) *Assessment in Early Childhood Settings: Learning Stories.* London: Paul Chapman.

Clarke, S. (1998) *Targeting Assessment in the Primary Classroom.* Abingdon: Hodder and Stoughton.

Clarke, S. (2002) *Formative Assessment in Action: Weaving the Elements Together.* Abingdon: Hodder Murray.

Department for Education and Skills (DfES) (2004) *Excellence and Enjoyment, Assessment for Learning.* Nottingham: DfES Publications.

Department for Education and Skills (DfES) (2006) *2020 Vision: Report of the Teaching and Learning in 2020 Review Group.* Nottingham: DfES Publications.

Department for Education and Skills (DfES) (2007) *Statutory Framework for the Early Years Foundation Stage: Setting the Standards for Learning Development and Care for children from birth to five* (EYFS). Nottingham: DfES Publications.

Drummond, M.J. (2003) *Assessing Children's Learning,* 2nd edn. London: David Fulton.

Drummond, M.J., Rouse, D. and Pugh, G. (1992) *Making Assessment Work: values and principles in assessing young children's learning.* Nottingham: NES Arnold in association with the National Children's Bureau.

Fisher, J. (2002a) *Starting from the Child: Teaching and Learning from 3–8,* 2nd edn. Maidenhead: Open University Press.

Fisher, J. (ed.) (2002b) *The Foundations of Learning.* Buckingham: Open University Press.

Hutchin, V. (2003) *Observing and Assessing for the Foundation Stage Profile.* Abingdon: Hodder and Stoughton.

Overall, L. and Sangster, M. (2006) *Assessment: A Practical Guide for Primary Teachers.* New York: Continuum.

Qualifications and Curriculum Authority (QCA) (2001) *Planning for Learning in the Foundation Stage.* London: QCA.

Qualifications and Curriculum Authority (QCA) (2003) *Foundation Stage Profile Handbook.* London: QCA.

Qualifications and Curriculum Authority (QCA) (2004) *Building a Picture of What a Child can Do.* London: QCA.

Qualifications and Curriculum Authority (QCA) (2005a) *Seeing Steps in Children's Learning.* London, QCA.

Qualifications and Curriculum Authority (QCA) (2005b) *Observing Children: Building the Profile,* London: QCA.

Qualifications and Curriculum Authority (QCA) (2007) *Assessment and Reporting Arrangements: Key Stage 1: Foundation Stage, years 1 and 2.* London: QCA.

Smidt, S. (2005) *Observing, Assessing and Planning for children in the Early Years.* Abingdon: Routledge.

Appendix 1

The following observation schedule, proposed by Hutchin (2003) and cited in *Observing Children: Building the Profile* (QCA, 2005b), can be used for a planned focused assessment in an early years setting.

Child:	Date:	Time:
Observation:	Observer:	

Assessment: what did you find out about the child's learning with regard to any of the following areas of learning? What was significant for the child?

Personal, social and emotional development (DA; SD; ED)

Communication and language (CLT; LSL) and literacy (R and W) (Include, if possible, anything the child said which seems significant as well as your assessment of this.)

Mathematical development (NLC; C; SSM)

Knowledge and understanding of the world

Physical development

Creative development

Child's comment (Try to make an opportunity to ask child about what they were doing, telling them about your observation.)

Planning: What next?

Planning is usually informed by observation in early years. Once you have observed a child/children within a setting you can use the following schedule to plan an activity.

Planning

Plan an activity for four year olds in a nursery setting. You will need to use the *Foundation Stage Profile Handbook* (QCA, 2003: ch. 2) and *Seeing Steps in Children's Learning* (QCA, 2005a). You should use the following as an outline (from the *Foundation Stage Profile Handbook*, QCA, 2003: 98–99).

Activity:

Key scale points:

Curriculum context:

Resources:

Outline of activity: How the activity was introduced – learning objectives/intentions:

Number of children:

Assessment opportunities:

Observations what the children said and did:

10 The Role of the Practitioner in Developing Personalised Learning

By the end of this chapter you will be able to answer the following questions:

- Which government policies direct practitioners to personalised learning?
- What are the underlying concepts of personalised learning?
- What does it mean to challenge and stretch the children in practice?
- How do practitioners address individual needs?
- Why is it important to lead learning and to enhance the development of the child?
- What are described as Additional Educational Needs?
- How does assessment operate within the framework of personalised learning?
- What is the role of the practitioner in an early years setting?

This chapter will support your understanding of the following Standards *(see Appendix 1)*:
- **Knowledge and understanding:** S01 ■ **Effective practice:** S07, S08, S10, S12, S13, S14 and S22
- **Relationships with children:** S26 and S27.

Introduction

Put simply, personalising learning and teaching means taking a highly structured and responsive approach to each child's and young person's learning, in order that all are able to progress, achieve and participate. It means strengthening the link between learning and teaching by engaging children – and their parents – as partners in learning.

(DfES, 2006: 6)

Child-centred pedagogy: teaching which focuses on the child's cognitive and affective learning needs.

Personalised learning: the adaptation of teaching and the curriculum to meet the learning needs of the individual child.

Assessment for learning: the involvement of the child in his/her learning.

Government policy, as developed in their recent document, *2020 Vision: Report of the Teaching and Learning in 2020 Review Group* (DfES, 2006) and the *Statutory Framework for the Early Years Foundation Stage: Setting the Standards for Learning Development and Care for children from birth to five* (EYFS) (DfES, 2007), presents a new framework for a **child-centred pedagogy**, founded on the holistic development of the individual. **Personalised learning, assessment for learning**, partnership working and the continuing professional development of practitioners which are the cornerstones of the government's agenda for change in education. Within this framework, the work of the early years practitioner is developed and sustained within a wide spectrum, where practice develops in response to the changing demands of the role. In essence, it means developing effective teaching techniques within the following broad framework:

- providing appropriate support and care which enhances the development of each child
- having positive attitudes towards diversity and difference
- developing positive attitudes towards diversity and difference in the child
- removing barriers to learning, achieving and participating
- stretching and challenging all children
- creating and developing partnerships
- closing the gap between learning and care
- enabling children to develop a love for learning
- enabling children to become lifelong learners
- planning for personalised learning, through ongoing observation and assessment
- adapting quickly to individual learning needs
- promoting children's health, safety and well-being
- managing children's behaviour
- giving consideration to children's social and emotional development (which can include spiritual, moral and cultural aspects)
- communicating and engaging with children in an effective and appropriate manner
- sharing information
- taking responsibility for continuing professional development.

Through case studies and practical worked examples this chapter will consider the role of the early years practitioner within the government's framework of personalised learning, where assessment, working in partnership with the child and continuing professional development all have a central part to play in contributing to its effectiveness in practice.

Empowering children for learning

Enabling children to take ownership of their learning is key to participation, learning and achievement. In essence, practitioners need to promote positive attitudes to learning, helping children to develop the necessary confidence and competence to be proactive participants in their learning. This section considers, through examples of good practice, how this can be addressed within the setting.

The government document *2020 Vision* emphasises the importance of 'instilling in all children and young people the belief that they can succeed' (DfES, 2006: 41). This supports Whitehead's (2003) idea of 'empowering' children. Children, he suggests, learn best when they feel in control: 'The feeling of empowerment is fundamental to children developing positive attitudes to themselves, and particularly to themselves as learners' (2003: 8). The government endorses and promotes personalised learning as an effective means of taking a more 'structured and responsive' approach to each child's learning. The government's emphasis is on *engaging* children and enabling them to 'develop the knowledge, skills, understanding and attitudes they need to thrive throughout their lives'. The way practitioners engage with a child or when they engage convey powerful messages within the child's world.

Shirley Clarke (2003: 85), a lecturer in assessment and curriculum at the Institute of Education, University of London, citing the Gillingham project, a study carried out in 2001 where 15 primary schools participated in formative assessment, provides common examples of child–practitioner engagement. In her example Clarke highlights the centrality of 'creating the right climate for feedback' in a one-to-one situation. She gives the following as a typical example of a reception class teacher:

Photo 10.1
Communicating with babies, through eye contact and by talking to them, enhances their development

Pearson Education Ltd. Jules Selmes © Pearson Education Limited 2004

When teachers opened with 'Now remember you did this wonderful drawing' and shared it with the child, they set the scene for a positive episode for children. Then children made a number of contributions to the dialogue. In contrast opening with 'Show this to me', 'What have you drawn?', 'Can you remember what we are doing this work for?' seemed like the onset of an assessment and children were noticeably more reticent.

(Clarke, 2003: 85)

By identifying the strengths, the practitioner/teacher has immediately created a positive situation, enabling the child to participate in ongoing dialogue. The following Case study provides further examples where children's learning has been supported within early years settings.

CASE STUDY

Babies

We use every opportunity to enable the babies to make close eye contact, looking at and sometimes touching each others' faces and ours. We sometimes lie on the floor with babies so that they can see and touch and talk with us easily. We constantly use their names to them and to the other babies.

Toddlers

Observation: Two boys who are brothers (one is three and the other four) are arguing over a toy car. They begin to fight. A member of staff kneels between the boys and talks to them quietly. She listens to the boys and one relinquishes the car to the other. He is praised for giving up the car.

The same two boys later fight again. The older tells an observer that he 'hates' his brother. A member of staff intervenes. She kneels in front of the older boy. She makes eye contact and talks quietly. She says that she understands that he is feeling cross with his brother but that he shouldn't say that he 'hates'

him. After talking to the older boy, the two are encouraged to make up. The younger extends his arms to hug the older (who declines) but the two now play together with toy cars and a garage. The member of staff sits near to them on the floor and lets them play together. She responds to their questions when they turn to speak to her but she does not interrupt them.

Older children

Observation: M [staff member] sat on a low sofa to welcome her group at the beginning of the session. Next to the sofa is a display entitled 'Growing'. The display includes a low table on which is placed a butterfly growing tent and a fish tank with some tadpoles inside. Next to the fish tank are toy frogs and toy cocoons. A couple of story books are placed on the table, one of which is *The Very Hungry Caterpillar*. One child and his mum look at the display and they talk with M about what is there. The boy (aged 4 years) is interested in the tadpoles. M gives him a magnifying glass and encourages him to look through it. They talk about what he can see, involving his Mum in the discussion.

Once the parents have left and the children are playing, one boy (3 years) sits down next to M with the *Very Hungry Caterpillar* book and asks her to read it to him. M and the boy hold the book together and look at the title words and the cover picture. M reads the words, pointing to them as she reads. She says she remembers reading the story when she was a little girl. The boy repeats the book title. They open the book together. The boy turns the page with excitement. M reads the story and together they discuss the pictures. M waits patiently for the boy as he struggles to 'weave' a toy caterpillar through holes in the book. Sometimes she helps him when the caterpillar gets stuck in the holes. Together they count the pieces of food the caterpillar eats each day and M asks the boy to identify the food. They discuss their preferences. As they reach the end of the story two older girls (aged 4) arrive and squeeze onto the sofa. They ask M to read the story to them. M begins again. Once again they look at and discuss the pictures and story. M asks the girls to count the food themselves which they do. M asks the girls questions about the story and about the food. They talk about how the caterpillar has changed. The girls agree that the butterfly looks completely different from the caterpillar. M reaches for a toy cocoon from the display and they look at this, discussing the transformation from caterpillar to butterfly.

(Goouch and Powell, 2006)

REFLECT AND RELATE TO PRACTICE

For each of the three Case studies list the nature and type of practitioner intervention. Consider the definition of personalised learning given at the beginning of this chapter. Which of the practitioner interventions you have listed would you consider to be examples of personalised learning?

☆ ☆ ☆

Having read the Case study, make a list of the practitioner interventions which you consider to be examples of personalised learning? Why do you think they exemplify personalised learning? For each one consider: Did the intervention help to 'empower' the child? Did it help to engage the child? Did it help the child to take ownership of the work? Do you think these interventions positively supported the child's learning? As an early years practitioner how would you have responded to the children in each of these Case studies?

Enabling children to progress and helping them to feel that they are progressing means paying close attention to the holistic development of the child. Many of the factors which contribute to this are not evident in the formal curriculum, but are to be found in both the formal and informal way a practitioner communicates with the child. Cheminais (2006) considers this within the following personalised learning framework, which has been adapted for an early years setting:

- Enable the child to know that you have high expectations because you know he/she can achieve.
- Start from the child – build on his/her knowledge, interests and aptitudes.
- Plan for learning – develop a repertoire of strategies, pacing the learning experience to make it challenging and enjoyable for each child.
- Involve children in their own learning – share objectives and feedback.
- Inspire children – enable them to see/experience your passion for learning.
- Enable children to become confident, co-operative learners.
- Consider progression – enable children to develop the skills they will need beyond the setting.

(adapted from Cheminais, 2006: 42)

Stretch and challenge

Various learning and teaching strategies have long been associated with challenging and stretching children, namely, questioning or the development of thinking skills through purposeful reflection. In practice it means having a structured, well thought out approach to each child's learning needs. In essence, it means knowing each child, supporting each child in his/her learning and starting from where he/she is. This section will consider, primarily through research evidence and case studies, the type of approach practitioners should employ when planning appropriately challenging learning experiences for children within their setting.

Challenge:
a difficult task
which stimulates
interest or
encourages
effort.

The word **challenge** is often used in educational circles, with little recourse to what it means in practice. The Chambers (1983) dictionary defines it as 'a difficulty which stimulates interest or effort; a task, undertaking; to test one's powers and capabilities to the full'. Although this definition provides some insight into the 'practice' of 'challenge', it still leaves much open to interpretation and the initiative of the practitioner. In practice stretching and challenging children is dependent on their individual capabilities and the practitioner's judgement of their capabilities. Consideration should be given to the way in which children are challenged – a perceived 'challenge' for one child may raise achievement, but may hinder progress for another. It requires careful thought both in planning for learning and on a moment-by-moment basis when supporting children in their learning experiences. In practice, it will entail finding a balance between helping children to engage fully with an activity and developing the skills and confidence to think through problems and find possible solutions and knowing when to intervene with appropriate support.

The government document, *Curriculum Guidance for the Foundation Stage* (QCA, 2000), underlines the centrality of employing activities which interest the children as a means of stretching their thinking. Using activities familiar to the children, that is, within their 'comfort' zone, often heightens their interest and provides a firm foundation from which more challenging learning experiences can be developed. For example, role play or stories can be presented at a level which demands more of the child, but will still be within their capabilities (QCA, 2000: 22). Developing routine practices, repeated at the same time each day, can also add to the children's feeling of security and provide further opportunity for introducing short activities, discussions or questioning which can help to stretch or challenge children to move beyond their current level. Engaging children in dialogue about their work, their enjoyment of an activity or what they feel they have achieved from an activity provides opportunity not only for reinforcing their learning, but for developing their communication and social skills. Through questioning – for example, if you had more time what would you have done next or why do you think that happened? – practitioners can help children to think more deeply about their learning experiences and enhance their skills, knowledge and/or understanding.

This is also supported by the results from both the *Effective Provision of Pre-School Education* (EPPE) study and *Researching Effective Pedagogy in the Early Years* (REPEY) study. Documented by Sylva et al. (2007: 58), they suggest that practitioners working in 'good quality' early years settings 'focus more on challenging activities, take an active role in teaching through pedagogical practices which include scaffolding children's learning through play, modelling activities/interactions and questioning'. The results further highlighted the benefits of a 'thoughtful, structured approach to everyday activities', which lead to better 'cognitive and linguistic outcomes for children'. Consider the following Case study which contrasts the case of two learners in a nursery setting, both aged 3 years but with differing abilities:

CASE STUDY

Natalie was . . . physically well developed. She . . . resisted any help when offered. She was a confident user of the nursery environment. She selected a broad range of opportunities for herself . . . She particularly enjoyed using the telephone. She could often be seen . . . having a lengthy and usually very loud conversation. . . . Natalie's language consisted of one or two recognisable words and a considerable amount of babble of the kind most usually associated with children of a younger age. She could imitate the intonation patterns. But when trying to communicate with adults or other children in the nursery, she became very frustrated because she was unable to express anything other than very basic needs in a way that others could understand. This was . . . difficult for her because she was . . . a sociable child.

Occasionally her frustration led to severe temper tantrums.

John was a quiet, gentle, articulate child. He was . . . not confident in making use of the nursery environment. He sometimes seemed nervous of other children . . . and was unable to stand his ground if another child challenged him for a piece of equipment. In these situations he would let the other child have the toy and move quickly away . . . Most of all he liked to look at books, preferably with an adult. John could read simple repetitive stories and was interested in discussing the words in books. There were one or two children in the group who John enjoyed playing imaginative games with, but he was always watchful of those other children he seemed to consider to be a threat.

(Edgington, 1998: 58–59)

REFLECT AND RELATE TO PRACTICE

Consider each of the children in the above Case study. List the skills, knowledge and/or understandings which they have attained. What areas of their learning are weak? For each child select one of the areas you consider to be weak and consider how, in practice, you would help them to develop in that area.

How would you stretch and challenge each of these children to enhance their learning and enable them to progress?

To date, there is scant research evidence from the field of 'successful practice' in early years and even less in relation to good practice in terms of appropriately stretching and challenging all children according to their needs and ability level. However, there are various approaches, widely acknowledged as good practice and commonly found across settings. Siraj-Blatchford (2004: 141) commenting on pedagogical aspects of the following models of exemplary practice – Developmentally Appropriate Practice (DAP), High/Scope (USA), Reggio Emilia (Italy), Movimento da Escola Moderna (MEM) (Portugal), Te Whariki (New Zealand) and Quality in Diversity (UK) – highlights the use of 'pedagogic instructional techniques, the encouragement of affective involvement and the encouragement of cognitive engagement or co construction' as features common to all the models and of central importance in early years learning. Table 10.1 provides a brief summary of the more commonly cited of these models of exemplary practice.

Connect & Extend

Look up each of these models (see Table 10.1 for references) and consider what techniques are employed or promoted by each one to stretch and challenge children. Would you employ these techniques? Why/why not?

In England and Wales the introduction of the early years Foundation Stage (EYFS) curriculum (DfES, 2007) reaffirmed the government's intention of closing the gap between education and care. Although the idea of an outcomes based curriculum for young children remains a contested area, there are many who support it, arguing that it provides clear guidance for practice. The government's educational programme, driven by demographic, social, economic, environmental and technological change, is underpinned by the increasing need for all nation states to be active competitors in the global market. In England, the overarching aim is for a quality early years provision, which reduces the gap between education and care and brings together the educational and developmental aspects of both areas of practice. The EYFS (DfES, 2007: 7) acknowledges the government's commitment to consistency and raising standards across the early years. The expectation is that through a single framework, practitioners will be able to 'plan for effective care, learning and development' which will ensure a 'consistent approach from birth to the end of the Foundation Stage' (DfES, 2006: 54) (i.e. at the end of the reception year).

Table 10.1 Early years models of exemplary practice

Developmentally Appropriate Practice (DAP) grew out of the early twentieth century child study movement in America, developed by G. Stanley Hall, the first American to obtain a doctorate in psychology (Follari, 2007: 28). The emphasis is on the development of an appropriate curriculum through observation of the child and a consideration of their developmental stage (see Kostelnik et al., 2006; NAEYC, 2008; the NAEYC was established in the USA in 1926 to promote the well-being of young children).

The High/Scope (USA) curriculum developed in the 1960s in response to the educational needs of young children in deprived areas. It is based on the idea that, through practitioner/parent support, children can plan their own work, do their own work and review it (known as plan–do–review) (see Holt, 2007).

Reggio Emilia (Italy): in response to the atrocities of the Second World War, parents in the little town of Reggio Emilia in Italy grouped together to start a pre-school for their children. From simple beginnings in 1945, the idea has been widely modelled. Based on the following principles (Follari, 2007: 198), there is a strong emphasis on the creation of an attractive learning environment:

* children's rights and capabilities
* collaboration among all members of the school community
* relationships among children, teachers, families, experiences and materials.

(See Abbott and Nutbrown, 2001; Thornton and Brunton, 2007.)

Movimento da escola moderna (MEM – the modern school movement) (Portugal): MEM developed in Portugal in the 1960s as a movement for teachers and educators during the dictatorship. Inspired by Celestin Freinet, the French pedagogue, it is founded on the principles of co-operation, communication and participation. Since 1974 and the beginning of democratic rule in Portugal, the movement has been influential in the formation of early years and primary education policy. (You can find out more about this movement through the following website: **www.movimentoescolamoderna.pt/**.)

Te Whariki (New Zealand) is the early years national curriculum, a requirement for early childhood services since 1998. It is based on principles (empowerment, family and community, holistic development and relationships), strands (well-being, belonging, contribution, communication and exploration) and goals which weave the strands and the principles together to give clear guidance to both learners and practitioners. There is a strong focus on the affective development of the child. (See the International Review of Curriculum and Assessment Frameworks Internet Archive, founded by the Qualifications and Curriculum Authority (QCA) in England to provide information on education policy (including curriculum details) in a number of countries, available at: **www.inca.org.uk**.)

Meeting individual needs

The nature of learning and teaching is changing – practitioners are being encouraged to design a curriculum to meet the individual needs of the learner within the context of national requirements. Despite the changes in approach, the social dimensions of the setting remain unchanged, i.e. the daily interaction of the children, practitioners and parents. By addressing the fundamental aims of teaching, this section will help you to consider the values-led purpose of education and care.

Individual learning can place the practitioner at the centre not of a single model, but 20 to 30 models of learning, depending on the number of children within the setting. To design a curriculum that responds to individual learning needs requires detailed knowledge of the subject matter and a clear understanding of the pedagogy required. It is important not to lose the familiar structure of the curriculum and learning environment that takes the learner through repeated patterns. However, through the five outcomes of *Every Child Matters*, early years settings can accommodate the broader, more varied curriculum that includes the academic, social and emotional needs of individuals. In this way, there is every opportunity that the learner will achieve.

DISCUSSION POINT

The idea of an outcomes-led, National Curriculum for the early years is a contested issue amongst practitioners, educationalists and academics. Some argue that it overlooks the importance of play and the strong affective dimension of children's development, while others argue that early years education needs the focus of a subject-based, outcomes-led curriculum and that the EYFS provides a good framework for practice. What is your view? You will need to look up the EYFS (DfES, 2007: 7).

Affective dimension: this relates to the emotional development of children and their ability to control their emotions.

The social element of educational settings that prepares learners for society remains a constant throughout periods of change. Settings can provide the opportunities for children to interact. Irrespective of curriculum content or style of delivery, there is an ethical, values-led purpose to education. What happens in an educational setting should enhance the capacities of children to learn and their motivation to learn. If this happens, children succeed and are initiated in lifelong learning for their own development. In essence, the characteristics of effective learning are to encourage children to:

Heuristic play: the term used to describe how children learn through exploration.

- be questioning and challenging (e.g. to ask why something happens/to think of alternative solutions to problems/to question why something worked/did not work)
- make connections and see relationships (e.g. **heuristic play** (discovery through exploration), with children of 18 months – by letting them select everyday objects from a basket and explore what they are used for)

- envisage what might be (help children to be creative, not only in art or music, but in their problem-solving and day-to-day activities. Ask children what they think will happen and why.)
- explore ideas (e.g. through a science activity – young children like to experiment with water)
- reflect on ideas, actions and outcomes (e.g. children can be helped to develop social skills through stories or role play of real life situations – love, bullying or helping others – which are followed by questions relating to why something happened and would they do the same thing, was it wrong/right or how would they have reacted and why? etc.).

The Curriculum

The National Curriculum acts as a guide and can provide a firm foundation for developing a learning programme to meet the needs of all children. This section examines how, through planning which considers the holistic development of the child, practitioners can effectively develop personalised learning in the setting.

A practitioner will be a skilled leader of a unique environment and a conductor of learning. It is fundamental that practitioners should have the ability to plan, select and arrange activities. Rosemary Rodger (2003: 24), an educational consultant and primary registered inspector of schools, suggests that what matters is the 'appropriateness of the experiences on offer to children'. Planning appropriate activities for children is the central skill of teaching. When considering the appropriateness of the curriculum, it is important for the practitioner to be able to predict children's responses and pace of work. Educators need to be consistent, particularly in having specific expectations of the children within their setting. Within the curriculum framework a practitioner will be alert to the contents and the extended curriculum and be able to select areas which can be used to stretch or challenge children when necessary.

Leading learning

The style of setting leadership, curriculum and child behaviour all have a direct relationship on child learning. The successful management of the curriculum – planning, delivery, monitoring and evaluation – is vital for ensuring a positive response from all children. The essential ingredients of the curriculum and teaching styles are all relevant to an early years setting.

In an early years setting, the management of the curriculum will be negotiated. Practitioners should not feel pressured into teaching material with which they are uncomfortable. Children need to be excited by the curriculum, and it is essential that educators do not become bored by a repetitive curriculum that lacks direction and cohesion. A creative approach to teaching should be tempered by the need for children to learn. Children need to be stimulated by the curriculum and not just learn to sit still. Successive 'lessons' involving similar activities will contribute to behaviour problems. Curriculum problems, in content or delivery, need to be managed collaboratively; curriculum planners need to understand that there are children who do not learn as expected and that they need special interventions. The meaning and application of support will need to be understood by practitioners in order that it becomes an effective curriculum tool to aid children with identified learning and/or behavioural problems. Methods for motivating children, remediation and special support need to be developed, implemented, monitored and evaluated. Collaboration is the key to curriculum management. Rodger (2003: 28) offers the following framework for 'working towards good practice in the reception class':

- Split the elements of the literacy and numeracy strategies and teach throughout the day.
- Give a high priority to personal, social and emotional development, communication, language and literacy and mathematical development.
- Always include the classroom assistant or nursery nurse in focused teaching activities.
- Nursery class and reception class may be combined in an early years unit.
- Do not differentiate between work and play.
- Include planned opportunities for learning in the outdoor environment for all areas of learning.
- Identify a specific learning intention in your planning for adult-focused activities and indicate the role of adults on your plans.
- Check how often you expect your children to sit all together on the carpet.
- What strategies have you introduced to involve parents?

Photo 10.2
Why are outdoor activities important in the context of personalised learning?

Pearson Education Ltd. Jules Selmes © Pearson Education Ltd. 2004

DISCUSSION POINT

Look up and consider the EYFS. Do you agree with Rodger? Would you add/remove anything from this list for a reception class? Make your own (general) framework for 'good practice' in terms of curriculum planning and implementation.

You can do this activity for 0–2 year olds, 3–5 year olds and/or 5–7 year olds. For 5–7 year olds, you will need to look up the National Curriculum Key Stage 1.

Enhancing the development of the child: creating independent learners

Practitioners would undoubtedly agree that helping each child to achieve his/her full potential should be at the centre of any teaching endeavour. How this is achieved in practice is largely dependent on the skilled, timely and appropriate intervention of practitioners. By considering some of the underlying issues, this section will address the idea of 'appropriate intervention' in practice.

To achieve their full potential, children need to be appropriately supported in an environment which nurtures individual talent. Although it is widely acknowledged that supporting children's learning promotes and enhances their development, there is no general consensus as to how or when the practitioner should intervene. At the same time, however, Drake (2005: 3) highlights the relevance of both 'timing and nature of adult interventions' to the 'quality' of the child's learning experience. For the practitioner this is perhaps one of the most challenging areas of teaching. Policy documents promote the idea of developing **independent learners** (this is discussed more fully in Chapter 15). Although this does not mean leaving children to manage their own learning, it does mean knowing when to initiate or direct learning, when to prompt or intervene and when to remain on the outside of the child's world. The following Discussion point, taken from an observation made by Edgington (1998: 172–173), provides a good example of subtle support in an early years setting. In addition it underlines the need for a suitably trained early years workforce.

Independent learner:
a learner who has the belief in him/herself to think through learning activities, problems or challenges, make decisions about his/her learning and act upon those decisions.

DISCUSSION POINT

A secondary trained teacher, who had returned to teaching after a career break and had been placed in a nursery without the benefit of any retraining, commented to her colleagues that she thought the nursery must be very boring for children. She felt that, because the staff had created a learning environment

▶

where everything had a definite place and where children could operate autonomously, children would get bored because the rooms always looked essentially the same. This view took no account of the fact that the experienced staff adapted the learning environment in subtle ways in response to their observations, or of the fact children were using the environment very confidently and with ever developing competence. A colleague asked her 'Do you think the children look bored?' After thinking for a moment she said: 'no they always look very busy and involved. But I would be bored if I was them.'

(Edgington, 1998: 172–173)

What do you think?

Having read this research brief, what were your thoughts on the continuing professional development of practitioners? The secondary trained teacher was bored. Why was she bored? What strategies/measures had the staff taken in this early years setting to support the children's learning? What sort of approach to teaching/supporting children might the secondary trained teacher have taken?

The EYFS (DfES, 2007) emphasises the importance of creating *enabling environments* – both physically and emotionally. It further underlines the need for the early years practitioner to 'get to know' each child within his/her care. Observing children formally and informally allows the practitioner to plan accordingly for both the type of support and the extent of support required by the individual child.

Drake (2005: 4) advocates the following when considering how best to support children; ultimately, however, it will depend on both the individual child and the personal attributes of the practitioner:

- Praise children's attempts and achievements.
- Listen to, and share information with parents and carers.
- Be prepared to support children's ideas and interests by adding resources to areas of provision or by planning an appropriate focus.
- Set high but realistic expectations. Make sure that your expectations are always appropriate to the child's stage of development and are rooted in observation-based assessments.
- Encourage children to be independent. Support them in making choices and decisions.

- Use questioning to challenge children's thinking and extend their learning. Use open-ended questions, for example: What will happen if . . . ? Why did you . . . ? How can we . . . ?
- Recognise when not to intervene in children's play.
- Acknowledge that children sometimes need time to observe before they are ready to join in.

Additional educational needs

In practice, it is important not only to recognise a child's specific pedagogical needs, but also to respond constructively to those needs. This section provides a summary of the common problems or difficulties with which children may present in an early years setting and shows how, through practitioner reflection (individually or in teams), appropriate interventions can minimise or at best remove children's barriers to learning.

The following are the more common types of additional educational needs which may arise in an early years setting. Tables 10.2–10.4 provide advice on how, as a practitioner, you can both recognise a child's specific pedagogical needs and respond to them.

Table 10.2 Behavioural, social and emotional difficulties	
General symptom	• Difficulty concentrating • Distracting peers • Inattentiveness • Disregard for practitioner/peers • Being subjected to/instigating bullying • Fighting • Lack of self-esteem
Suggestions for inclusive and effective setting management	• Assign a mentor (in a nursery setting: key worker; in a primary school: TA, Teaching Assistant) • Set achievable tasks to raise self-esteem • Liaise with the SENCO, Special Educational Needs Coordinator (if available), and, if required, parents to understand child's needs • With keyworker/TA (as appropriate) devise a weekly diary to co-ordinate their tasks, progress, goals and misdemeanours • Plan for their learning – collaborate with the SENCO/TA/key worker (as appropriate)

Table 10.3 Speech, language and communication difficulties

General symptom	• Difficulty with word and sentence formation – oral and written • Comprehension difficulties • Problems with expressing thoughts • Difficulty concentrating, understanding and staying on task • Reading difficulties (4–7 year olds) • Easily distracted • Impaired spatial awareness • Low self-esteem
Suggestions for inclusive and effective setting management	• Simplify tasks and ensure that instructions are clear (make them available orally, visually and in writing as appropriate) • Use sign language communication aids such as British Sign Language, Makaton, Picture Exchange Communication System and electronic aids • If needed, obtain input and support from a speech and language therapist • Plan for their learning – collaborate with the SENCO/TA/key worker (as appropriate)

Edgington (1998: 76) highlights the advantage for early years settings where there is a bilingual member of staff. However, she advocates the following for all settings, where she advises that practitioners should put themselves in the place of a person who is learning English as an additional language:

• How do families know how to apply for a place?
• How welcoming is the setting?
• How effectively is information communicated (parents to staff as well as staff to parents)?

It is important for practitioners to address these issues collectively within the setting, along with the ways they communicate with parents and children. This can help to illuminate values and attitudes amongst staff and provides opportunity for considering the extent to which the ethos of the setting is supportive of and includes all learners. When determining practitioner and team views in relation to inclusion, the following reflect and relate to practice (after Table 10.4) provides a useful framework.

Table 10.4 English as an additional language (EAL)

General symptom	Children from families that do not speak English at home and need assistance in accessing services and support. The following are basic indicators of children with EAL: • Slow to speak English • Difficulty staying on task • Isolation from peer group • Difficulties with most subjects • Subjected to and/or instigator of bullying • Behavioural, emotional and social difficulties
Suggestions for inclusive and effective setting management	If the child has 'asylum seeker' or refugee status, your setting leader will have made contact with the Ethnic Minority Achievement Service and located the child's named support worker. This is a Service that works with pupils to tackle underachievement in minority groups • Use multi-sensory teaching approaches (e.g. signs and symbols, visual materials, audio and ICT) to support the child's understanding and subsequent communication with practitioner and peer group • Praise efforts and successes for the child • Be gentle in any necessary disapproval • Build upon the child's previous knowledge and interests • Keep a log of the child's language and communication development • Plan for their learning – collaborate with the SENCO/TA/key worker (as appropriate)

REFLECT AND RELATE TO PRACTICE

• Do I include all my learners?
• How do I/should I support all my learners?
• How do I make my teaching productive for all my learners?
• How do I make my early years setting a just setting? (e.g. do I treat all learners with the same respect/equally? Do I help children to respect each other, irrespective of differences?)

Assessment: personalised learning through ongoing observation and assessment

Before completing this journey through personalised learning in practice it is appropriate to consider the place of Assessment for Learning. In essence, assessment for learning involves practitioners using the information from setting/classroom observation, to involve the children in deciding their learning objectives and how best they can meet them. Although AfL is discussed in Chapter 9, this section provides an overall summary of what it means in the context of personalised learning.

In recent years there have been many debates focusing on assessment and reporting issues in education (see Chapter 9). Prompted by research, most notably that of Black and Wiliam (1998), which addressed raising standards through classroom assessment, there has been a move away from assessment of learning towards assessment for learning (Ofsted, 2003: 1). The Assessment Reform Group (2002) define assessment for learning as: 'The process of seeking and interpreting evidence for use by learners and their teachers to decide where the learners are in their learning, where they need to go and how best to get there.' They recommend that assessment for learning should:

- be part of effective planning for teaching and learning
- focus on how children learn
- be recognised as central to practice
- be regarded as a key professional skill for practitioners
- be sensitive and constructive because any assessment has an emotional impact
- take account of the importance of learner motivation
- promote commitment to learning goals and a shared understanding of the criteria by which children will be assessed (for young children it may not be appropriate to to share/make known the criteria for assessment)
- provide constructive guidance for learners about how to improve
- develop learners' capacity for self-assessment and recognising their next steps and how to take them (for young children self-assessment and/or recognition (child) of next steps is not always appropriate)
- recognise the full range of achievement of all learners.

Ofsted (2003), in response to advice from the Qualifications and Curriculum Authority (QCA), underline the centrality of the practitioner for the effective implementation of assessment for learning. The skills, knowledge and understanding of practitioners will have a direct bearing on raising standards. Ofsted (2003) highlight the following benefits of a skilled workforce which leads to improved outcomes for children:

- improved focus on the quality of teaching and learning
- greater clarity of objectives and expectations in the classroom/setting
- clearer understanding of national standards
- greater consistency and rigour in the assessment process
- improved understanding among children of how they can learn most effectively
- better appreciation among parents of how they may support their children's learning.

It is important in early years settings that there is a shared understanding of what is to be assessed and by what criteria. Brook (2003: 103) suggests that when 'writing' assessment into planning, it should include the *aims* and *objectives* of the assessment. She cites the example of planning for children to be able to discuss their work and the consequent need for the practitioner to plan for time to listen to them. Practitioners need to have a good understanding of both curriculum levels and child development. Although regular assessment may be for the purposes of improving children's learning on a day-to-day basis, the process of building up evidence of their attainments over the course of a longer period is fundamental to good practice and a statutory requirement since the introduction of the Foundation Stage Profile (QCA, 2003) – the statutory **summative assessment** for all children at the end of the Foundation Stage (i.e. at end of the reception class year). In practice, the fundamental principles of assessment are:

Summative assessment: a summary of a learner's achievements at a given moment in time.

- assessment over each setting/key stage
- integrating assessment, teaching and learning
- drawing on evidence from
  - ongoing setting work
  - observation
  - homework (more appropriate for KS1)
  - written work (more appropriate for 3–5 year olds and 5–7 year olds)
- record keeping
- retaining evidence
- setting policy on assessment.

The following Case study documents Brook's (2003: 103) experience of observing children in a number of Reggio Emilia settings in Italy. The Reggio Emilia system places an emphasis on art education.

CASE STUDY

Each school has an art teacher and an atelier, where the children can choose to spend time working with different materials, and they are allowed to make decisions concerning their own activities and materials. They will often spend long periods working through their ideas, observed and supported (as necessary) by the art teacher. The emphasis is placed on the children's first-hand experiences, and art is described as one of the languages of children – a particularly important means of expression for those who are not yet reading and writing. Art is considered one of the ways in which children learn, one of the expressions they can give to their growing understanding of the planned school experience.

REFLECT AND RELATE TO PRACTICE

Consider the above Case study. In planning for this type of activity, what would you have considered in relation to assessing the children's progress?

You should consider that the children make decisions relating to their work, that they work through their ideas, that art is a vehicle for self-expression and how you will support them/question them/discuss their work.

☆ ☆ ☆

How would you assess children's progress in this type of activity?

You should consider the following:

- planning for assessment (what will you look for, how will you support/question the children and discuss their work with them?)
- can marking and feedback be made purposeful and useful for assessment?
- can previous experience be shared between practitioners?
- how can the breadth of child achievement be celebrated, recorded and supported by evidence?
- what mechanisms can be set up to use the same work as evidence to support assessment in more than one area?
- how could I make records accessible/useful to parents and children?

The role of the practitioner in developing personalised learning: bringing it together

For the early years practitioner, the personalisation of learning, within the government's framework for education as discussed in this chapter, presents new challenges and at the same time demands new ways of thinking. However, a closer examination of the role of the practitioner in an early years setting can bring greater focus to personalised teaching and learning in practice. By considering teaching within the context of pedagogy, Siraj-Blatchford (2004) and Sylva et al. (2007) provide a broad overview of the principles supporting personalised learning in practice. Siraj-Blatchford (2004: 138) suggests that pedadgoy is an 'interactive process between teacher and learner and the learning environment', which also includes the wider environment of the child. Sylva et al. (2007) define pedagogy for the purpose of their paper 'Curricular quality and day-to-day learning activities in pre-school', which draws on results from the *Effective Provision of Pre-School Education* (EPPE) study and *Researching Effective Pedagogy in the Early Years* (REPEY) study. They define it as 'the practice [of art/science/craft] and creation of a stimulating environment for play and exploration in which children will learn without adult guidance' (Sylva et al., 2007: 53). Citing Siraj-Blatchford et al. (2002) they suggest that pedagogy within this context requires careful planning 'rather than merely reacting to spontaneous activities in an unthought-of or ad hoc manner'

(Sylva et al., 2007: 54). What is clear from these definitions is that effective person-alised learning is dependent on the timely and appropriate interventions of skilled, knowledgeable practitioners, with a good understanding of children's development and learning.

DISCUSSION POINT

Consider the four cornerstones of the government's agenda for change in education, mentioned at the beginning of the chapter – personalised learning, assessment for learning, partnership working and the continuing professional development of practitioners.

Having read the chapter, what do they mean to you? How will they shape your practice as an early years practitioner? (you should start by defining each of the four terms)

SUMMARY

Empowering children for learning (p. 203)

How can an early years practitioner effectively involve children in their learning?

Enabling children to take ownership of their learning is key to participation, learning and achievement. The way practitioners engage with a child or when they engage conveys powerful messages within the child's world. In essence, practitioners should build on what a child knows, have high expectations of their ability as learners and involve them in their own learning.

Stretch and challenge (p. 206)

What are the key issues in stretching and challenging children?

Although various teaching strategies have long been associated with challenging the child, namely, questioning or developing thinking skills in children, in practice it means knowing each child, supporting each child in his/her learning and starting from where he/she is.

Meeting individual needs (p. 210)

What do we mean by the centrality of the practitioner?

To devise a curriculum that responds to individual learning needs requires detailed knowledge of the subject matter and a clear understanding of the pedagogy required. Good practice means encouraging children to be questioning and challenging, make connections and see relationships, envisage what might be, explore ideas and reflect on ideas, actions and outcomes.

The Curriculum (p. 211)

What are the key issues in developing a stimulating curriculum for an early years setting?

A well-planned curriculum with relevant activities will be challenging, rewarding and appropriate to children's ability and intellectual development. Planning appropriate activities for children is the central skill of teaching. When

SUMMARY *CONTINUED*

considering the appropriateness of the curriculum, it is important for the practitioner to be able to predict children's responses and pace of work.

Enhancing the development of the child: creating independent learners (p. 213)

What are the principal issues in helping children to achieve their full potential?

It is vitally important that early years practitioners 'get to know' each child within their setting. Observing children formally and informally allows the practitioner to plan accordingly for both the type of support and the extent of support required by the individual child.

Additional educational needs (p. 215)

What is the importance of recognising a child's pedagogical needs?

Government policy is underpinned by the idea of 'inclusive' learning environments, that is,

settings created by practitioners who recognise the learning needs of each child and respond accordingly. Some children may present in an early years setting with special educational needs. It is vital that practitioners both recognise and respond to those needs. Effective personalised learning means helping each child to come closer to realising their full potential as learners.

Assessment: personalised learning through ongoing observation and assessment (p. 218)

What is assessment for learning?

Assessment for learning is at the centre of the government's plan for a more personalised approach to learning. For this to be effective, it should be part of day-to-day practice in settings, where practitioners are continuously seeking evidence of children's learning and reflecting upon how best to help children progress and are involving children in that process.

Glossary

Affective dimension: this relates to the emotional development of children and their ability to control their emotions. Emotional development, in an appropriately supportive environment, will help children to have a higher self-esteem and to feel confident in their learning individually and with others.

Assessment for learning: practitioners use the information from setting classroom observation, to involve the children in deciding their learning objectives and how best to meet them.

Challenge: a difficult task which stimulates interest or encourages effort.

Child-centred pedagogy: teaching which focuses on the child's cognitive and affective learning needs.

Heuristic play: an activity for young children, usually between the ages of 10 months and 2 years, where they are enabled/allowed to explore, to discover and to find out what objects are used for.

Independent learner: a learner who has the belief in him/herself to think through learning activities, problems or challenges, making decisions about his/her learning and acting upon those decisions.

Personalised learning: the adaptation of teaching and the curriculum to meet the learning needs of the individual child. It is based on the collaborative approach of the practitioner, child and his/her parents or carers, where practitioners are continuously collecting and evaluating evidence of learning, with a view, through discussion with the child, to engaging him/her

in his/her learning to achieve the best possible outcomes for the child both emotionally and academically.

Summative assessment: a summary of a learner's achievements at a given moment in time (e.g. the result from a written test).

Find out more

Rodger, R. (2003) *Planning an Appropriate Curriculum for the Under Fives: A Guide for Students, Teachers and Assistants*, **2nd edn, London: David Fulton.**
This is a useful book to use for planning in conjunction with the *Statutory Framework for the Early Years Foundation Stage: Setting the Standards for Learning Development and Care for children from birth to five* (EYFS) (DfES, 2007). The book offers ideas, materials and examples of good practice for each of the early learning goals. This second edition also considers effective target setting for 3–5 year olds and assessment in practice.

Department for Education and Skills (DfES) (2006) *2020 Vision: Report of the Teaching and Learning in 2020 Review Group*, **Nottingham: DfES Publications.**
This document defines personalised learning (p. 6) and, by outlining the government's vision, provides a good consideration of what personalised learning means in practice. Although it tends to focus on personalised learning in schools, the underpinning principles are equally applicable in early years settings.

Wilmot, E. (2006) *Personalising Learning in the Primary Classroom: A practical guide for teachers and school leaders*, **Carmarthen, Wales: Crown House.**
Elaine Wilmot, an educational consultant and former headteacher, considers what personalised learning means to primary school practice. Although the book is written for those working in primary schools, many of the strategies can be employed directly with nursery or pre-school children or can be adapted for that age group. The book is useful, in that the examples have been 'tried and tested' in practice.

West-Burnham, J. and Coates, M. (2005) *Personalizing Learning*, **London: Continuum.**
The authors, John West-Burnham and Max Coates, are respected academics within the area of leadership. In many ways this book approaches personalised learning from that perspective. In giving good consideration to what personalised learning means for practitioners, learners and the curriculum, they highlight the centrality of the affective dimension of the person.

References

Abbott, L. and Nutbrown, C. (2001) *Experiencing Reggio Emilia: Implications for Pre-school Provision*. Milton Keynes: Open University.

Allan, J. (2003) Productive pedagogies and the challenge of inclusion, *British Journal of Special Education*, Vol. 30, No. 4: pp. 175–179.

Anning, A., Cullen, J. and Fleer, M. (eds) (2004) *Early Childhood Education: Society and Culture*. London: Sage.

Assessment Reform Group (ARG) (2002) *Assessment for learning: 10 principles –.research-based principles to guide classroom practice*. London: ARG.

Black, P. and Wiliam, D. (1998) *Inside the Black Box: Raising Standards Through Classroom Assessment*. London: King's College.

Brook, A. (2003) Art: 'Swirly. It's all swirly!', in Cooper, H. and Sixsmith, C. (eds) *Teaching Across the Early Years 3–7: curriculum coherence and continuity*. London: RoutledgeFalmer.

Chambers (1983) *Chambers 20th Century Dictionary*. Edinburgh: Chambers.

Cheminais, R. (2006) *Every Child Matters: A Practical Guide for Teachers*. London: David Fulton.

Clarke, S. (2003) *Enriching Feedback in the Primary Classroom*. Abingdon: Hodder and Stoughton.

Croll, P. and Moses, D. (1998) Pragmatism, ideology and educational change: the case of special educational needs, *British Journal of Educational Studies*, Vol. 46: pp. 11–25.

Department for Education and Skills (DfES) (2006) *2020 Vision: Report of the Teaching and Learning in 2020 Review Group*. Nottingham: DfES Publications.

Department for Education and Skills (DfES) (2007) The *Statutory Framework for the Early Years Foundation Stage: Setting the Standards for Learning Development and Care for children from birth to five* (EYFS). Nottingham: DfES Publications.

Drake, J. (2005) *Planning Children's Play and Learning in the Foundation Stage*. London: David Fulton.

Edgington, M. (1998) *The Nursery Teacher in Action*. London: Paul Chapman.

Follari, L.M. (2007) *Foundations and Best Practices in Early Childhood Education: Histories, Theories and Approaches to Learning*. Columbus, OH: Pearson/Merrill Prentice Hall.

Goouch, K. and Powell, S. (2006) *Case Studies for Early Years Professional Standards 2.1–2.7*. Canterbury: Canterbury Christ Church University.

Holt, N. (2007) *Bringing the High/Scope Approach to Your Early Years Practice*. London: Routledge.

Kostelnik, M., Soderman, A. and Whiren, A. (2006) *Developmentally Appropriate Curriculum: Best Practices in Early Childhood Curriculum*, 2nd edn. Upper Saddle River, NJ: Prentice Hall.

National Association for the Education of Young Children (NAEYC) (2008) *Developmentally Appropriate Practice in Early Childhood Programs*. Washington, DC: NAEYC.

Ofsted (2003) *Good Assessment in Secondary Schools*. London: HMI.

Qualifications and Curriculum Authority (QCA) (2000) *Curriculum Guidance for the Foundation Stage*. London: QCA.

Qualifications and Curriculum Authority (QCA) (2003) *Foundation Stage Profile Handbook*. London: QCA.

Rodger, R. (2003) *Planning an Appropriate Curriculum for the Under Fives: A Guide for Students, Teachers and Assistants*, 2nd edn. London: David Fulton.

Siraj-Blatchford, I. (2004) Quality Teaching in the Early Years, in Anning, A., Cullen, J. and Fleer, M. (eds) *Early Childhood Education: Society and Culture*. London: Sage, pp. 137–148.

Siraj-Blatchford, I., Sylva, K., Mattock, S., Gilden, R. and Bell, D. (2002) *Researching Effective Pedagogy in the Early Years*, Research Report No. 356. London: DfES.

Sylva, K., Taggart, B., Siraj-Blatchford, I., Totsika, V., Ereky-Stevens, K., Gilden, R. and Bell, D. (2007) Curricular quality and day-to-day learning activities in pre-school, *International Journal of Early Years Education*, Vol. 15, No. 1, March: pp. 49–65.

Thornton, L. and Brunton, P. (2007) *Bringing the Reggio Approach to Your Early Years Practice*. New York: Routledge.

PART 3 Enhancing Learning Practice

Part 3 focuses on enhancing learning practice primarily through the Continuing Professional Development of those involved in children's learning, development and well-being during the Early Years Foundation Stage and Key Stage 1. By considering the learning community, the collaboration of all those involved, including practitioners, children, parents, governors, professionals from the social and health services and those from the wider local community, Part 3 addresses the importance of practitioners' personal professional development for raising children's aspirations and achievements.

11 Professional Development

By the end of this chapter you will be able to answer the following questions:

- What issues need to be considered when a new member of staff joins a setting?
- How can performance management lead to improved outcomes for children in all settings?
- What factors contribute to the development of an effective self-evaluation process?
- What are the most important issues for effective time management?

This chapter will support your understanding of the following Standards *(see Appendix 1)*:
■ **Teamwork and collaboration:** S33 and S34 ■ **Professional development:** S38 and S39.

Introduction

The government's vision for education includes a well-qualified early years workforce, with 'clear professional roles for **children's centres** and full day care settings' (DfES, 2006: 30). Results from the *Effective Provision of Pre-school Education Project* suggested that **quality** was directly related to better outcomes for children. The results further suggested that the following key factors contribute to this:

> Leaders with high qualifications
> Trained teachers working alongside and supporting less qualified staff
> Staff with a good understanding of child development and learning.
>
> *(DfES, 2006: 29)*

This chapter will consider how everything from welcoming a new member of staff into an early years foundation stage setting to encouraging high levels of practice, involves acknowledging their professional development needs. For both the new recruit and the experienced practitioner, this marks the beginning of the continuing process of self-evaluation, centred on improved teaching and learning and enhanced self-management.

Children's centres: centres which provide health, education and social services in one location to young children (0–5 years) and their parents.

Quality: the term used to describe the merits of teaching and learning within a setting.

DISCUSSION POINT

Results from the *Effective Provision of Pre-school Education Project* (DfES, 2006: 29*)* highlighted the above key factors as directly contributing to *better outcomes* for children.

In a group of three or four discuss why you think these factors are central to raising standards and improved outcomes for children in early years settings.

Identity and belonging: welcoming staff

Early years settings are communities of practice for all their members and as such develop processes and practices according to the place and level of engagement by each practitioner which is determined by role and job description. Staff are welcomed and enabled to develop a sense of belonging where they identify with the ethos and values of the setting. By identifying the issues or areas with which a new member of staff needs to be familiar and by considering the essential elements of a programme of induction, this section will show how individual settings can effectively welcome new members of staff.

Working in early years settings can be both challenging and stimulating. All staff need to know that the contributions they make are valued. In addition, the government's drive for a more integrated delivery of children's services, with a strong emphasis on partnership working, gives greater responsibility to the individual working within the early years setting. Consequently, practitioners, to a lesser or greater degree, depending on their role, share in the responsibility of ensuring that outcomes are achieved. This reinforces the need for all staff to know their role and place in the setting and for employers to ensure that appropriate training is given.

When a new member of staff joins the setting, the following list helps to identify what they will need to know:

- job description
- his/her position in the team/setting
- settings aims, polices and procedures (written copy), including those related to safeguarding and promoting the welfare of children
- relevant documentation (written copy), including statement of 'safe practice and standards of conduct and behaviour expected of staff and children in the setting and [other] relevant personnel procedures [e.g.] disciplinary, capability and whistle-blowing' (DfES, 2005: 17)
- reporting and assessment procedures
- members of team – introduce colleagues
- identities of vulnerable pupils (as appropriate, according to data protection)
- child protection training, if appropriate for the position.

REFLECT AND RELATE TO PRACTICE

Imagine you have just been appointed as a newly qualified practitioner in an early years setting. You receive the above documents and information. What would you do next? You should consider how you will use the documents and information in practice and any questions you might want to ask.

In addition, new members of staff should have access to one or more of the support mechanisms and relevant information illustrated in Figure 11.1.

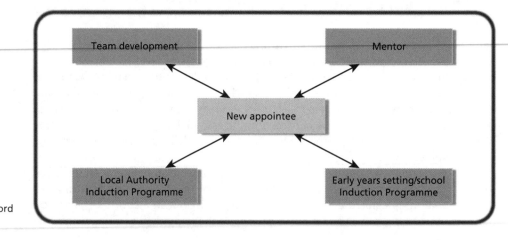

Figure 11.1 Areas of support for newly appointed staff

Source: Blandford (2002) p. 262

Photo 11.1
Children help the new member of staff identify with the community

Pearson Education Ltd. Jules Selmes © Pearson Education Ltd. 2004

Induction needs to be planned but flexible. The following actions can be employed effectively:

- appoint a mentor
- identify the training, development and personal needs of the new appointees
- negotiate with your new colleague the most appropriate personal and professional support
- develop a climate of mutual support
- create an environment which is open; respect the needs of others
- promote job shadowing and observation, laying the foundation for reflective practice
- ensure that the newly appointed member of staff can identify with their team
- ensure that the new appointee will know their role, managers and team
- if necessary, consider external factors such as accommodation, transport and social needs to assist with work/life balance
- ensure that support and professional guidance are relevant
- provide access to external support networks; support groups; advisers.

Performance management

Performance management is an essential element in the development of the wider workforce in early years and educational settings. Its purpose is to provide an opportunity for performance enhancement that motivates and develops individuals. By outlining the wider objectives of performance management, this section will show that when it is implemented effectively and linked with the setting improvement plan, it can enhance the overall performance of the setting.

Performance management and review should improve the quality of education and care for children by assisting practitioners to realise their potential and to carry out their duties more effectively.

CHECKLIST: WHAT IS THE PURPOSE OF PERFORMANCE REVIEW?

- To raise standards through target setting that enhances performance, and to improve provision for children and practitioners.
- To link the review cycle to:
  - LA or company (independent sector) development plans
  - Early years setting/school management procedures
  - Ofsted – action plan
  - annual reviews and development plans
  - individual staff development plans
  - induction and assessment.
- To plan the professional development of the setting workforce within the local LA, company (independent sector) and national frameworks.

Performance review: whereby one professional holds him/herself accountable to him/herself in the presence of another professional.

A working definition of **performance review** is one professional holding him/herself accountable to him/herself in the presence of another professional. The review may improve the management of teaching and learning within the setting by helping practitioners to identify ways of enhancing their skills and performance and supporting them in the identification of achievable targets. Performance review should assist in planning professional development individually and collectively within the framework set by the **setting improvement plan**. In addition, this will enhance the overall management of the setting and provide an opportunity to consider the management of change. Performance review should also support the promotion of equal opportunities.

Setting improvement plan: a plan which focuses on all areas within the setting/ school where improvement is needed.

To this end, a performance review is open and based on the mutual understanding by all staff within the setting of its context, purpose, procedures, criteria and outcomes. The process and procedures adopted should be fair and equitable and should be seen to be so, both in general and by respecting equal opportunities, particularly in relation to gender and ethnicity. The process and procedures supporting performance review should also be acceptable to all staff. The setting workforce should benefit from participation in the scheme. There should be the opportunity for objective judgements to be made concerning the management of the institution.

The scheme should be integral to the setting's development strategy and attempt to balance the demands of professional development and public accountability. A rigorous system of review is one that raises standards, key elements of which are trust, training, resourcing, time, support and commitment. For performance management to have any meaning it should be seen to inform the setting development process. To this end, settings should aim to have in place a co-ordinated procedure for ensuring that:

- mechanisms exist for collating professional development needs identified through individual reviews
- there is co-ordination of training needs and related development opportunities
- there are contingency plans for coping with those whose performance is perceived as poor for a variety of reasons, e.g. stress, lack of skills.

As performance review is an annual process, there is an opportunity to agree targets with staff in the light of targets within the setting improvement plan, which will itself be influenced by key points for action in Ofsted reports and benchmark information from national data collected by Ofsted and the local authorities (LAs) and company educational development plans (EDPs).

DISCUSSION POINT

Consider what you have read within this section, especially the checklist. How does performance review of an individual practitioner link to the overall performance of the setting?

Self-evaluation

Self-development is systematic; we never stop learning and developing. The art of self-evaluation is to be continually learning. Senge makes it clear:

> People with a high level of personal mastery live in a continual learning mode. They never 'arrive'. People with a high level of personal mastery are acutely aware of their ignorance, their incompetence, their growth areas. And they are deeply self-confident. Paradoxical? Only for those who do not see that the journey is the reward.

(1990: 142)

By considering how self-evaluation works in practice, this section encourages the reader to consider their values, beliefs and practices and examine the extent to which they need to correspond to those of the setting in order to improve self-performance and ultimately outcomes for all children.

The culture of the teaching profession and the role of the support staff in educational settings is changing, reflecting the changing society in which we live, with its proliferation of cultures, beliefs and values. Effective teaching and learning in settings are based on shared beliefs and values. The setting community works towards a common goal, reaching for and achieving targets. In practice, staff need to relate their actions to their beliefs and values. If the two do not equate, staff should consider their position in the setting in relation to children's needs. Educational settings should be places in which success is celebrated. How does this happen? Do staff willingly participate in the change process, or are they passive in their response to the dominant ideology of the day? While these are matters of sociological debate, self-evaluation and effective self-development should influence practice in a positive way.

A fundamental issue will be the individual's ability to recognise where they are in relation to where they would like to be. As Senge indicated, the most successful among us will never reach their destiny. Self-assessment is also relevant for practical appreciation. Carr and Kemmis (1986: p. 31) suggest that self-evaluation of:

> **Professional competence is, therefore, to be judged not by the ability to articulate and defend moral principles, nor as a matter of traditional conformity or technical accountability. Rather it is assessed in terms of moral and prudential answerability for practical judgements actually made within the context of existing educational institutions.**
>
> *(Carr and Kemmis, 1986)*

Theory and knowledge can transform staff's beliefs and values. In the process of self-reflection, interaction with educational theory may not dictate practice, but it may transform the outlook of the practitioner. Providing individuals with new concepts is a means not merely of offering them a new way of thinking, but also of offering them the possibility of becoming more aware of their thoughts and actions. The full task of self-reflection and evaluation requires staff to collaborate in decision-making that will

Photo 11.2
Theory and knowledge can transform staff's beliefs and values

Pearson Education Ltd. Jules Selmes © Pearson Education Ltd. 2006

transform their situation. The process of self-evaluation encompasses the interaction of staff with the setting. Staff should consider whether they are in the right setting for them, i.e. do they share the objectives, values and culture?

DISCUSSION POINT

Practitioner self-evaluation questions:

- What do I value?
- What is my present situation?
- Where would I like my career to lead?
- How might I get there?
- What help is available?

Personal qualities needed – do I have:

- the ability to self-manage?
- clear personal values?
- clear personal objectives?
- an emphasis on continuing personal growth?
- effective problem-solving skills?
- the capacity to be creative and innovative?

A means of developing the skills required for self-evaluation is to consider the following range of knowledge (adapted from Carr and Kemmis, 1986: 3i) that exists regarding educational practice; this will enable staff to develop their own practice:

- common-sense knowledge about practice that is simply assumption or opinion, for example the view that students need discipline
- folk-wisdom of staff, like the view that children get restless on windy days
- skill knowledge used by staff: how to line children up, or how to prevent children speaking while instructions about a task are being given
- contextual knowledge: the background knowledge about this group of children, this community or this child, against which aspirations are measured
- professional knowledge about teaching and learning strategies and curriculum
- educational theory: ideas about the development of individuals, or about the role of education in society
- social and moral theories and general philosophical outlooks: about how people can and should interact, the uses of knowledge in society, or about truth and justice.

As a process, self-evaluation should inform practice day to day. An effective professional practitioner will be effective in their evaluation of themselves. In practice, self-evaluation will involve making sense of ourselves in the situations shown in Table 11.1.

Table 11.1 Situations for self-evaluation

Team work:
- listening
- attitude
- flexibility

Relationships with:
- parents
- colleagues
- children

Knowledge of:
- current publications
- equal opportunity issues
- learning styles

Preparation of:
- activities lessons
- monitoring procedures
- assessment

DISCUSSION POINT

Consider each of the four categories shown in Table 11.1. Discuss how you could give your 'best performance', in practice. For each item listed consider how it impacts on improved outcomes for children.

A model of self-evalaution

We have just considered the centrality of self-evaluation in improving personal performance and ultimately the learning experiences and outcomes of children. Through a model of self-evaluation this section takes that a step further. By encouraging the reader to closely examine his/her work practices and related attitudes the section shows how effective self-evaluation can lead not only to improved performance, but a better balance between work and home.

A practice-based approach to self-evaluation is shown in Figure 11.2. In this example questions relate to the practitioner making sense of themselves in a range of situations.

REFLECT AND RELATE TO PRACTICE

Look at Figure 11.2 and ask, where am I in this process? You should consider the questions in relation to where you are now, basing your answers on theoretical knowledge or practical experience.

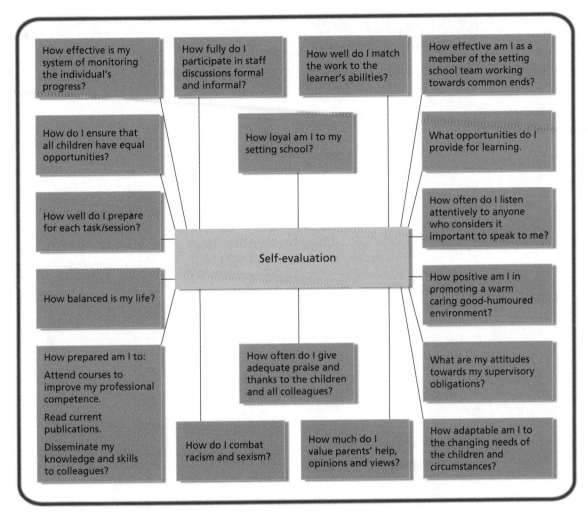

Figure 11.2 A model of self-evaluation

Source: Blandford (2006) p. 292; adapted from Manchester LEA (1986)

CHECKLIST: SELF-DEVELOPMENT – KEY ISSUES FOR CONSIDERATION

- Relationship with self (self-evaluation)
- Ability to develop
- Level of empowerment – status, value
- Choices available
- Opportunity for individualistic activities.

DISCUSSION POINT

Discuss the above checklist in relation to your own practice.

Self-development involves learning and understanding where you are within your job and career. Staff should have a clear view of what their job is about. Staff should also have an understanding of their position in relation to those they manage. For each member of staff, self-development can be difficult. All staff face many demands, including:

- government demands: to deliver the curriculum, to register children, parents' evenings, Ofsted
- colleagues' demands: requests for assistance, information or help from others at a similar level or within your team
- children's demands: to inform and liaise
- parents', governors' and trustees' demands
- externally imposed demands: social services, police, agencies that work for and with young people
- system-imposed demands: line managers (LMs), LA, company budgets, meetings and social functions, which cannot be ignored.

In addition, there will be other demands such as family, friends, hobbies and social commitments. It is important to understand that practitioners and support staff need a balance between their professional and personal lives.

Self-management

Self-evaluation informs self-management. Therefore, it is important to have a clear view on how to manage and organise the workload. In order to manage time effectively you will need to identify how to use time and determine goals. By considering the centrality of personal planning and the need to set goals and prioritise work, this section provides an overview, from which you can develop your own framework of the issues which need to be considered to do this effectively.

In practice, this means adopting systems to aid personal and developmental organisation. The majority of practitioners will have a full commitment in their engagement with babies, toddlers and young children, consequently their organisational systems need to involve:

- day-to-day planning, diary keeping
- 'in tray', dealing with post and decision-making
- retrieval of information and filing
- organisation of the workspace
- administration
- management of stock

- management of children's materials and work
- organisation of curriculum materials
- stress management.

It is also worth identifying how time is wasted, for example:

- procrastination
- delegating inefficiently
- mismanaging paperwork
- holding unnecessary meetings
- failing to set priorities.

Personal planning

Practitioners will have many things to fit into a day's work. Therefore they will need to recognise which part of the day or night is the most productive, the time when they may have the most creative ideas, or can concentrate best. For the majority of people, this time is early in the day, when they are freshest, and before the events of the day start to crowd in and push away ideas. A minority of people do their best work late at night.

It has been suggested that about 20 per cent of personal time is prime time, and that, used correctly, it should produce about 80 per cent of the most creative and productive work. The rest of the time is likely to be of lower quality and is nowhere near as productive.

Creative thinking, and the most difficult jobs, deserve high-quality time. If you try to do them at times when there are likely to be many interruptions or the need to catch up, this will lead to frustration. In this low-quality time, it is better to do things which are easy to pick up after interruptions, or jobs which have a positive outcome. Apart from the advantage to the individual in using prime time effectively, there are wider implications – for example, the timing of meetings. Important decisions need some of the team's prime time, not the traditional slot of low quality at the end of the teaching day. It is advisable for settings to timetable team meetings earlier in the day, when vital and creative thinking is needed. In sum:

- your prime time is when you do your best work
- seek to understand how *you* work, and then . . .
- plan your day accordingly as far as you are free to do so
- allow incubation time for the subconscious to work on problems.

Setting goals and priorities

One way in which time management can be improved is to review the way in which goals or tasks are identified. This will include both routine matters to attend to and/or some longer-term issues. Whatever they are, it is best to divide them into workable units of activity by using the acronym SMART. The task needs to be *specific*, clearly defined. It needs to be *measurable*, so that it is easy to see when it has been completed.

It should also be *attainable*. Unrealistic targets are depressing. They also need to be *relevant*, or appropriate, to current and future needs. And finally, tasks should be *time-limited* with defined deadlines. Open-ended tasks have a habit of not getting done.

Once a SMART list of things that need to be done has been drawn up, the next task is to prioritise them. If this is not done, it is easy to feel helpless and stressed in the face of so many things that need to be done simultaneously. Organising tasks into some sort of order not only makes it easier to finish one thing before going on to the next, but it also legitimises the fact that some of the things have to be put off until later.

Dilemmas arise when the urgent, but unimportant, regularly pushes out the important but less urgent. Schedules need to be readjusted to fit in new and urgent items. This may entail being firm about the time planned for important tasks. To add to the dilemma, individual perceptions of what is important may differ from individual to individual. In sum:

- make a list of daily tasks
- prioritise the tasks according to their urgency and importance
- be ruthless with the order by which tasks are dealt with
- examine why tasks are not getting done, and do something about it!

DISCUSSION POINT

Using the criteria listed above, relate it to your present work. How could you use your time more efficiently?

This is a good exercise to help you manage your time more effectively.

Stress

All work, to a lesser or greater degree, will have a certain level of stress. This should not necessarily be viewed within a negative framework. Stress can be both a catalyst for effective work and at other times a negative force. By defining what is meant by stress in practice and considering its causes, this section will show how practitioners can effectively manage stress within the day-to-day life of early years settings.

Practitioners are exposed to many stresses in their working life. There are constant challenges within the workplace. However, challenges are also opportunities which result in responses placed on a continuum from excitement to excessive tiredness (see Figure 11.3). Everard et al. (2004: 125) highlight the need for some stress in all jobs. They suggest that it 'provides challenge and motivation, helps to raise performance and is an ingredient of job satisfaction'.

Individuals should know their energy levels. If a challenge cannot be met and creates energy loss, inevitably stress will occur. The consequences of stress can be debilitating. Stress can be exhibited in many ways, for example, irritability, tiredness,

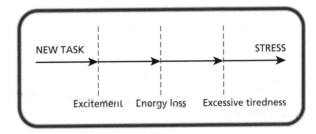

Figure 11.3
Stress levels

Source: Blandford
(2006) p. 298

excessive drinking and depression. Practitioners should be aware of stress in the workplace; it is important to acknowledge personal stress levels and identify and support those who find work stressful.

Stress can be overcome if the imbalances that exist are redressed, for example, by raising low energy levels. Practitioners need to look after their own welfare, and remain in control. Control may also mean evaluating the use of time, ensuring that no one activity makes excessive demands. More specifically, a model of stress will serve to illustrate the effect of stress in a practitioner's working life (see Figure 11.4).

The following stress levels are described by Lifeskills Associates (1995):

- *Optimum level*: when practitioners are at their optimum level they are likely to be alert and self-confident. In practice, they will think and respond quickly, perform well, feel well and be enthusiastic, interested and involved in the task which they will carry out in an energetic, easy manner.
- *Overstressed*: alternatively when practitioners are overstressed they are likely to have feelings of anxiety and mental confusion. In this condition they will not think effectively or solve problems clearly or objectively. They will forget instructions, and be inclined to panic. Physically, there will be symptoms such as increased heart rate and blood pressure, excessive perspiration, churning stomach and indigestion. In addition co-ordination will be impaired and reflexes slowed.

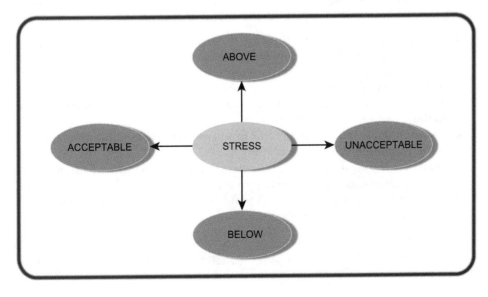

Figure 11.4
A model of
stress levels

Source: Blandford
(2006) p. 298

- *Understressed*: if practitioners are understressed they are likely to experience a lack of interest or enthusiasm for the task. They can have feelings of futility or depression and believe that nothing matters any more – even a simple job can seem a huge task. They will be bored and lacking in energy. To them the world will look drab and grey and it will be hard to summon up energy to start new jobs or create fresh interests.

Causes of stress

In her *Times Educational Supplement* review of 'What really stresses teachers', Emma Burstall (1996) highlighted the following causes of stress in teachers:

Work:
- lack of time to do the job
- lack of parental support
- lack of resources
- national curriculum/irrelevant paperwork
- rate of change
- lack of LA support
- poor status of profession
- staff relationships
- government interference
- pressure of meetings.

Home:
- worries about own children
- worries about elderly parents
- lack of time with family
- untidiness of others
- family illnesses
- housework
- guilt over not meeting all family's demand
- in-laws
- having to take work home
- lack of private space,

Managing stress

Having identified the causes, practitioners should then attempt to manage stress. Brown and Ralph (1995: 95–105) offer the following advice:

1 *Examining beliefs and expectations*: are these realistic and achievable? Is there a need to set more attainable goals?
2 *Time management*: can time be used more effectively? Techniques such as prioritisation, delegation, objective setting can be considered.
3 *Assertion*: learning how to communicate more confidently at all levels and to deal positively with conflict.
4 *Communication*: looking at patterns of interpersonal communication and self-presentation skills.
5 *Relaxation techniques* of all kinds, such as physical exercise, meditation, yoga, aromatherapy, and collection of biodata.
6 *Support networks*: it is important to build and maintain support networks of family, friends and colleagues, both within and outside the work setting.

Brown and Ralph (ibid.) also indicate the importance of how the setting as an organisation can help practitioners to address the problem of stress. They suggest a variety of ways in which practitioners can approach this issue:

1 Helping to *destigmatise* the idea of stress by putting it on the agenda for discussion.
2 Encouraging the establishment of *self-help groups* to explore group problem-solving of setting school stress factors and to develop appropriate solutions where possible.
3 Developing an *empathetic ethos* and offering support for self-help management techniques.
4 Identifying and liaising with *people who can help* within the local authority and other relevant organisations.
5 Drawing up a setting *action plan* after school-wide staff consultation. Factors to consider might include workloads, resources, discipline, relationships, environment, career progression, future staff development and training needs, parental and community pressure.
6 Providing *appropriate staff development*, either within the setting/school or at an outside venue.
7 Making available information about *counselling services* and encouraging staff to use them where necessary.

In sum, Brown and Ralph (1992, 1994, 1995) found that practitioners are unable to destigmatise stress and that organisational needs must be met before personal needs. Change issues (e.g. new responsibilities, a change in leader/leadership style) also emerge as a significant factor in contributing to stress levels in settings.

Brown and Ralph (1995: 105) conclude that practitioners need to recognise and analyse openly for themselves signs of stress at work. They emphasise the need for an organisational approach to the management of stress. In particular, practitioners need to be reassured that they will not lose professional esteem or promotional opportunities by admitting to stress.

DISCUSSION POINT

What is your view on stress? Do you see it in a positive/negative light?

Do you think personal factors causing stress should be discussed in an open climate?

As a practitioner in an early years setting, what factors would you 'put in place' to minimise personal stress?

As a leader in an early years setting, what factors would you 'put in place' to minimise stress for your team?

Preparing leaders for early years settings

In the field of continuing professional development, the government has placed strong emphasis on having a well-qualified children's workforce. To this end they endorsed the National Professional Qualification for Integrated Centre Leadership (NPQICL). The programme was developed following a project carried out by the Pen

Green Leadership Centre and addresses leadership issues related to large budgets, multi-professional groups and challenging targets that are required for the role of Children's Centre Leaders. This section will provide an outline of the course leading to the NPQICL.

The starting point is a set of standards. The National Standards for Leaders of Integrated Centres for Children and Families are similar to the standards for school leaders and centre on six key areas:

1 Shaping the present and creating the future
2 Leading learning and development
3 Building and strengthening teams
4 Being accountable and responsible
5 Developing strong families and communities
6 Managing the organisation.

The programme content was developed by staff from Early Excellence Centres and leaders from a range of services and sectors including Sure Start projects, family centres, nursery schools, primary schools, Neighbourhood Nursery Initiative schemes and children's centres. Wider representation also came from the National Centre for Healthcare leadership, the National College for School Leadership, Social Care Institute for Excellence, Pen Green Leadership, Early Years Regional Leadership Centres, Sector Skills Council, Skills for Care and Development and the Department for Children, Schools and Families. The purposes of NPQICL are to:

• provide for early years integrated centre leaders a programme and qualification equivalent to the National Professional Qualification for Headship;
• create opportunities for integrated centre leaders to consider leadership implications of their roles;
• examine the nature of multi-professional services and their implications for integrated centre leadership;
• create a forum for reflection, dialogue and discussion about leadership practice in integrated centres;
• examine how leadership is defined and described in the literature of leadership and to relate theory to practice;
• guide and support practitioner research into the leadership issues in participants' own centres; and
• develop leadership capability.

The actual programme spans a year and consists of a 13- or 19-day taught programme with additional time being spent on intersessional activities, online activities and assignments. Participants can select between a research or a study route depending on their academic experience. The structure and processes of the NPQICL programme can be found in Table 11.2 whilst the NPQICL Learning Journey over an academic year is illustrated in Table 11.3.

Eligibility to participate in the programme includes entry requirements for Masters-level study and the ability to be assessed in the workplace against the standards. As an integral part of the programme successful participants will gain 60 credits at Masters level at the end of the programme. To fulfil the workplace assessment participants need to be in a children's centre environment.

Table 11.2 Structure and processes of the NPQICL programme

	Elements			
Programme plan	Induction Introduction to research	Study route	Leadership symposium	
		Research route		
Essential philosophy	Andragogy	Constructivist pedagogical leadership	Isomorphism	Challenge and containment
	Living the learning	Reflection	Transformation	Tutor/mentor roles
	Learning community			
Tasks	Leadership contract	Community contract	Personal Professional Development Record (PPDR)	
	Academic study	Learning journal	Assignments	Working in teams
Learning processes	Praxis	Enquiry	Reflection	Journaling
	Challenge	Self-evaluation	Self-awareness	
Specific techniques	Sculpt	Life and learning journeys	Micro project	Goldfish bowl
Building the community of practice	Co-construction	Practitioner knowledge	Theory	Action research
	Celebrating diversity			
Supporting growth of the participants	Mentor	Assignments at Masters level	Initial assessment	Final assessment

Table 11.3 The NPQICL Learning Journey

Element	Explanation
Induction	Where concepts of the programme are introduced along with the Personal Professional Development Record (PPDR). Participants begin to identify the most appropriate route for them (Study or Research). Participants are also introduced to University procedures, registered as University students on a Post Graduate Certificate and are introduced to the Virtual Learning Environments.
Initial based assessment	The participant and line manager are guided through the PPDR, by an assessor, where leadership-learning priorities are identified.
Introduction to study and research methods	These two days begin to raise participants' awareness the world of academic study at Masters level.
Study route	This aspect of the programme consists of two five-day blocks with two themes: Exploring the Leadership Experience, and Leading Across Professional Boundaries. Having set a leadership learning contract the work is geared towards the assignments through micro projects.
Research route	Participants are given two two-day blocks of time to work with a tutor on building a significant research project that leads to a dissertation-type submission at Masters level.
Final assessment	The participants' leadership capability is assessed through their PPDR, portfolio of evidence and witness statements.
Mentor visits	Each participant has three mentor visits during the year.
Tutor support	The tutor(s) delivering the NPQICL give participants support throughout the year.

DISCUSSION POINT

In 2006/07 400 funded places were available on the NPQICL programme across the country with the south east having 36 of those places. This number did not match the numbers of children's centres that were operational by 2008 according to government figures. Bearing in mind that the Centre leaders are required to have the NPQICL qualification, do you think a lack of leaders with the NPQICL qualification will affect the way children's centres have developed/will develop?

Some people say 'leaders are born', while others say 'leaders develop'. What is your view in the context of managing a children's centre? Would you consider following the NPQICL programme?

Professional development: bringing it together

Central to the management of discipline in settings/schools is the level of self-esteem, knowledge, skills and understanding that emanates from the practitioner. Practitioners with low levels will be unable to participate in the workplace in a meaningful way. Practitioners can gain confidence by adopting a few straightforward procedures to meet their needs. The following Activity has been taken from a worked example of an In-Service Education and Training (INSET) programme focusing on the first of the areas, self-esteem. It provides the reader with guidance on how to prepare for practice and also includes evaluative questions on children's experience of learning.

ACTIVITY

Developing self-esteem

Practitioners can reduce stress and gain confidence by adopting the following few straightforward procedures to meet their needs:

- *Preparation*: reflect on the successes of the previous activity/lesson, repeat these strategies, prepare activity/lesson content around available resources, note any particular problems with children.
- *Starting the day*: arrive early and take time to check whether everything that is required is at hand, rehearse tasks/lessons mentally and aim to make a good, confident start to each activity/lesson; allow time to consult with colleagues about individual children.
- *Colleagues*: be a good team player by making well-researched suggestions on strategies to overcome difficulties with disruptive children, listen to advice when offered, collaborate with all agencies to gain support, be assertive when appropriate.
- *Managers*: do not waste time discussing their failings as managers or your own perception of their attitude towards your work, but find ways of working with them. They are busy people who may not feel that it is appropriate for them to deal with every discipline-related incident that occurs in their setting/school. Be pleasantly assertive when you feel that your needs are not being met.
- *Keep things under control*: learning and teaching is filled with false starts, incomplete conversations, children that arrive at the wrong time, children that behave in an irrational manner. Do not strive for all-round perfection, make priorities and be ready to say no; work within your limits.

▶

- *Children*: if discipline is a problem it must also be made a priority before it starts to cause unacceptable stress. Do not cover it up; seek support from a mentor or understanding colleague and from sympathetic senior managers. A major difficulty with a particular child should be a whole-setting/school issue and not a private problem. Be assertive, ask for time to talk about the problem, and make it clear that you need support. Try hard not to take a child's misbehaviour as directed personally to you. Take opportunities to discuss discipline problems with colleagues, managers and support agencies.
- *Colleagues*: give feedback to them when you have received help; this will make both of you feel better and encourage others to support you.
- *Get a life*: not participating in anything other than setting/school is a downhill step and bad for self-esteem, for mental health and for the ultimate well-being of children.
- *Keep fit*: feeling fit is good for self-esteem and helps to get you through a tiring week.
- *Focus on the manageable*: move the focus from teaching to particular teaching tasks. An alternative approach to thinking a group is difficult and beyond your ability to cope is to start thinking what, and who, makes the group difficult, then devise ways of dealing with these individual issues.
- *Change direction*: if a setting/school or area is not suited to you, move.
- *Celebrate success*: it is in the nature of conscientious people that they dwell on things that go wrong. Try to think what has gone well; this will give you the energy to deal with problems as they arise.
- Remember, a practitioner's perception of themselves will impact on the self-esteem and confidence of their children.

(Blandford (2004); adapted from Haigh, 1997: 20–21)

DISCUSSION POINT

Consider the above Activity. Why is it important for practitioners to have a positive self-image?

How could you develop this in yourself, in a way which will lead to improved outcomes for children?

SUMMARY

Identity and belonging: welcoming staff (p. 227)

How does the 'welcoming' procedure initiate professional development?

Staff are welcomed and enabled to develop a sense of belonging, through which they identify with the ethos and values of the setting. All staff need to know that the contributions they make are valued. Practitioners, to a lesser or greater degree, depending on their role, share in the responsibility of ensuring that outcomes are achieved. This reinforces the need for all staff to know their role and place in the setting and for employers to ensure that appropriate training is given.

Performance management (p. 229)

How can performance management lead to improved outcomes for all children across the setting?

Performance management is an essential element in the development of the setting/school workforce. Its purpose is to provide an opportunity for performance enhancement that motivates and develops individuals. Performance management and review should improve the quality of education and care for children by assisting practitioners to realise their potential and to carry out their duties more effectively.

Self-evaluation (p. 231)

What factors influence the development of an effective self-evaluation process?

The art of self-evaluation is to be continually learning. Effective teaching and learning in settings is based on shared beliefs and values. In practice, staff need to relate their actions to their beliefs and values. If the two do not equate, staff should consider their position in the setting in relation to children's needs. Self-evaluation and effective self-development should influence practice in a positive way. A starting point for this process could inform practitioners about their individual aspirations in terms of their career.

Self-management (p. 236)

What are the most important issues for effective time management?

Self-evaluation informs self-management. Therefore, practitioners need to have a clear view on how to manage and organise their workload. In order to manage time effectively practitioners will need to identify how to use time and determine goals. In essence, they need to adopt systems to aid personal organisation.

Stress (p. 238)

How can practitioners reduce personal stress?

Practitioners are exposed to many stresses in their working life. However, stress can be both a positive and negative issue. There are constant challenges within the workplace. Individuals should know their energy levels. If a challenge cannot be met and creates energy loss, inevitably stress will occur. Practitioners should be aware of stress in the workplace; it is important to acknowledge personal stress levels and identify and support those who find work stressful.

SUMMARY *CONTINUED*

Preparing leaders for early years settings (p. 241)

Qualifying for leadership

The government places a strong emphasis on having a well-qualified children's workforce. To this end they endorsed the National

Professional Qualification for Integrated Centre Leadership (NPQICL) for those who lead early years multi-agency children's centres. This section provides an outline of the course leading to the NPQICL, placing it within the context of continuing professional development.

Glossary

Children's centres: centres which provide health, education and social services in one location to young children (0–5 years) and their parents.

Performance review: whereby one professional holds him/herself accountable to him/herself in the presence of another professional.

Quality: the term used to describe the merits of eaching and learning within a setting. It covers a broad area, encompassing teaching to the early learning goals to

meet the individual needs (affective and cognitive) of each child and responding to learners as individuals. This is a contested area, particularly when determined by externally imposed standards. Quality should be internally driven.

Setting improvement plan: a plan, aimed at improving the quality of teaching and learning, which focuses on all areas within the setting/school where improvement is needed. It considers the vision/mission, the values, past achievements and government policy.

Find out more

Cunningham, B. (ed.) (2008) *Exploring Professionalism*, London: Institute of Education.
This book is timely in that it considers the role of the 'professional' in education – from identity through learning to meeting the changes in education.

Pickering, J., Daly, C. and Pachler, N. (2007) *New Designs for Teachers' Professional Learning*, London: Institute of Education.
This book, through the insights of those who have considerable experience in continuing professional

development (CPD), addresses it from both a theoretical and practical stance, offering sound ideas for practice.

In terms of personal development, it is also important to keep up to date with current research. You will find the following academic journals useful for this:

Education 3-13: International Journal of Primary, Elementary and Early Years Education.
International Journal of Early Years Education.

References

Blandford, S. (2004) *Professional Development Manual*. London: Pearson Education.

Blandford, S. (2006) *Middle Leadership in Schools: Harmonising Leadership and Learning*. London: Pearson Education.

Brown, M. and Ralph, S. (1992) Towards the identification of stress in teachers, *Research in Education*, Vol. 48: pp. 103–110.

Brown, M. and Ralph, S. (1994) *Managing Stress in Schools*. Plymouth: Northcote House.

Brown, M. and Ralph, S. (1995) The identification and management of teacher stress, in Bell, J. and Harrison, B.T. (eds) *Vision and Values in Managing Education*, London: David Fulton.

Burstall, E. (1996) What really stresses teachers, *Times Educational Supplement*, 16 February.

Carr, W. and Kemmis, S. (1986) *Becoming Critical: Education, Knowledge and Action Research*. Lewes: Falmer Press.

Department for Education and Skills (DfES) (2005) *The Common Assessment Framework*. Available at www.dfes.gov.uk.

Department for Education and Skills (DfES) (2006) *Effective Provision of Pre-School Education Project*. Available at www.dfes.gov.uk.

Everard, K.B., Morris, G. and Wilson, I. (2004) *Effective School Management*, 4th edn. London: Paul Chapman.

Haigh, G. (1997) 'Don't worry, be happy', *Times Educational Supplement* (First Appointments) 10 Jan: pp. 20–22.

Lifeskills Associates Limited (1995) *Stress Levels*. London: Lifeskills Associates Limited.

Senge, P.M. (1990) *The Fifth Discipline: The Art and Practice of the Learning Organization*. New York: Doubleday: p. 142.

12 In-Service Education and Training

By the end of this chapter you will be able to answer the following questions:

- How do I plan an INSET programme?
- How do I select issues to be addressed?
- How do I evaluate and monitor new initiatives I have established as a result of INSET?
- How do I relate children's learning needs to INSET?

This chapter will support your understanding of the following Standards (see Appendix 1):
■ **Knowledge and understanding:** S01 ■ **Professional development:** S37, S38 and S39.

Introduction

Effective practice in the early years requires committed, enthusiastic and reflective practitioners with a breadth and depth of knowledge, skills and understanding.

Therefore, through initial and ongoing training and development, practitioners need to develop, demonstrate and continuously improve their:

- **understanding of the individual and diverse ways that children develop and learn**
- **practice in meeting all children's needs, learning styles and interests**
- **work with parents, carers and the wider community**
- **knowledge and understanding in order to support actively and extend children's learning in and across all areas and aspects of learning**
- **work with other professionals within and beyond the setting**
- **relationships with both children and adults**

(DfES, 2005: 11)

The training of staff is critical to the development of an early years or school setting. The above, taken from the government document, *KEEP – Key Elements of Effective Practice* (DfES, 2005), reflects a commitment to and vision for a well-trained and effective children's workforce and highlights the important areas for development within early years settings. In the past, in-service training for practitioners was considered by the government to be a suitable mechanism to implement development and, more specifically, change. Following the Education Reform Act 1988, five days per academic year have been allocated for staff development in all schools; there were no similar statements for early years settings. The majority of this time has been utilised to accommodate whole-school **INSET** programmes. The effectiveness of such training programmes in terms of impact on practice has been limited. The limitations are due, in part, to lack of planning and management.

INSET: In-service Education and Training.

INSET is most likely to have an impact if it is matched to organisational aims and objectives. In the great majority of settings where INSET has led to change, INSET needs had been systematically identified and the expected outcomes of training were clearly identified. INSET is a very important part of professional development and its management should ensure:

- goals are identified in consultation with all staff
- the means to reach those goals are agreed both collectively and within teams and also with individuals as appropriate
- realistic targets in terms of time and resources are agreed
- the goals and means of reaching them are monitored and evaluated; the goals are modified accordingly.

By addressing how organisational in-service training can be effectively established in practice, this chapter will consider the centrality of ongoing continuing professional development for all staff working in early years educational settings. It follows a slightly different format to the other chapters, in that it finishes with an appendix offering worked examples for INSET.

Planning

Planning for INSET will require several months of review and consultation. Staff should not be expected to accommodate suggestions immediately. As professionals, practitioners should view the place in which they work as a place of learning. Within the framework of continuing professional development, self-development and staff development are essential prerequisites to effective management and effective settings. Equally, a precondition and an outcome of effective continuing professional development policies is a culture that encourages reflection and development. This section will consider how to plan a relevant and effective INSET for practitioners and other staff within an early years setting.

Practitioners and support staff should be trained in a professional manner. The style, content and relevance of INSET should be complemented by appropriate management. The exemplars of good practice have shown the importance of teaching and learning styles in training programmes.

INSET programmes should be planned by a team representing the views of all staff (examples of worked programmes are given in the appendix at the end of this chapter). Once planned, the programme should be circulated and views sought from

Photo 12.1 How do staff needs directly relate to children's learning needs?

Pearson Education Ltd. Jules Selmes © Pearson Education Ltd. 2007

colleagues on appropriate approaches to each element. The final details should reflect staff needs and concerns. These should relate directly to learner needs. INSET is only part of the process of developing, implementing and reviewing change. It is not a remedy for all ills but should be placed in the context of practice. If change is needed, it should be considered within the priorities of the **organisational improvement plan**, a plan aimed at improving the quality of teaching and learning, which focuses on all areas within the setting/school where improvement is needed. It considers the vision/mission, the values, past achievements and government policy.

Organisational improvement plan: a plan which focuses on all areas within the setting where improvement is needed.

Anyone who considers that a 'stand and deliver' approach to training will encourage staff participation could be considered naïve. Staff need an approach that is supportive in order to feel confident that their contribution will be respected and valued. Staff should be given the opportunity to reflect individually and in groups on the material presented during training. Relevant information should be circulated in advance to enable staff to consider their position in relation to important policies, procedures and practice.

The presentation of the material should be varied and interesting. A lot of printed words will generate little response from staff with busy professional lives. Relevant information should be presented in a succinct, accessible style. Long lists or meaningless prose will not be appreciated. Staff need to engage with key issues in an informed way. Staff need to know and understand the essential points that relate to their practice in order to make a judgement.

INSET should focus on issues that are relevant to the individual setting/school and which will lead to a confirmation or change of practice. Staff need to feel confident that they are working with colleagues they trust, if they are to be open about such an emotive subject. INSET co-ordinators need to plan their groups with care, not allowing dominant individuals who do not 'have a problem' to lead or intimidate others. All staff should be committed to an open, honest approach to discussing individual and whole-setting/school problems. The use of case studies will enable staff to share concerns about a particular problem. All discussions should be solution-orientated.

The frequency of INSET days, half-days or twilight sessions will also impact on the quality of the programme and subsequent outcomes. Isolated days that are scheduled in a random manner throughout the year will not promote active, all-inclusive debates on policy, procedure and practice. Time needs to be invested in building a positive, supportive atmosphere among staff. Given the restrictions of the setting/school day, whole days of training followed by twilight sessions may provide the most appropriate structure. Managers and INSET teams would have to consider this aspect of organisation in their planning.

The venue is also important. It is sometimes beneficial to have an off-site venue to generate the right atmosphere for staff to feel confident. When INSET is setting/school-based, the careful selection of rooms, chairs, tables and display equipment is important. The room should be large enough to accommodate the group, without being too large. Chairs should be comfortable; not at varying heights, or in rows. Tables should be provided if staff are expected to write. Display equipment (video, overhead projector and flip charts) should be visible to all. Technical equipment should be checked before the session. If staff require pens/pencils and paper, these should be available.

CHECKLIST: CRITERIA FOR EFFECTIVE INSET

- recognition on the part of practitioners of their training needs in relation to organisational objectives
- support of the manager/headteacher and other staff
- a coherent organisational policy
- precise targeting of provision
- choice of an appropriate form of INSET, whether setting/school-based or externally based
- fulfilment of appraisal performance targets
- choice of appropriate length of course and mode of attendance
- practical focus
- appropriate expertise on the part of the higher education institutions offering INSET
- appropriate follow-up.

DISCUSSION POINT

In a group of three or four, plan an INSET day for staff in a nursery setting.

You will need to consider all the factors/issues mentioned in this section. It might be appropriate to start by doing a summary outline of issues to be considered when planning an INSET. You should select a specific topic/area to cover.

Teaching for Learning – practice-based INSET

This section considers how an INSET programme, which focuses on effective or improved practice for learning, has a positive impact on practitioners and ultimately on children's learning experiences.

In the great majority of early years settings and in most areas of the curriculum, practitioners have sufficient command of the subject areas they teach and adequate pedagogical skills to teach them satisfactorily to the children assigned to them. However, there are some subject areas where practitioners' command may be weak or where there are serious weaknesses in key aspects of methodology, such as the appropriateness of activities and the pace and challenge of activities. Local circumstances and national shortages mean that some settings are unable to provide specialist teaching, where appropriate, with the result that practitioners are obliged to engage in curriculum (learning and play) areas in which they lack adequate experience. In early years foundation stage settings, where all staff are engaged with children in all curriculum areas, it can be difficult to provide sufficient guidance in all areas. There is often a lack of confidence and knowledge. Additionally, many practitioners are ill-equipped to deal with the need to teach basic skills (personal and educational).

In all subject areas, the knowledge required of practitioners evolves continuously; for some, maintaining sufficient level of skill demands opportunities for practice beyond the teaching situation. Changes in curriculum content also need to be understood and applied. Rapid technological change, particularly in ICT, likewise demand that practitioners keep abreast of the possibilities these offer to improve the teaching of the subject areas (see Chapter 6). For all these reasons, regular and systematic subject-specific staff development through in-service training, both for specialists and non-specialists, remains a major concern if settings/schools are to maintain and improve their effectiveness.

The following checklist relates teaching for learning-based INSET to setting practice.

CHECKLIST: INSET

Where INSET is seen to be having positive effects, these include:

- a more confident grasp of knowledge (in all personal and educational areas)
- a heightened awareness of different teaching methods
- a sharper approach to matching work to children's needs
- more effective questioning techniques
- better curriculum documentation
- closer collaboration between support staff and practitioners.

The characteristics of such INSET are:

- detailed planning and close match to identified need
- clear objectives agreed with participants
- clear relationship to setting needs
- use of practitioners' prior knowledge and experiences
- adequate provision of follow-up activity
- a mutually supportive but self-critical staff, committed to the raising of standards
- support, encouragement and realistic expectations by managers/headteachers.

DISCUSSION POINT

To what extent and in what ways can lack of personal and educational knowledge and effective teaching methods impact on children's learning experiences and achievement?

Issues

Although the arrangements for, and impact of, staff development in many settings will be adequate, there is always room for improvement. This section addresses the importance of ongoing training and development for improving practice and considers the need for it to be reinforced through follow-up activities.

In most settings, the monitoring of INSET and the evaluation of its effectiveness and impact on practice are unsystematic. Where these are undertaken, it is crucial to use the results to inform future planning. Too little attention is given to the impact such training has on practice and especially on raising standards. Arrangements for dissemination need to be carefully considered. In planning INSET, the following might be of help:

- how to monitor INSET provision more closely and systematically
- how they might evaluate INSET, to determine its impact on children
- giving greater attention to dissemination and to follow-up activity, to sustain the momentum of training, to broaden expertise and to share good practice
- making IT an INSET priority: practitioners require sufficient familiarity with a range of IT facilities and the skill to apply these to the teaching of their subject
- the INSET needs of the workforce concerning provision for children with special educational needs.

Photo 12.2 How can you evaluate the impact of INSET on children's learning?

Pearson Education Ltd. Lord and Leverett © Pearson Education Ltd. 2007

DISCUSSION POINT

In a group of three or four, consider the points raised above. Imagine that you are the INSET management team in a nursery for 3–5 year olds. How would you act on this advice?

INSET and appraisal

Whole-setting/school in-service training for practitioners should relate directly to the **appraisal** process (i.e. evaluation of an individual's performance, which involves future target setting). This section provides an overview of factors which need to be considered when planning an appraisal-related INSET.

Practitioners' needs should be identified and targets set in the context of the setting/school improvement plans. It is important to identify these needs and where possible, plan INSET to accommodate training. This ensures that the appraisal cycle is completed and that INSET is relevant. The following points should be considered as factors central to effective appraisal-related INSET:

Appraisal: evaluation of performance, which involves future target setting.

- Training needs are identified at setting/school level following performance management and/or the drawing up of the organisational improvement plan.
- The practitioners, whose needs are identified, are the ones selected for training. There are no substitutions. More than one practitioner attends from each setting.
- Managers are fully aware of the purpose of the training and the expected outcome.
- The training forms part of a coherent programme and is not a 'one-off'.
- The training requires preparatory work by the practitioners.
- The training is sufficiently extensive to allow work in the setting before and between sessions, to enable reflection and consolidation.
- Trainers are fully briefed.
- Training groups are comparatively homogeneous or the training is targeted to the identified needs of the participants and sufficiently differentiated to take account of their varying levels of expertise.
- The range of provision includes on- and off-site courses, guided reading, setting support, support groups and distance learning materials.
- Dissemination strategies are built into the course, participants are given the time to disseminate what they have learned and encouraged to do so.
- Training is followed up by some form of support in the setting.

REFLECT AND RELATE TO PRACTICE

How does target setting (for individual practitioners), considered in the context of the organisational improvement plan, impact on outcomes for children?

INSET and behaviour management

Through an example of good practice INSET, which addressed behaviour management and emanated from a collaborative approach in a large suburban co-educational primary school, this section will show how effective INSET programmes can be initiated and developed in early years settings (Blandford, 2004, pp. 161–162).

In this large suburban co-educational primary school practitioners had expressed concern over increasing problems with individual pupil and classroom management. They felt that the existing discipline policy and procedures did not meet pupil needs. As a consequence practitioners were highly stressed, and staff and pupil absenteeism was prevalent. The headteacher, in consultation with LA support agencies and his staff, devised a course that focused on managing behaviour. The course programme was based on a series of case studies on video and covered:

- positive correction
- consequences
- prevention
- repair and build.

The course ran during twilight sessions over a six-week period. The following statement introduced the courses:

> Behaviour management is an important area when considering raising
> expectations. Issues about behaviour and discipline are in the frame each and
> every working day and new and proven strategies are surely welcome to [all
> practitioners].

The value of this course lies in its common-sense, jargon-free strategies of helping teachers prepare for dealing with the situations which are likely to occur in the classroom, such as:

- the child who refuses to leave the room
- the child who answers back
- the noisy classroom.

The case studies are all the more convincing and absorbing because the presenter comes across as a colleague, speaking from experience and explaining strategies which clearly work in the classroom. The programme addressed the following areas:

WHAT HAPPENS IN PRACTICE?

Positive correction

The presenter states the painfully obvious truth that most practitioners under stress will correct a child from feelings of anger rather than in a reasoned, calm and rational way. It is explained that behaviour management is an emotional issue, but that there are more efficient and successful methods of correction than resorting to intrusive and confrontational ways. Amongst the strategies discussed and demonstrated in classroom settings are the following:

- tactical ignoring by teachers
- distraction and diversion
- cool-off time and rule reminders.

'Take-up-time' is also defined; this gives pupils enough time to do what the teacher asks them and enough time to allow both of them to save face.

Consequences

The presenter deals with the emotive issue of bullying and how to deal with a child who rushes out of the classroom. It highlights the importance of children being helped to make connections between their behaviour and the result which has come about. It also emphasises the importance of 'certainty' rather than 'severity', and by this stresses crucially that there is always follow-up by the teacher after an incident, even if it is not possible at the end of the lesson or day.

Prevention

The presenter looks at how schools can maximise positive behaviour by way of a structured framework and approach, used and agreed by all staff.

Repair and rebuild

The presenter explores skills and strategies to encourage children to respect the rights of others and to take responsibility for their own behaviour. It also deals with how teachers can restore strained relationships and break the cycle of attention-seeking and power games.

The case studies are eminently suitable for staff discussion on behaviour management. If staff could be encouraged to attend more INSET training in this area, the head-teacher was confident that the case studies videos would form the basis for very worthwhile discussion as they provide a visual, rather than written, stimulus that is a welcome and accessible source on the subject.

DISCUSSION POINT

Before reading the discussion below relating to this behaviour management course, reflect on why you think this INSET was positively received by the practitioners who participated.

Discussion

There are several important features of the approach adopted by the managers when implementing the behaviour management course. The programme was an outcome of discussions that focused on practitioner and child needs; something needed to happen. The programme involved case studies that were real and related directly to practice. Practitioners were able to reflect individually (blank paper was provided) and to discuss with colleagues in small groups their thoughts and feelings emanating from behaviour management issues. No judgements were made and practitioners felt confident with the process and the outcomes of each session. The atmosphere was collegial, supportive and directed to meeting the challenge of the escalating problems in their school.

The course provided strategies for resolving these problems. The strategies were not solutions in themselves, but were a focus for teachers to reflect on their own practice. The course culminated in a review of the existing discipline policy and procedures. Practitioners felt confident in expressing the view that there needed to be a period of review, that changes were necessary, but that these had to be planned. The initial impetus for the course was based on fear, confusion and stress; the outcome was an emphatic celebration of good practice. Practitioners were able to share their strengths in preparing a programme of change. A key factor was the collegial approach and collective response to the difficult, multifaceted issue of managing discipline in schools.

SUMMARY

Planning (p. 252)

What factors/issues do you need to consider in developing an effective INSET programme?

Planning for INSET will require several months of review and consultation, where venue, approach and staff needs are all taken into consideration. Staff development needs should be considered within the context of the setting/school improvement plan.

Teaching for learning-based INSET (p. 254)

Can you be a good practitioner without a good knowledge base in all subject areas?

Early years practitioners need to have a good subject knowledge in all areas of practice, along with sound and effective strategies.

Issues (p. 256)

Why are monitoring and evaluation central to effective INSET?

The monitoring of INSET and the evaluation of its effectiveness and impact on practice should be systematic. Where these are undertaken, it is crucial to use the results to inform future planning. Too little attention is given to the impact such training has on practice and especially on raising standards. Arrangements for dissemination need to be carefully considered.

INSET and appraisal (p. 257)

Why should target setting (for individual practitioners) be considered in the context of the school/setting Improvement Plan?

In-service training for practitioners should relate directly to the appraisal process. Practitioners'

SUMMARY *CONTINUED*

needs should be identified and targets set in the context of the setting/school Improvement Plan. It is important to identify these needs and, where possible, plan whole-setting INSET to accommodate training.

INSET and behaviour management (p. 258)

What factors influence the development of a good INSET programme?

An example of good practice is a course that emanated from a collaborative approach to INSET in a large suburban co-educational primary school. Teachers had expressed concern over increasing problems with individual pupil and classroom management. The headteacher, in consultation with LA support agencies and his staff, devised a course that focused on managing behaviour.

Glossary

Appraisal: evaluation of performance, which involves future target setting.

INSET: In-Service Education and Training.

Organisational improvement plan: a plan, aimed at improving the quality of teaching and learning, which focuses on all areas within the setting where improvement is needed. It considers the vision/mission, the values, past achievements and government policy.

Find out more

The National College for School Leadership (NCSL) website has a good section on personalised learning (**http://www.ncsl.org.uk/personalisinglearning-index.htm**). Through a framework for leading personalised learning in educational settings, case studies, short documentary films and training activities for those engaged with personalised learning in practice, the website provides material and ideas for developing an effective INSET programme. A number of activities offer thought-provoking 'reflections', e.g. 'how have you made a difference to the success of learners?', which can be used for both group INSET or as questions to help you think about how you can improve the way you personalise learning in practice.

Ofsted (2006) *The Logical Chain: continuing professional development in effective schools*, London: HMI.

This document examines the professional development of staff in 29 schools where exemplary practice within the area of Continuing Professional Development was identified. By highlighting good practice, the document is not only informative, but will also give you ideas, based on sound evidence, for developing effective CPD and INSET programmes in practice.

In 2005 the Training and Development Agency (TDA) took over the responsibility from the government of providing guidance and support for developing CPD in educational settings. Their Continuing Professional Development pages, which are both helpful and useful, can be accessed at: http://www.tda.gov.uk/.

The following books have been selected because of their relevance to and centrality in effective teaching and learning in the early years. As their titles suggest, they encompass recurring and important themes in education, which need to be addressed in the earliest years of education. In addition, they provide excellent themes for INSET.

Brownhill, S. (2007) *Taking the Stress out of Bad Behaviour: Behaviour Management for 3–11 year olds.* **London: Continuum.**

Brighouse, T. (1978) *Starting Points of Self-Evaluation.* **Oxford: Oxfordshire Education Department.**

Hart, S., Dixon, A., Drummond, M.J. and McIntyre, D. (2004) *Learning Without Limits.* **Maidenhead: Open University.**

MacBeath, J. and Mortimore, P. (2001) *Improving School Effectiveness.* **Maidenhead: Open University.**

Wilson, G. (2006) *Breaking Through Barriers to Boys' Achievement.* **London: Continuum.**

References

Blandford, S. (2004) *Professional Development Manual*, 3rd edn. London: Pearson.

Blandford, S. (2006) *Middle Leadership in Schools: Harmonising Leadership and Learning*, 2nd edn. Harlow: Pearson.

Department for Education and Employment (DfEE) (1994) *Code of Practice*. London: HMSO.

Department for Education and Stills (DfES) (2005) *KEEP – Key Elements of Effective Practice*. Nottingham: DFES.

General Teaching Council for England and Wales Trust (GTC) (1993) *The Continuing Professional Development of Teachers*. London: GTC.

Appendix 1

Having read this chapter the following section will help you to reflect on the issues developed in the chapter by considering a number of worked INSET programmes.

1 INSET programme: the management team

This presents a worked programme for managers and teams. The development of in-service training should begin with an analysis of shared values and beliefs.

Friday:

6.00	Welcome
6.15	Beliefs and values
6.45	Vision and mission
7.15	Teams
7.45	Dinner

Saturday:

9.00	Learning
10.00	Targets
10.45	Break
11.00	Staff development
11.30	Communication
12.30	Lunch
1.15	Planning
2.15	Evaluation – health checks
3.15	The way forward? Roles and responsibilities
4.15	Summary and action plan

2 Values Statement

This provides examples of pro formas that can be completed to examine staff values and beliefs. A shared understanding of colleagues' values and beliefs will provide a starting point for organisation development. Where differences occur these should be accepted and respected.

Ref	What we value	What we do	Comment

Ref	Value	Behaviour statement	Comment

3 Management and learning

The following has been adapted from a worked example of INSET. It provides the reader with a series of evaluative questions that enable practitioners to develop a shared understanding of the relationship between management and learning. Practitioners may consider their role in terms of children, parents, school and community. Questions relating to setting/classroom management and learning could be structured in an objective way as shown in the following (Brighouse, 1978).

Practitioner with children

- To what extent am I aware of, and do I take account of, individual needs?
- Am I aware of children with particular problems?
- How do I deal with them?
- How do I respond to poor attendance?
- How do I respond to behavioural problems?
- How well do I know my children?

Practitioner with parents

- Do I know the parents?
- How effectively do I communicate with parents?
- Is there a shared understanding of how their child should behave, and about attendance?
- Is the home situation stable or changing?
- How well do I know the family?

Environment

- What is the general appearance of the setting like – playground, corridor, rooms, classroom lavatories, playing fields?
- Who ensures that displays are of quality and reflect all children's work?
- What is the manner in which children move around the setting/school between lessons tasks, during breaks and at the start and end of the day?
- How would the noise level be described?

Practice

- What is the provision for children with behaviour problems?
- How are teaching and non-teaching staff supported when dealing with discipline-related matters?
- What staff training opportunities are there?

- How well does the setting school communicate with LA support agencies and advisers?
- How effective is the discipline policy?
- Does policy reflect practice?
- Are there sufficient discipline procedures and practices to support staff and children?
- Praise, rewards and sanctions – what are used and why?
- What opportunities are given for the development of initiative and responsibility?
- What is the procedure for checking lateness and absence?

Communication

- How does the setting school communicate with members of the wider community?
- Are there adequate opportunities for all members of the community to express their views?
- What consultative process is used to help arrive at policy decisions related to discipline?
- What are the links with the EWO, educational psychologist and schools' advisory service?

Parents

- How is a parent first introduced to the setting?
- How do parents personally meet members of staff?
- Are there opportunities for parents to meet staff:
  - as a matter of routine?
  - at their own or the setting school's request?
- Is there a parents' association? What are its functions? Is it effective?
- What are the various kinds of meetings held for parents? What proportion of parents attend meetings and how is information communicated to those who do not attend?
- Do parents know and understand the discipline policy, procedures and practices in this setting?
- How are parents aided and encouraged to be interested in helping their children to achieve their potential?
- Is there a home–setting contract?
- How does the setting meet family needs?
- Is information to parents communicated appropriately, in a language and style that is understood by members of the family for ethnic groups, translated into their own language?

Community

- Does the setting school see itself as a focus of the community? How does it promote such an image?

- How does the setting school ensure good relationships with the local community?
- What is the relationship between the organisation and its community?
- Are children involved in any way with local community service?
- Does the setting school have regular contact with the local family centre?
- How closely does the setting school work with social services in order to meet community needs?
- How well does the setting school relate to the cultural aspirations of the community in terms of behaviour, respect and family values?

The list of points to be considered in the evaluation is by no means conclusive. All settings have their own needs that should be identified and the setting's response to each evaluated. Much of the above is objective and setting-orientated. However, practitioners will have their own belief and value systems that also need to be evaluated (Adapted from Brighouse (1978)).

4 A questionnaire for practitioners

The questionnaire examines outcomes, but also focuses on learning. This would provide managers with a lead into discussing teaching and learning styles.

A QUESTIONNAIRE FOR PRACTITIONERS

Rate the following on a 1–5 scale (1 = agreement):

1   My job is to get across the facts.
2   What do the children need to know to increase their knowledge?
3   Essentially, I have to be in control of the setting.
4   I have to decide on the learning outcomes.
5   It's up to me to decide on whether the children have learnt something.
6   I have to be in charge of the resources.
7   The children do not need to know the end point; they just have to cope with each step.
8   If the children do not learn something, they just need to work harder.
9   There is a lot of material that the group must get through – that is the main task.
10   I must look for the right answers.

5 Developing communication skills

Aim: To outline the different methods of communication
       To assess their effectiveness
Time: 45 minutes

Stage 1   5 minutes

Tick the appropriate column on the following table to show how frequently you make use of each.

	Daily	Weekly	Half-termly	Termly
Formal meeting				
Informal meetings				
Interviews				
Briefings				
Information sheets				
Memos				

6 Organisation development plan – raising achievement

Aim: To examine aims
       To examine teaching and learning styles/differentiation
       To identify areas of weakness in resourcing
Time: 1 hour

Stage 1   5 minutes

Brainstorm the context that you are working in (size of team/school/local authority) – consider all factors inside and beyond the setting school – write on a flip chart.

Stage 2   10 minutes

Divide into two groups. Look at the setting school aims. Write down on a flip chart what the aims should be – how can you implement these aims?

Stage 3   5 minutes

Share your ideas with your team/department.

Stage 4   20 minutes

Discuss strategies for raising achievement through planning/completing tasks/teaching and learning styles. List.

13 The Learning Community

By the end of this chapter you will be able to answer the following questions:

- What factors influence the development of an inclusive learning community?
- What is the role of the key person and to what extent does he/she contribute to the learning, development and well-being of the children to whom he/she is assigned?
- Why is communication central to effective practice within an early years setting?
- How can I involve parents as partners in their children's learning?

This chapter will support your understanding of the following Standards *(see Appendix 1):*
■ **Knowledge and understanding:** S03 ■ **Effective practice:** S07, S08 and S18 ■ **Relationships with children:** S25 and S27 ■ **Communicating and working in partnership with families and carers:** S29, S30, S31 and S32 ■ **Teamwork and collaboration:** S33.

Introduction

Inclusive education: practitioners teach to the learning needs of each child, where each child is welcomed and included.

The government's vision is clear – an **inclusive education** which gives every child the opportunity of achieving his/her full potential:

> to achieve this children need to feel loved and valued, and be supported by a network of reliable and affectionate relationships. If they are denied the opportunity and support they need to achieve these outcomes, children are at increased risk not only of an impoverished childhood, but also of disadvantage and social exclusion in adulthood.
>
> *(The Stationery Office, 2006: 31)*

Since 2003, early years settings have embraced the five outcomes of *Every Child Matters* (DfES, 2003); every child will be healthy; stay safe; enjoy and achieve; make a positive contribution; and achieve economic well-being. Within the setting the balance of activities is shared amongst the workforce (i.e. where appropriate; for example, this will not be the case for childminders) – leaders, other educators, support staff, administrators, external agents and the voluntary sector. The government endorses the idea of an inclusive learning community, which focuses on the learning, development and well-being of each child. Reflected in the quote at the beginning of the chapter, this is founded on the development of good collaborative relationships. By addressing the importance of building and sustaining good working relationships with the children, their parents and those who work within the setting, this chapter will consider how early years settings are, in essence, learning communities that guide and support all members of the community.

An inclusive learning community

Communities of educational practice are based on agreeing and implementing good conditions for learning and development, but recognise that to achieve the highest standards and sustain improvement, the social interactions, curriculum (formal and informal/hidden) and other learning experiences of the child should be considered as a whole. In creating an environment which supports the learning, development and well-being of all children, the collaborative practice of the staff within the setting needs to be founded on shared values and beliefs. This section explores the principles underlying the idea of an inclusive community, where all childrenare valued and supported as unique individuals and in which they feel a sense of belonging.

Inclusion is perhaps best understood in terms of what it means and what it aims to do within the context of early years practice. The Centre for Studies on Inclusive Education (CSIE) (2000: 1) explains what inclusion in education means:

- Valuing all children and staff equally.
- Increasing the participation of children in, and reducing their exclusion from, the cultures (see Chapter 18), curricula and community of the setting.

- Restructuring the cultures, policies and practices in the setting, so that they respond to the diversity of children in the locality.
- Reducing barriers to learning and participation for all children.
- Learning from attempts to overcome barriers to the access and participation of particular children to make changes for the benefits of children more widely.
- Viewing the differences between children as resources to support learning, rather than as a problem to be overcome.
- Acknowledging the right of children to an education in their locality.
- Improving educational settings for staff as well as children.
- Emphasising the role of educational settings in building community and developing values, as well as increasing achievement.
- Fostering mutually sustaining relationships between educational settings and communities.
- Recognising that inclusion in education is one aspect of inclusion in society.

The role of the practitioner is fundamental to fostering understanding of inclusive thinking and practice in the educational community. In doing so, it is necessary that the practitioner has an understanding regarding the opinions, attitudes and experiences of colleagues, parents and children. Julie Allan (2003), professor of education at the University of Stirling, who has written widely on inclusive education, argues: 'Becoming inclusive . . . means becoming political; listening to what children and their parents say about what inclusion means to them; and recognising the way in which we ourselves are implicated in practices that exclude' (2003: 178).

> ### DISCUSSION POINT
>
> Consider the above list of what inclusion in education means (CISE, 2000). Do you think it would be possible to create an inclusive learning community in a setting if all staff did not share these values or principles? Why/why not?

In early years settings and schools, practitioners and teachers play the role of **loco parentis**. They are not there solely to bestow knowledge on children, they are also there to assist in the children's fuller development as social beings and to work as part of a team in the construction of an effective and inclusive educational community. It is important that practitioners listen to the voices of children. Lewis and Lindsay (2000) and Roberts (2000) comment on the importance of hearing the child's voice and providing room for practitioners to develop a perspective on the children's world. Roberts explains: 'It is clear that listening to children, hearing children and acting on what children say are three very different activities, although they are frequently elided as if they were not' (2000: 238).

Creating an inclusive learning context is not to be viewed or understood as an end point. It is not a product which emerges when a practitioner or educational community uses a particular formula for the management of teaching and learning. Nor is it a restrictive scientific theory; inclusive thinking and practice results in a constant

Loco parentis: acting in the place of parents.

Photo 13.1 Is inclusive practice embedded in your day-to-day practice?

Pearson Education Ltd. Tudor Photography © Pearson Education Ltd. 2004

developmental process, where decisions are made and action taken on the basis of inclusion – to be included. Such processes will result in the establishment of an effective learning community. The following 'What happens in practice?' provides examples of inclusive practice in a nursery setting.

WHAT HAPPENS IN PRACTICE?

Babies

We realise that it can be difficult for some babies when they make the move from the baby room to the toddler room. Although the rooms are separate, we have low windows and a gated opening between the two so that the babies and toddlers can see and interact with each other as they choose. When we feel that a baby is ready to move to the toddler room they spend short periods of time in there for the first few sessions with their new **key person**. Also, we tend to have staff move between the rooms and we are all together outside so all the babies and children know all of us well. We think this familiarity and chance to build relationships with us and the older children helps the babies when they move to the toddler room.

Key person: a staff member who is responsible for one child observing and spending time with them to support their learning.

Toddlers

J has cerebral palsy. He now has a specially designed chair for the nursery, with appropriate restrainers and cushioning. This chair also has a large tray that can be fitted to the front.

The chair helps J, the other children in the nursery and us, in a range of ways. Firstly, it is identical to his chair at home and so he is familiar and comfortable in it. You'll see him smile when he is lifted into the chair. Secondly, it really helps him to be in the same position as other children when they are in their high chairs to eat and drink. It also enables J to have close eye contact as we draw his chair close to others.

His parents worked tirelessly to arrange for this chair to be provided and its benefits are becoming really evident.

Older children

We don't have a specific time for parents to bring their children to nursery, although we are open from eight o'clock. We feel it is important to acknowledge that families have different routines in the morning and that children have different sleep patterns and rhythms. So parents sign in when they arrive and we welcome children into whatever activity is going on when they come.

(Goouch and Powell, 2006)

REFLECT AND RELATE TO PRACTICE

For each setting list the ways in which these practitioners have addressed the idea of inclusion. Do you think it was effective? Would you have approached these situations in the same way? What, if anything, would you have done differently?

Community: place and function

Critically, education in early years settings should be concerned with education within and for communities, not of communities (Poster, 1982). Community education begins with and for the individual. By considering a case study outlining the development of a community music centre, this section will address the idea that learning communities are underpinned by place and function. Stoll et al. suggest:

> everything people do on a daily basis, within the school and in relation to parents and the local community, is underpinned by a sense of belonging and collective commitment to each other's learning and ensuring that the school is a moving school.

(2003: 136)

The principles, on which community provision is built, are based on certain assumptions that also relate to inclusive learning communities (Blandford and Gibson, 2005):

- education relates to other branches of social provision; it does not exist only as an academic entity
- social provision is determined by the prevailing social and economic framework of society
- both social and educational provision have become more centrally controlled
- there has been a move towards devolution of power reflecting the need to provide community-type activities led by the community
- there is a greater emphasis on participation that contributes to the emancipation of the educator.

The following 'What happens in practice?' considers how a learning community was developed through a music initiative:

WHAT HAPPENS IN PRACTICE?

Community music centres

Many schools and communities have a history of music-making. These have been established over time through church and faith groups, the voluntary sector, schools and philanthropists. This case study describes two examples of a local centre and an international centre that have provided many opportunities for volunteers and students to develop a range of skills. The local centre originated in a large co-educational 11–18 comprehensive school in southern England; the other is a music centre in Lisbon, Portugal.

Within the school, community music started with a choir for pupils and children from neighbouring schools which led to the formation of a school wind band which evolved into a Community Music Centre (CMC) and now exists as an independent charity organisation within the local community. In Portugal, the music centre provides an opportunity for young people to join a musical ensemble that rehearses in languages with which participants are most familiar, i.e. English and Portuguese. The centre sympathises with the internationally mobile student and caters for students from a variety of musical backgrounds. As a community group, the International Music Centre (IMC) is unrestricted by involvement in a national music system and open to all.

Blandford and Duarte (2004) found that the social benefits motivated and sustained membership of both centres. Social skills are enhanced by participation in a musical community through the development of friendships, improved self-confidence and, in many cases, facilitated transition into a new environment.

In terms of learning, participants developed transferable skills associated with learning and taking responsibility. Through teaching and guiding younger members, the participants were able to gain understanding of their own needs, particularly in the areas of intonation, aural perception, notation and ensemble proficiency. The experience of inclusion moves beyond notions of class, ability, race or creed as has been demonstrated by research, practice and music-making. In terms of inclusion, it would appear that by moving out of school and into the community the codes that limit our understanding of community are broken.

Participation in a musical community is fully inclusive. Children with learning and physical disabilities are supported and stimulated by the group. Students from different nationalities, cultural backgrounds, abilities and a wide age range are able to combine their efforts to the common good of the community.

All players reported how much they had enjoyed the experience of participating in a musical community. As reflected in the words of the music educator, Isaac Stern (Guaspari, 1999), the aim of music-making is:

> not to make 'musicians' out of everyday performers, but more important, to make them educated, alert, caring inquiring young people, who by playing music feel a part of the connective tissue between what the mind of man has been able to devise and the creativity of music . . . in other words, become literate, and part of the culture of the whole world.

DISCUSSION POINT

1 How could you develop music activities for/within an early years setting?
2 How can musical communities help children develop social skills?
3 How do Community Music Centres help children's learning and development?

Setting, home and the community: theoretical framework

The connection between the early years setting and the community is not fixed but exists on a continuum, which is guided by the practices within the setting, particularly the extent to which parents are involved. In essence, the continuum extends from a 'closed door pattern' of connection or links between the setting, home and community, to an 'open door' pattern, with a 'balanced pattern' falling somewhere in the middle. In practice, settings will borrow from one or more of the patterns. This section will consider what this means in practice.

The three possible patterns of connection between the setting and the local community can be described as follows:

Closed door pattern: the early years setting deals with all the child's educational and social problems, while community involvement and intervention is minimal.

1 **The closed door pattern**: the early years setting deals with all the child's educational and social problems, while community involvement and intervention is minimal. Within a closed system, as in the second law of thermodynamics, the total energy of the system will deteriorate. According to Friedman (1986), the closed door policy towards the community lacks feedback and will waste energy without the right guidance. In the absence of input from the parents and the community, the setting will be unaware of changes occurring in these systems, and hence will be unable to adapt itself and its curricula to these changes and will keep degenerating.

Open door pattern: the early years setting and the parents operate as open systems, so that information flows freely in both directions.

2 **The open door pattern**: the early years setting and the parents operate as open systems, so that information flows freely in both directions. The setting with an open door policy makes the parents partners in their children's educational process and strives to become an influential factor in the life of the community. A basic assumption of systems theory is that the open system is designed to process the inputs of its external environment and return the processed product to the environment for its use and benefit. The exchange of energy occurs in a cyclic nature. The final and improved product serves as a new source of energy passing from the environment to the system. In this way the deteriorating process is stopped (Katz and Kahn, 1978). According to Friedman (1986), the setting with an open door policy receives its children from the parents, teaches them and raises their level of education, in order to return them to their community. In their adult life they will produce a new generation of children, whose contribution to their children's education is expected to be greater than that of their parents' generation.

Balanced pattern: the early years setting and the parents set the degree of closeness or distance between them, in order to achieve their educational and social goals to the optimal extent.

3 **The balanced pattern**: the early years setting and the parents set the degree of closeness or distance between them, in order to achieve their educational and social goals to the optimal extent. When the distance is large, the setting has to bridge the gap and reach out to the community; when the distance is small, the school has to some extent to close its gates.

DISCUSSION POINT

To what extent are these theoretical patterns reflected in early years government policy?

Do you think the government wishes to promote a certain type of pattern? Why?

Identity and belonging: welcoming the child

Each child is unique, which will be reflected in the way he/she settles into a new setting. By addressing the transition from home to setting and setting to school, this section will consider the extent to which present practices welcome the child and help him/her to settle in and become part of the community.

The transition from home to setting can be a difficult time for both children and parents. To make it easier and to maintain a support system for the child and his/her family, early years settings employ a key-person approach, whereby a member of staff is assigned to the new child and his/her family on entry; a different key person is assigned to the child as he/she moves through the setting. In addition, to meet the challenges that a rota system can pose in a setting (necessitated by the staff 'shift' system which operates in many early years settings to accommodate the longer day, which can extend from 8am to 6pm), children are usually assigned a second key person with whom they become familiar. Elfer et al. (2003) define the key-person approach as:

> a way of working in nurseries in which the whole focus and organisation is aimed at enabling and supporting close attachments between individual children and individual nursery staff. The key person approach is an involvement, an individual and reciprocal commitment between a member of staff and a family.

(2003: 18)

This can have enormous benefits for the child in what may seem like an alien environment. From the perspective of the child, who will also have contact with a number of other practitioners within the setting on a daily basis, the key person is an adult whom they can trust. The following 'What happens in practice?' is an example of practice within a children's centre and shows the role of the key person in the wider context of reassuring the mother when she has to leave her child at the setting.

WHAT HAPPENS IN PRACTICE?

A mother brought her seven month old son into the setting and stayed to show some photographs to her key person. . . . The key person sensitively included a two year old in this looking and talking session, helping her to be gentle with the photographs, while chatting to the mother and keeping a vigilant eye on her seven month old son as he crawled around and played happily on the floor. When the photographs had been looked at, the mother stayed for a further chat – her son was playing contentedly but she was eager to stay for her own sake.

(Marsh, 1997: 99)

REFLECT AND RELATE TO PRACTICE

Do you think the key person in the above example dealt with this situation effectively and appropriately? Why/why not?

Would you have dealt with this situation differently? If this is the case, how would you have dealt with this situation?

The key-person system is underpinned by the development of meaningful relationships between the adult and the child. Children learn, develop and grow in confidence in an environment where they feel cared for, respected and know that they matter. Although there has been some criticism of the key-person approach, documented by Elfer et al. (2003) and centred on the idea that the key person can inadvertently displace the parent or take the role of the parent (see Chapter 2), or that the child can become too attached to the key person, the government endorses this approach. The government views the role within a strong professional framework, where 'attachment' to the child is seen as part of 'sharing care' with the parents which enables the child to learn and develop as an independent individual. The key person, who is usually assigned to a number of children, within the setting is responsible for:

- meeting the needs of the children to which he/she is assigned, responding sensitively to their feelings, ideas and behaviour
- talking to parents to make sure that their child is being cared for appropriately within the setting
- keeping records of the child's development and progress which he/she will share with the parents, child and other professionals as required.

(adapted from DCSF, 2008)

The assigning of one person to a particular child, who will work with him/her for specified periods of time each day, provides the opportunity for closer bonds to develop between the child and the adult. Although children can cope with a number of different adults taking care of their learning and development, research has shown that at critical times (e.g. if they are upset on arrival) children find it more reassuring and comforting to be with a familiar adult. It was mentioned earlier within the section that there has been some criticism of the key-person approach. The following is a summary (Elfer et al., 2003: 8–9) of the views of four experienced practitioners, who put forward their argument against the approach:

- It brings staff too close to a parental role and they risk becoming over-involved.
- If children get too close to any one member of staff, it is painful for them if that member of staff is not available.
- It can be threatening for parents who may be jealous of a special relationship between their child and another adult.
- The key person approach is complex to organise and staff need to work as a team, not as individuals.
- It undermines the opportunities for children to participate in all nursery–community relationships.

DISCUSSION POINT

Do you agree with the criticisms of the key-person approach? Why/why not?
What is your view? Do you think the key-person approach is an effective and appropriate way of supporting children and their families? Why/why not?

Photo 13.2
The key person approach should complement the role of the parents
Pearson Education Ltd. Jules Selmes © Pearson Education Ltd. 2004

The early years are vital for laying the foundations for the kind of people we become. Acknowledging the centrality of early years education in the development of the child, practitioners need to consider the type of environment they are creating. Settings should be communities of engagement. From the physical surroundings through to the staff, curriculum and **hidden curriculum**, they need to be inviting, welcoming, supporting and secure. Edgington emphatically states that it is at this time that children 'must develop the resources they need to cope with the emotional, social, physical and intellectual challenges they will meet as they grow older' (1998: 57). Earlier in this section we considered the transition from home to setting and considered some of the difficulties for the child and his/her parents. The following activity addresses factors which should be considered in the transition from setting to school:

Hidden curriculum: that which is learned tacitly within the setting.

ACTIVITY

Margaret Edgington (1998: 80–81), who is known for her work on educational practice in early years, offers suggestions for managing the transition from setting to school. The following issues have been developed from her work:

- Admissions policies should be developed in a manner which enables teachers to get to know and respond to each child as an individual.

▶

▶

- Aspects of classroom life which are likely to be stressful for children starting at school for the first time should be considered.
- Consider how stress can be minimised – a child should be able to adjust gradually to the new environment and expectations.
- Consider how you could involve a child's parents/guardians in supporting a child during the transition.
- Consider how you can help children to approach new experiences and new challenges with confidence.
- Consider how an early years team can work together to ensure that the transfer from an early years setting to the next class/setting can be as stress free as possible.

DISCUSSION POINT

Consider Edgington's advice. How would you prepare a child to move from your setting into the reception class at a local school?

Communication

In developing a secure, inclusive environment which responds to the learning needs of all children, open channels of communication at all levels are central to effective practice. By considering the idea of communication through three case studies, presented as 'What happens in practice?', this section will highlight how poor communication between practitioners, parents and children can directly impact on the children's learning and development.

Communication is central to effective operations within an early years setting. According to the National Policy Board for Educational Administration's (NPBEA) *Principles for our Changing Schools*:

> communication underlies all organisational and administrative situations, and is essential to decision-making and effective leadership. . . . At the heart of communication lies the opportunity to resolve contradictions, quell rumours, provide reassurance, and, ultimately, instil meaning in the complex but engaging task of education.

(1993: 16-4)

In early years settings, staff and leader practitioners use different methods of communication for different purposes; some are more successful than others. Why is it that communication always seems to flow more smoothly in some settings and teams than others? One reason is the current and/or established communication climate. The conditions in which ideas, information and feelings are exchanged directly influence the extent to which communication is a positive or negative force in a setting. The following 'What happens in practice?' provides three examples of 'communication' within a nursery setting.

WHAT HAPPENS IN PRACTICE?

Babies

O is asleep in the pram outside the door here on the patio, in the sunshine. Her Mum does this at home. We know that this is part of her regular routine at the moment as we have a very effective form of contact diary that works here. Both the parents and staff at the nursery use this on a daily basis and we are all very happy with it. One family is especially supporting this system as the grandparents bring and collect their grandchild. The contact diary helps the parents to get a good picture of their daughter's day and helps them to tell us important information directly. We also get to know if there has been a difficult night or feeding problems which would affect her day with us.

Toddlers

A photograph book is developed during the time the child is in nursery. The photographs are taken once a week in school and/or at home. A Polaroid camera is in the nursery for this purpose. The photographs are intended to illustrate a significant change or piece of development that occurs. For example a parent exclaimed out loud when she saw her child toddling up the climbing frame steps on his own, 'Look that's the first time he's done it and he's laughing!' The parents talk with us [staff] about what development and learning is happening, about why they have taken the photo, and together we decide on a caption to reflect this.

Older children

We decided that having everybody [staff] standing in a line, first thing in the morning when we opened the doors, was effectively blocking off parents from the nursery, forming a boundary. We changed our practice so that the nursery room was opened up as soon as they came in, the activities were visible and parents felt they could move more freely with their children. We gave ourselves places to sit around the room so that we are visible and accessible. This way, the

◗

parents seemed to find it easier to join in with their children to begin with, to take them off to the toilet, to put on aprons if necessary and just generally to settle their child before leaving. Parents seem to feel more welcome to just join in which makes that transition from home to nursery more relaxed. It also gives us the opportunity to talk with the parents informally and more regularly. Pictures are often brought from home and book swaps take place then too.

(Goouch and Powell, 2006)

REFLECT AND RELATE TO PRACTICE

What strategies/practices have been developed in each of these examples which either reflect good methods of communication or have opened up the channels of communication?

☆ ☆ ☆

Do you think they have been effective?
Would you have taken a different approach? Why/why not?

Parents: developing partnerships

Parental involvement in the early years setting enriches the child's world and extends their horizons because when the parents take part in the educational process, children are exposed to a variety of people who represent different worlds in terms of life experience, age, occupation, interests and attitude; these encounters afford many opportunities for learning, enrichment and identification (Noy, 1984). By addressing why parents should be partners in their children's learning and how this partnership can be developed and enhanced by practitioners, this section will consider practical ways of involving parents which can contribute to both the child's advancement and that of their parents.

Since the late 1990s there has been a strong movement in England by the government to encourage parents to become more actively involved in their children's learning. Busher (2000: 90) suggests that this coincided with the increased body of recent research which highlighted the impact parents have on enhancing their children's learning. The benefit of parental involvement is also manifested in the child's personality and behavioural variables, such as improvement of the self-image and of learning habits, reduction in disciplinary problems and absenteeism, and rise in motivation (Raywid, 1984).

The interaction between home circumstances and setting practices is important. Opportunities for practitioners and parents to talk about their child and share information can help guide practitioners in their planning for behaviours for learning. Partnerships with parents play a key role in promoting a culture of co-operation between parents, educational setting, LAs, early learning organisations and others; this is important in enabling children to achieve their potential.

Parents hold key information and have a critical role to play in their children's education. They have unique strengths, knowledge and experience to contribute to the shared view of a child's needs and the best ways of supporting them. It is therefore essential that all professionals (early years setting, LAs and other agencies) actively seek to work with parents and value the contribution they make. The work of professionals can be more effective when parents are involved and account is taken of their wishes, feelings and perspectives on their children's development. All parents should be treated as partners. They should be supported to be able and empowered to recognise and fulfil their responsibilities as parents and play an active and valued role in their children's education. This is particularly so when a child has special educational needs.

Sometimes a child may be with a foster parent or residential worker or with another relative because of a court order. These carers also have a general responsibility to work with the educational setting and the child. They may have as much to contribute in terms of understanding why a child is behaving poorly and what might be done to improve matters.

Early years settings should provide welcoming environments for parents. Settings can use prospectuses and other communications to convey and reinforce the notion of home–setting (and home–school) partnerships. Contact with parents should not be confined to formal meetings, e.g. parents' evenings for those whose children are at primary school and meetings with key persons or leader practitioners in settings; it should be an integral part of setting and school life. It may be possible to bring together groups of parents to discuss problems in an atmosphere of mutual support.

Practitioners, teachers and governors should be alert to the difficulties and pressures which can arise from unstable family relationships and the impact of unemployment, homelessness, family bereavement, racial tension and illness. Sometimes family breakdown may result in children having very disrupted lives and moving between different homes or moving out of areas where they have established friendships. For some children, the educational setting may be the only secure, stable environment.

It has been shown that when children have relationships outside the family in which they feel valued and respected, this acts as a protection against adversity within the family. Children may nonetheless feel inhibited about discussing changes in their lives such as family breakdown. Problems within the family can have an adverse effect on children's emotional and educational development. The educational setting's processes for recording and identifying children with problems should be sensitive to possible links between behaviour and other experiences in a child's life. This may lead to the need to involve other agencies or support services in order to assist the child's development (see Chapter 17).

Good behaviour, as well as bad, will need to be drawn to parents' attention, and early notice given of any particular strengths or difficulties with an individual child. The setting's behaviour policy should make clear the matters considered of sufficient importance to require notification of parents.

Educational settings have found home–setting (and home–school) contracts to be of significant benefit in involving parents constructively in considering children's behaviour. Such contracts, which specify the expectations of children, parents and the educational setting, have proved useful in setting out for parents their particular responsibilities in relation to their child and in defining the educational setting's role and policies. These are likely to work best if they offer the prospect of benefits as well as sanctions, and can form part of the admissions process.

In practice parents need accurate information and regular feedback about what is happening in the educational setting. The information should be clear, comprehensive and user-friendly. It should also be communicated in a style and language appropriate to its audience (e.g. can parents read, do they speak a different language, etc.?). Parents and carers should also have an influence on the way the settings are managed. Clearly, all parents should be involved in partnership with practitioners. It is the organisation's responsibility to develop confidence in parents to enable this to happen.

DISCUSSION POINT

It was not until the late 1990s that the government launched a drive to involve parents in the early education and care of their children. This coincided with the increased body of research which highlighted the benefits of involving parents and the publication of the government's National Childcare Strategy which put early years education more firmly within the political arena. Consider the following statement: 'Government policy did not need to emphasise the centrality of working in partnership with parents – early years settings have always involved parents in their children's learning and development.' Do you agree with this statement? Why/why not? Do you think that the political drive to involve parents in their children's learning and development has altered the way we view parental involvement both in theory and practice?

Communicating and working in partnership with parents

Positive attitudes to parents, user-friendly information and procedures and awareness of support needs are important. There should be no presumption about what parents can or cannot do to support their children's learning. Stereotypic views of parents are unhelpful and should be challenged. All staff should bear in mind the pressures a parent may be under because of the child's needs. To make communications effective professionals should:

- acknowledge and draw on parental knowledge and expertise in relation to their child
- focus on the children's strengths as well as areas of additional need
- recognise the personal and emotional investment of parents and be aware of their feelings

- ensure that parents understand procedures, are aware of how to access support in preparing their contributions, and are given documents to be discussed well before meetings and within meetings
- enable parents to be supported at meetings
- respect the validity of differing perspectives and seek constructive ways of reconciling different viewpoints
- repect the differing needs parents themselves may have, such as a disability or communications and linguistic barriers
- recognise the need for flexibility in the timing and structure of meetings.

Parents will also benefit from their involvement, which enables them to deepen their knowledge of their child's world, the teaching methods and effective forms of negotiation with children. Involvement in their child's education may help the parents to develop their own personalities and satisfy their needs. In the school they may find an outlet for their talents and tendencies which are not expressed in other places. By 2010, all mainstream and special schools should be delivering extended services which include:

> parenting support including information sessions for parents at key transition points, parenting programmes run with the support of other children's services and family learning sessions to allow children to learn with their parents.
>
> *(DfES, 2005: 8)*

Parents gain satisfaction from the experience of expressing their needs and skills, from the new opportunities opened to them for self-expression and realisation, and from the opportunity to share in the educational process and the gratitude and praise they receive for their participation and involvement (Noy, 1984; Hituv, 1989).

Early years practitioners benefit from parental participation in the educational work in the setting. Noy (1984) reports on four main areas in which parental involvement makes a substantial contribution: physical help, connections and contacts, the educational sphere and creativity. This also strengthens the educator's professional, social and personal image, relieves the feeling of solitude that can accompany the educator's work and increases his/her motivation to persevere and refresh professional knowledge.

The Community Education Development Centre (CEDC) (2000: 32) suggest the following effective ways of involving parents:

- provide materials to support children's learning at home
- make effective use of the voluntary assistance of parents within the school (or setting)
- make work with parents and the community an integral part of staff recruitment, induction and CPD
- actively encourage parents to offer support to their children and suggest possible ways of doing this
- make information available in a form which is accessible to all parents
- provide regular guidance and training to parents who participate in the co-education of their children within the school (or setting)
- provide curriculum workshops (Early Years Foundation stage)
- facilitate the election of parent governors to represent parents on the school's governing body.

The following example of 'What happens in practice?' documents how one primary school developed an initiative which both supported and involved parents.

WHAT HAPPENS IN PRACTICE?

Highfield Primary School in Efford, Plymouth, has converted two empty classrooms into a community room. The community room offers 'whizart' classes, in which parents work alongside their children on art activities one afternoon a week. After school, ICT sessions are available for parents and children. Parents wishing to develop their ICT skills can take part in a 15-week training course. The head teacher explained: 'Many of the parents here had bad experiences at school. They still find school a threatening environment. It's a way of getting parents in and getting them to spend time learning and talking with their child.' As a result of the school's success in involving parents, children are more likely to ask their parents for help with homework.

(DfES, 2005)

DISCUSSION POINT

Highfield Primary School has developed a programme for actively involving parents. Imagine you were the practitioner responsible for initiating and implementing the programme; how might you have developed it?

Consider how you would initiate, implement and run another activity for parents and children to learn together.

Other examples of parental engagement with early years settings have been those which centred on the parents themselves, such as aerobics clubs for parents/practitioners. During the aerobics parents developed the confidence to ask questions about their children. These provide opportunities for parents to fully engage in the learning community.

The learning community: bringing it together

Effective learning communities are founded on good working relationships between those involved in the child's learning, development and well-being, most notably the child him/herself, the parents and the practitioner. Early years leaders will contribute to building a culture within the setting that utilises the richness of the resources that exist within and beyond it, and ensure that learning experiences are integrated into the wider community. The change in culture will also contribute to the development of an early years system that will lead to innovation in all areas through the sharing of good practice. The effectiveness of building partnerships within the learning community and the wider local community is based on long-term planning through consultation and identification of needs. The sustainability, however, of these partnerships (children, parents, practitioners and the wider community) will be dependent on the innovative practices of those involved in the learning, development and well-being of the child.

SUMMARY

An inclusive learning community (p. 270)

Do we need to question our values in developing an inclusive learning community?

The practitioner is fundamental in fostering understanding of inclusive thinking and practice in the educational community. In inclusive learning communities, practice is founded on shared values and beliefs.

Community: place and function (p. 273)

What is the role of the extended community?

Learning communities develop within and for those they serve, who in turn develop a sense of belonging through shared participation in a common interest.

Setting, home and the community: theoretical framework (p. 275)

Which theoretical framework do you think would be the most effective in practice?

The connection between the early years setting and the community is not fixed but exists on a continuum from the open door pattern (welcoming to the whole community) through to the closed door pattern (not welcoming to the extended community).

Identity and belonging: welcoming the child (p. 276)

What are the key factors in engaging children in the community?

Acknowledging the centrality of the early years of education in the long-term development of the child, practitioners need to create an environment which is supportive, welcoming and engaging. This is founded on the development of good relationships between those involved, which can be enhanced by the key person, responsible for engaging with the child and his/her family.

Communication (p. 280)

Why is the centrality of effective communication so important?

In early years settings, staff and leader practitioners use different methods of communication for different purposes; some are more successful than others. Developing open and effective channels of communication between practitioner and parents can enhance the children's learning and development.

SUMMARY *CONTINUED*

Parents: developing partnerships (p. 283)

Government policy did not need to emphasise the centrality of working in partnership with parents – early years settings have always involved parents in their children's learning. Discuss.

Government policy places emphasis on the development of effective partnerships particularly between practitioners, children and parents. This is supported by research evidence, which highlights the benefits for children's learning development and well-being.

Glossary

Balanced pattern: the early years setting and the parents set the degree of closeness or distance between them, in order to achieve their educational and social goals to the optimal extent.

Closed door pattern: the early years setting deals with all the child's educational and social problems, while community involvement and intervention is minimal.

Hidden curriculum: that which is learned tacitly within the setting. It is most closely addressed through the ethos of the setting and describes the outcomes of the educational experience which are not openly addressed through the formal curriculum.

Inclusive educational settings: practitioners teach to the learning needs of each child, where each child is welcomed and included.

Key person: a member of staff assigned to a particular child who is responsible for welcoming him/her each day, observing the child on a formal basis and spending some time working with him/her to support his/her learning.

Loco parentis: acting in the place of parents.

Open door pattern: the early years setting and the parents operate as open systems, so that information flows freely in both directions.

Find out more

Elfer, P., Goldschmied, E. and Selleck, D. (2003) *Key Persons in the Nursery: Building Relationships for Quality Provision*, London: David Fulton.
Chapter 2, What is the Key Person Approach?, provides a good insight into the work of a key person. Through case studies it delineates the role of the key person in a child's learning and development.

Whalley, M. and the Pen Green Centre Team (2001) *Involving Parents in their Children's Learning*, London: Sage.
This book provides an insight into practice in the Pen Green Centre in Corby. Established in 1983, the centre is well known for its early years practices. The book provides comprehensive coverage of parental involvement in their children's learning – from involving fathers to examining the impact of the involvement on the lives of families/carers.

References

Allan, J. (2003) Productive pedagogies and the challenge of inclusion, *British Journal of Special Education*, Vol. 30, No. 4: pp. 175–179.

Blandford, S. and Duarte, S.J. (2004) Inclusion in the Community: a study of community music centres in England and Portugal, focusing on the development of musical and social skills within each centre, *Westminster Studies in Education*, Vol. 27, No. 1, Abingdon: Taylor and Francis.

Blandford, S. and Gibson, S. (2005) *Special Educational Needs Management in Schools*. London: Sage.

Busher, H. (2000) Developing Professional Networks: Working with Parents and Communities to Enhance Students' Learning, in Busher, H. and Harris, A. with Wise, C., *Subject Leadership and School Improvement*. London: Paul Chapman: pp. 89–102.

Centre for Studies on Inclusive Education (CSIE) (2000) *Index for inclusion: developing learning and participation in schools*. Bristol: CSIE.

Community Education Development Centre (CEDC) (2000) *Building Learning Communities: Making it Happen*. Woodpark School, Coventry: CEDC.

Department for Children, Schools and Families (DCSF) (2008) *The Early Years Foundation Stage: Principles into Practice*. Available at: **www.standards.dcsf.gov.uk**.

Department for Education and Science (DfES) (2003) *Every Child Matters: Summary*. Nottingham: DfES Publications, Ref: DfES/0672/2003.

Department for Education and Science (DfES) (2005) *Extended Schools: Access to Opportunities and Services for All: A Prospectus*. Nottingham: DfES Publications, Ref: DfES/1196/2005.

Edgington, M. (1998) *The Nursery Teacher in Action*. London: Paul Chapman.

Elfer, P., Goldschmied, E. and Selleck, D. (2003) *Key Persons in the Nursery: Building Relationships for Quality Provision*. London: David Fulton.

Friedman, Y. (1986) *School, Home and Community in Israel: Alienation and Openness in the Educational Space*. Jerusalem: Henrietta Szold Institute (in Hebrew).

Goouch, K. and Powell, S. (2006) *Case Studies for Early Years Professional Standards 2.1–2.7*. Canterbury: Canterbury Christ Church University.

Guaspari, R. (1999) *Music of the Heart*. New York: Hyperion.

Hituv, M. (1989) The community school – principles, trends and methods of action, *Dapim*, Vol. 8: pp. 87–93.

Katz, D. and Kahn, R.L. (1978) *The Social Psychology of Organisations*. New York: John Wiley.

Lewis, A. and Lindsay, G. (eds) (2000) *Researching Children's Perspectives*. Buckingham: Open University Press.

Marsh, C. (1997) Developing positive relationships with parents and children, in Abbott, L. and Moylett, H. (eds) *Working with the Under-3s: Training and Professional Development*. Buckingham: Open University Press: pp. 95–106.

National Policy Board for Educational Administration (NPBEA) (1993) *Principles for our Changing Schools*. Virginia: NPBEA.

Noy, B. (1984) *Parent Participation in the Educational Work of the School*. Jerusalem: Emanuel Yaffe College for Senior Teachers (in Hebrew).

Poster, C. (1982) *Community Education*. London: Heinemann.

Roberts, H. (2000) Listening to children and hearing them, in Christensen, P. and James, A. (eds) *Research with Children: Perspectives and Practices*. London: Falmer Press.

Raywid, M.A. (1984) Synthesis of research on schools of choice, *Educational Leadership*, Vol. 41, No. 7: pp. 70–78.

Stainback, S., Stainback, W., Esat, K. and Sapon-Shevin, M. (1994) A commentary on inclusion and the development of a positive self-identity by people with disabilities, *Exceptional Children*, Vol. 60: pp. 486–490.

Stoll, L., Fink, D. and Earl, L. (2003) *It's About Learning (and it's About Time): What's In It For Schools?* London: RoutledgeFalmer.

The Stationery Office (TSO) (2006) *Working Together to Safeguard Children*. London: TSO.

CHAPTER 14 Collaborating to Promote Learning

By the end of this chapter you will be able to answer the following questions:

- How is children's learning in the early years enhanced through collaborative working?
- Why is effective teamwork of staff central to effective practice?
- How can I involve the parents of children with special educational needs in their learning and development?
- How can I engage children in sustained shared thinking?

This chapter will support your understanding of the following Standards (see Appendix 1):
■ **Knowledge and understanding:** S06 ■ **Effective practice:** S10, S14, S16, S22 and S23
■ **Relationships with children:** S25 and S26 ■ **Communicating and working in partnership with families and carers:** S29 and S31 ■ **Teamwork and collaboration:** S33, S34, S35 and S36.

Introduction

The collaborative working of all those involved in the early years of a child's life is strongly endorsed by the government. This includes the parents, practitioners and other professionals from health, education and social services. By considering collaborative working with parents, colleagues and children this chapter will provide practitioners with an overview of what this means for daily practice in the setting.

Collaborating with parents to promote children's learning

Research evidence highlights the strong benefits for children's long-term learning and development when parents engage positively with their children during the early years. Further evidence suggests a direct link between brain development and the amount of stimulation a child receives (DCSF, 2008: 8). This is reflected in government policy, which emphasises the importance of early years settings establishing and maintaining relationships with parents. Although this has already been discussed (see Chapters 2 and 13), little mention has been made of developing relationships with the parents of children with special educational needs (SEN). This section will give consideration as to how, in practice, the parents of children with special educational needs can be given a voice in the early education of their children.

Photo 14.1 What are the benefits of parents positively engaging with their children in the early years?
© SuperStock. Brand X Pictures www.agefotostock.com SuperStock. Brand X Pictures

Before considering this area, it is important to reflect on the results from the Effective Provision of Pre-School Education (EPPE) Project. The findings suggested that 'what parents do' is more important than who they are. The findings further suggested that parents who did engage in a number of activities with their children tended to have 'higher intellectual and social/behavioural scores' (DCSF, 2008: 9).

DISCUSSION POINT

As a practitioner in an early years setting, what would these findings suggest to you?

That is: 'what parents do' is more important than who they are and that parents who did engage in a number of activities with their children tended to have 'higher intellectual and social/behavioural scores' (DCSF, 2008: 9).

What would you do about it if this was the situation in your early years setting?

The findings from the EPPE study further highlighted that parents who engaged in activities with their children tended to engage in one or more of the following activities:

- Reading with their child
- Teaching songs and nursery rhymes
- Painting and drawing
- Playing with letters and numbers
- Visiting the library, museums and other places
- Creating regular opportunities to play with friends.

(DCSF, 2008: 9)

REFLECT AND RELATE TO PRACTICE

Reflecting on the above list (DCSF, 2008: 9), what could/would you do to help all parents of the children in your early years setting to engage in one or more of the activities with their child?

In considering children with SEN, it is important to be aware from an early stage what their particular area of need might be. One important area to consider is that of speech, language and communication. Recent research showed that in some areas of the UK approximately 50 per cent of children enter school with language or communication problems (DCSF, 2008: 4). If a child with such a difficulty enters an early years setting and either the problem or the cause of the problem has not been diagnosed then practitioners will have to consider how best to help that child advance in his/her learning. Although for a number of children there is no clear cause of the problem, a recent document, published by the Department for Children, Schools and Families, highlights the following as possible causes of speech, language and communication difficulties:

- Ear infections – if a child has many ear infections, they may be unable to hear words, or hear distorted sounds, or find it confusing and tiring to focus on verbal communication;
- Specific difficulties in using their oral muscles effectively, which may affect their speech – for example, if a child has cerebral palsy;
- difficulties that are passed down through families;
- problems during pregnancy or birth that affect children's developing brains and contribute to their speech and language difficulties as part of a wider developmental delay;
- a recognised syndrome or disorder that causes communication difficulties;
- a lack of stimulation and support to provide the rich language experiences necessary to develop their speech, language and communication skills.

(DCSF, 2008: 9)

The sooner an assessment can be made, the more quickly practitioners can develop a programme to help them develop alongside the other children. There may be no reason why the parents of children with SEN cannot be helped to do some or all of the activities highlighted by the EPPE study. In effectively evaluating the needs of those with SEN and subsequent learning support required, it is important that early years practitioners liaise with the children's parents. The revised Code of Practice (CoP) (DfES, 2001) makes clear that accessing and working with parents or, in the case of '**looked after children**' (see Chapter 17), guardians, is fundamental. The CoP explains:

> Partnership with parents plays a key role in promoting a culture of co-operation between parents, schools, Local Authorities and others. This is important in enabling children and young children with SEN to achieve their potential.
>
> *(DfES, 2001: 16)*

Table 14.1 summarises research findings on the importance of hearing the parents' voice. The revised CoP (DfES, 2001: 2:7) outlines what **inclusive** educational settings (practitioners teach to the learning needs of each child, where each child is welcomed and included) should be endeavouring to achieve in accessing the parents' voice.

In considering how to put some of these ideas into practice it is important that there are open channels of communication between practitioners within the setting and parents. Mittler (2000, 153) emphasises the centrality of having home–setting policies which 'go beyond fine words'. He further suggests that 'they must include concrete proposals for achieving better working relationships with . . . parents and the local community' (ibid.). Table 14.2 suggests the necessary roles and responsibilities of the inclusive educational setting towards parents. (Since the revised CoP (DfES, 2001: 2:16) parent partnership services have been a mandatory aspect of LA provision.)

Looked after children: a child 'looked after by a local authority if he/she is in their care or is provided with accommodation for more than twenty-four hours by the authority' (DfES, 2006d: 3).

Table 14.1 Listening to parents

Reference	Research findings
Solity (1992: 120)	Parents are increasingly seen as consumers within the education system and so it is important that parents and practitioners establish an effective rapport with each other.
Hornby (1995: 20–21)	A partnership model: practitioners are viewed as experts on education and parents are viewed as being experts on their children.
Kelley-Laine (1998: 345)	High achieving well-ordered settings are characterised by good home–setting relationships.
Kenworthy and Whittaker (2000: 221–223)	Ending the segregation of children depends on achieving a consensus, shared conviction between young people, parents, survivors of segregation, educationalists and policy makers.
Mittler (2000: 151)	Parents of children with exceptional needs have a particularly great need for working relationships with practitioners based on understanding and trust.

As educators, practitioners, teachers and managers of early years settings, there needs to be an awareness of the whole community in day-to-day practice. What are its values? What are the current tensions? What do practitioners hope to achieve for children in their care? How can it be done in an inclusive way, i.e. working both in and with the community? In order to answer these questions practitioners must locate themselves as individuals within the community, becoming aware of their specific roles in helping the community to function inclusively and successfully.

How do practitioners fit into the government's plan for inclusive education and how do they ensure that they are the architects rather than mere recipients of any new plans? In attempting to build a positive attitude and experience of inclusive education, which might challenge any negative attitude to SEN, setting communities need to allow space and time for practitioners to share views, feelings and experiences. This should take place in an open and supportive climate as the importance and benefits of colleague interaction, support and peer review cannot be overstated. Specifically, practitioners should be given time and space to collaborate in developing collective attitudes towards all learners. Such informal, reflective meetings would allow practitioners to:

- share tips and insights and consider how they might involve children and parents
- feel secure enough to respond to and work with questions being asked of their practices, beliefs, understandings and professional knowledge.

Table 14.2 Inclusive educational settings: Responsibilities to parents

Recommendations	Establishing and evaluating
To ensure the following are made available on request and that parents are aware of their rights to this information	<ul><li>Setting SEN policy</li><li>Support available in the setting and the LA</li><li>Procedures for acting on parental concerns</li><li>How to complain if they are unhappy with the setting's/school's arrangements</li><li>LA services</li><li>Local and national organisations that may be able to offer further advice and information.</li></ul>
To ensure parents are made aware and involved from the start of a child's SEN identification	<ul><li>SENCO (if appropriate) or named representative in setting to keep a file on parent and child details, recording and tracking all communication and details regarding a child's SEN identification and assessment.</li></ul>
Home–setting contracts making clear the role(s) and responsibilities of the SEN person/team and parents	<ul><li>SENCO/named representative and parents to discuss contracts as part of regular meetings to evaluate child's SEN and Individual Education Plan (IEP) (if appropriate).</li></ul>
To ensure that parents are provided with regular feedback regarding their child's progress	<ul><li>SENCO/named representative to ensure copies of all files relevant to child's SEN identification and assessment (e.g. those compiled by the setting practitioner, LA and in some cases educational psychologist (EP)) are sent to parents.</li></ul>
To ensure that parents understand the processes their child is going through in order that their setting meets their SEN effectively	<ul><li>SENCO/named representative to make regular contact with parents either by home visits or telephone calls. To liaise with the parents in a sensitive manner, enabling them to share if they are feeling intimidated, threatened or confused.</li></ul>
Where problems do occur with breakdown in communication, to make contact and work closely with LA parent partnership service	<ul><li>SENCO/named representative to be aware of the parent partnership service in their LA. To note named officer(s) and ensure that, if needed, regular and recorded communication takes place.</li></ul>

Consider the following, which is taken from an interview with an early years leader practitioner in a nursery in Thanet. It provides a good example of how practitioners in this setting have reflected on ways of involving parents in their children's learning.

WHAT HAPPENS IN PRACTICE?

We include songs and rhymes from the children's own background and family culture by asking parents to model the kinds of songs they use, for example, when they are helping a baby to sleep. We take it for granted that we all use the same songs but they are often very different and yet this is a really important way of settling a baby and helping them to feel safe and secure.

REFLECT AND RELATE TO PRACTICE

In what ways will this have been beneficial to the babies? Do you think this was a good way of involving the parents?

In this setting, practitioners have asked parents which songs they sing to the children. By bringing the familiar from home to the setting, this has provided a means of bridging the gap between home and setting. How else could you bridge the gap between what happens at home and what happens in the setting which would also involve parents? (Consider babies and toddlers.)

DISCUSSION POINT

The following summarises the importance of dialogue in the establishment of an inclusive setting community, where the voices of children, parents and practitioners are heard and listened to:

- To feel respected 'one' needs to be heard.
- To respect the 'other' 'one' needs to listen.
- To establish a learning community with shared values and aims 'one' needs to work with the 'other'.
- To establish 'our' common aims we need to work 'together'.
- To openly share 'our' fears and insecurities.
- To openly share 'our' values and attitudes.

- To openly share 'our' strengths and weaknesses.
- To agree on communal goals and ways in which to achieve them.
- To evaluate and revise 'our' practices regularly.

Do you agree with this list? Should we be so open in discussing the issues mentioned?

What further suggestions would you make in establishing an inclusive learning community?

Collaborative working with colleagues

Ofsted highlighted the 'collaborative working of practitioners' as a key feature of effective settings:

> Adults work effectively together to encourage children. In well-organised settings, adults work well together as a team to promote children's learning. They are warm and enthusiastic towards children and their high aspirations promote children's achievements. Staff are involved in planning and making decisions about children's welfare, learning and development. Key areas of responsibility are shared effectively. Good adult-to-child ratios enable sustained interactions that help children to flourish.
>
> *(Ofsted, 2008: 23)*

Well-organised settings of the type referred to by Ofsted (2008) depend on good leadership, which employs a collaborative approach to working. This type of collaborative approach to leadership is referred to as **distributed leadership** and is discussed in Chapter 19 and consequently will not be mentioned within this chapter. That said, in considering how practitioners can work together as a **team**, support each other through mentoring and work with other professionals through multi-agency teams, leader practitioners will establish the framework for practice. This section will consider how these areas can be developed in practice and how, when adults work together effectively, it leads to improved outcomes for all children.

Distributed leadership: leaders delegate tasks and responsibility to team members, giving them the authority to make and act on a decision.

Team: a group of people working together to achieve a common goal.

Mentoring

Mentoring is a widely recognised means of enabling staff to develop both individually and as team members. Mentoring generally means the positive support offered by staff with some experience to staff with less experience of the setting. This experience can extend over a wide range of activities, or be specific to one activity. Mentoring will differ according to need and includes enhancing the mentee's skills and professional development, helping to develop a set of educational values, consulting to help the mentee to clarify goals and ways of implementing them, helping to establish a set of personal and professional standards, and networking and sponsoring by providing opportunities for the mentee to meet other professionals.

Mentoring is time consuming. Mentees should select their mentor based on professional needs, present and/or future. It is important to understand that mentoring is a continuous staff development activity which, once the system is established, takes place during the normal day-to-day life of the early years setting. Mentors need to know and understand the essential elements of a mentoring relationship.

The following provides a useful summary of the essential features of the mentoring process:

- a recognised procedure, formal or informal
- a clear understanding of the procedure and the roles of mentor and mentee
- trust and a rapport between both parties
- the credibility and genuineness of the mentor as perceived by the mentee
- confidentiality and discretion
- a relationship based on the mentee's perception of his/her own needs
- a suitable range of skills used by the mentor: counselling, listening, sensitive questioning, analysis and handing back responsibilities
- an appropriate attitude by both parties, for example the ability of the mentor to challenge the mentee, and the self-motivation of the mentee to take action when necessary
- in addition, teachers should be aware of equal opportunity issues that need to be addressed in the selection and training of mentors.

DISCUSSION POINT

As an early years leader, how would you establish and sustain an effective mentoring system for your team? You might need to consider where, when and how frequently mentors–mentees will meet and with what agenda.

Effective teams

In developing effective teams within early years settings, leader practitioners should consider that teams do not act as teams simply because they are described as such. Everard et al. defined a team as:

> a group of people with common objectives that can effectively tackle any task which it has been set to do. The contribution drawn from each member is of the highest possible quality, and is one which could not have been called into play other than in the context of a supportive team.

(2004: 163)

Team leadership has attracted many commentators and academics. Northouse (2004: 210), a respected author in the field of leadership, particularly relating theory to practice, emphasised the need for team leaders to focus on 'what makes teams effective or what constitutes team excellence'. He suggested that leaders cannot improve groups without a clear focus on team goals or outcomes. Employing the criteria for group effectiveness proposed by Hackman and Walton (1986) of Harvard University, and characteristics for team excellence proposed by Larson and LaFasto (1989), Northouse proposed a framework for developing an effective team:

- Clear elevating goals – the team should be kept focussed on the goals and outcomes can be evaluated against the objectives.
- Results-driven structure – teams should find the best structure to accomplish their goals.
- Competent team members – team members need to be provided with the appropriate information and training to carry out their job effectively and to be able to work collaboratively within the team.
- Unified commitment – effective teams do not just happen. They are carefully designed and developed. Involving team members in the various processes can enhance the sense of unity.
- Collaborative climate – founded on trust out of which develops honesty, openness, consistency and respect, where integration of individual actions is seen as one of the fundamental characteristics of effective teams.
- Standards of excellence – need to be clear and concrete where team members feel a certain pressure to perform well. An effective leader can facilitate this process by requiring results – make expectations clear, reviewing results – provide feedback to resolve performance issues and rewarding results – acknowledge superior performance.
- External support and recognition – provide teams with the necessary resources to carry out the required tasks and reward team member performance, rather than individual achievement.
- Leadership of effective teams – leaders influence teams through four processes: cognitive – helps the team to understand the problems with which they are confronted, motivational – unites the team and helps the members to achieve the required standards, affective – helps the team to cope with difficult situations by providing clear goals, assignments and strategies and co-ordination – matches individual skills to roles, provides clear objectives, monitors feedback and adapts to changes.

(Northouse, 2004: 211–215)

DISCUSSION POINT

As a leader in an early years setting, how would you establish and develop a strong team?

Building the team

Developing team skills will involve a balance between concern for team, concern for the task and developing the individual. Few leaders are able to achieve this effective balance. Everard et al. (2004: 163) highlight the 'ineffective way tasks are handled' when teams do not 'gel'. Referring to educational settings, they further suggest that 'when . . . groups . . . fail to work at peak efficiency the effectiveness of the whole organisation suffers' (ibid.). A leader within an early years setting may find identifying the characteristics of his/her team difficult. The nature of the task and the ethos of the setting will influence the working habits of team members. Equally, pressure from external agencies will affect the quality of the team. Family commitments, hobbies and political initiatives are areas of influence on leaders' lives; these, in turn, will influence the individual's commitment to the team. In essence, the quality of the relationships within the team will determine the quality of the task.

Leaders within early years settings should aim to lead and participate in effective teams which agree aims, share skills, realise potential and reduce stress and anxiety. A leader should avoid the pitfalls of weak management which include:

- overemphasis on people
- overemphasis on task
- overemphasis on agendas, not processes
- reacting to events, not anticipating them
- failure to celebrate success, individual and team.

The following research briefing (what happens in practice?) addresses collaborative working within a Sure Start local programme and provides a good example for this type of practice within an early years setting.

WHAT HAPPENS IN PRACTICE?

Multi-agency working: professionals from the health, social and education services working together to meet the needs of children and their families.

The initial aim of the Director at Sure Start Millmead was to *create a* 'multi-skilled, **multi-agency**, multi-disciplinary peripatetic team of workers able to respond to local needs in creative and innovative ways, able to evaluate services provided and change services and approaches as needed' (West and Carlson, 2007: 126). To achieve this aim the director proposed an 'open, non-hierarchical management style', founded on respect and a 'willingness to listen and learn', where views of parents and team members were valued. Time and money was invested in staff training and weekly meetings were chaired by different members of the team. Staff were encouraged to take on different roles within the centre and critique the cultures of established service providers. In addition, they were encouraged to be 'innovative' in their approach to work and to see themselves as active participants in building a 'new culture of professional practice'. Staff were relatively free to work under their own initiative within a 'no-blame culture'.

Considerable attention was given to recruitment and suitable applicants who supported the Sure Start ethos of 'openness and respect' were employed. Funding to Sure Start was provided on an annual basis, which made it difficult to employ people on long-term contracts. 'The team was composed of six community workers, a mental health support team including a midwife, a health visitor, a social worker, an early years educator, a librarian, a careers advisor and a speech and language therapist.'

There was generally good collaboration between the professionals from different disciplines and although most valued the relative autonomy they were given to develop programmes and carry out their work, there were some staffing issues which were resolved as they arose by the director. There was effective inter-professional working between the speech therapist and the early years educator, which is described here because of its particular relevance to education. The early years educator found the multi-agency approach difficult at the start and took time to adjust to having to create her own timetable. The experience, however, she said has given her a 'huge outlook'. Initially, there were many changes to her job and she visited many nurseries to assess what was needed. In the final synthesis she wanted to be a 'facilitator of more play based learning'. To this end she worked closely with the speech therapist to assist the relatively large number of children with speech difficulties. She did a drop-in session for parents jointly with the speech therapist at the local nursery. Parents were able to discuss ways of supporting their children at nursery in relation to reading, writing, maths and talking skills. While the speech therapist said 'she was learning what she called a more holistic perspective from her Early Years and Social Worker colleagues, the educator began to consider herself as part of a team in relation to families'. Both started to look at families and their needs in a more integrated way. The educator learnt to recognise specific speech problems and could advise staff in other nurseries about referral procedures. The speech therapist said she learnt to work in a 'more family responsive way' and liked the way services could be delivered within the Sure Start programmes more 'efficiently' because problems were identified earlier. She recognised the importance of parents as partners in their child's education. 'Their input is vital, if not more vital than what we do. I often say to a lot of the parents that I have worked with, who would say oh thank you so much for what you have done and I would say well I haven't done anything. I have just given you the advice and you have actually done the work. So it is recognising that we are here to help in certain ways and not to actually cure. And in terms of working with other professionals, I think again you have got to stop looking at your little bit in a box because children aren't you know. They are not this little bit is health, this little bit is education, this little bit is social services, it is actually how we all work together to help that child be a whole person in the environment that they are in.' Both the speech therapist and the educator addressed the issue of staff development and support for other nursery staff. A new Code of Practice was subsequently developed and both now jointly run sessions for parents and children.

(West and Carlson, 2007: 143–149)

REFLECT AND RELATE TO PRACTICE

What strategies were employed to build an effective team?

You will need to consider how the director developed her own leadership style and the involvement of parents and practitioners from different professional disciplines.

☆ ☆ ☆

Imagine you are a practitioner in an early years setting which employs this type of leadership model (distributed leadership). How might this impact on the way you carry out your job?

You should consider your thoughts in relation to extra responsibilities and your continuing professional development and also how it would impact on teaching and learning. Are you in favour of the distributed leadership model in early years settings? Why/why not?

Multi-agency teamwork

Professionals engaged in early years childcare and educational settings are encouraged to take a 'pro-active' role in working within the new multidisciplinary framework. This supports both the government's vision for a more integrated provision of services for children and the broader understanding of children's learning which is not confined to formal educational settings. Edwards (2006: 55) suggests this provides strong grounds for 'multi-professional collaboration'. This, she further suggests, along with 'strong reciprocal links between home and early education settings' enables children's 'dispositions to engage' and to be 'supported across settings'. This section will consider multi-agency working in practice and the skills needed by early years practitioners in order to be able to work effectively as part of a multi-professional team.

The government consultation document, *The Early Years Foundation Stage* (DfES, 2006a: 10), highlights the following key professionals who may be part of the team: 'speech and language therapists, occupational therapists and physiotherapists, social workers, health visitors, midwives, portage workers, dieticians, and specialist teachers working with children with visual and hearing impediments'. Although LAs are responsible for supporting those involved in the delivery of services within the multi-agency/inter-agency framework, Anning (2006: 16) underlines the difficulties faced by many professionals working within multidisciplinary teams. Citing the findings from the Multi-Agency Team Work for Children's Services (MATCh) project (Anning et al., 2006), she highlights the difficulty in moving from being a specialist within a single-agency context to becoming a generic worker with team responsibilities. However, the findings indicate, she states, that when 'differences in beliefs, values and approaches . . . were acknowledged, confronted and reconciled' teams were able to move forward more effectively. The following research brief (see 'What happens in practice?'), which has been adapted from the MATCh project (Anning et al., 2006), is considered because of its relevance to leadership and teamwork. The MATCh project explored the delivery of public and voluntary sector services through multi-agency teamwork. The research was carried out between 2002 and 2004 and focused on five different, but typical multi-agency teams within these sectors. The following provides an example of multi-agency working within a nursery setting, with 40 children (0–4 years) on roll, all with learning disabilities.

WHAT HAPPENS IN PRACTICE?

On entry, following discussion between parents and practitioners, children were assessed and individual learning plans were drawn up for each child. Provision for children included play-based learning activities, physiotherapy, speech therapy and organised visits to various local amenities. Adults were offered parenting and support sessions. Health workers provided direct work with children and parents, but were increasingly expected to 'train' nursery staff in their specialist knowledge by modelling activities with children in the main classroom. Outreach work in family homes was carried out through the 'Portage' home visitor scheme. The nursery staff group comprised a head of nursery, counsellor, senior nursery nurse, three nursery nurses, a nursery escort/assistant, an administrative assistant, an ethnic minority development worker, a minibus driver, cleaner and assistant cleaner, bookkeeper, fundraising and development manager and fundraiser as well as a Portage home visitor. In addition, there were two part-time physiotherapists, one part-time speech therapist and a full-time training officer. There was also a range of voluntary workers contributing to cooking, driving and working with the children.

Within the core nursery team there was a clear hierarchy with strong leadership from the nursery head in the style of a full managed team. Nursery staff had strong links with other agencies such as the local child development team.

Because of the wide range of skills and backgrounds represented in the team, team managers and leaders were often unable to provide support or supervision to some team members and separate arrangements were made for this to be provided by someone more appropriate. Staff exchanged knowledge both informally, through chats in the corridor, and formally through arranged meetings. The results further suggested that the teams had developed a number of joint activities to facilitate effective multi-professional working, with considerable time and effort going into team building and team development activities. In relation to the way multi-professional teams are organised and managed the findings suggested that all team members need to be line managed and have their work co-ordinated with other members of the team. All team members need to have appropriate support for personal and professional development. Above all, team members need to have absolute clarity about who is performing each of these tasks for themselves and for their team colleagues. All agencies need to develop formal structures for liaison with other agencies responsible for a multi-agency team and to agree collectively how the team and its members will be managed. These agencies all need to provide clarity about the aims and objectives of the team if the team is to organise itself to deliver these objectives.

(Anning et al., 2006)

DISCUSSION POINT

Do you think this team worked together effectively? Why/why not?

You will need to consider their aims, purpose, how they were organised and achievement of goals.

In your opinion, what personal characteristics are key to being an effective team player within the new multi-agency/inter-agency framework?

Collaborative working with children

The positive effects on a child's learning, development and well-being when adults collaborate with them in the process are well documented in research literature and are supported by the government. The type of approach required and the benefits for the child are addressed at some length in Chapters 5 and 10 and will not be mentioned in detail within this chapter. That said, there is one area which has been given only scant attention within Chapter 5 and is deserving of greater consideration, the area of **sustained shared thinking**. This section will consider how practitioners can develop this type of learning activity with the children within their setting and also consider how heuristic play offers a valuable means of enabling younger children to start developing as effective thinkers.

Sustained shared thinking is strongly endorsed by the government as a means of effectively engaging with children to help them advance in their learning, and development and research shows the longer-term benefits for children in terms of developing as independent thinkers and learners. Siraj-Blatchford et al. (2002) define it as 'an episode in which two or more individuals "work together" in an intellectual way to solve a problem, clarify a concept, evaluate activities, extend a narrative etc. Both parties must contribute to the thinking and it must develop and extend.' It is perhaps best understood within the following framework developed by the government:

Sustained shared thinking: an episode in which two or more individuals 'work together' in an intellectual way to solve a problem, clarify a concept, evaluate activities, extend a narrative, etc. (Siraj-Blatchford et al., 2002).

- Adults are aware of the child's interests and understandings, and the adult and child work together to develop an idea or skill.
- In the most effective settings, practitioners support and challenge children's thinking by getting involved in the thinking process with them.
- There are positive, trusting relationships between adults and children.
- The adults show genuine interest, offer encouragement, clarify ideas, and ask open questions, supporting and extending children's thinking and helping them to make connections in learning.

(DCSF, 2008: 53)

By providing opportunity for sustained shared thinking, children learn to work through quite complex problems, employing a number of valuable skills in the process. Although the **plan–do–review** approach of the **High Scope curriculum**, whereby children are appropriately supported in the selection and planning of an activity, which they carry out themselves and review after thorough discussion with practitioners and other children, provides numerous opportunities for sustained shared thinking, this type of collaborative approach (child–practitioner) of thinking through issues and problems can be planned and implemented with relative ease in an early years setting. The important factor is to think of the type of questions which are sensitively asked to help children develop a feeling of being in control or being the 'director' of their learning. These might include: That's good, how does it work . . . ; That's interesting, why did you . . . ?; You're good at thinking, can you think of another way of doing that . . . ? It is important to ask the question with interest and enthusiasm about the child's work. You need to show that they are the 'expert' and you would like to know about it too. In addition, you must give time to the child to think through

Plan–do–review: children are appropriately supported in the selection and planning of an activity, which they carry out themselves and then review after thorough discussion with practitioners and other children.

High Scope curriculum: a guided curriculum, whereby educators support children in developing and carrying out plans and in choosing activities, but not in their actions (Bridge, 2001).

Photo 14.2 Practitioner questioning should help children to feel that they are the 'director' of their own learning

Pearson Education Ltd. Jules Selmes © Pearson Education Ltd. 2008

their response. You might find that they need an additional question to help them get to where they need to be. However, in addition to asking questions, there are other ways to develop sustained shared thinking. It should not be separated as an activity which can only be carried out during formal learning experiences. It should be part of integrated practice, where opportunity is provided throughout the day to help children engage with you in this type of thinking.

Siraj-Blatchford (2005) offers the following ways of developing sustained shared thinking. An example of how each might be approached in practice has been added to this list. They provide a framework for promoting sustained shared thinking as a cross-curricular element and will help you to reflect on how you could find opportunities throughout the day to help children engage in thinking:

- inviting children to elaborate (e.g. that's interesting, tell me about it)
- re-capping (e.g. can you remind me what you have just said about . . . ?)
- offering your own experience (e.g. I usually wear Wellington boots when it rains; they keep my feet dry)
- clarifying ideas (e.g. so you think a piece of wood will float if I put it in the water?)
- suggesting (e.g. I wonder if you did . . . what would happen . . .)
- using encouragement to further thinking (e.g. that's so interesting, tell me how you thought of . . .)
- offering an alternative viewpoint (e.g. ask them 'can you think of a different way of doing that?')
- speculating (e.g. I wonder what she would have done if she saw that the new girl was on her own in the playground)
- asking open questions (e.g. how . . . ?, why . . . ?)
- modelling thinking (e.g. I have to think what I need to do when I go shopping – I need to think what I want to cook this week, look at the recipe books, make a list of the ingredients, make sure I have my money and go to the supermarket).

REFLECT AND RELATE TO PRACTICE

For each of the above sustained shared thinking processes, can you provide a different example of how you might carry it out in practice?

Heuristic play: an activity for young children, usually between the ages of 10 months and 2 years, where they are enabled/ allowed to explore, to discover and to find out what objects are used for.

For younger children, **heuristic play** provides a good means of helping this age group to start thinking more deeply – it is the beginning of children's questioning. Young children enjoy exploring objects (e.g. spoons, empty tins, sieves, plastic jars and slot-in lids) and through this type of activity will start to make connections between the object and its purpose. Practitioner questions, prompts, comments and discussion with the child can be adapted to his/her developmental stage and learning needs. The following, adapted from an interview with an early years leader of practice at a nursery in Thanet, provides an example of how heuristic play and explorative activity can be extended by questioning.

WHAT HAPPENS IN PRACTICE?

I put together some treasure baskets which included lots of natural objects like large pebbles, cones and feathers. You need to tune into the child's thinking and watch and see what they choose to explore or play with. You do not need to bombard them with questions – watch carefully to see what interests them. Only when they start to get bored should you support and extend their thinking by, for example, blowing a feather and gently talking about what is happening.

REFLECT AND RELATE TO PRACTICE

In what ways do you think that this activity has helped the young children to develop as thinkers?

You need to consider how it would have helped them if the practitioner had not intervened and what the practitioner added by intervening.

In planning for this activity the practitioner would have considered the nature and type of support he/she would have given to the children (e.g. when to intervene with a comment or question, the types of questions or comments and other ways the child's learning could be supported/developed). For the above example, can you outline, in the way described, how you would have planned for this exercise?

Consider children of 10 months, 18 months and 2 years.

Collaborating to promote learning: bringing it together

Collaborative working in the early years depends on the continuing effort of practitioners to sustain an established culture of collaboration with each other, the children, the parents and other professionals within the multi-agency framework. That said, on a final note the following examples of what happens in practice probably best serve to illustrate the importance of collaboration in promoting children's learning and development.

WHAT HAPPENS IN PRACTICE?

Babies

In this nursery, the health visitor is here one morning a week. She brings scales etc. and parents are welcome to have their baby checked and/or weighed if they choose.

We find that this helps parents firstly as they can combine bringing their child/ren to nursery with a health check, and secondly because, in this informal, friendly environment, it seems they find it less threatening than going to the clinic. So then, some families that have been described as 'hard to reach' are getting some help. We find that this also helps people to talk about their babies with other parents, in conversation.

We dedicated a play worker to be involved in these sessions so that toys and resources were available in the same area as the health checks and our play worker was on hand to play with the babies and to give friendly advice.

Toddlers

When J came to nursery we quickly realised that he wasn't getting as much from our provision as he could. We felt that we were ill equipped, both in terms of knowledge and resources, to support his development, because of his complex needs. We looked on the internet for as much information as we could find about his condition. Luckily, we had help from a Portage worker, who came and showed very specific examples of how to promote J's learning and development safely.

We used to lean him against the lion (big floor soft toy) for most of the session, but now we know how to use other things and work in different ways to give J (and us) more choices. The Occupational Health representatives have also visited J at home and his parents have relayed even more information now to us so that we can be of more help to J.

Older children

At this nursery we make home visits before the children start. The parents are always asked if they are happy for us to do it and mostly they agree. We started to notice though that some of the families in short-term Bed and Breakfast accommodation were amongst those not happy for us to visit. We make special efforts now, as a team, to make individual contact with the parents when they come in the morning and work hard to quickly build the strong relationship with these children and their families that we feel we have already established with the others we had visited at home.

This has helped us to establish that children in this group were benefiting from the nursery provision to the same degree as other children. And also close contact has helped us to direct families towards other sources of support that may be available. Access to multi-professional teams helps us to understand the range of support in practice that is around.

(Goouch and Powell, 2006)

REFLECT AND RELATE TO PRACTICE

Consider each of the above examples. How does each demonstrate collaborative working?

Consider what happens and who is collaborating with whom.

Consider the ways that collaborative working was developed in each of these examples. Do you think it was effective? Why/why not?

Consider who was collaborating with whom and what they were hoping to achieve. Would you have approached it differently? Why/why not?

SUMMARY

Collaborating with parents to promote children's learning (p. 291)

How would you involve the parents of children with SEN?

Research evidence highlights the strong benefits for children's long-term learning and development when parents engage positively with their children during the early years. It is vitally important for practitioners to consider how they can involve parents in their children's learning, particularly the parents of children with SEN.

Collaborative working with colleagues (p. 297)

Why does the effective collaborative working of adults (in a setting) lead to improved outcomes for children?

In essence, effective leadership is dependent on the development of strong teams. Teams do not act as teams simply because they are described as such; they are purposefully developed. Practitioners need to consider the skills needed, particularly communication skills, for taking a 'pro-active' role in working within the new multidisciplinary framework. Staff can be supported in developing the right skills through mentoring. This is defined as the positive support offered by staff with some experience to staff with less experience within the setting.

SUMMARY *CONTINUED*

Collaborative working with children (p. 304)

How would you define sustained shared thinking?

Children are the focus of all work endeavour in an early years setting. Sustained shared thinking provides a means of helping them to develop as confident learners with the skills, knowledge and understanding to be able to think and act for themselves.

Glossary

Distributed leadership: leaders delegate tasks and responsibility to team members, giving them the authority to make and act on a decision.

Heuristic play: an activity for young children, usually between the ages of 10 months and 2 years, where they are enabled/allowed to explore, to discover and to find out what objects are used for.

High Scope curriculum: a guided curriculum, which originated in America in the 1960s whereby educators support children in developing and carrying out plans and in choosing activities which enable them to carry out the activity themselves (Bridge, 2001).

Looked after children: a legal term, defined by the Children Act 1989 as a child 'looked after by a local authority if he/she is in their care or is provided with accommodation for more than twenty-four hours by the authority' (DfES, 2006b: 3).

Multi-agency working: professionals from the health, social and education services working together to meet the needs of children and their families.

Plan–do–review: a characteristic of the High Scope curriculum, whereby children are appropriately supported in the selection and planning of an activity, which they carry out themselves and review after thorough discussion with practitioners and other children.

Sustained shared thinking: an episode in which two or more individuals 'work together' in an intellectual way to solve a problem, clarify a concept, evaluate activities, extend a narrative, etc. Both parties must contribute to the thinking and it must develop and extend (Siraj-Blatchford et al., 2002).

Team: a group of people working together to achieve a common goal.

Find out more

Baker, J. (2004) Disabled children, in Wyse, D. (ed.) *Childhood Studies: an introduction*, Oxford: Blackwell: pp. 244–248.

Although this is a very short chapter, by challenging the reader to consider how he/she views disabled children, Jane Baker considers some of the elements developed within the section on collaborating with parents.

References

Anning, A. (2006) 'Setting the national scene', in Anning, A. and Edwards, A. *Promoting Children's Learning from Birth to Five: Developing the New Early Years Professional*, 2nd edn, Maidenhead, Berkshire: Open University Press/McGraw-Hill: pp. 1–16.

Anning, A., Cottrell, D., Frost, N., Green, J. and Robinson, M. (2006) *Developing Multi-professional Teamwork for Integrated Children's Services*, Maidenhead: Open University Press/McGraw-Hill.

Bridge, H. (2001) Increasing parental involvement in the Preschool Curriculum: what an action research case study revealed, *International Journal of Early Years Education*, Vol. 9, No. 1: pp. 6–21.

Department for Children, Schools and Families (DCSF) (2008) *Every Parent Matters*. Nottingham: DCSF Publications.

Department for Education and Skills (DfES) (2006a) *The Early Years Foundation Stage*. London: DfES Publications, HMSO.

Department for Education and Skills (DfES) (2006b) *Supporting Looked After Learners: A Practical Guide*. London: DfES Publications, HMSO.

Department for Education and Skills (DfES) (2001) *The Code of Practice for Special Educational Needs*. London: HMSO.

Edwards, A. (2006) 'Young children as learners', in Anning, A. and Edwards, A. *Promoting Children's Learning from Birth to Five: Developing the New Early Years Professional*, 2nd edn, Maidenhead: Open University Press/McGraw-Hill.

Everard, K.B., Morris, G. and Wilson, I. (2004) *Effective School Management*, 4th edn. London: Paul Chapman Publishing.

Goouch, K. and Powell, S. (2006) *Case Studies for Early Years Professional Standards 2.1–2.7*. Canterbury: Canterbury Christ Church University.

Hackman, R. and Walton, R. (1986) 'Heading groups in organisations', in Goodman, P. (ed.), *Designing Effective Workgroups*. San Francisco: Jossey-Bass.

Hornby, G. (1995) *Working with Parents of Children with Special Educational Needs*. London: Cassell.

Kelley-Laine, K. (1998) Parents as partners in schooling: the current state of affairs, *Childhood Education*, Vol. 74, No. 6: pp. 342–345.

Kenworthy, J. and Whittaker, J. (2000) Anything to declare? The struggle for inclusive education and children's rights, *Disability and Society*, Vol. 15, No. 2: pp. 219–231.

Larson, C.E. and La Fasto, F.M.J. (1989) *Teamwork: What Must Go Right: What Can Go Wrong*. Newbury Park, CA: Sage.

Mittler, P. (2000) *Working Towards Inclusive Education: Social Contexts*. London: David Fulton.

Northouse, P. (2004) *Leadership: Theory and Practice*. Thousand Oaks, CA: Sage.

Ofsted (2008) *Early Years Leading to Excellence*. London: Ofsted.

Siraj-Blatchford, I., Sylva, K., Mattock, S., Gilden, R. and Bell, D. (2002) *Researching Effective Pedagogy in the Early Years*, Research Report No. 356. London: DfES.

Siraj-Blatchford, I. (2005) *Quality Interactions in the Early Years*, paper delivered at the TACTYC annual conference Birth to Eight Matters! Seeking Seamlessness – Continuity? Integration? Creativity?, 5 November, Cardiff.

Solity, J. (1992) *Special Education*. London: Cassell.

West, L. and Carlson, A. (2007) Claiming Space: An in-depth auto/biographical study of a local Sure Start project. Centre for International Studies of Diversity and Participation, Department of Educational Research: Canterbury, Christ Church University, New Zealand.

By the end of this chapter you will be able to answer the following questions:

- What characterises independent learning?
- Why does teaching for independent learning need to be a cross-curricular dimension of the curriculum?
- In what ways does creating the right learning environment contribute to children's ability to develop as independent learners?
- How can knowledge of children's learning and development enhance teaching for independent learning?
- What does collaborative working for independent learning mean in practice?

This chapter will support your understanding of the following Standards *(see Appendix 1)*:
- **Effective practice:** S07, S08, S11, S15, S19 and S22 ■ **Relationships with children:** S25, S26, S27 and S28
- **Communicating and working in partnership with families and carers:** S29.

Introduction

CASE STUDY

The things we value here are helping children to have self-confidence and develop their own feeling of self-competence. That is, the children themselves feel that they are competent problem-solvers. Helping children to develop their own feeling of competence is more important than confidence. We do that through staff, resources and by having a safe and secure environment. I don't just mean safe and secure in the traditional understanding of the word but also in the way we structure their personal (learning) zones. For example, they can get to where they want to go without being interrupted – e.g. in a corridor or if they are working on something another child will not come and take their equipment. We talk a lot about personal zones and depth of engagement in that children feel safe and secure so that they can engage in what they are doing. That is facilitated by adults. It could be an adult or child initiated activity, but the important thing is the meaningful interaction with the adult which makes it meaningful for the child.

We want children to be aware of the needs of other children. Children should respect each other's personal space and personal zones. We help them to develop the ability to focus on something and to see it through rather than flit from one thing to another. So it's an ability to be determined and focused. We are facilitating learning through the way we structure their personal learning zones.

(Personal learning zones refers to the child's 'space' – no child will take a resource from another child if they are using it.)

*(Adapted from an interview with
the head of a pre-prep school in Yorkshire)*

Independence means thinking and acting for oneself. As the above Case study shows, creating the right learning environment in helping children to develop the necessary skills, attributes or emotional integrity for independent learning is very important for practice. However, as Hendy and Whitebread (2000) found, in their study of independent learning in the early years, practitioners all agreed on the importance of promoting independent learning in children, but held differing opinions as to what this meant in practice. Their findings further suggested that practitioners' understanding of the concept tended to focus on the development of *independent children* rather than encouraging independent learning; where the latter concept acknowledges the important role of the practitioner. In essence, independent learning involves learning how to think and act for oneself, where the necessary skills, knowledge, understanding, dispositions and emotions should be developed in the earliest years of education.

DISCUSSION POINT

Reflect on the learning objectives for this chapter and identify the skills, knowledge, dispositions and emotions that are associated with an independent adult.

The idea of independent learning is endorsed by the government and reflected in many of their documents related to the early years; it underpins the *Statutory Framework for the Early Years Foundation Stage: Setting the Standards for Learning Development and Care for children from birth to five* (EYFS) (DfES, 2007). A close look at the early learning goals reveals how few are not directly related to the concept of independent learning.

ACTIVITY

Look at the early learning goals in EYFS (DfES, 2007: 12–16). Make two lists – those directly related to independent learning and those which are not directly related to independent learning. (EYFS is available at **www.teachernet.gov.uk/publications**.) You can review this at the end of the chapter.

WEB

You will find a table of the government documents which are relevant for this chapter on our **website**.

You will probably have noticed, having completed this activity, that it is not always evident which early learning goals relate to the concept of independent learning. However, one thing is clear; for effective pedagogy, practitioners not only need to know the skills, knowledge, understanding, dispositions and emotions that constitute independent learning, but also need to know how to integrate the necessary techniques into everyday teaching practice. This chapter will consider the characteristics associated with independent learning and show how in many ways they are dependent on practitioners creating the right learning environment to teach for and enable children to become independent learners.

From theory to practice

What characterises independence in adulthood is inner integrity, self-belief and an ability to work co-operatively with others. This section addresses the characteristics of independent learners and considers ways of helping children to develop these characteristics in practice.

You will have discovered from the activity at the beginning of the chapter that it is relatively easy to identify characteristics associated with independence. Your list may have included some or all (or more) of the following: motivation, confidence, creativity, determination, perseverance, self-discipline, emotional well-being, good communication skills, systematic or reasoned thinking, initiative, enthusiasm, adaptability, feeling in control, knowledge of personal strengths and weaknesses, explorative, critical discernment and an ability to participate with others. Independent adults think well of themselves and have a positive outlook on life, even in the face of failure. They understand that setbacks are part of life for everyone and what matters is the way they are handled. Peter Jones from the television programme *Dragon's Den*, in his analysis of successful entrepreneurship, highlights the benefits of changing your *perception of failure*. He believes that:

there are no failures in this world, only events that give you feedback. I see every outcome as having value, and if I do not get the result I set out to get, I take a look at the result I did get and explore what it is telling me. I focus on what I did right and assess and alter what I didn't. This means I am better equipped to have another go; it also means I have learned something really valuable from a so-called failure that will help me in the future.

(Jones, 2008: 20)

Connect & Extend

Look up Williams' study of independent learning which is discussed in her *Promoting Independent Learning in the Primary Classroom* (2003). What is your opinon?

Although much of this may seem like common sense, the question for practitioners is how to help young children develop the necessary skills to be able to think positively and in essence to become independent learners. In practice, this is not without its challenges. In part, this is attributable to the differing views of independent learning. Williams (2003: 10), in her study of independent learning, based on the views of 80 primary school teachers, noted the emergence of two ideas – the **interactionist view** and the **isolationist view**.

Although both promote the development of certain dispositions associated with independent learning, the latter denies children any form of *interaction* and *encouragement*. Williams suggests, however, that there is overlap between the two views and in practice teaching for independent learning means adapting the curriculum to give 'children the chance to make choices, organise themselves and respond with energy and enthusiasm' (2003: 130). What is clear from Williams' delineation of independent learning is that the necessary skills etc. need to be integrated into daily practice and

Interactionist view:
'where children are motivated, good problem solvers, effective communicators and able to seek help as appropriate' (Williams, 2003: 10).

Isolationalist view:
'where children are trained to develop skills for self-sufficiency and to work alone' (Williams, 2003: 10).

Photo 15.1 To what extent should independent learning steer a path between the interactionist and isolationist view?

Pearson Education Ltd. Jules Selmes © Pearson Education Ltd. 2008

Photo 15.2 What skills do children develop through interactive work?

Pearson Education Ltd. Jules Selmes © Pearson Education Ltd. 2008

developed as cross-curricular elements. That said, there is no reason why the necessary skills cannot be developed as an additional discrete subject. Following Socrates' dictum of 'know thyself', independent learning as a discrete subject would provide children with further opportunity to know and build on their strengths, understand that weaknesses can be overcome, become aware of their potential, believe in themselves and come to a greater understanding of how they learn.

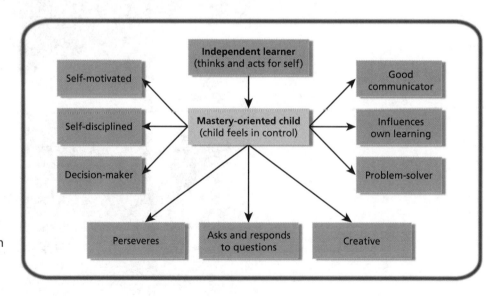

Figure 15.1 Qualities of an independent learner

Firstly, it is important to clarify what characterises an independent learner. Figure 15.1 identifies the qualities which belong to an independent child. Practitioners would undoubtedly agree that this is the type of learner they would like to develop in their setting. In practice this means:

- creating a positive learning environment
- developing good pedagogical practice
- working collaboratively.

Creating a positive learning environment

The idea of learning should permeate the setting. This involves nurturing an environment where all children share in decisions relating to their learning and learning environment. This section will consider how, through both the physical and broader learning environment (i.e. the way practitioners relate to the children, communicate the importance of learning and plan for learning etc.), children's learning can be enhanced: 'The generic term "environment" refers to the physical learning space and to the people and ideas that contribute to learning' (Williams, 2003: 71).

The idea of creating a learning environment which both promotes learning and encourages each child to be an active participant in his/her learning is the beginning of creating the right environment for independent learning. The role of the practitioner in this process needs to be given careful consideration; supporting learning in an ineffective manner can inadvertently make the child overly dependent on the practitioner, incapable of thinking or acting independently. Practitioners need to consider how they can provide both a physical environment which supports and stimulates the children and at the same time develop an interactive approach to teaching, which is supportive of and stimulates children's learning.

DISCUSSION POINT

What sort of outcomes do you think practitioners are expecting when they speak of stimulating children's learning?

Consider, firstly, the physical environment in the context of independent learning. The physical environment should overtly transmit to children the message that learning is important, learning is for everyone and that 'you' are part of 'this' learning environment.

REFLECT AND RELATE TO PRACTICE

In terms of the physical environment, what would you do to transmit the message to all children that learning is important, learning is for everyone and that 'you' are part of 'this' learning environment? Consider displays, resources, furnishings etc.

Practitioners need to nurture an environment where all children share in decisions relating to their learning and learning environment. The art of decision-making is encouraged by allowing children to put forward their opinion in an environment where they know their opinion matters. It is vital to develop a strong framework for practice, within which children can become competent and confident learners. Asking children for their opinion gives them the feeling of being in control, of shared responsibility and of owning their learning.

In terms of sharing in the ownership of their physical environment, Julie Fisher (2002: 90), formerly a lecturer in early Childhood Education at Reading University and presently an early years adviser in Oxfordshire, suggests that children can be *involved in the planning and arrangement* of:

- their space
- naming work areas
- selecting resources
- categorising resources
- sorting resources
- labelling resources
- locating resources.

This list is not exhaustive. For example, for young children (0–2 years), rewarding the tidying away of resources can have a powerful effect on a child's feeling of independence.

REFLECT AND RELATE TO PRACTICE

Can you add to the list presented by Fisher (2002)? You need to consider ways of helping children to become decision-makers either through the physical learning environment or through sharing in the ownership of the physical learning environment.

Williams highlights the benefits of 'a learning environment which promotes independence' in terms of providing 'a framework for children's developing self esteem and responsibility' (2003: 71). By involving children in the development of the physical learning environment, the practitioner will have enabled them to exercise choice and initiated some of the thinking skills needed for solving problems. For example:

- Which resources to use and why?
- Where to find the resources and why?
- How to use the resources.

This is the basis of independence of thought and action in young children. Practitioners will initiate the process in their setting by stimulating the child through verbal, physical and emotional communication. As children develop, the ability to make choices becomes more of an extended thought process. However, this is gradual, as it is the process which is important and is ultimately dependent on effective and appropriate practitioner interaction with the child. The following examples of what happens in practice show how two early years settings set up interactive play areas for the children:

WHAT HAPPENS IN PRACTICE?

A lot of children come with challenging behaviour and little experience of outdoor play. The garden has 'transition zones' which are made with textured flooring. This causes children to slow down and adjust their behaviour as they move through the garden. Children love the garden; they grow food all year round and harvest and eat it. Multicultural aspects are well promoted outdoors, for example by building a sukkah for the Jewish festival of Sukkot. Children have freedom to move in and out of doors when they wish as they use all-weather clothing. Children love to play in the puddles and watch them evaporate. Water and sand play is very creative with various tiers, a small waterfall and a pump. Children gain enormous confidence through their outdoor play.

(Adapted from Ofsted, 2008: 23)

A **sensory room** was set up, to help children to discover a range of sensations and become more aware of touch, light, colour, sound and smell in a relaxing environment away from the noisy action of the playroom. It is used regularly for babies and the youngest children. Older children with emotional difficulties, physical problems or global developmental delay also access it. The facility is also used by the wider community. The stimulation received from the multi-sensory experiences in this room benefits a range of users with additional needs.

(Ofsted, 2008: 24)

Sensory room: a room set up with various objects which a child can use/play with/explore to discover a range of sensations and become more aware of touch, light, colour, sound and smell.

REFLECT AND RELATE TO PRACTICE

In what ways were these learning environments stimulating for the children?

☆ ☆ ☆

In what ways were these learning environments interactive? Do you think they will stimulate the children? Why/why not? Design an interactive outdoor play area for 1–2 year olds.

Various widely accepted approaches to early years learning – High Scope Curriculum, Reggio Emilio and Montessori – have a specific focus on enabling children to become independent learners. For example, in the Montessori system, the deliberate and careful introduction of resources by the practitioner, with time for the children to try them out, enables the children to *select and work* with the resources in their own way (Follari, 2007: 228). The *plan–do–review* (children plan and carry out an activity, reviewing it and the outcomes after; at each stage they would be appropriately supported by practitioners) approach of the High Scope Curriculum is particularly good for enhancing a child's ability to engage with and take ownership for their learning. Allowing the children time to plan how they might use a particular resource, how they might work together as a team (if this is relevant) and what outcomes they expect gives them a feeling of control and confidence. Time for reflection after the activity gives the children the opportunity to consider the strengths, weaknesses, areas for improvement and why something worked or did not work. However, the role of the practitioner is crucial to the success of the activity. The following 'What happens in practice?' provides an example of a child, in a pre-school setting which follows the High Scope Foundation approach, planning her activity. On a daily basis, within this setting, the children are provided with the opportunity to plan an activity, carry it out for two hours and reflect upon it after. The practitioners move around the setting while the children are carrying out their plans. Consider the questioning techniques employed by the practitioner. The children have just selected their activity from a poster, presented to them by the practitioner and detailing, in words and pictures, the various available work areas and related activities.

WHAT HAPPENS IN PRACTICE?

Karissa: I want to work with blocks.
Teacher: Karissa, you want to work with blocks again like yesterday? What do you want to do with the blocks? Are you going to build something today?
Karissa: I want to build a bridge for the cars to go under.
Teacher: A bridge? Great! What kind of blocks do you think you will need?
Karissa: Um . . . long ones for across I think. (Pause.)
Teacher: OK. How do you think the cars will fit underneath the long . . .
Karissa: (Bursts in) And tall ones for the sides!
Teacher: OK. So you're going to the block area to build a bridge for the cars to go under and you're going to try using long blocks and tall blocks. Great! Let's see how it works!

(Follari, 2007: 151)

The following shows the type of questions asked by the practitioner during reflection time after the activity.

WHAT HAPPENS IN PRACTICE?

Teacher: Karissa, I noticed you started using some different shaped blocks today. Why did you decide to do that?

Karissa: I saw a picture in the Thomas book of a bridge for the trains. Underneath it was where cars go. But the tall parts weren't just straight like my tall blocks on the sides. They were curved in the book.

Teacher: And you wanted to make the tall part of your bridge look curved like the book?

Karissa: Yes.

Teacher: How did you do that?

(Follari, 2007: 152)

REFLECT AND RELATE TO PRACTICE

For practitioner questioning to effectively promote independent learning in children, careful thought has to be given to the way questions are worded, when they are posed and how they can be used to reinforce the children's responses.

How has the practitioner in the above example, both during the planning and the reflection stages, done this?

☆ ☆ ☆

For each teacher intervention in this example can you think of an alternative?

Do you agree with the way this teacher has approached this activity? Would you have approached it differently? In what way?

This type of activity provides children with the opportunity to independently think through their course of action. They will consider what resources are available, what they need and identify the most appropriate for their chosen activity. Making provision for this type of learning experience on a regular basis enables the children to become familiar with a routine which they have independently carried out. By repeatedly allowing them to take control of the situation, they are more likely to think through and correct errors in the choice of resources. This again is where the role of the practitioner is important. Featherstone and Bayley suggest that for children to become *self-determined* they need 'repeated opportunities to plan and initiate their own activities. They need to set goals for themselves, and these goals need to be their own, worked out in partnership with – but not imposed by – an adult' (2006: 58). They further highlight the importance of practitioner support in helping children to develop the necessary *review skills* and having the 'spontaneity to adapt what they are doing on the way to achieving their goals'. At the planning stage children can be asked to consider other approaches to the problem or other resources which could be used. During reflection time they might be asked to consider how the problem could have been approached differently or how it could be improved upon. The important issue is that there are often different or more efficient approaches to the same problem.

However, working through an activity or problem until the end is vital if children are to learn how to persevere, particularly in difficult situations. Repeatedly allowing children to *plan–do* and *review* their activities provides many opportunities to weigh up the pros and cons of making an error of judgement. If, for example, within a short period of time after embarking on an activity, a child realises that he/she has chosen the wrong resource for the desired outcome then the reselection of a more appropriate resource should be considered. But what happens if the resource a child has selected will give the desired outcome, but a different resource would have been better? These are the types of issues which should be discussed with the children. What is their view? Remember the advice earlier in the chapter – 'there are no failures in this world, only events that give you feedback' (Jones, 2008: 20). For the practitioner, it is a matter of altering children's perceptions of decision-making – an error of judgement, for example in the choice of resource, is not a failure. Supported in this way, children will independently change an inappropriate resource and happily continue their activity.

Connect & Extend

In what ways do the following models promote independent learning (you can relate this to the 'connect and extend' in chapter 14):

High/Scope (Holt, N. (2007) *Bringing the High/Scope Approach to Your Early Years Practice*, UK, Routledge)

Reggio Emilio (Abbott, L. and Nutbrown, C. (2001) *Experiencing Reggio Emilia: Implications for Pre-school Provision*, Milton Keynes: Open University and Thornton, L. and Brunton, P. (2007) *Bringing the Reggio Approach to Your Early Years Practice*, New York: Routledge).

Montessori (Monessori, M. (1989) *The Montessori Method*, N.Y; London: Schocken and Montessori, M. (1965) *Dr. Montessori's Own Handbook*, N.Y: Schocken).

ACTIVITY

The activity in Table 15.1, which is more appropriate for children at Key Stage 1, can be used as a way of helping children to become aware of the skills etc. they need to develop to become independent learners. You can put this on the wall as a display. On a weekly basis have a specific thought and/or action which addresses one of the skills, e.g. self-motivation. Children will then be encouraged to practise that all week. This activity can be enhanced by having a system of awards/rewards. Complete Table 15.1 as a group and consider the different types of 'action' you would expect of children to help them develop the particular independent learning skill.

Although your setting may not adopt one of the approaches referred to in Connect & Extend, by becoming familiar with them, you will be able to use and adapt certain elements of each one, integrating them into your practice as appropriate.

The one overriding factor in creating an environment which promotes independent learning is the development of positive and supportive practitioner–child relationships. Williams suggests that 'with an affective climate and mutual concern for well-being', both practitioners and children 'will be better prepared to achieve personal and national targets' (2003: 130).

Table 15.1 Becoming an independent learner	
An independent learner	**Action**
Self-motivated	Work hard to achieve a specific goal
Self-disciplined	
Decision-maker	
Perseverance	
Creative	
Asks and responds to questions	
Problem-solver	
Directs/influences own learning	
Good communicator	Listens to others without interrupting

Whitebread et al., in their study in Cambridgeshire, which examined the development of independent learning in the early years, highlighted the following comment made by one of the practitioners; it reaffirms the need for a strong learning environment from which children can develop as independent learners:

> Learning is intrinsic to life and because it is this important children need to be owners of their own learning; they won't see it as intrinsic to life if they don't own it themselves – everything they do must have a purpose which makes sense to them.

> *(Whitebread et al., 2005: 40)*

This tends to place the responsibility on the practitioner; where the central question is why do children need to carry out/participate in a particular activity? If it serves no purpose would you want to do it? Then why should they/would they want to do it? Every activity should have a purpose, including the revisiting of early learning goals in different ways. This should be central to planning; familiarising children with the subject content builds their knowledge, skills, understanding and ultimately their confidence. If practitioners help children to build self-confidence, there will be a natural progression from ownership of learning to directing and influencing their own learning. Children who can direct or influence their own learning have a strong sense of self and others within their immediate world and tend to be proactive in the learning process – physically, intellectually and emotionally. The following outlines some of the more important factors which should be taken into consideration when planning for children's independent learning:

- Develop a pool of resources which are relevant and inviting – are they appropriate for the child's needs and experiences? Do they help promote independent learning? (e.g. for 0–2 year olds a basket of toys – dolls, teddy bears etc. – will be inviting; 1–2 year olds can be given the opportunity to select a toy of their choice at a particular time each day, which can provide practitioners with the opportunity to discuss their choices with them).
- Give children time to think on their own when they are engaged in an activity – both practitioner-led and child-initiated. Remember personal reflection will be fruitless unless the child has been taught how to think constructively.
- Practitioners need to consider how they will support children in making choices; you want them to be able to independently make choices in the future.
- Support children appropriately – encourage, reward, challenge, value them and their achievements – are you helping them to become independent learners (in thought and action) or are you helping them to become independent workers dependent on your thought and your action? Whitebread et al. highlight the 'important distinction between praise (which produces teacher pleasers) and encouragement (which gives information/feedback and supports independence)' (2005: 47).

To a large degree all practitioners aim to develop children who can influence and direct their own learning; it is a hallmark of independence in adulthood. To develop this type of learner in the setting, children need to be provided with the opportunity to try out their own ideas. The foundation for this is creativity. Towards the beginning of this chapter you were asked to consider what outcomes practitioners expected by providing an environment, in the generic sense, which stimulates children's learning. In essence they would be expecting children to be creative in their thought processes. They would want to encourage children to be creative, to develop their own ideas.

The Robinson Report, *All Our Futures: Creativity, Culture and Education* (National Advisory Committee on Creative and Cultural Education (NACCCE), 1999), emphasised the importance of creative development and cultural education across the curriculum. This is acknowledged by the government in the *Statutory Framework for the Early Years Foundation Stage: Setting the Standards for Learning Development and Care for children from birth to five* (EYFS) (DfES, 2007), where creative development is one of the six early learning goals and educational programmes. Teaching should address the related learning goals within the following relatively broad educational programme:

> Children's creativity must be extended by the provision of support for their curiosity, exploration and play. They must be provided with opportunity to explore and share their thoughts, ideas and feelings, for example through a variety of art, music, movement, dance, imaginative and role-play activities, mathematics and design and technology.
>
> *(DfES, 2007: 13)*

Creative development has already been addressed in Chapter 7 and will only be considered briefly in this chapter. That said, it is important to remember that creative development involves enabling the child to think creatively. Some children will be spontaneous and others will need a more supportive and conducive learning environment for their creative talents to begin flourishing. Creative thinking involves freedom of thought, reflection and stimulation. For the practitioner, this means considering how the activity is initiated, the type of activity selected, the interaction with the child, the questions you will ask and when and the responses you will give to the child. It is important to remember that creativity of thought requires 'space'; you do not want to inadvertently stifle that thought process. The following example of what happens in practice shows how one nursery helped young children to develop their creativity:

WHAT HAPPENS IN PRACTICE?

As part of a topic on transport a practitioner has set up a creative activity. The children are provided with a range of paints they have assisted in mixing, and a selection of brushes. Pencils and marker pens are also provided. The children are invited to select paper from a range of textures, colours and sizes. Around the area are displayed drawings and photographs of buses and some model buses. Included are some particular photographs taken on a recent visit to the local bus depot. As the children arrive at the table, the adult reminds them about the recent visit. They discuss what they saw in terms of size, shape, and colour. She reminds them as well of the slippery, shiny surface of the bodywork and of the smell of the engines. She talks to them about the photographs, paintings and models set out around the area.

(Hodson, 2002: 56)

REFLECT AND RELATE TO PRACTICE

In what ways did this activity help children to develop their creativity?
   You will need to list the different strategies used by the practitioner, including at the planning stage, to help the children develop their creative talent.

Do you think this was a good activity to help children develop their creative talent?
   You will need to consider that creative thinking involves freedom of thought, reflection and stimulation. For the practitioner, this means considering how the activity is initiated, the type of activity selected, the interaction with the child, the questions you will ask and when and the responses you will give to the child.

Look at the EYFS (DfES, 2007). Using the Creative Development learning area (pp. 15–16), plan an activity for 2 year olds to help them develop their creative talents.
   Using the Key Stage 1 Curriculum, plan an activity for 7 year olds to help them develop their creative talents.

For younger children, providing the opportunity to explore mechanisms leading to the stage where they make up their own song, story or picture about what they did in their holidays is a good medium for the development of creative talents. Allow them to tell their 'neighbour' about their plans and encourage a class presentation after completion. For older children, activities which focus on forming groups/councils allow them the opportunity for planning decision-making, debating and finding solutions. For example, small groups of children could develop a plan for improving the setting/school environment (e.g. removal of litter, new pond, play area, more displays of their work). By developing the project together they engage in setting goals and are challenged to think of both practical and innovative ways of implementing their plan. For practitioners, this means choosing a 'real' or imagined event and making it clear to the children that the intention is to carry through their suggestion. In the study carried out by Whitebread et al. they highlighted the following important finding in relation to curriculum planning: 'Children differ between those who respond well to open-ended, child-initiated tasks and those who like a supportive structure established by an adult; both kinds of opportunities need to be provided' (2005: 47). To enable children's creative talents to develop there should be ample opportunity for exploration and play.

Developing good pedagogical practice

Improving outcomes for children is dependent on practitioners having good knowledge, skills and understanding not only in relation to children's developmental needs and subject knowledge but also in relation to new or recognised good pedagogic practice. This section will consider some of the essential elements in developing good pedagogical practices.

Creating an effective context for independent learning is largely dependent on how practitioners approach teaching and learning and the extent to which they make it a cross-curricular element, central to practice. The government document, *KEEP – Key Elements of Effective Practice* (DfES, 2005), highlights the importance in early years education of not only developing good relations with children, parents and other related service providers, but the need for practitioners to:

- Understand how children develop and learn;
- Know about the curriculum – the 'subject knowledge' that is as important in the Foundation Stage as in later stages;
- Know about and be able to use the range of teaching strategies appropriate to this distinct stage;
- Understand how to promote and support child-initiated learning.

(DfES, 2005: 6)

The greater practitioner knowledge in these areas, the easier it will be to develop an effective context for independent learning. That said, knowledge is further developed through observing children in the setting and discussing their learning with other practitioners. Planning, especially at the long-term stage, provides a good time to deepen your knowledge base. Although continuing professional development will be provided for in the setting, it is always a good idea to develop your own skills, knowledge and understanding. Personal reading on the above mentioned areas will provide new ideas for teaching, for helping children to be creative and most importantly will challenge and stimulate you. Remember, children see practitioners as role models; a strong knowledge base and an enthusiasm for learning will have an extremely positive impact on children's ability to develop as independent learners.

Understand that each child is unique

The best starting point is in acknowledging that each child is unique. In the way that children have different talents, they also respond differently to learning situations. This is dependent not only on their natural stage of physical, intellectual and emotional development, but can be influenced by their position within their family and the extent to which their parents communicate with them. For example, the youngest of four children may be more mature at two years old than their eldest sibling at the same age. The question for practitioners is how to make learning fun for each child. The learning experience will then be meaningful for the child and engagement and a sense of achievement will follow. These dimensions of learning underpin the idea of helping children to become self-motivated learners, characterised by a desire to learn, understand and achieve goals. This is not always an easy task. A simple analogy might be the lock and key. For every lock there is a key. The practitioner needs to find the right key to unlock the child's potential to enjoy and succeed. In practice, this involves observing the child, knowing the child, how he/she learns and the extent to which his/her learning depends on the type and amount of support you give him/her.

Knowing and using different teaching strategies

Children respond best to a number of short activities, which should be presented in different learning styles, e.g. visual, audio, kinaesthetic etc. (see Chapter 5). Young children need the stimulation practitioners give them. During their time in the setting the practitioner is a very important connection with their external environment – physical, social and emotional. For very young children (0–2 years) communication is the stimulus for learning, which must involve action on their part. The following 'What happens in practice?' has been adapted from an interview with the manager of a nursery in York and highlights the type of skills independent learning aims to develop in young children (0–2 years) and how this can be done:

WHAT HAPPENS IN PRACTICE?

We try to help young children develop the following independent learning skills:

- self-esteem
- individual enjoyment of learning alone and as part of a group

▷

- involvement in decision-making
- giving children choices
- empowering them to make choices.

In practice we do this by involving the children in decision-making. For example, what snack they have and how much to have. There are no set activities as such for this age group. We have baskets of toys in the room and the children are free to choose which toys to play with and when. We encourage free-play with an adult around. As we have a ratio of 9 children to 4 adults where standard practice is 3:1, we can give more time to individual children. For example, there is always an adult to encourage them and develop their thinking by asking them relevant questions.

REFLECT AND RELATE TO PRACTICE

Consider the above case study. What strategies have been employed to help these young children develop as independent learners?

 ☆ ☆ ☆

Would you use the same strategies as those employed within this nursery to help children develop the necessary skills for independent learning? What would you do differently? What strategies would you keep or develop further?

The following 'What happens in practice?' has been adapted from an interview with a senior lecturer in education at a university in the north of France and highlights the importance of understanding how older children (3–7 year olds) learn and develop when planning for independent learning. Although she describes the techniques she uses when teaching English and German as foreign languages to children, many of the techniques can be used or adapted for other subject areas.

WHAT HAPPENS IN PRACTICE?

Smaller children want to grow. They very often play at being an adult. They like to imitate grown-ups, to play roles. Also they are building their own mother tongue. They are used to not understanding everything. Not understanding does not bother them as much as it bothers grown-ups or educators. They are quite satisfied if they roughly get the gist of things. And if they don't, they invent their own inner story. They guess. They infer the meaning. Even in their mother tongue they are proud to use new words, to master the pronunciation of a sound.

I always plan a surprise in the lesson. They quickly begin to understand that there will be something strange, funny, good during the lesson, but they do not know when to expect it. As a result they always concentrate to make sure they do not miss the fun. For example I will do a role play. I bring in a funny hat. To play the specific role the children have to wear the hat. Everyone wants to play the specific role so that they can wear the hat.

In another role play, after creating a story with them, I encourage them to learn and play the roles. In the story, one character (a child) springs on his bed during the absence of his father. I just use an old mat to represent the bed. But when the children can spring on it, for them it is as much fun as the forbidden action on a real bed.

To teach thank you, I bring sweets.

Once we played setting the table. I invented a game that made children ask for a plate, a glass etc. I brought my own doll's dinner party set from when I was a child. It was real china and much nicer than the ugly plastic things they have now. That made them very proud and curious and careful.

When colouring a picture I give strange orders or encourage them to fantasise, e.g. to paint blue lemons or yellow crocodiles.

Children love nonsense!

REFLECT AND RELATE TO PRACTICE

What teaching strategies have been employed in this example of early years practice in France? Do you think that they will help the children to become independent learners?

☆ ☆ ☆

What does this example of early years practice in France tell you about the way children learn and develop?

Do you think that the pedagogical practices employed will help children to develop as independent learners?

Would you use this type of approach to teaching in an early years setting in England? Why/why not?

Taking responsibility: the step-by-step approach

One central feature of making learning fun is that children are more likely to want to engage with it. Children are more likely to develop the habit of self-discipline if they feel empowered to approach whatever task they are given and feel that there is some chance of personal success. Areas which may be perceived as 'difficult' by some children provide an opportunity for practitioners to 'break down' the learning process. Children should be taught how to approach a problem step by step, which brings greater focus to their thought process and their sense of achievement. Each step provides a small opportunity for success.

For practitioners this involves not only making learning fun, but starting from the individual child. With personal effort, determination and perseverance everyone can achieve their potential. Children need to be made aware that learning self-discipline is an acquired habit. Learning to control desires and thoughts and persevering with the task in hand is the foundation for self-discipline. Featherstone and Bayley (2006) underline the importance of not leaving this *subtle* aspect of independent learning to *chance*. They further emphasise that 'when we support children in acquiring self-discipline we help them to understand that they, and not other people, are responsible for what they do and for carrying out certain obligations' (2006: 58). One possible way of ensuring that this aspect of independent learning is developed as a cross-curricular theme is to have consistently high expectations of the children which should be exercised in a consistent manner. For example, how do you help children to respect self and others and encourage kindness and friendship?

Photo 15.3 How do you teach children a step-by-step approach to problem-solving?

Feeling a sense of achievement

Children who persevere do not give up in the face of failure. They realise that in life we learn from our mistakes. They will know that by persevering they not only achieve their goals, but can also improve on them. Such a child will feel confident to try again until he/she arrives at his/her goals. In practice this means enabling children to develop the habit of perseverance. Children adapt their learning to meet practitioner expectations. If practitioners have high expectations and appropriately encourage, support or challenge the children in their setting, they will be able to develop the necessary skills to meet these demands. Remember that you want the child to enjoy the learning experience and to feel a sense of achievement. Questions are asked to help children become independent learners capable of persevering in the face of difficulties. The way you interact with the child is crucial. It is a good idea to make a list of possible ways you can reinforce children's responses. This might be both verbally and through a system of rewards or praise. Equally important are the questions the children ask you and to each other. This should be encouraged. One possible way might be to read them a story. Prior to starting the story ask each child to listen carefully and by the end of the story have one question they would like to ask. You will call upon them to ask the question to the group at the end of the story. Creating a calm, supportive and organised climate provides a firm base for children to develop their talents.

REFLECT AND RELATE TO PRACTICE

Complete Table 15.2. It will help you integrate the necessary skills for independent learning into daily practice.

In completing the table you should reflect more deeply on some of the issues raised within the chapter so far.

Learning the 'art' of perseverance hinges on following through plans and ownership of learning; children should be encouraged to complete tasks. The following framework for planning, developed by Williams (2003) from research findings in 80 primary schools, provides a valuable framework for enabling older children to develop the inner integrity to persevere in learning:

- Allow children to plan some of their activities and give them opportunities for negotiation in the order of tasks for the week;
- Give children use of a 'planning board' on which to organize their tasks;
- Remember that children need to have the opportunity to work at personal tasks;
- Encourage the development of personal action plans;
- Use posters and flow charts to remind children how to solve particular problems;
- Ensure that all tasks in the setting give opportunities for children to contribute ideas, exercise independence and maintain at least some cultural identity.

(Williams, 2003: 19)

Table 15.2 Reflective Practice: Teaching for independence

Independent learning skill	Characteristics	How can this be developed in practice?
Self-motivation		
Self-discipline		
Decision-making		
Perseverance		
Creative		
Asks and responds to questions		
Problem-solving		
Influences own learning		
Good communicator		

DISCUSSION POINT

Consider the above framework for planning (Williams, 2003: 19). Use it to plan an activity for a group of children between the ages of 5 and 7 years (i.e. a reception class or Key Stage (KS) 1 class). You can choose any area of the Early Years Foundation Stage or the National Curriculum Key Stage 1. Remember your planning must consider teaching for independent learning.

Working collaboratively

Good communication skills are essential for children to be able to work effectively with others and to progress as independent learners. Encouraging children to to work co-operatively is a feature of good practice. This section will address the centrality of good communication skills in children's abilty to participate effectively in collaborative work and consider possible ways practitioners can help children to develop these skills.

Collaborative working at all levels is strongly endorsed by the government and supported by recent research. Whitebread et al. (2005) in their study of independent learning in the early years highlighted, amongst others, the following relevant findings, all of which relate to collaborative working:

The children learnt a great deal by watching one another.

Sometimes when an adult became involved in an activity the children were more inclined to say they couldn't do something, but if they were working with another child they were less likely to question their abilty, and often mimicked the other child, gaining confidence in their abilities.

Sometimes it is best for adults not to intervene in children's disputes and disagreements in collaborative play, but give them time and space to resolve issues themselves.

(Whitebread et al., 2005: 47)

Collaborative working is based on good communication. To be a good communicator means being good at transmitting information you want someone else to know. Children not only need to feel confident to do so, but need to have developed a number of skills to be able to do this effectively. The following list has been adapted from the EYFS (DfES, 2007: 13). Children need to be able to:

- interact well with others
- negotiate situations
- listen to and respect others' point of view
- ensure others listen to them when they speak
- be able to respond to questions
- present others with ideas, feelings or events which they have organised, sequenced and clarified
- speak clearly, audibly and confidently.

For practitioners, this means creating a climate where communication and co-operation are encouraged. Enabling children to develop good communication skills is dependent on the frequent provision of the type of learning experiences recommended by the EYFS (listed above). This can be achieved by making time for children to work in groups, teams or in pairs, both on a formal and informal basis. Equally, communication skills flourish when children have time to work alone, time to think, reflect, question and imagine. For younger children, working at a table together or playing together encourages them to communicate with each other. For older children, planning activities together provides opportunity for discussion and the sharing of ideas. Feedback to the group at large should be encouraged. Children need to start presenting their ideas 'publicly' at a young age. Encourage one child to present the group's findings. Encourage them to speak loudly and clearly. They could present a poster or a play. These types of activities promote the development of a number of very valuable independent learning skills. They should be frequent occurrences in the setting. In this way children grow accustomed to speaking and presenting in front of others. After or during the presentations made by the children, practitioners need to reaffirm the positive aspects, by making a serious comment or by asking a serious question.

For young children, helping them to develop their vocabulary base is an important dimension of good communication. There are various ways this can be done. For example, for older children, when reading a story to a group, practitioners could ask each child to think of a question to ask at the end. Children should also be encouraged to ask the meaning of words they do not understand, which should be referred to repeatedly by the practitioner. Allowing children time to make up their own stories not only helps their communication skills but offers opportunity for creativity. They should be encouraged to tell their story either to their 'neighbour' or to the group.

The following 'What happens in practice?' provides a good example of collaborative working in practice. It has been adapted from an interview with a senior lecturer in education at a university in the north of France and considers how children and practitioners can work together to develop some of the skills discussed. Although she describes the techniques she uses when teaching English and German as foreign languages to young children (3–7 year olds), many of the techniques can be used or adapted for other subject areas.

WHAT HAPPENS IN PRACTICE?

The smaller the children the more important singing is for them. They like it! Of course the songs must have gestures to help memorisation.

Games are of course also very important. They provide a very useful means of repeating the same sentence very often without boring children. And what's more, it makes even the shyest child speak because everyone wants to win!

One other important means is of course story telling. Everybody likes a good story, even grown-ups! But of course story telling has to be adapted, prepared, mimed, illustrated. The technique for the success of this is very important. Small children can't concentrate their listening for more than one or two minutes; so one has to use many different techniques to sustain their attention.

What children also like is videos of real life in the country of the learnt language if the subject is adapted to their interest.

REFLECT AND RELATE TO PRACTICE

List the collaborative strategies which have been used in the above example of 'What happens in practice?' to help the children's learning.

How do the collaborative activities mentioned contribute to the development of the children's communication skills? Would you use these types of activities to help children develop communication skills? What would you do differently?

One final and very important area to consider is that of enabling children to develop the art of rational argument. Children should be encouraged to give reasons for a particular statement they make. This provides an opportunity to show that an individual is entitled to his/her opinion as long as he/she can give reasons to support it. In practice, this means asking children to identify why they hold that opinion or why they think it is worth carrying out a particular activity. Other children need to be encouraged to respect that; they need to listen to the opinion of the others. It can then be opened to the rest of the group, where opportunity is provided for the other children to agree/disagree and give their opinion. The important issue for the practitioner is that of creating an ethos which always encourages children to support their opinions with a rational argument.

Independent learning: bringing it together

In essence enabling children to develop as independent learners must be an integral part of the formal and informal hidden curriculum. Effective practice in this area of learning means engaging with, committing to and planning for, the necessary understanding, skills, dispositions and emotions associated with independent learning. Although every child is unique he/she is capable of taking ownership for his/her own learning. Careful consideration should be given to independent learning with the early years setting:

- Practitioners could develop a list of skills, dispositions and emotions which they consider to be associated with independent learning. These should be clearly defined. In addition, there should be consensus over what type of independent learner they wish to develop.
- Have an INSET day, where a specialist/member of the setting focuses on how the necessary skills, dispositions and emotions can be developed alongside curriculum content. Remember independent learning is a process and the focus should be on developing habits.
- Practitioners should review the curriculum as a team and consider where these skills, dispositions, understandings and skills are being addressed and where they could be integrated.
- Practitioners develop new units of work to address the related area. Remember the necessary skills, understandings, dispositions and emotions should be addressed as cross-curricular strands, but can also be addressed as a discrete subject. Opportunities for question-asking, problem-solving, creativity, decision-making, making choices, rational argument, respect etc. should all be written into the curriculum.

SUMMARY

From theory to practice (p. 314)

What characteristics does an independent learner possess?

What characterises independence in adulthood is inner integrity, self-belief and an ability to work co-operatively with others. Independent adults think well of themselves and have a positive outlook on life, even in the face of failure. They understand that setbacks are part of life for everyone and what matters is the way they are handled.

SUMMARY *CONTINUED*

Creating a positive learning environment (p. 316)

What are the advantages, in terms of promoting independent learning, in allowing children daily opportunities to plan–do–review their learning?

The idea of learning should permeate the setting. The physical environment should overtly transmit to children the message that learning is important, learning is for everyone and that 'you' are part of 'this' learning environment. This involves nurturing an environment where all children share in decisions relating to their learning and learning environment.

Developing good pedagogical practice (p. 326)

What are the key elements in developing good pedagogical practices?

The government document, *KEEP – Key Elements of Effective Practice* (DfES, 2005: 6), highlights the importance in early years education of developing good relations with children, parents and other related service providers and the development of knowledge, skills and understanding of children's development and learning. The greater practitioner knowledge in these areas, the easier it will be to develop an effective context for independent learning.

Working collaboratively (p. 332)

What skills are required to be able to work collaboratively?

Collaborative working is based on good communication. To be a good communicator means being good at transmitting information you want someone else to know. Children not only need to feel confident to do so, but need to have developed a number of skills to be able to do this effectively. This can be encouraged in the setting through group and pair work and by providing the opportunity for the children to present their work to the group/class.

Glossary

Inclusive: practitioners teach to the learning needs of each child.

Independent learning: means having the belief in yourself to think through learning activities, problems or challenges, make decisions about your learning and act upon those decisions.

Interactionist view: 'where children are motivated, good problem solvers, effective communicators and able to seek help as appropriate' (Williams, 2003: 10).

Isolationalist view: 'where children are trained to develop skills for self-sufficiency and to work alone' (Williams, 2003: 10).

Sensory room: a room set up with various objects which a child can use/play with/explore to discover a range of sensations and become more aware of touch, light, colour, sound and smell. It is usually a quiet room away from the main teaching and learning rooms.

Find out more

Porter, L. (2005) *Gifted Young Children: a Guide for Teachers and Parents*, **2nd edn. Buckingham: Open University Press.**
This book considers how to enhance the social participation of talented children (0–8 years) and how to help and support them in valuing themselves as people.

Hutchinson, N. and Smith, H. (2004) *Intervening Early: Promoting Positive Behaviour in Young Children*, **London: David Fulton.**
This book developed out of a joint project in 1999 between Bristol's Educational Psychology Service and the Behaviour Support Service. It

provides practical examples of how to develop positive learning dispositions in children. Part II, Ideas for support, is particularly good in this respect.

Costello, P. (2000) *Thinking Skills and Early Childhood Education*, **London: David Fulton.**
The author, Patrick Costello, covers the broad area of 'thinking skills' in early childhood education from philosophical thinking through to the skills of argument. Chapter 5 provides worked examples for developing thinking skills in relation to personal, social and moral development.

References

Abbott, L. and Nutbrown, C. (2001) *Experiencing Reggio Emilio: implications for pre-school provision*. Milton Keynes: Open University.

Department for Education and Skills (DfES) (2005) *KEEP – Key Elements of Effective Practice*. London: DfES.

Department for Education and Skills (DfES) (2007) *Statutory Framework for the Early Years Foundation Stage: Setting the Standards for Learning Development and Care for children from birth to five* (EYFS). Nottingham: DfES Publications.

Featherstone, S. and Bailey, R. (2006) *Foundations for Independence: Developing Independent learning in the Foundation Stage*, 2nd edn. Lutterworth: Featherstone Education.

Fisher, J. (2002) *Starting from the Child*. Maidenhead: Open University Press/McGraw-Hill Education.

Follari, L.M. (2007) *Foundations and Best Practices in Early Childhood Education: Histories, Theories, and Approaches to Learning*. Columbus, OH: Pearson/Merrill Prentice Hall.

Hendy, L. and Whitehead, D. (2000) Intepretations of independent learning in the Early Years, *International Journal of Early Years Education*, Vol. 8, No. 3: pp. 245–252.

Hodson, E. (2002) Planning to meet the physical and creative development needs of young children, in

Keating, I. (ed.) *Achieving QTS – Teaching Foundation Stage*. Exeter: Learning Matters.

Holt, N. (2007) *Bringing the High/Scope Approach to Your Early Years Practice*. London: Routledge.

Jones, P. (2008) *Tycoon*. London: Hodder and Stoughton.

Montessori, M. (1965) *Handbook*. New York: Schocken.

Montessori, M. (1989) *The Montessori Method*. New York: Schocken.

National Advisory Committee on Creative and Cultural Education (NACCCE) (1999) *All our Futures: Creativity, Culture and Education*. Sudbury: DfEE.

Ofsted (2008) *Early Years Leading to Excellence*. London: OPSI.

Thornton, L. and Brunton, P. (2007) *Bringing the Reggio Approach to your Early Years practice*. New York: Routledge.

Whitebread, D., Anderson, H., Coltman, P., Page, C., Pino Pasternak, D. and Mehta, S. (2005) Developing Independent Learning in the Early Years, *Education 3–13*, March.

Williams, J. (2003) *Promoting Independent Learning in the Primary Classroom*. Buckingham: Open University Press.

PART 4 Learning Futures

Part 4 considers key aspects of developing professional practice which will influence learning in the future. Effective leadership is fundamental to early years practice, raising standards and improving outcomes for all children. The collaborative approach which is beginning to emerge as the favoured model within the early years sector means that all members of the learning community share in the day-to-day leadership and management of the setting. In exploring the concept of 'distributed leadership', Part 4 shows how all those who work within the setting contribute to the development of its culture, the day-to-day and longer-term planning for children's learning and shape the partnerships which develop within the setting and beyond.

Grade school © photodisc

By the end of this chapter you will be able to answer the following questions:

- Why is strategic planning different from operational planning?
- Where is the best starting point for an Improvement Plan?
- What is long-term planning and how do I prepare a long-term plan?
- How does long-term planning inform medium-term planning, which in turn informs short-term planning?
- Why is ongoing observational assessment central to short-term planning?

This chapter will support your understanding of the following Standards *(see Appendix 1):*
■ **Knowledge and understanding:** S01, S02, S03, S05 and S06 ■ **Effective Practice:** S08, S09, S10, S11, S12, S13, S14 and S21 ■ **Relationships with children:** S26 ■ **Teamwork and collaboration:** S33, S34 and S35 ■ **Professional development:** S38.

Introduction

Children who begin their education in a learning environment that is vibrant, purposeful, challenging and supportive stand the best chance of developing into confident and successful learners. Effective learning environments are created over time as the result of practitioners and parents working together, thinking and talking about children's learning and planning how to promote it.

(QCA, 2001: 2)

Developing an effective cycle for learning is founded on good planning. As discussed in Chapter 9, assessment is inseparably linked to the planning process. Fisher describes this 'continuous cycle, [where] assessment [informs] planning which informs assessment which influences planning' (1998: 42). Fisher supports the widely held view, also endorsed by government policy on assessment, that planning is not 'effective unless assessment is effective'. Planning, a multi-layered process, provides the building blocks for what happens in the setting on a day-to-day basis. The Qualifications and Curriculum Authority (QCA) (2001), as shown above, highlight the centrality of planning in terms of meeting the learning needs and helping the child to achieve his/her full potential as an independent learner.

In essence, effective planning leads into effective engagement. Although planning consists of long-, medium- and short-term plans, the focus is always that of the child. Alvestad, in her research on pre-school teachers' understandings of educational planning and practice in Norway, suggests that planning should focus on 'learning, which needs to be connected to the children as active participants in authentic meaningful activities in a shared practice' (2004: 93). This chapter will address planning across the setting/school and show how planning at all levels, from the Improvement Plan through to day-to-day planning, is connected to and impacts on teaching and children's learning experiences.

DISCUSSION POINT

1 In a group of three or four discuss what you think are the principal differences between long-, medium- and short-term planning.
2 Reflect on Alvestad's (2004) comment about learning. Why does practitioners' understanding of learning in the early years influence their planning?

You can review these issues at the end of the chapter.

The planning process

Long-term plan: an overview of children's learning covering all areas of the curriculum.

Medium-term plan: concerned with the curriculum, they cover specific areas of learning.

Short-term plan: a working document detailing daily teaching practice.

The development of **long-, medium- and short-term plans** provides a natural gradation in the planning process, leading the practitioner from a broad overview to a more precise focus on the individual child. As stated in Chapter 9, what is clear, however, about all planning – long, medium and short term – is that it needs to: be founded on and intertwined with assessment for learning; consider the vision and mission statements of the setting; and provide a number of opportunities for children to revisit the early learning goals and educational programmes. This section provides a step-by-step guide to planning, guiding the reader through the various practical issues which present in practice.

There is no template for planning. Each person will develop a way of planning to suit their needs. This will be dependent on the vision, mission, aims, culture, ethos and policy of the setting, influenced in turn by the staff:child ratio, the age range of the children and the time they spend in the setting. That said, there are certain generic rules which can be applied to planning to make it a manageable process which is both central to and enhances teaching and learning. In practice, the principal issue is that of where to start. Although the focus of planning is the child, it goes without saying that basic plans for teaching and learning will have to be in place even before you will have met the child; it is acknowledged that all children can be given certain learning opportunities relevant to their age group which are clearly set out in the *Statutory Framework for the Early Years Foundation Stage* (EYFS) (DfES, 2007). Consequently, the starting point for planning is the curriculum – the six areas covered by the early learning goals, educational programmes and the assessment scales as set out in the EYFS. This document reaffirmed the government's commitment to quality provision in the early years and provides a strong framework within which practitioners can focus their understanding of children's learning and construct and direct their teaching in practice. As a reminder, the following areas are covered by the early learning goals and educational programmes:

- personal, social and emotional development
- communication, language and literacy
- problem-solving, reasoning and numeracy
- knowledge and understanding of the world
- physical development
- creative development.

Underpinning these six areas are the following descriptors of learning which were mandated by the Childcare Act 2006 and in essence, more precisely define the type of learning opportunities planning needs to consider:

- the early learning goals – the knowledge, skills and understanding which young children should have acquired by the end of the academic year in which they reach the age of five;
- the educational programmes – the matters, skills and processes which are required to be taught to young children;

- the assessment arrangements – the arrangements for assessing young children to ascertain their achievements.

(DfES, 2007: 11)

Practitioners may feel daunted by the prospect of developing effective plans which provide each child with worthwhile learning opportunities. This does not have to be the case. The development of long-, medium- and short-term plans provides a natural gradation in the planning process, leading the practitioner from a broad overview to a more precise focus on the individual child.

Fisher (1998: 23) suggests that-long term planning is about the *curriculum*, whereas short-term planning is about the *child*. In essence it is about both the child and the curriculum. Planning is a practical activity based on the following established principles:

1 Planning is a cyclical process.
2 Planning is both analytical – thinking things through involving calculation and individual reflection – and social – motivating and drawing on the contributions and commitment from all staff.
3 When determining objectives be **SMART** (Tuckman, 1965). Remember, objectives should be: **S**pecific, **M**easurable, **A**ttainable, **R**elevant and **T**imed.

From this broad view of the planning process, it is important to consider in more detail the intricacies of effective planning for children's learning which will involve practitioners working in an early years setting. Before embarking on this process it is

Photo 16.1
Short-term planning starts with observation of the child

Pearson Education Ltd. Jules Selmes © Pearson Education Ltd. 2004

Table 16.1 Planning: Government documents

Document	Summary
Statutory Framework for the Early Years Foundation Stage: Setting the Standards for Learning Development and Care for children from birth to five (EYFS) (DfES, 2007)	This document sets out the early learning goals and educational programmes, along with the assessment scales (appendix 1).
Seeing Steps in children's learning (QCA, 2005a)	This document considers more precisely the skills etc. that children need to learn to achieve the early learning goals. By focusing on continuity and progression, it provides valuable information for helping children to meet achievable targets (for children aged 3–5 years old).
Curriculum Guidance for the Foundation Stage (QCA, 2000)	This document addresses effective teaching and learning in practice and provides useful advice on how to provide steps to help children meet learning objectives (for children aged 5–7 years).
Foundation Stage Profile Handbook (QCA, 2003)	Considers assessment in practice, detailing, through case studies, both how to make judgements on children's achievements and how to standardise assessment in the setting.
Observing Children – Building The Profile (QCA, 2005b)	This document considers the centrality of observation in enabling practitioners to know children well, with the aim of adapting teaching to meet individual learner needs.
Improving outcomes for children in the Foundation Stage in maintained schools (DfES, 2006)	This document focuses on effective target setting in the early years, which should be used to inform short-term planning.
Planning for learning in the foundation stage (QCA, 2001)	This document provides five very clear examples of planning in practice from the long-term planning process, through to how **observational assessment** informs short-term planning.

Observational assessment: practitioners observing and evaluating children's learning, either planned or as incidental observation.

worth considering the government documents which will be useful for planning in practice (see Table 16.1). It goes without saying that this list will have to be updated as new policies are issued.

Long-term planning

The goal of the long-term plan is that of ensuring that each child is provided with a 'broad, balanced and purposeful curriculum' (QCA, 2001: 3). This section will examine the various aspects of teaching, learning and the curriculum which should be considered by the long-term plan.

Long-term planning aims to provide an overview of the children's learning. Prepared weeks, months or even a year in advance, usually by the leadership team, its focus is that of the curriculum. Like all plans, it acts as a guide to teaching and learning and needs to be flexible enough to allow for the unplanned, such as the arrival of a new pet animal in the setting. This can provide a new learning experience for some children and activities related to the happening should be integrated into the short-term plan. Unlike the short-term plan, the long-term plan makes provision for the group of children, acknowledging that many areas of the curriculum are relevant for a particular age range, irrespective of other factors which may influence children's learning. Fisher, however, is quite scathing about the benefits of long-term planning in relation to 'the developmental needs of individual children' (2002: 51–52). She further suggests that long-term plans are concerned with 'children's entitlement to the curriculum' and merely act as a framework for considering the 'breadth and balance of children's experiences during their time in the setting' (ibid.). This view is supported by a number of practitioners who see long-term planning in terms of providing a broad overview of curriculum provision. Drake (2001), on the other hand, in her delineation of long-term planning implies greater depth to the process than Fisher (2002) would suggest. For Drake, children's learning, in long-term planning, should be 'defined in terms of curricular aims, resources, organization, adult role, and potential learning experiences' (2001: 39). This tends to offer scope for considering such issues as the type of questions practitioners might ask children to support their learning or the extent to which they will intervene in activities. What is clear, however, is that long-term planning needs to cover all areas of the curriculum, covering most areas a number of times during the course of the year; the same topic should be reiterated in different ways.

The best starting point for the long-term plan are the six areas of learning outlined by the early learning goals and educational programmes. These are clearly stated in the EYFS (DfES, 2007). In addition, it will be helpful to use the Assessment Scales (EYFS: Appendix 1), which although they show what aspects of the learning goals and educational programmes need to be assessed, present the essential areas of the curriculum within a more precise framework for planning. In addition, the Qualifications and Curriculum Authority document, *Seeing Steps in Children's Learning* (QCA, 2005b), is a useful document for planning. It is important to consider at this stage particular areas which might be difficult to cover. Extra time spent on reflection in the long-term planning process can reduce the workload for medium- and short-term planning, when the pressures of time might be a strong constraint. It is at this stage that practitioners should consider the type of activities which will be employed – child-initiated, adult-led etc., the different way children learn (see Chapter 5), the inclusivity of the curriculum and opportunities for assessment. The long-term plan should include opportunities for focused assessment which can also be used to inform assessment for the Foundation Stage Profile. In relation to gathering evidence for the Profile, the QCA document *Observing Children – Building the Profile* (QCA, 2005a: 29) suggests that practitioners should consider as a group the type of activities which could be usefully and effectively employed with the children to adequately cover areas of the curriculum which might be deemed difficult. The document provides the following example in relation to *cultures and beliefs*: through group work, practitioners may suggest that this area of the curriculum can be adequately covered through 'discussions at circle time, using persona dolls, displaying and discussing appropriate artefacts, use of appropriate information books and stories or through role play' (ibid.).

It is worth bearing in mind (see Appendix 1) that the long-term plan provides the foundation for both the medium- and short-term plans. Consequently, they should be built within a strong framework; this will be your initial working document. In addition, a number of children will attend the setting on a part-time basis, while others will be in the setting for a number of years. Practitioners will need to ask themselves during the long-term planning process: How can I make allowance for the part-time children and how can this plan be altered next year to ensure that children's learning will be equally stimulating? The following 'What happens in practice?' describes the approach to long-term planning taken by a private inner city nursery. It has a staff of eight, one of whom is part-time, and 24 children (2–4 years). Some children attend on a part-time basis.

WHAT HAPPENS IN PRACTICE?

At first we met up every month to plan our curriculum. Having worked together for two years, we have experience of the planning process and a collection of long- and short-term plans to draw on. Now, we meet every three months to discuss, evaluate and adjust them if necessary.

We begin our planning cycle in September. At this point in the year, we discuss last year's long-term plan and evaluate how successful our themes have been in capturing the children's interests and imagination and helping them to make progress. It has taken two years of working together with parents and using our knowledge of the children to reach a stage where we are confident in our approach to long-term planning. We are always looking out for fresh ideas to motivate and engage the children as they move through the nursery. Each area of learning is given equal emphasis and there are opportunities to revisit each aspect at least three times a year.

(QCA, 2001: 11)

REFLECT AND RELATE TO PRACTICE

In what ways does this reflect good long-term planning practice?
Is there anything which has not been mentioned which you would consider?

Prior to completing the plan it is worth considering the following checklist. Ask yourself: have I provided:

- an indication of when you plan to teach aspects/areas of learning?
- an indication of how regularly and frequently you plan to teach aspects/areas of learning?
- an indication of how you will link aspects/areas of learning in a relevant and interesting way for the children?
- special events and activities that provide a meaningful context and enhance learning (e.g. a visit to a city farm, a cultural or religious festival)?
- for a balanced curriculum – i.e. including all aspects of learning, a balance within and between the six areas of learning and sufficient opportunities for the children to revisit all aspects of learning regularly and frequently?

(QCA, 2001: 4)

DISCUSSION POINT

The QCA document, *Planning for Learning in the Foundation Stage* (QCA, 2001), gives a number of examples of long- and short-term plans in practice. Look up these examples (available at **http://www.qca.org.uk/**). Discuss them. Using this document and the documents recommended for long-term planning produce your own long-term plan for a nursery setting for children aged 3–5 years.

Medium-term planning

In practice, medium-term plans are drawn from the long-term plan and are usually prepared on a termly, half-termly or monthly basis. This section will address the place of medium-term planning within the context of planning for teaching and learning and considers the extent to which they differ from long-term plans.

Having considered some of the conflicting positions on long-term planning, it has probably become evident that diverging opinions amongst practitioners and researchers as to what constitutes effective planning are commonplace. This is a certain truth when it comes to medium-term plans. Some choose to abandon the idea of medium-term planning, working instead from the long-term plan, while others develop detailed medium-term plans covering a broad spectrum of issues related to children's learning. Fisher (2002) is of the opinion that medium-term planning, like long-term planning, is also related to the curriculum. She sets her opinion within the framework of children's development. Although practitioners will know many of the children by this stage in the planning process, Fisher (2002: 52) suggests that their developmental needs will not be evident so far in advance. She delineates medium-term planning within the context of *continuity* and *progression*, where the plans should address these issues 'from one stage in each area of learning to the next, and from one setting or class to the next' (Fisher, 1998: 24). In essence, medium-term plans cover a specific area/theme of learning. As it will inform the short-term plan it is a good idea to include as much detail relating to the curriculum and teaching and learning as possible and present it in weekly blocks to facilitate short-term planning. Drake (2001) suggests that the medium-term plan should include

> focus activities and anticipated experiences linked to e.g. predictable interests (festivals, seasons, outside visits), a curricular focus or theme. [In addition it should identify] assessment opportunites, key area(s) of learning, early learning goals, enhancement to provision and intended outcomes for the end of the period.
>
> *(2001: 39)*

It is perhaps a good idea to fine-tune planning at this stage and consider in more detail what is meant by the 'curriculum'. The government document, *A Training Support Framework for the Foundation Stage* (DfES, 2002), defines 'curriculum'

> as the educational programme, or what you want children to learn; what you plan and provide to help them learn. [The document further states that] it's more than that. It's everything the children do and see and hear and feel while they're with you in the setting. It includes unplanned as well as planned activities.
>
> • Firstly the activities and experiences that you have thought out for children and the work you do with them – the planned and offered, or taught curriculum.
> • Finally, the things that children get to know and understand – the received or learned curriculum.
>
> *(2002: 11)*

There is a tendency in planning just to focus on the formal academic curriculum. However, it is vitally important to consider not only the knowledge, understanding and concepts you want children to learn, but the types of skills and attitudes they need to develop to become competent and independent learners. It should be remembered that:

> Young children develop confidence in themselves as learners and their emerging skills progress rapidly across all six areas of learning, but they are dependent on adults to create the right emotional and physical learning environment.
>
> *(DfES, 2006: 11)*

Alvestad (2004), in her work on pre-school teachers' understandings of educational planning and practice in Norway, noted the different focus of practitioners. While some focused planning on the educational content others focused on the affective dimensions of the child. Both are relevant and while it is often easier to found planning on a knowledge base, it is important to consider how personal, social and emotional development can be incorporated into planning to support children's learning and help them to become independent learners.

DISCUSSION POINT

Why do you think there are conflicting views on medium-term planning? What areas/issues would you address in a medium-term plan? Why?

Short-term planning

The short-term plan is 'the working document'. Usually prepared a week in advance, it can change on a daily basis as practitioners observe or learn something new about a child's development or learning needs. This section will address the centrality of ongoing observational assessment in short-term planning and consider how this type of assessment can be integrated into day-to-day practice within the setting.

Short-term planning focuses on the child. Fisher suggests that it is concerned with '**differentiation** and planning for the needs of specific groups and individual children' (1998: 24). The short-term plan is usually prepared a week in advance, but is altered on a day-to-day basis to meet the learning needs of each child as they arise. It is in the short-term planning that the immediacy of the cyclical nature of planning is apparent. On a daily basis practitioners will be observing children, primarily on an informal basis, and using this information to alter the learning experience the child/children will have the following day. In practice, it is most effective to have a sheet with the children's names listed and a column to make notes throughout the day. The sheet may include prompts to help you, for example, the possible questions you might ask the children. At the end of the day, practitioners will then reflect on their notes and consider how this information can be best used to help the child/children to advance in their learning. Although short-term plans draw on the long-term plan, they are continuously informed by ongoing observational assessment and need to consider target setting. The government document, *Improving outcomes for children in the Foundation Stage in maintained schools* (DfES, 2006: 8), defines target (also known as next steps or goals) as 'an area for development, improvement, enhancement – building on one's previous best'. It further adds that the purpose of a target is 'to improve the quality of involvement, engagement and well-being of all those involved'. In setting targets for children's learning and development, start from the learning goals and educational programmes set out in the Early Years Foundation Stage; this document can be supported by *Curriculum Guidance for the Foundation Stage* and *Seeing Steps in Children's Learning*. Ultimately, however, target setting is informed by ongoing observational assessment and practitioners need to consider the following questions when setting targets and planning for children's learning on a short-term basis:

Differentiation: relates to the adaptation of the curriculum to meet the learning needs of each child.

- What types of activity engage and motivate this child?
- Is it best to plan the provocations for learning outdoors or indoors?
- What are the most appropriate next steps in learning that will best support, extend and develop this child's skills, knowledge and understanding?

(DfES, 2006: 12)

The following 'What happens in practice?' is adapted from an interview with the head of a pre-prep school in Yorkshire and shows one way of seeking and interpreting evidence for learning (3–5 year olds).

WHAT HAPPENS IN PRACTICE?

You need a baseline assessment for all areas. That's what we do. Staff carry out detailed observations, both formally and informally, so that it can be recorded for individual children. The important thing is the individual child. We have activities structured in such a way that we can see children in a variety of activities. We would look at the early learning goals (EYFS) and then try to match them by using the Foundation Stage Profile (QCA, 2003). We also use the North Yorkshire Early Years curriculum, which is similar. These observations are not one-off. We look at a trend over time. Staff do a number of observations and track the child's progress over time.

DISCUSSION POINT

Why do you think it is important to do a number of observations of children in assessing their progress?

You should list as many reasons as you can and also consider the various reasons for both formal and informal observations.

It is clear from the above example that children need a number of opportunities to achieve the early learning goals. Observing a child participating in a specific activity will indicate to the practitioner which learning goals have been achieved; many children achieve a number during one activity. However, some children will need support to achieve the leaning goal/goals and will be given further opportunity to revisit the specific area of learning through a number of different activities. In planning for short-term learning, the QCA (2001) suggests that plans should consider the following:

- Clear learning intentions for individual or groups of children informed by observations and based on the stepping stones/early learning goals
- A brief description of the range of experience and activities
  - adult directed and child initiated
  - indoors and outdoors
- How experiences and activities can be adapted for individual or groups of children
- How the children will be organised
- The role of the adult(s), including parents
- The resources and equipment needed.

(QCA: 2001: 4)

In addition the document suggests that the short-term plan should consider:

- Opportunities for observations of individuals or groups of children
- Questions and/or vocabulary that the adult(s) will use during the activity
- Opportunities for informal assessments of individual or groups of children.

(ibid.)

The following 'what happens in practice?' describes the approach to short-term planning taken by a private inner city nursery. It has a staff of eight, one of whom is part-time, and 24 children (2–4 years). Some children attend on a part-time basis.

WHAT HAPPENS IN PRACTICE?

At our weekly meeting, we develop our short-term plan for the week ahead, based on the previous week's observations and the aspects of learning we plan to promote. We meet informally each day to agree our roles and responsibilities, so we know what we need to prepare for the next day. We plan to use the activities more than once during the course of the week, to enable all children to have the opportunity to take part, including those who attend for a limited number of sessions. We encourage children of all ages and stages of development to participate in the activities. The adult present will adapt the activity to challenge each individual child.

(QCA, 2001: 12)

REFLECT AND RELATE TO PRACTICE

Do you agree with the way this setting approaches short-term planning? What would you add or do differently?

Strategic planning

Strategic plan: an expression of how an organisation intends to achieve its aims in a deliverable form beyond the current year.

A **strategic plan** is an expression of how an organisation intends to achieve its vision, mission, and aims in a deliverable form for a period beyond the current setting or financial year. In essence, a strategic plan takes a long-term view. This section will consider the centrality of the strategic plan in both managing and developing the setting/school thus providing the context for the cycle of learning.

An effective setting will have plans and policies that support the leadership and management of learning. In an effective setting, a strategic plan will be a working document used by staff and governors in the delivery of agreed aims and objectives. The plan will consider where the setting wants to be and how it aims to get there. A deliverable plan will encompass all the activities of the setting.

Strategic planning takes into consideration the strengths and weaknesses of the setting as an organisation and also external factors such as government directives. Fidler (2002) suggests 'that strategic thinking is a mental attitude which tries to keep long-term objectives constantly in mind and considers all short-term decisions in this long-term perspective' (2002: 13). Leaders have a critical role in articulating organisational goals. These goals will reflect personal values as determined by vision and mission. Preparing a strategic plan might encompass a framework for all activities as shown in Figure 16.1.

The format of the strategic plan will depend upon the individual needs and circumstances of the setting. Ideally the plan should cover a period of three to five years and be reviewed and modified on an annual rolling basis so that a medium-term planning horizon can be maintained. It should, as Fidler suggests, 'include implications for both what to do and also what not to do. In short . . . , it should indicate (implicit) priorities' (2002: 25). It should be a coherent and comprehensive document showing the relationship between financial and academic years. Settings should develop their own planning cycle and timetable which allows for:

- a review of past activities, aims and objectives – did we get it right?
- definition or redefinition of aims and objectives – are the aims still relevant?
- development of the plan and associated budgets – how do we go forward?
- implementation, monitoring and review – how do we make the plan work and keep it on course?

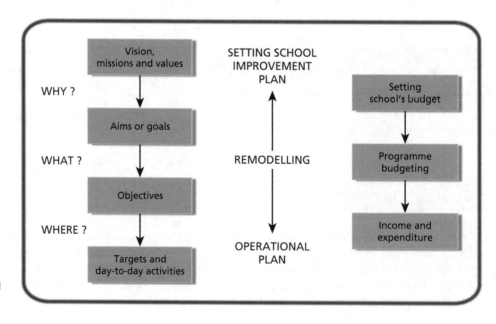

Figure 16.1
Strategic plan

Source: Blandford (2006) p. 79

- feedback into the next planning cycle – what worked successfully and how can we improve?

Operational planning

Operational planning is about tasks underpinned by policies and targets and relates directly to the role of all staff in the setting: who does what, when and how. This section will consider the issues addressed by an effective operational plan.

Operational planning is detailed. It aims to achieve a particular set of objectives within a given time and is concerned with making things happen in the short term. The planning, implementation and evaluation of professional development programmes in a setting should take account of the setting's strategic plan, priorities and available resources. A useful framework for developing and implementing an operational plan is provided by the National Occupational Standards (Management Standards Centre, 2004). For effective outcomes the Standards recommend the following:

- Balance new ideas with tried and tested solutions
- Balance risk with desired outcomes
- Make sure your plans are consistent with the objectives
- Make sure the plan is flexible and complements related areas of work
- Develop and assign objectives to people together with the associated resources
- Win the support of key colleagues and other stakeholders
- Monitor and control your plan so that it achieves its overall objectives
- Evaluate the implementation of your plan and make recommendations that identify good practice and areas for improvement.

Operational planning provides the details that turn strategies into actions and aims to achieve a particular set of objectives within a given time. The process of developing a setting's operational plan should be collaborative.

The process of planning is often more important than the plan. In terms of the innovation itself, an action plan might address a range of questions including who will benefit from the plan: children, colleagues? What will the costs be for those affected? Will additional resources be required to monitor the additional resources? It is also worth considering: is the change easy to communicate to those concerned and will they see its purpose? If this is not agreed, will it be possible to adapt what is intended to suit specific circumstances? Whose support will be needed? Will key people have a sense of ownership of the change?

> **Operational plan:** this is a plan about tasks underpinned by policy and targets and relates directly to the staff.

Photo 16.2
Operational
planning should
balance risk with
desired outcomes

Pearson Education
Ltd. Lord and
Leverett
© Pearson
Education Ltd.
2007

DISCUSSION POINT

How does an operational plan differ from a strategic plan?
How does an operational plan inform long-, medium- and short-term curriculum planning?

Improvement Plan (IP)

Improvement plan: This provides a framework for strategic planning where staff can identify long- and short-term objectives to manage themselves effectively.

The **improvement plan** provides an operational focus for the implementation of strategic planning in which staff can identify long- and short-term objectives to manage themselves effectively. The main purpose of an IP should be to improve the quality of learning for children. This section will consider the preparation process for an IP, including the centrality of the audit to this process, and examine the idea of an action plan for its implementation.

An IP should relate to the setting's vision or mission, its achievements, government policy and LA policies and initiatives. The IP should be central to the management of the setting, involving all staff. Hargreaves and Hopkins stated that:

> The production of a good plan and its successful implementation depend upon a sound grasp of the processes involved. A wise choice of content for

the plan as well as the means of implementing the plan successfully will be made only when the process of development planning is thoroughly understood.

(1991: 4)

As the main purpose of an IP is to improve the quality of learning for children, Stoll et al. (2003: 153) underline the need to 'see patterns and discern connections between seemingly unconnected events' in improvement planning. They further suggest that effective Improvement Plans consider 'connectedness', where they get 'below the surface of the actions or explore what happens when all of the priorities are being worked on at one time' (ibid.). Skelton et al. (1991) advocate that the format of IPs should:

- demonstrate involvement
- provide a focus for action
- provide a means of presenting the plan
- provide a link to staff development
- provide a means of assessing progress.

The value of an IP as an operational tool will rest with the leadership team. An understanding of the planning process is a necessary prerequisite to participation in the development of the IP. A model of the planning process will aid improvement planning, illustrated in Figure 16.2.

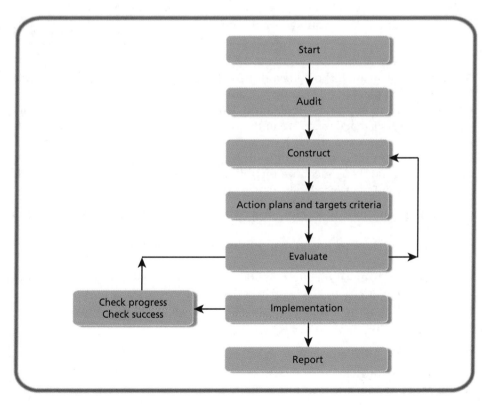

Figure 16.2
The planning process

Source: Blandford (2006) p. 84

Audit

To begin, IPs might identify strengths and weaknesses in the various relevant areas. In essence an audit will provide a basis for selecting priorities for development. The context of the audit will be:

- values, vision, missions, aims and objectives of the setting
- policies and initiatives
- inspections and reviews
- staff appraisals
- views of all stakeholders: staff, governors, parents, children and community.

A full audit will be time consuming; a programme of specific small-scale audits may be more practical and achievable within the setting. An audit might include:

- interviews with colleagues
- practitioner observation – where appropriate
- review of documentation
- writing up findings.

REFLECT AND RELATE TO PRACTICE

Imagine you have been asked to carry out the audit for the improvement plan in a nursery setting. Consider how you would organise it. Whose views would you want to consider? What questions would you ask?

The outcomes of an audit should reveal strengths and weaknesses in order to provide a basis for action planning. The audit will also identify priorities for development.

The success of an improvement plan will depend upon the planning process. Fidler (2002: 26) suggests that developing an IP involves a hierarchial planning process. He recommends, at the first planning level, a consideration of the impact of the strategic plan on the 'organisational structure and the decision-making' processes within the setting. Fidler (2002: 26) identifies the following areas for inclusion within the IP, where detailed sub-plans need to be drawn up:

- curriculum (and child outcomes) plan (what we intend to contribute to children's learning)
- staff planning (how we intend to recruit and develop people with the skills to do it)
- financial (and material resources and premises) plan (how we intend to acquire and spend the money to help us achieve it)
- marketing plan (how we intend to obtain the resources and support of others to enable us to achieve it).

The plan might include:

- aims of the setting
- proposed priorities and their time-scale

- justification of the priorities in the context of the setting
- the plan draws together different aspects of planning
- methods of reporting outcomes
- broad financial implications of the plan.

As a strategic plan, the IP should consider the changes needed to improve the effectiveness of the setting. Planners should recognise that the urgent and unavoidable linking of priorities will lead to increased collaboration between staff and other stakeholders.

DISCUSSION POINT

The main purpose of the improvement plan (IP) is to improve the quality of learning for children. What do you think should inform the planning stage for a focused and effective IP?

Implementing the IP

Once the IP has been completed, detailed action plans can be drawn up. This will involve colleagues deciding on the way forward to implement the IP. Action plans are a means of operationalising the strategy. Action plans should contain:

- the agreed *priority* area
- the *targets* – specific objectives for the priority area
- *success criteria* against which progress and achievement can be judged
- the *tasks* to be undertaken
- allocation of *responsibility* for tasks and targets – with *time-scales*
- *resources* required.

Action plans should prepare the way forward for the implementation of the IP. How this will work will depend on several factors. Hargreaves and Hopkins (1991: 65) identify the following activities required to make the plan work:

- sustaining commitment during implementation
- checking the progress of implementation
- overcoming any problems encountered
- checking the success of implementation
- taking stock
- reporting progress
- constructing the next development plan.

Planning a cycle for learning: bringing it together

Planning may involve going around in circles as various combinations of objectives, actions and resources are considered, while ensuring that all elements are included. In successful settings, improvement plans focus on strategies to improve the quality of teaching and learning and thereby raise children's levels of achievement. Successful settings often display:

- a shared vision and high expectation about children's achievement
- an agreement on effective teaching practices and their impact on children's achievement
- agreed and acknowledged arrangements to ensure the setting is managed effectively and efficiently
- a strategy to develop, monitor and review curriculum and associated learning and teaching policies and schemes of work
- a coherent approach of monitoring and evaluation, assessing children's progress and recording and reporting their achievements.

Planning can be challenging, enjoyable even; it can also be difficult (LaGrave et al., 1994: 5–24). Practitioners need to be able to plan a variety of events that happen in the life of the setting, and specifically within their area of responsibility. The majority of practitioners will experience the limitations of finance and other resources. There will also be time factors to consider in the preparation and implementation of the plan. It may be necessary to alter the plan in order to accommodate these challenges.

Planning will also be constrained by the need to meet deadlines. This must be included in the development of plans. More specifically, problems may arise if objectives are vague, circumstances change, or if there are difficulties with people and local politics. The planning process is perhaps best summarised as in Table 16.2, which can provide a framework for all planning within a setting.

Table 16.2 Planning stages

Objectives	Stage 1	*Define the objectives*	What are you aiming to achieve?
	Stage 2	*Generate and evaluate objectives/actions*	What are the courses of action available? Which one will best achieve your objectives?
Actions	Stage 3	*Identify the actions*	What is required to implement your objectives?
	Stage 4	*Sequence the actions*	What is the best order?
Resources	Stage 5	*Identify the resources*	What resources are required?
Review	Stage 6	*Review the plan*	Will it work? If not, return to stage 2 or 3.
Preparation	Stage 7	*Prepare plans and schedules*	Who will do what and when?
Audit	Stage 8	*Monitor and evaluate*	Re-plan if necessary.

SUMMARY

The planning process (p. 342)

What is the starting point for planning?

The development of long-, medium- and short-term plans provides a natural gradation in the planning process, leading the practitioner from a broad overview to a more precise focus on the individual child. What is clear, however, about all planning – long, medium and short term – is that it needs to: be founded on and intertwined with assessment for learning; consider the vision and mission statements of the setting; and provide a number of opportunities for children to revisit the early learning goals and educational programmes.

Long-term planning (p. 344)

What aspects of the curriculum and teaching and learning should be considered by the long-term plan?

The goal of the long-term plan is that of ensuring that each child is provided with a 'broad, balanced and purposeful curriculum' (QCA, 2001: 3). The long-term plan makes provision for the group of children, acknowledging that many areas of the curriculum are relevant for a particular age range, irrespective of other factors which may influence children's learning.

Medium-term planning (p. 347)

How do medium-term plans differ from long-term plans?

In practice, medium-term plans are drawn from the long-term plan and are usually prepared on a termly, half-termly or monthly basis. In essence, they cover a specific area/theme of learning.

Short-term planning (p. 349)

How does assessment inform short-term planning?

The short-term plan is usually prepared a week in advance, but is altered on a day-to-day basis to meet the learning needs of each child as they arise. Although short-term plans draw on the long-term plan, they are informed by ongoing observational assessment and need to consider target setting.

Strategic planning (p. 351)

What issues/areas are considered by a strategic plan?

In an effective setting, a strategic plan will be a working document used by staff, governors and trustees in the delivery of agreed aims and objectives. The plan will consider where the setting wants to be and how it aims to get there.

Operational planning (p. 353)

How does an operational plan inform short-, medium- and long-term curriculum planning?

Operational planning is about tasks underpinned by policies and targets and relates directly to the role of all staff in the setting: who does what, when and how.

Improvement Plan (IP) (p. 354)

Why is an audit so important in developing an IP?

The IP provides a framework for strategic planning in which staff can identify long- and short-term objectives to manage themselves effectively. The main purpose of an IP should be to improve the quality of learning for children.

Glossary

Differentiation: relates to the adaptation of the curriculum to meet the learning needs of each child. Differentiation can be by input – where different tasks, determined by a child's ability, are selected by the practitioner prior to the activity – or by output – where all children do the same activity and the differences in the way children carry out and/or complete the activity are considered.

Improvement plan (IP): provides a framework for strategic planning in which staff can identify long- and short-term objectives to manage themselves effectively. An IP should relate to the setting's vision or mission, its achievements, government policy and LA policies and initiatives.

Long-term plan: an overview of the children's learning, covering all areas of the curriculum and detailing when learning areas will be revisited.

Medium-term plan: concerned with the curriculum. In essence, it covers a specific area/theme of learning.

Observational assessment: practitioners observing and evaluating children's learning, either as a planned observation or as an incidental observation.

Operational plan: Operational planning is about tasks underpinned by policies and targets and relates directly to the role of all staff in the setting: who does what, when and how.

Short-term plan: a working document, detailing daily teaching practice and all related aspects. It is informed by ongoing observational assessment and is often altered on a day-to-day basis.

Strategic plan: an expression of how an organisation intends to achieve its vision, mission, and aims in a deliverable form for a period beyond the current setting or financial year.

Find out more

The following government documents are recommended for writing/preparing workable plans. It is a good idea to read them in advance to help you become a competent planner:

Qualifications and Curriculum Authority (QCA) (2005) *Observing Children – Building the Profile*, London: QCA.
Qualifications and Curriculum Authority (QCA) (2001) *Planning for Learning in the Foundation Stage*, London, QCA.

Fidler, B. (2002) *Strategic Management for School Development*, London: Paul Chapman.
Although this book considers strategic management/planning for schools rather than early years settings, it provides a detailed account of strategic management in practice. Building on what you have already read in this chapter, Brian Fidler's book will give you a broader picture of the whole area of strategic management, including planning.

Petersen, E. (2003) *A Practical Guide to Early Childhood Curriculum: Linking Thematic, Emergent and Skill Based Planning to Children's Outcomes*, Harlow: Pearson.
This book provides good advice on long- and short-term planning to meet the learning outcomes of young children.

References

Alvestad, M. (2004) Preschool teachers' understandings of some aspects of educational planning and practice related to the National Curricula in Norway, *International Journal of Early Years Education*, Vol. 12, No. 2, June.

Blandford, S. (2006) *Middle Leadership in Schools: Harmonising Leadership and Learning*. Harlow: Pearson.

Department for Education and Skills (DfES) (2002) *A Training Support Framework for the Foundation Stage*. Nottingham: DfES Publications.

Department for Education and Skills (DfES) (2006) *Improving outcomes for children in the Foundation Stage in maintained schools*. Nottingham: DfES Publications.

Department for Education and Skills (DfES) (2007) *Statutory Framework for the Early Years Foundation Stage: Setting the Standards for Learning Development and Care for children from birth to five* (EYFS). Nottingham: DfES Publications.

Drake, J. (2001) *Planning Children's Play and Learning in the Foundation Stage*. London: David Fulton.

Fidler, B. (2002) *Strategic Management for School Development*. London: Paul Chapman.

Fisher, J. (1998) The Relationship between Planning and Assessment, in Siraj-Blatchford, I. (ed.) *A Curriculum Development Handbook for Early Childhood Educators*. London: Trentham Books.

Fisher, J. (2002) *Starting from the Child: Teaching and Learning from 3–8*, 2nd edn. Maidenhead: Open University Press.

Hargreaves, D.H. and Hopkins, D. (1991) School effectiveness, 'school improvement and development', planning, in Preedy, M. (ed.) *Managing the Effective School*. London: Paul Chapman.

LaGrave, J., Mole, R. and Swingler, J. (1994) *Planning and Managing Your Work*, B600 The Capable Manager. Open Business School: Open University Press.

Management Standards Centre (2004) The National Occupational Standards. Available at **www.management-standards.org** (Accessed: 9 January 2006).

Qualifications and Curriculum Authority (QCA) (2000) *Curriculum Guidance for the Foundation Stage*. London: QCA.

Qualifications and Curriculum Authority (QCA) (2001) *Planning for Learning in the Foundation Stage*. London: QCA.

Qualifications and Curriculum Authority (QCA) (2003) *Foundation Stage Profile Handbook*. London: QCA.

Qualifications and Curriculum Authority (QCA) (2005a) *Observing Children – Building the Profile*. London: QCA.

Qualifications and Curriculum Authority (QCA) (2005b) *Seeing Steps in Children's Learning*. London, QCA.

Skelton, M., Reeves, G. and Playfoot, D. (1991) *Development Planning for Primary Schools*. Windsor: NFER/Nelson.

Stoll, L., Fink, D. and Earl, L. (2003) *It's About Learning (and it's About Time): What's In It For Schools?* London: RoutledgeFalmer.

Tuckman, B.W. (1965) 'Development sequence in small groups', *Psychological Bulletin*, Vol. 63, No. 6: pp. 384–399.

Appendix 1

The following section will help you to relate planning to practice. Planning for resources is very important in the teaching and learning process. Review the long-term plan you should have prepared. Using the framework below, adapted from *Observing Children – Building the Profile* (QCA, 2005b: 30), consider, within the context of your long-term plan, what issues you need to consider to address each of these questions, what resources are needed and why (if applicable). Also consider how you would set up the resources. Would you have a number of learning areas, would you have others in boxes, on shelves etc.?

Points to consider	Issues to consider/resources	Other notes
How many aspects of areas of learning (or profile scales) are potentially covered by the provision and resources?		
What is available to support children's interests? What attracts and motivates children to participate most?		
Is it set up in a way to challenge children to investigate and develop their thinking and be curious?		
Do resources and equipment support and celebrate inclusion and diversity?		
Do displays support and celebrate inclusion and diversity?		
Are resources accessible to the children (e.g. storage units well positioned and well labelled etc.)		
How does ethos and teaching encourage children to care for resources and equipment?		
Do/can all children make good use of displays to support their learning (e.g. children learning English as an additional language, gifted and talented children, children with SEN, boys/girls etc.)		

17 Extending Partnerships

By the end of this chapter you will be able to answer the following questions:

- Why is the collaborative working of all stakeholders central to the realisation of the government's vision for early years education?

- What skills and knowledge are needed for effective partnership working within a multi-agency context?

- How do I access, implement and monitor external support provided by agents/organisations for children who require it?

- How will I know when it is not appropriate to share information relating to a child?

This chapter will support your understanding of the following Standards *(see Appendix 1)*:
- **Knowledge and understanding:** S03, S04 and S06 ■ **Effective practice:** S13, S14, S20 and S23
- **Relationships with children:** S26 ■ **Communicating and working in partnership with families and carers:** S32 ■ **Teamwork and collaboration:** S33 and S36.

Introduction

Mutual engagement involves not only our competence, but also the competence of others. It draws on what we do and what we know, as well as on our ability to connect meaningfully to what we don't do and what we don't know – that is the contributions and knowledge of others.

(Wenger, 1998: 76)

Sure Start Children's Centres: aim to provide access to health, education and social services in one location to young children (0–5 years) and their families living in deprived communities.

Effective partnership working is at the centre of the government's programme for educational change. The publication of *Choice for Parents, the best start for children: making it happen – An action plan for the ten year strategy:* **Sure Start children's centres**, *extended schools and childcare* (DfES, 2006a) set out the government's vision for an **'integrated provision'** of services – health, social and education – to improve outcomes for all children and enable parents to create a good balance between their work and family life. Integrated working means a number of people, groups or organisations working together to provide an effective means of supporting children and families with additional needs. By considering the government's vision for an integrated service provision in early years settings, this chapter will explore the idea of partnership working and what this means for early years practice. You will find a table of the relevant government documents on our **website**.

Integrated working: a number of people, groups or organisations (within the health, social and educational services) working together to provide an effective means of supporting children and families with additional needs.

Partnership working

As early years practitioners you will understand that the government's vision for the integration of services is an ambitious project and it is important that there is a clear understanding as to what is intended. The programme involves a change in the way that settings both see themselves and are seen within the community. It is through this initiative that the government recognised that environment and circumstances have a significant impact on a child's learning, attainment and future life chances and that the effective engagement of parents, guardians and other related agencies has a positive impact on children's achievement. By addressing the idea of the provision of services through multi-agency teams, this section will consider what partnership working means for early years practice. The following highlights the three principal areas where you will experience and/or be responsible for partnership working within early years settings (that of working in partnership with the child is not included below as the idea of working with children in early years settings assumes partnership):

- Where children receive education and care in more than one setting, practitioners must ensure continuity and coherence by sharing relevant information with each other and with parents. Patterns of attendance should be a key factor in practitioners' planning.
- Close working between early years practitioners and parents is vital for the identification of children's learning needs and to ensure a quick response to any area of learning difficulty. Parents and families are central to a

child's well-being and practitioners should support this important relationship by sharing information and offering support to learning in the home.

- Practitioners will frequently need to work with professionals from other agencies, such as local and community health services, or where children are looked after by the local authority, to identify and meet needs and use their knowledge and advice to provide children's social care with the best learning opportunities and environments for all children.

(DfES, 2007: 10)

DISCUSSION POINT

Consider these three areas for partnership working developed in the *Statutory Framework for the Early Years Foundation Stage: Setting the Standards for Learning Development and Care for children from birth to five* (EYFS) (available at: **www.teachernet.gov.uk/publications** or **www.everychildmatters.gov.uk**).

In your opinion, what are the key issues relating to practice?

The government emphasises the importance of an integrated provision of services as an efficient means of meeting the needs of children and families. For this to be effective, the collaboration of all stakeholders is of central importance. In essence, integrated working is the 'joined up' working of personnel from the health, education and social services. However, this does not necessarily mean that they are co-located within the same physical place, although this is the case with children's centres. In practice, it means the development of open channels of communication between the service providers and is best understood within the following framework which clearly shows the government's aims for the integration of services:

- to provide more comprehensive approaches to prevention and early intervention in universal settings; [i.e. noticing early that children may need a speech therapist or psychologist etc.]
- to provide services that are personalised around the needs of individual children and their parents; [i.e being able to provide or give parents access to the particular service needed for their child's well-being]
- to make sure that everyone supporting individual children, together with their parents, shares high expectations of them to succeed;
- to provide better co-ordination and a single point of contact for families;
- to reduce the likelihood that children or young people who are at risk of harm, or are putting others at risk, go unnoticed by the system; and
- to start to move towards a system where it is service users, not just the services themselves, who drive design and delivery and where it is children, families and young people themselves who are empowered to take responsibility for their own outcomes.

(DfES, 2008: 42–43)

Key person:
the practitioner responsible for developing links with and forming a close relationship with a particular child and his/her family in an early years setting (0–5 years old).

In practice, every child and his/her family/carers will have someone who knows them and with whom they can talk. In early years settings this may be the **key person** (see Chapter 13), leader practitioner or a practitioner. In primary schools it is very likely to be the class teacher. In practice, many children will not need to access any further services than that with which they are provided within their early years setting or school. However, sometimes the needs of children and their families/carers are beyond what can be provided on a day-to-day basis in the setting/school (e.g. if a child has behavioural or speech problems). Further measures are required and it is important that practitioners recognise the additional need and act. Table 17.1, adapted from the government document *Building Brighter Futures: next steps for the children's workforce* (DfES, 2008: 45), highlights when practitioners will need to take further action to ensure the health, safety, well-being and achievement of children.

DISCUSSION POINT

Consider the above framework (DfES 2008). What are the implications for practice?

What do you need to do, be aware of etc. to ensure that you would be able to put the above framework into practice?

Meeting the holistic needs of all children requires the flexible working of statutory (government or government backed) agencies. Educational settings need to develop policies and protocols that ensure that there is a seamless service. However, early years

Photo 17.1
Practitioners need to recognise the additional needs of some children and act

Pearson Education Ltd. Jules Selmes © Pearson Education Ltd. 2008

Table 17.1 Recognising the additional needs of children

The voice of the child	The response of the service providers
If I have a need – someone in my setting works with me and my family/carers to understand my needs and helps me and my family/carers to decide what is best for me.	Identifies needs early – a practitioner/leader practitioner/key person within the setting/school who knows the child and his/her family identifies a problem and knows how to respond to it and access the wider services. (May implement Common Assessment Framework – see section 'Practical issues: information sharing and looked after children' within this chapter.)
If I need more support – someone I trust works with me and my family/carers to work out an action plan and decide who can help me.	Assesses those needs and provides information and advice – a trained practitioner works with the child and his/her family to develop a personalised action plan. (If appropriate they will be supported by the multi-agency team.)
If I need more people to help – someone brings together all the people I need to support me and my family/carers and makes sure we get the support and can access it.	Form the team around the child – where the child needs the services of more than one practitioner, someone (practitioner/leader practitioner/practitioner) will select the people most able to help and support the child from the multi-agency team and specialists from the various service providers. To ensure that the services are delivered they are co-ordinated by a lead practitioner.
If I have been receiving support – someone talks to me and my family/carers to see if the support has helped me or if I need something more.	Reviews progress – the child and his/her family/carers will be involved in a regular review of progress.

Source: Adapted from DfES (2008) p. 45

settings do not work alone in providing services (education, care, health and social), but are supported and guided by the Local Authority (LA). In 2005, the government published *Championing Children* (2005) which outlined the remit of the LA and the skills, knowledge and behaviours required by managers of the integrated services. Figure 17.1 shows how the management of services by the LA involves an integrated approach at each level from integrated governance (one department within the LA to deal with matters relating to children and families – education, health and social), through to an integrated approach (planning for how all services will be provided and by whom), through to the delivery of services for families and children (i.e. through an early years setting, children and their families will have access to education, care, health and social services, where open channels of communication operate between the service providers).

For early years practitioners, this means working supportively and in partnership with parents and children to ensure that everyone involved understands the responses

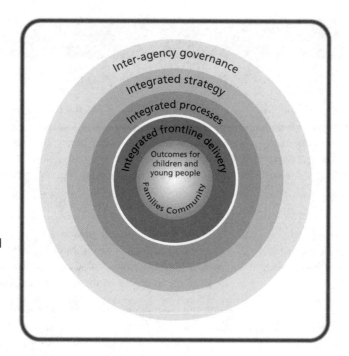

Figure 17.1
Championing
children:
focus for Local
Authority
managers of
integrated
services
Source: DfES
(2006) p. 4

of the professionals concerned. In theory, this will lead to a better quality, more mean-ingful provision. It should be recognised that external support services (a list of local support services can be accessed through the LA) play an important part in helping set-tings identify, assess and make provision for all children. It is self-evident that all services for all children should focus on identifying and addressing needs to enable them to improve their situation through:

- early identification of need
- continual engagement with the child and parents
- focused intervention – in response to the need
- dissemination of effective approaches and techniques.

The objective is to provide integrated, high-quality, holistic support that focuses on the needs of the child. Such provision should be based on a shared perspective and should build on mutual understanding and agreement where all voices are heard. Services should adopt a flexible child-centred approach to service delivery to ensure that the changing needs and priorities of the child and their parents can be met at any given time. The coming together of service providers to support a child with an identified problem is referred to as **multi-agency** working and 'can range from a group of practitioners deciding informally to work together to support a child or family, right through to a large-scale venture like different services coming together in a Sure Start children's centre' (DCSF, 2008: 9).

All agencies, which might include health services delivering health advisory and support services (e.g. speech and language therapists, occupational therapists and physiotherapists, as well as doctors and nurses and social workers) will need to

Multi-agency:
a group of
individuals
from different
disciplines
working together
to support a
child and
his/her family.

recognise the need for effective collaboration of services involved with the children and parents. Consultative responsibilities and effective communication systems at management and practitioner levels will then be clearly identified. Developments in organisational structures and working practices will need to reflect this principle. Joint planning arrangements would then:

- take account of good practice
- ensure consultation with all relevant services
- agree priorities
- publicise decisions to parents and professionals
- regularly review policies and objectives.

In practice, the three principal models of multi-agency working with which you might be involved are:

1 Multi-agency panel: members remain with their agency but meet regularly to discuss children with additional needs who would benefit from multi-agency input. Panel members might do case work or take a more strategic role.
2 Multi-agency team: members are seconded or recruited into the team with a leader and common purpose and goals. They may still get supervision and training from their home agency, but have the opportunity to work with a range of different services.
3 Integrated services: different services such as health and education are co-located to form a highly visible hub in the community. Funded by the partner organisations and managed to ensure integrated working, they are often based in schools or early years settings.

(DCSF, 2008: 9)

Sector Skills Council

The publication of *Every Child Matters; Change for Children* (DfES, 2004a) set out a national framework for local change programmes to build services around the needs of children and young people in order to maximise opportunity. The following year the government published *The Common Core of Skills and Knowledge for the Children's Workforce* (DfES, 2005b) outlining the core skills and knowledge required for those working within the children's workforce, where mutual engagement and collaborative working underpin the type of partnership working developed by the document. This section will consider the areas of expertise outlined by the government for those working within a multi-agency context.

In consultation with employers, user groups and employees, the DfES developed the following six areas of expertise as a framework for practice within a multidisciplinary context:

- effective communication and engagement with children, young people, their families and carers
- child and young person development

- safeguarding and promoting the welfare of the child
- supporting transitions
- multi-agency working
- sharing information.

(DfES, 2005b)

The document reflects the new child-centred focus of the government's change programme, which is not concerned with the provision of services per se, but with providing services to meet the needs of the child. For practitioners this means responding to both need and demand at the individual and community level. Successful practice, within a multi-agency, multidisciplinary context means being:

clear about your own role and aware of the role of other professionals; you need to be confident about your own standards and targets and respectful of those that apply to other services, actively seeking and respecting the knowledge and input others can make to delivering best outcomes for children and young people.

(DfES, 2005b: 18)

The following, underpinned by the Common Core of Skills and Knowledge, provides a good example of partnership working in practice; it has been adapted from an interview with the manager of a nursery in York.

WHAT HAPPENS IN PRACTICE?

We have a shared partnership in York which has been running now for three years. Once a term all childcare providers – childminders, nurseries, pre-schools, nursery schools and primary schools – get together. The team is predominantly those providing childcare and education, although we also have a Development Worker. The meetings provide an opportunity to discuss various issues relating to individual children. For example some children will attend more than one setting and we can share helpful observations or thoughts relating to those children. We don't discuss best practice or training at these meetings. However, we are one of three nurseries in the York Childcare charity and we meet once a week to share our thoughts on best practice and training needs. Although we don't currently have in-house training days, we do have two evenings a year when everyone comes together [*from the three nurseries*] for training in a specific area of practice.

REFLECT AND RELATE TO PRACTICE

Consider the above example of what happens in practice. To what extent is this type of partnership working effective for the child? Why/why not? If you were a member of the shared partnership would you want to improve on the model? Why/why not?

DISCUSSION POINT

Consider the type of skills you need to develop and what you need to know to work effectively and efficiently within the framework being developed in early years settings for multi-agency working. You will need to look up the government document *Core Skills and Knowledge for the Children's Workforce* (DfES, 2005b): Chapter 5, Multi-agency Working (pp. 18–20), available at: **www.teachernet.gov.uk/publications**. Make a list of the specific skills and knowledge you need to develop for effective multi-agency working. How would you develop the skills and knowledge needed?

You might like to create your own tables – one for skills and one for knowledge.

Integrated services in practice

The government aims to make England the 'best place in the world for children and young people to grow up' (DCSF, 2007: 3), where the services provision meets the needs of all children and helps to unlock the full potential of every child. This section will consider the government's vision for children in England and how this will impact on those working within the early years sector.

Local Authorities (LAs) have a key role in assisting early years settings in the implementation and development of the government's holistic vision for education – **personalised learning** programmes to meet the needs of the individual child. The framework for change, developed from the 2004 Children Act, promoted the idea of agency partnerships and integrated services. There was to be a 'shared sense of responsibility across agencies for safeguarding children and specialised help to promote opportunity, prevent problems and act early and effectively' (DfES, 2004a). The Childcare Act 2006 conferred new duties on LAs to deliver the government's plan. *The Children's Plan: Building Brighter Futures* (DCSF, 2007) developed this further, setting out the government's broader plan for children:

> **Personalised learning:** the adaptation of teaching and the curriculum to meet the learning needs of the individual child.

- Happy and healthy: secure the well-being and health of children and young people
- Safe and sound: safeguard the young and vulnerable
- Excellence and equity: individual progress to achieve world class standards and close the gap in educational achievement for disadvantaged children
- Leadership and collaboration: system reform to achieve world class standards and close the gap in educational achievement for disadvantaged children
- Staying on: ensure that young people are participating and achieving their potential to 18 and beyond

- On the right track: keeping children and young people on the path to success
- Making it happen: an integrated provision of services which will not only provide a safety net for the vulnerable but also a means of unlocking the potential of every child.

DISCUSSION POINT

For each of the statements above consider one way of putting it into practice in: (a) an early years setting for 6 month–2 year olds, (b) an early years setting for 3–5 year olds, (c) a reception class and (d) Key Stage 1 in a primary school.

You will need to look up the *Statutory Framework for the Early Years Foundation Stage: Setting the Standards for Learning Development and Care for children from birth to five* (EYFS) (DfES, 2007), available at: **www.teachernet.gov.uk/publications**, and the Key Stage 1 National Curriculum.

Lead professional: the person responsible for implementing, monitoring and co-ordinating the provision of extra support required by certain children and their families/carers.

Children's Trusts: the bringing together at Local Authority level, both strategically and operationally, of education, social care and health departments to function as one under the internal management of a children's trust.

Integrated working has put greater emphasis on practitioners knowing all the children within their setting, being able to monitor their progress (including their well-being) and identifying any problems which may require extra support. Some issues can be sorted out within the setting and practitioners will not need to seek outside support for the child. However, open channels of communication within the settings are vital, where children's progress etc. can be discussed. The setting is responsible for knowing when outside support is required for a particular child. However, within settings, there will be designated members of staff who will be responsible for completing Common Assessment Frameworks (CAF) (see Chapter 1), acting as a **lead professional** and liaising with the local Children's Trust. Local Authorities provide good training and advice to enable practitioners to act and work effectively in identifying when children need extra support and how to access, implement and monitor the support.

Children's Trusts

The intention of **Children's Trusts** is for education, social care and health departments to function as one, both strategically and operationally, under the internal management of a Children's Trust. This section addresses the rationale behind Children's Trusts and considers the extent to which they support both daily and specific practices within the early years.

Children's Trusts provide a more integrated framework for the services that embrace the social, educational and economic well-being of children as determined by *Every Child Matters* (DfES, 2003). It builds on existing schemes that have rationalised local authorities in terms of role. Underpinning this change is the rationale that local authorities will commission, monitor and review services rather than be the point of delivery (i.e. interaction with the child). Each of the authorities has developed strategically in response to local need and it is important to consider local needs as the first point of reflection prior to establishing change.

In practice this offers a partnership approach to the delivery of services and gives early years settings more of a voice in the community. They can 'feed their views into local service planning', will work with Children's Trusts to find places for 'hard-to-place children' and can expect greater support from LAs in promoting the 'educational achievement of **looked after children**' (DfES, 2004b). LAs and Children's Trusts will also engage with early years settings, schools and other providers to ensure that all children in their local area are being effectively supported.

It is intended that integrating services will mean more effective support for children with complex needs who require multi-agency support, where early years settings will work closely with the Children's Trust. The following shows what this means in practice:

> **Looked after children:** a child 'looked after by a local authority if he/she is in their care or is provided with accommodation for more than twenty four hours by the authority' (DfES, 2006b: 3).

- early years settings are responsible for knowing the children they work with, monitoring their progress, identifying when they may need additional support and, where possible, providing it;
- early years settings, with the support of the Children's Trust, are responsible for assessing needs requiring wider services from the Children's Trust (usually through the Common Assessment Framework) and engaging with the Children's Trust to have those services provided;
- early years settings and Children's Trusts together are responsible for the provision of joined up services, including by agreeing together who should be the lead professional to co-ordinate activity and be the main contact for families;
- individual services are responsible for providing timely high quality services in their service area.

(DfES, 2008: 47)

The wider workforce

The wider workforce encompasses a range of practitioners whose professional and voluntary activities focus on the child. This section outlines the government's vision for a well-qualified and skilled early years workforce.

The need to raise professional standards in the early years sector reflects on the difficulties experienced by the workforce which include:

- professional experience which is limited by short-term retention of staff thus reducing the time to develop skills and expertise
- limited finance to attract and sustain long-term appointments of suitably qualified staff
- poor communication between childcare and education services
- the inspection process which can be demotivating
- poor leadership and management.

It is not surprising that schools and early years settings are experiencing problems in recruiting and retaining the right staff. In response to these issues, the government have developed initiatives for the professional development of the wider workforce including accessible progression routes for the existing workforce. There are also plans to attract and retain sufficient staff by reducing turnover and encouraging men and members of ethnic minority groups into the professions. The career framework includes Early Years Professional Status (EYPS) for those working in early years settings and the National Professional Qualification in Integrated Centre Leadership (NPQICL) for graduates managing and leading children's centres. By 2015 the government envisages that every full day care setting will have at least one graduate Early Years Professional leading the setting, with two in disadvantaged areas (DCSF, 2008). The aim being to create a teaching profession from 0 to 19 years that combines learning with care.

DISCUSSION POINT

In what ways will having a graduate EYP leader in each day care setting by 2015 impact upon the day-to-day practice? Do you think EYPs should be graduates? Why/why not?

Within the context of *Every Child Matters*, the workforce extends beyond educational organisations and encompasses all agencies whose function it is to support and develop children. A clear and pragmatic description of the government's vision for the children's workforce is provided in the Introduction to *Children's Workforce Strategy: Building a world class workforce for children, young people and their families* (DfES, 2006c) and is as follows:

- Strives to achieve the best possible outcomes for all children and young people, and reduces the inequalities between the most disadvantaged and the rest
- Is competent, confident and safe to work with children and young people
- People aspire to be part of and want to remain within – where they can develop their skills and build satisfying and rewarding careers; and
- Parents, children and young people trust and respect.

(DfES, 2006c: Introduction)

Children's Centres

Children's centres provide a means for education, social and health care to function as one, both operationally and strategically. This section will consider if, in practice, children's centres meet the government's ideal for an integrated provision of services.

Since 1998 Sure Start Local Programmes (SSLP) have been providing early learning, family services and health programmes in deprived areas. Building on their success, the government implemented the programme nationally through the initiative referred to as Sure Start Children's Centres. The idea of the children's centre is to respond to the social needs of a child or his/her family. In practice children's centres provide a service beyond the school for those families requiring additional support. Schools, where appropriate, will need to work closely with health advisers and centre co-ordinators to ensure clarity of communication. This extends beyond case conferences and enables all practitioners to be proactive and reactive to a family's needs. This is not new: in areas of need, children's centres are often located on school sites. Child psychologists and paediatricians may also contribute to work in this area. In essence, the focus of the Sure Start Children's Centres is to provide 'a one stop shop of help advice, childcare and early education for children under five and their families' (DfES, 2006a: 19).

The rapid expansion of individual children's centres has led to them becoming complex organisations. Children's centre leaders are required to create new partner-ships within their own community, with other Integrated Centres (IC), between their Integrated Centre and the wider community and with other agencies. Figure 17.2 highlights the different types of partnerships which need to be considered.

Creating these new relationships and building effective communities of practice will require new knowledge, skills, behaviours, relationships, processes, actions and outcomes. The centres themselves have provided a fundamental shift from offering a range of local initiatives to becoming a mainstream service. Subsequently, this has brought a greater focus to leadership of and within the centres. The idea of a 'super-leader' is also emerging as an alternative, mirrored by schools with Executive Heads being appointed over two or more schools in a federated or trust format. This in turn puts pressure on headteachers (Primary, Special and Secondary) to have a better

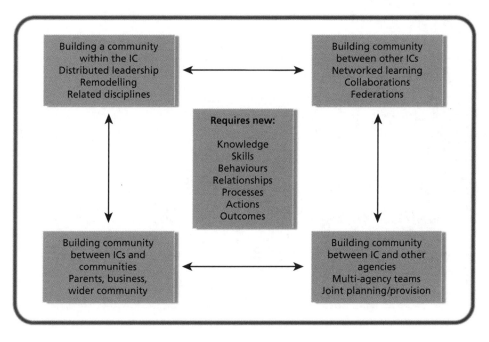

Figure 17.2 Relationship of leadership requirements with building effective communities of practice

Photo 17.2
A one-stop shop for health, social and educational services under one roof: are children's centres effective?

Pearson Education Ltd. Jules Selmes © Pearson Education Ltd. 2004

understanding of how children's centres work and ultimately will require the whole area of governance to be brought into line with a multi-agency institution and a more secure form of funding to offer stability.

WHAT HAPPENS IN PRACTICE?

The following exerpt is taken from an interview with the Director of a Sure Start Children's Centre. Since 2001 she has managed the children's centre and sees her role as 'enabler across all areas of the' delivery. She gives her view of what an integrated provision of services means in the day-to-day practice in a children's centre and how teams have developed in response to that:

In the past we had what I call parallel working. Every agency knew what they were doing, like a jigsaw. Everything was very distinct in training, objectives and philosophies back then and the focus was on services and on which agency would provide. Now we have integrated working – a team coming together to agree a vision of what you are going to provide and how. [In essence it is] an integrated philosophical approach with the child at the centre. There isn't the demarcation you got in the jigsaw. For example a health visitor and a volunteer parent might deliver a programme of support. The following term, it might be a teacher or a community worker, whoever is in the team and has the skills to do it. So it is focused on what parents need. The focus is not on the service.

We have four trading wings in our social enterprise, [one of which is] childcare and early education and includes a 50 place nursery for children up to age 5. We have a crèche in that. That section is managed by a manager who has an early years background. There are 18 members of staff. A number would have NVQs in childcare, about five have health backgrounds, some have been doing adult education. We have a big integrated children's centre team and there isn't particularly a division between health and education [in terms of professional role]. Our teams have evolved. By the time our building opened in 2003 we had our teams together. An integrated team started when I started in 2001. I was meticulously careful in the recruitment process. I wanted to recruit people from the local area who had the potential. There was a great gap in social and healthcare. For example in the childcare and early education 'wing' we have a pre-schools advanced teacher. She has worked with the manager on staff development, on modelling good practice, ensuring we deliver the early stage foundation curriculum, implementing the Ofsted suggestions, considered policy and procedures and looked at leadership in the nursery. She has just qualified as an early years professional.

[Interviewer: It is documented that the manager's role in children's centres has more to do with managing adults than children. Is this how you see your role?]

Yes, I have very little to do with children. I go into the café and the nursery and see how provision impacts on children and I see that it is a comfortable, happy place for children. So I look at quality and inclusivity. I look at how the rooms are organised, how accessible the resources are to the children, how open the staff are to the children's needs, how nurturing the environment is and how welcoming particular parts of the programme are to the parents. I can empathise with that.

[Interviewer: Do you delegate tasks?]

I delegate tasks all the time, it is part and parcel of distributed leadership and it enables people to take on responsibility. If they don't there's no criticism. We don't want people who are stuck, to stay in that position. So if there are issues blocking them we need to know and help them. We have peers in place who can help. That is a very important part of the programme.

REFLECT AND RELATE TO PRACTICE

Having read the interview presented above, list the ways in which daily practice within the centre is managed in order to provide an integrated service (social, health and education).

☆ ☆ ☆

Would you have taken a different approach? In what way? Why/why not?

Practical issues: information sharing and looked after children

Information sharing

Practitioners should reflect on when and how they should share confidential information and how to support looked after learners in the setting. This section will examine information sharing and looked after children from a practical stance and consider the importance of knowing when to share information and how to support looked after learners.

Legal and ethical issues are at the root of sharing what may be defined as confidential and/or sensitive information with others to whom it may be relevant. Issues relating to information sharing in the implementation and preparation of a Common Assessment Framework (CAF) (see Chapter 1) are equally applicable for related situations. Consent of the individual is an important aspect of the CAF. The ways in which the information supplied for a CAF will be used should be explained to the individual concerned and/or their parent/carer and permission should be sought from the individual to use the information accordingly. Confidential information can only be disclosed on the CAF if the individual concerned is in agreement. Sharing confidential information can be a complex area, requiring the judgement of the practitioner. In certain circumstances confidential information should be disclosed. Details of when this situation can arise and other matters relating to the sharing of information is available in the government document *Information Sharing: Practitioners' Guide* (DfES, 2006b; available at **www.everychildmatters.gov.uk/informationsharing**). However, the following key issues, adapted from this document, should always be considered:

1 Explain openly and honestly at the outset what information will or could be shared, and why, and seek agreement – except where doing so puts the child or others at risk of significant harm.
2 The child's safety and welfare must be the overriding consideration when making decisions on whether to share information about them.

3 Respect the wishes of children or families who do not consent to share confidential information – unless in your judgement there is sufficient need to override that lack of consent.
4 Ensure information is accurate, up-to-date, necessary for the purpose for which you are sharing it, shared only with those who need to see it, and shared securely.
5 Always record the reasons for your decision – whether it is to share or not.

(DCSF, 2008: 3)

However, as the following quotation, from Georgina Nunnery, a solicitor in Lewisham, clearly highlights, if there is any doubt, particularly if the child is at risk, a practitioner should seek advice: 'No inquiry into a child's death or serious injury has ever questioned why information was shared. It has always asked the opposite' (DCSF, 2008: 3).

> **Connect & Extend**
>
> Information sharing is an important issue. Look up the following document: *Information Sharing: Practitioners' Guide* (DfES, 2006b), which is available at **www.everychildmatters. gov.uk/informationsharing**. Consider when you would not share information relating to a child and when you would share information and with whom. Why do you think it is such an important area?

Looked after children

The delivery of more integrated services will require new ways of working and a significant culture change for staff used to working within narrower professional and service-based boundaries. One such area is the education and well-being of looked after children. The Children Act 1989 specifies that 'a child is looked after by a local authority if he/she is in their care or is provided with accommodation for more than twenty four hours by the authority' (DfES, 2006c: 3). Early years settings provide a place of stability for looked after learners. Those involved in their teaching and learning should keep them focused on task while at the same time being aware of their extra needs. The *Framework for the Inspection of Schools* (Ofsted, 2005) considers the extent to which the education provided contributes to a child's well-being, with a specific focus on looked after children. Assessment criteria will include 'attainment, personal development, well-being, care and support'. Settings will need to provide evidence that there is an 'effective Personal Education Plan' (a statutory requirement for all children in care in addition to setting records) in place for looked after children and that action is taken to maximise their attendance, avoid exclusions and monitor their experiences on an individual basis (DfES, 2006c: 8). The government document, *Supporting Looked After Learners – a practical guide for governors* (DfES, 2006d: 9), underlines the responsibilities incumbent on schools in relation to the education of looked after learners:

- schools should have an overview of the educational needs and progress of looked after children
- school policies should be reviewed from the point of view of looked after children
- resources should be allocated to match priorities for looked after children
- schools need to know the number of children within their school who are in care
- how they are performing in comparison to their peers.

For looked after learners in schools, there is a designated teacher, usually a senior member of staff, who is responsible for:

- receiving personal education plans from social workers and co-ordinating the development of the plan
- providing a central point of contact for all professionals working with looked after children.

(DfES, 2006d: 10)

In addition, however, *Supporting Looked After Learners* (DfES, 2006d) underlines the need for schools to have a clear policy in place for the professional development of all staff working with looked after or other vulnerable children.

Extending partnerships: bringing it together

The delivery of more integrated services will require new ways of working and a significant culture change for staff used to working within narrower professional and service-based boundaries. Easy and effective communication across current organisational and professional boundaries is a strong foundation for co-operation. Improving outcomes for children depends on the integrated working of multi-agency teams. The Children Act 2004 confers a duty on LAs to work with local statutory agents to promote a more integrated working relationship around the needs of children and young people; the partners will have a duty to co-operate with the LA. The children's trust arrangement will provide a formal system for key partners to work together, either providing services or procuring the services from other agents, under a common inter-agency management structure. The key partners involved will depend on local needs. However, the partnership could also include relevant representatives from the voluntary, community and private sector, young people and their families, other agencies with responsibility for front-line statutory services to children, such as job centres, colleges and faith organisations, Immigration Services who may come into contact with children, young people and their families (DfES, 2005a). The government document, *Statutory guidance on inter-agency co-operation to improve the well-being of children: children's trusts* (DfES, 2005c), underlines the need for partnerships to be sustainable, with supporting structures which maintain the 'momentum of change and set a clear direction of travel'. Effective inter-agency management will mean:

- Clear LA leadership
- Full engagement of all key partners, including the voluntary and community sectors
- Clear accountability and;
- Relationships built on trust, a shared vision and a determination to improve outcomes for children.

(DfES, 2005c: 21)

These reforms are far-reaching and, if successful, will lead to the celebration and enhancement of all professions allied to children and young people's learning. However, in addition to policies, there is a need for a change in culture, perception and the professional experience of the early years workforce. Personally, professionally, socially and educationally, the early years workforce needs to be valued.

DISCUSSION POINT

Having read the chapter, reflect on the following three principal areas of partnership working in the early years:

- Where children receive education and care in more than one setting, practitioners must ensure continuity and coherence by sharing relevant information with each other and with parents. Patterns of attendance should be a key factor in practitioners' planning.
- Close working between early years practitioners and parents is vital for the identification of children's learning needs and to ensure a quick response to any area of learning difficulty. Parents and families are central to a child's well-being and practitioners should support this important relationship by sharing information and offering support to learning in the home.
- Practitioners will frequently need to work with professionals from other agencies, such as local and community health services, or where children are looked after by the local authority, to identify and meet needs and use their knowledge and advice to provide children's social care with the best learning opportunites and environments for all children.

(DfES, 2007: 10)

You were asked at the beginning of the chapter to consider the key issues in partnership working in the early years. Has your view changed? Would you add anything more?

SUMMARY

Partnership working (p. 364)

Why does the government emphasise the importance of an integrated provision of services?

Such provision is aimed at early intervention and prevention and should be based on a shared perspective that builds on mutual understanding and agreement where all voices are heard. Practitioners do not work in isolation, but are supported and guided by the Local Authority which has been restructured to reflect the more integrated approach to the delivery of services.

Sector Skills Council (p. 369)

What are the six areas of expertise outlined by the government as requirements for working within a multidisciplinary team? Why are they important?

The core skills and knowledge required for those working within a multidisciplinary framework are founded on effective collaborative work.

SUMMARY *CONTINUED*

Integrated services in practice (p. 371)

What is the government's vision for children in England over the coming years? How will this affect those working within the early years sector?

In practice, the effective integration of services is dependent on practitioners knowing all the children within their setting, helping them to develop their potential and being able to identify any extra needs which require the support of external agencies.

Children's Trusts (p. 372)

How do Children's Trusts help/improve day-to-day practice in an early years setting?

The intention of Children's Trusts is for education, social care and health departments to function as one, both strategically and operationally, under the internal management of a children's trust.

The wider workforce (p. 373)

Do you think Early Years Professional Status (EYPS) for those working in early years settings will help to narrow the gap between education and childcare?

The wider workforce encompasses a range of practitioners whose professional and voluntary activities focus on the child. Any aspect of quality in education or childcare will be determined by the quality of the workforce.

Children's Centres (p. 374)

Do you think children's centres in practice meet the government's ideal for an integrated provision of services?

Children's centres provide access to health, education and social services under one roof. The co-location of services in one area can mean faster access to services for children and families requiring additional support.

Practical issues: information sharing and looked after children (p. 378)

What is the importance of information sharing and supporting looked after learners?

Practitioners should reflect on when and how they should share confidential information and how to support looked after learners in the setting.

Glossary

Children's Trusts: the bringing together at Local Authority level, both strategically and operationally, of education, social care and health departments to function as one under the internal management of a Children's Trust.

Integrated working: a number of people, groups or organisations (within the health, social and educational services) working together to provide an effective means of supporting children and families with additional needs.

Key person: a member of staff assigned to a particular child who is responsible for welcoming him/her each day, observing the child on a formal basis and spending some time working with him/her to support his/her learning.

Lead professional: the person, working within a multidisciplinary team, responsible for implementing, monitoring and co-ordinating the provision of extra support required by certain children and their families/carers. He/she could be a designated person within an early years setting.

Looked after children: a legal term, defined by the Children Act 1989 as a child 'looked after by a local authority if he/she is in their care or is provided with accommodation for more than twenty four hours by the authority' (DfES, 2006: 3).

Multi-agency: a group of professionals from the different disciplines – health, social and education – working together to support a child and his/her family.

Personalised learning: the adaptation of teaching and the curriculum to meet the learning needs of the individual child. It is based on the collaborative approach of the practitioner, child and his/her parents or carers, where practitioners are continuously collecting and evaluating evidence of learning, with a view, through discussion with the child, of engaging him/her in his/her learning to achieve the best possible outcomes for the child both emotionally and academically.

Sure Start Children's Centres: launched as a government initiative in 1998, with the aim of providing access to health, education and social services in one location to young children (0–5 years) and their families living in deprived communities.

Find out more

Department for Education and Skills (DfES) (2005) *The Common Core of Skills and Knowledge for the Children's Workforce,* **Nottingham: DfES Publications; available at: www.teachernet.gov.ac.uk/publications.** This document provides the framework for all those working within the children's workforce. Being familiar with the skills and knowledge required will help your professional development. You should read it and reflect on how you could develop and improve your own skills and knowledge to be an effective practitioner.

Department for Education and Skills (DfES) (2007) *The Early Years Foundation Stage – Effective practice: multi-*

agency working, **Nottinghham: DfES Publications; available at www.teachernet.gov.uk/publications.** This government document provides a good outline of multi-agency working in practice which will supplement what you have read in this chapter.

Broadhead, P., Meleady, C. and Delgado, M. (2007) *Children, Families and Communities: Developing Integrated Services,* **Maidenhead: Open University.** It is worth reading this book on integrated working in a children's centre (in Sheffield) which has developed into a centre of what is considered to be good practice. It will help you to build on what you have learnt within this chapter.

References

Department for Children, Schools and Families (DCSF) (2007) *The Children's Plan: Building Brighter Futures.* London: DCSF.

Department for Children, Schools and Families (DCSF) (2008) *Making It Happen: Working Together for Children, Young People and Families.* London: DCSF.

Department for Education and Science (DfES) (2003) *Every Child Matters: Summary.* Nottingham: DfES Publications, Ref: DfES/0672/2003.

Department for Education and Science (DfES) (2004a) *Every Child Matters: Change for Children.* Nottingham: DfES Publications, Ref: DfES/1110/2004.

Department for Education and Science (DfES) (2004b) *Every Child Matters: Change for Children in Schools.* Nottingham: DfES Publications, Ref: DfES/1089/2004.

Department for Education and Science (DfES) (2005) *Championing Children: A Shared Set of Skills, Knowledge and Behaviours for those Leading and Managing Integrated Children's Services.* Nottingham: DfES Publications.

Department for Education and Science (DfES) (2005a) *Extended Schools: Access to Opportunities and Services for All: A Prospectus.* Nottingham: DfES Publications, Ref: DfES/1196/2005.

Department for Education and Science (DfES) (2005b) *Common Core of Skills and Knowledge for the Children's Workforce*. Nottingham: DfES Publications, Ref: DfES/1189/2005.

Department for Education and Science (DfES) (2005c) *Statutory Guidance on Inter-agency Co-operation to Improve the Well-being of Children: Children's Trusts*. Nottingham: DfES Publications, Ref: 1680-2005DOC-EN.

Department for Education and Skills (DfES) (2006) *Championing Children.* Nottingham: DfES.

Department for Education and Skills (DfES) (2006a) *Choice for Parents, the best start for children: making it happen – An action plan for the ten year strategy: Sure Start children's centres, extended schools and childcare*. Nottingham, DfES Publications, Ref: 0356-2006DOC-EN.

Department for Education and Skills (DfES) (2006b) *Information Sharing: Practitioners' Guide*. Nottingham: DfES Publications; available at: **www.everychildmatters.gov.uk/informationsharing**.

Department for Education and Skills (DfES) (2006c) *Children's Workforce Strategy: Building a World-class Workforce for Children, Young People and Families.* Nottingham: DfES Publications.

Department for Education and Skills (DfES) (2006d) *Supporting Looked-After Learners: A Practical Guide for School Governors*. Nottingham: DfES Publications, Ref: 1929-2005DOC-EN.

Department for Education and Skills (DfES) (2007) *Statutory Framework for the Early Years Foundation Stage: Setting the Standards for Learning Development and Care for children from birth to five* (EYFS). Nottingham: DfES Publications.

Department for Education and Skills (DfES) (2008) *Building Brighter Futures: Next Steps for the Children's Workforce*. Nottingham: DfES Publications.

Office for Standards in Education (Ofsted) (2005) *Every Child Matters: Framework for the Inspection of Schools in England from September 2005*. London: HMI, Document Reference 2035.

Wenger, E. (1998) *Communities of Practice: Learning, Meaning and Identity*. Cambridge: Cambridge University Press.

18 Culture, Ethos and Practice

By the end of this chapter you will be able to answer the following questions:

- What is ethos?
- To what extent is culture influenced by the values and behaviours of those who work within the early years setting?
- Why is culture central to the way organisations work?
- How do vision and mission statements influence educational goals and practices?

This chapter will support your understanding of the following Standards *(see Appendix 1)*:
■ **Knowledge and understanding:** S03 and S04 ■ **Effective practice:** S07, S08, S09, S13, S15, S18 and S24
■ **Relationships with children:** S25, S26, S27 and S28 ■ **Communicating and working in partnership with families and carers:** S30 and S32 ■ **Teamwork and collaboration:** S33.

Introduction

People carry 'mental programs' that are developed in the family in early childhood and reinforced in schools and organisations . . . These mental programs contain a component of national culture. They are most clearly expressed in the different values that predominate among people from different countries.

(Hofstede, 2001: xix)

One of the key characteristics of educational settings, whatever their size, philosophy or constitution, is almost certain to be the mix of cultures represented among the staff and children. In the true spirit of international education, this can be hugely broadening, producing unexpected delights and sociological advantages. But this same characteristic can also present considerable challenges. This tension is perhaps best explained by Geert Hofstede's (2001) outline of differences between people stated above. Hofstede, who taught in the field of organisational anthropology and international management at Maastricht University and worked as a consultant to governments and international companies, is probably best known for his work *Culture's Consequences* (1980) – a study of the social interactions of people in over 50 countries. In this book he defines culture more succinctly as 'the collective programming of the "mind" that distinguishes the members of one group or category of people from another'. Reaffirming the definition of the well-known anthropologist, Kluckhohn (1951), Hofstede equates the 'mind' with 'the head, heart and hands', that is, for 'thinking, feeling and acting with consequences for beliefs, attitudes and skills'. (Hofstede, 2001: 9–10). By exploring the concept of **culture**, the factors affecting or influencing it and how it is developed in a setting, embodied by the setting's vision and mission statements and manifested through the **ethos** (the intangible atmosphere which develops as a result of social interactions and processes), this chapter will consider the practical implications of 'culture' for children's learning and development in early years settings.

Culture: can be defined as values and beliefs held by individuals, which distinguish them from other groups of individuals.

Ethos: the intangible 'atmosphere' which develops in a setting from values, attitudes, culture and policies promoted.

Ethos

Ethos can be defined as the 'atmosphere' which develops in a setting as the result of the social interaction (e.g. the way people show respect to others etc.) between the practitioners, children, parents and others involved in the day-to-day practices and processes (e.g. teaching, greeting people etc.). By considering ethos in a broad sense, this section highlights the difficulties in defining it in practice.

Ethos, a central feature of life within the setting, is frequently overlooked, or rather ignored on the grounds that it is diffuse, complex and difficult to address in a scientific and logical manner. Although there is no one single definition which can adequately describe ethos (see Chapter 1), it is highly relevant in any consideration of culture. Settings, like other communities, have their own characteristics and personalities. Differences between settings may be explained in terms of organisational (e.g. who is responsible for what etc.) and social structures (e.g. how practitioners interact and relate to one another in the process of work) which also reflect the interpersonal relationships that create ethos. The whole-setting 'feeling' exists to such an extent that it drives the setting as a community towards achieving goals. An intangible relationship between local and setting communities and setting ethos may exist but the link could be difficult to define. Yet the importance of ethos in the learning community is widely accepted.

McLaughlin (2005: 306–307) highlighted the better performance of educational settings which develop a strong ethos. He further suggested that ethos is becoming more prevalent in education policy. Donnelly (2000: 135–136), by offering two definitions which reflect differing views, highlights the difficulty in delineating ethos. Some, she suggests, view ethos as 'a formal expression of the authorities' aims and objectives for an organization'. Others, she suggests, 'see ethos as something which is more informal emerging from social interaction and process' (Donnelly, 2000: 150). The resultant reality in the learning community she suggests is that 'ethos is not a static phenomenon but rather . . . a "negotiated" process whereby individuals come to some agreement about what should and should not be prioritised' (ibid.). Although this may seem self-evident, arriving at consensus in multicultural communities may be fraught with difficulties. Leaders, managers, practitioners, parents, children, teachers and all staff create a setting's ethos through values and behaviours that reflect values portrayed in policies and practice. However, in many settings the various stakeholders may not share the same values or behaviours. The issue for leaders then becomes one of finding common ground from which the best possible approach to teaching and learning can be developed.

Culture

Defining culture can pose as many problems as defining ethos. By considering how culture is defined, this section will consider why addressing culture, in its broadest sense, is central to developing effective practice.

Culture is a word which only came into popular use with the rise of the sociological sciences at the end of the nineteenth century and is often used to more closely define a broader field (e.g. political culture, social culture, religious culture or national culture etc.) and refers to the values or beliefs underlying the area/system to which it refers, which are made known through the practices. Hofstede (2001) likened culture to an onion with different layers, where the core values are at the hidden centre and are made known through the practices which Hofstede (2001: 11) refers to as the rituals (e.g. how you greet people, how you show respect to others, religious ceremonies etc.), the heroes (i.e. the people, real or created, who are seen as models of behaviour) and the symbols (e.g. the language, words, gestures, pictures etc.), all of which are relatively easy to observe and to understand. The values are the assumptions inherent in the culture; they define the norms by which people of the same culture live, although they are often not articulated, or even overtly recognised, as they are taken for granted.

In the day-to-day life within settings, culture affects the manner in which all members of the community relate to each other. The culture may be visible and explicit, or vague and implicit. It may be strong and dominant, or virtually impotent. A helpful culture might be defined as the way in which all of us in this workplace agree to work together in order to provide the best service for the learners. It affects everything from the way decisions are made to the way children learn, and is in turn affected by these factors.

Attempting to analyse this further, the elements which affect education culture could be categorised into the following three groups:

- The *social environment*, i.e. the background against which the setting processes take place. This includes the cultures represented, the gender balance, the maturity and experience of staff, the geographical position, the physical nature of the buildings and the nature of the community from which the setting draws its intake. It has an underlying effect on the way people work, affecting the communities' expectations of each other and consequently impacts on the extent to which the aims are achieved.
- The formal *management systems, policies and structures*. Implicit and unintentional messages may be conveyed by the answers to questions such as:
  - to what extent do the support and learning systems cohere?
  - to what extent does the educational (as opposed to the profit) agenda drive decisions?
  - are staff encouraged to develop 'on-the-job', or are practitioners treated as expendable items that must be replaced with a model that is already trained for the latest development?
- The *actions and behaviours* of the people in the setting, as these determine ultimately how policy is implemented. This is hard to legislate for, as it depends on willingness and ability, which is closely linked with attitude and skills. As people are inevitably influenced by, and respond to, the way they themselves are treated, the responsibility of the setting leader to set an example and to create a conducive atmosphere is pivotal.

Together, these three elements affect the culture of the setting, and are, in turn, influenced by it.

DISCUSSION POINT

Consider the type of issues/misunderstandings which might arise in an early years setting with an international mix of staff and children (e.g. some staff may consider that children should be taught in a particular way or may consider that staff should have less/more 'attachment' to the children). Your remit is to find solutions to these issues/misunderstandings, either as preventative or interventionist measures. Reflect on how you might do this.

You need to make a list of all the possible issues/misunderstandings you can think of and consider how, on a one-by-one basis, you might address them in practice – remember you always have the best interests of the children at the centre.

You can review your thoughts when you have read the chapter.

Photo 18.1
How do you
develop a culture
which promotes
the learning and
development of
all children?

Pearson Education
Ltd. Jules Selmes
© Pearson
Education Ltd.
2004

Figure 18.1 clearly shows how the three elements of social environment, policy, systems and structures and actions and behaviours are linked. The relationship between the elements in Figure 18.1 determines the degree of consonance operating in the setting. Where there is a high degree of consonance, or consistency, the setting's values are more recognisable, and the setting is likely to provide an agreeable and productive atmosphere for learning. But where there is dissonance, or disharmony, between these elements, energy gets diverted away from the central educational task (e.g. it might be

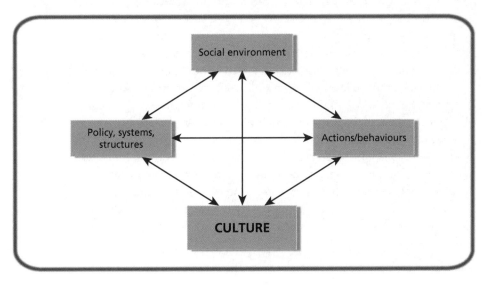

Figure 18.1
Factors
influencing
setting culture

Source: Blandford
and Shaw (2001)
p. 54

expended on such activities as mediating conflict or counteracting the consequences of suppressed resentment).

The following examples of what happens in practice (in a nursery setting in England) show how culture influences and directs the practice which develops in a setting.

WHAT HAPPENS IN PRACTICE?

Babies

The nursery manager arranged for there to be times when parents could join in short baby massage sessions with their new babies. The parents brought with them a changing mat and baby oil, sat on the floor with their baby lying on the mat in front of them while gentle music played in the background. The leader of the group demonstrated the simple stroking movements and the parents copied her. The session lasted for half an hour.

This session seemed to offer an opportunity and permission for intimacy between the mothers and their babies as they made close eye contact. Mothers said it was one of the few times in a busy day when you could sit down and dedicate time to building a special relationship with your baby. Other mothers described similar benefits. For example, one mother said that she uses these massage techniques now in the afternoons 'when he gets fractious' for her own and her baby's relaxation. Someone else commented that she used this massage more now because it helped to relieve her baby's colic.

Toddlers

In our setting each child has an A4 booklet of coloured paper designated for recording development. These books are called 'My Learning Journey'. They start with a photograph of the child. Any significant incidents noted during each day are recorded briefly and immediately on Post-it stickers which are then kept in the book. These are not confined only to key persons but are available for contributions from anyone helping in the nursery. We know that, however open we try to be, we sometimes make judgements about particular children that may not be fair. Other colleagues may have a completely different view of the same child and that's why it's important to share our observations and ideas.

Our team has an informal meeting every day over lunch to talk about children as well as formal recall and planning sessions once a week. Following these discussions, and with reference to the Post-it notes, records are then written in the book. Plans from these records are then devised for the following and subsequent weeks, so that the children's interests and development lead plans.

We try to find time to talk about the children as often as possible, and it's not difficult because there's something happening in their development all the time.

(Goouch and Powell, 2006)

REFLECT AND RELATE TO PRACTICE

For each of the above examples consider how practice has been influenced by the culture within the setting.

It might help to consider how they do this in other countries. In the example with the toddlers, how do they ensure that practice is not influenced by the individual culture of practitioners?

Developing culture: multicultural issues and practice

Ultimately, the culture of a setting is determined by individual and collective beliefs and values. Settings do not consist of homogeneous groups of people with shared identities; settings are collections of individuals within a shared culture. By outlining the four cultures defined by Charles Handy (1993) – the power, role, task and person culture – which in practice overlap, this section considers that although subcultures develop, the dominant culture, promoted by the setting, will be reflected by management structures.

The modelling of a setting will require **Improvement Plans** and policies that acknowledge established practice. A setting culture will manifest itself in many forms:

Improvement plans (IP): a framework for strategic planning in which staff can identify long- and short-term objectives to manage themselves effectively.

- practice – rites, rituals and ceremonies
- communications – stories, myths, sagas, legends, folk tales, symbols and slogans
- physical forms – location, style and condition of the setting buildings, fixtures and fittings
- common language – phrases or jargon specific to the setting.

Within each culture, subcultures exist with their own sets of characteristics. The setting culture may be the dominant culture or teams may create their own subcultures. Charles Handy (1993), renowned for his work in the field of management thinking, founded on his experience both in industry as an executive of Shell International Oil company and as a Professor of the London School of Business, offers a means of understanding the culture of organisations by identifying common characteristics. More specifically, he suggests that organisations are:

- collections of individuals
- political systems

joined together by:

- power and influence.

Handy (1993: 182) described how organisations differ according to the way they work, levels of authority, formality and control, planning, financial matters, rules and results. Handy also described the impact of the building; settings can certainly offer variety here. Most significantly, Handy focuses on the people within organisations, as it is people who create and work within the culture of an organisation. Handy

(1993: 183–191) defined four cultures which could provide a framework for analysing practice:

- power culture
- role culture
- task culture
- person culture.

These cultures are summarised below. Although they are shown as separate cultures, in practice, there is an overlap. The lists are not exhaustive; there may be other characteristics which could be applied. Equally, the characteristics may be more observable at different periods of the setting day, week or year!

The characteristics of a *power culture* are:

- web shape in design
- culture depends on a central power source, rays of power and influence spreading out from the central figure (e.g. a leader practitioner with an authoritarian style)
- organisation dependent on trust and empathy for effectiveness
- communication dependent on telepathy and personal conversation
- if whoever is at the centre of the web chooses the right people, they can be left to get on with the job
- few rules and procedures – little bureaucracy
- control is exercised by the centre, by occasional forays from the centre or summonses to the centre
- the quality of the person(s) at the centre is of paramount importance
- individuals employed by them will prosper and be satisfied, if they are power-orientated
- faith in the individual not in committees
- judges by results and is tolerant of the means
- low morale and high turnover in the middle layers – too competitive.

The characteristics of *role culture* are:

- can be pictured as a Greek temple
- logic and rationality
- strength is in its pillars

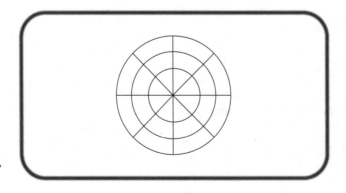

Figure 18.2
The power
culture

Source: Blandford,
(2006) p. 66

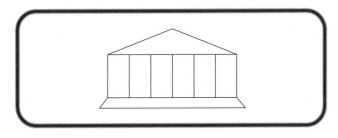

Figure 18.3
The role
culture
Source: Blandford
(2006) p. 67

- the work of pillars, and the interaction between the pillars, is controlled by:
  - procedures for roles (job descriptions, authority decisions)
  - procedures for communications (required sets of memos)
  - rules for the settlement of disputes
- co-ordinated at the top by a narrow band of senior managers
- role or job description is more important than the individual
- individuals are selected for satisfactory performance in the role
- performance over and above the role is not required
- position power is the major power source
- personal power is frowned upon and expert power is only tolerated
- rules and procedures are the major methods of influence
- offers security and predictability – clear career path
- slow to perceive the need for change

The characteristics of *task culture* are:

- groups, project teams or task forces for a specific purpose
- structure best described as a net
- some strands of the net are thicker and stronger than others
- emphasis on getting the job done
- influence is placed on expert power more than on person power
- utilises the unifying power of the group to ensure that individuals identify with the objective of the organisation
- high degree of control over work
- easy working relationships within the group with mutual respect based upon capacity rather than age or status
- appropriate where flexibility and sensitivity are important
- limited depth of expertise
- thrives where speed of reaction, integration, sensitivity and creativity are important

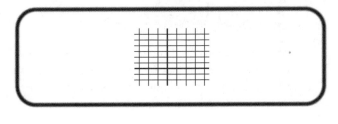

Figure 18.4
The task
culture
Source: Blandford
(2006) p. 68

Figure 18.5
The person
culture

Source: Blandford
(2006) p. 69

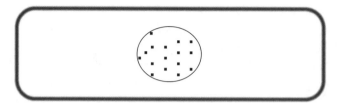

- control is difficult – by allocation of projects
- little day-to-day management
- not always the appropriate culture for the climate and the technology.

The characteristics of *person culture* are:

- unusual, individuals may cling to its values
- the individual is the central point
- it exists only to serve and assist the individuals within it
- structure best described as a cluster
- control mechanisms are impossible
- influence is shared; the power-base is usually expert, individuals do what they are good at
- generally only the creator achieves success
- individuals may exist in other cultures – not easy to manage
- little influence can be brought on them, not easily impressed.

Organisational culture will vary; settings are complex organisations with management structures that are determined by and are a reflection of the dominant culture, which in essence may be thought of as the one promoted by/within the setting. Tom Peters and Robert Waterman (2004: 75), both from a management consultancy background and renowned for their book *In Search of Excellence*, first published in 1982, highlight the 'dominance and coherence of culture' in strongly performing companies, where all employees share a common set of values. In most settings, leaders will need to understand the culture in the same way that they need to understand their own personalities. They will need to identify the culture of the settings in which they work and also the subculture within teams. This will be according to the collective beliefs and values of the setting community and their relationship to the community's own beliefs and values. As a subculture, do the characteristics and practice of the team reflect the culture of the setting or do they differ in any way? Setting and team culture ought to be compatible.

DISCUSSION POINT

Consider the models of culture outlined in this section (Handy, 1993). In practice, there will be overlap and leader practitioners may find certain elements of one effective and combine them with certain elements from another model. Imagine you are part of a team within an early years setting which has been given the task of developing an effective framework for practice, which is focusing on organisational structure (e.g. who reports to whom, or is leadership shared etc.). Which elements from each of the above would you select and try to put into practice? Why?

Effective settings require collective practices. Individuality may generate creativity. However, if the individual's values and beliefs are the antithesis of the setting's values and beliefs, this will result in negative behaviour; a situation which can prevail in any international setting. Conflict will inevitably ensue!

DISCUSSION POINT

To what extent do you think that an individual's values and behaviours in a setting will influence the ethos and culture which develops?

What are the implications for practice in an educational setting with a multicultural mix of children and staff?

The influence of Hofstede

Hofstede's seminal work (1980, 2001) is familiar to many. Hofstede surveyed 117,000 employees in a number of different countries worldwide. He found distinct differences in basic cultural assumptions which had an effect on the way people worked, and on the way they related to each other at work. By addressing the 'dimensions' Hofstede developed to compare the social actions and reactions of people within different national cultures, this section will consider how culture can be developed and develops in an early years setting.

Trying to make sense of the differences in core values between people of different cultures, Hofstede (1991) derived from his data a way of categorising them into various dimensions and then explored ways in which these interacted with each other. Different countries were found, through the research, to have different relative positions on these dimensions, and some understanding of values in that society may be deduced from their positions. These five dimensions he defined as:

- *individualism–collectivism*:

  The degree to which people see themselves or their collective group as more important. Individualistic societies tend to emphasise the 'I' above the 'we', while collectivist societies respect the goals of their own group more than individual achievement.

- *power distance (PD)*:

  The amount of emotional distance between employers and employees. In high power distance cultures, employees tend to prefer their managers to lead visibly, and paternal-autocratic leadership styles are seen as caring. In low power distance cultures, the opposite is true; employees express a preference for consultative management styles.

- *uncertainty avoidance (UA)*:

  The degree to which people feel threatened by uncertain or unknown situations. People with a high uncertainty avoidance index tend to prefer to know where they are, with rules of precision to guide them, while the opposite is the case with those with a low UA index, where more risks may be taken.

- *masculinity–femininity*:

  This is concerned with the degree of achievement-orientation built into the culture, taking its name (perhaps unhelpfully) from stereotypical gender expectations. High masculinity cultures value status, challenge and achievement, while high femininity cultures value good working relationships and co-operation.

- *Long-term vs. short-term orientation*:

  This dimension emerged after the others following studies of entrepreneurial development in East Asia, which did not fit into the previous dimensions. It represents an emergence of a long-term orientation (e.g. persistence, thrift, ordering relationships by, and observing, status, and having a sense of commitment to others) out of the more traditional short-term orientation (e.g. protecting 'face', respect for tradition).

Hofstede's work has had a strong influence on the way we view culture, but what does it mean for early years practice? In reality there is an overlap within each dimension. That is, in practice culture will develop on a continuum somewhere, for example, between individualism and collectivism. Consequently, an ethos may develop within a setting which reflects both individualism and collectivism or long-term and short-term orientation. The important issue within the setting is the type of cultural climate which is being developed, embodied in the mission and vision statements and reflected in the ethos. In essence it will develop through the collective efforts of leader practitioners, practitioners and even governors. Each of Hofstede's dimensions has been considered in the light of children's learning and development in early years settings and is presented below as statements or questions (the majority have already been addressed elsewhere within the book), for you to consider in the context of developing culture within the setting.

Individualism–collectivism:

- Respect children's views/beliefs/values from their home background.
- Treat all children equally (i.e. you are impartial).

- Help all children to develop their self-esteem.
- Encourage children to take the initiative (e.g. develop a thought).
- Encourage children to and develop a climate where children feel confident to speak in front of the group.
- Focus on each child as a unique individual (e.g. aware of the stages of cognitive development, which act only as a guide, you consider what each child can do and achieve him/herself and how you can help that development).
- How do you group children (e.g. by task and current needs)?
- Do you see the purpose of learning as 'learning how to learn' (i.e. you **personalise the learning** [see Chapter 10] for the children and help them to become independent learners)?

(Adapted from Hofstede, 2001: 237)

> **Personalised learning:** the adaptation of teaching the curriculum to meet the learning needs of the individual child.

Power distance:

- How independent (in learning) do you help the children to be/become?
- How do you show respect to the children/how do you teach them to show respect to you?
- Have you developed a child-centred education?
- Do you encourage children to communicate with you/peers?
- How do you transfer knowledge to your colleagues and to the children?
- How do you involve parents in their children's learning (i.e. parents are the primary educators/carers of their children, practitioners help to strengthen/develop that relationship)?
- Do you consider the quality of teaching and learning (e.g. having up-to-date subject knowledge and knowledge of effective practice, having open channels of communication – practitioner–child–parent, personalising learning and empowering children)?
- Is the practitioner–child–parent relationship authoritarian/more of a partnership?
- Do you give children 'thinking time and space' (e.g. time to be creative, time to develop confidence in their creativity – for young children providing opportunity for heuristic play)?
- Do you employ technology to complement teaching and not replace it (see Chapter 6)?

(Adapted from Hofstede, 2001: 107)

Uncertainty avoidance (you want to develop low uncertainty avoidance so that children learn to cope with new situations):

- Provide open-ended learning situations (i.e. the learning outcomes are unknown at the start) and a lot of time for discussion (practitioner–child, child–child or parent–child).
- Teach children that some things/situations do not have yes/no answers.
- Make children aware of what to expect (where possible) and let them know that they are not alone – many children/people will experience what they are experiencing/will experience.
- Help children to attribute success/achievements to their own ability.
- Help children to develop a feeling of self-efficacy (self-competency).
- Ask parents for their ideas (i.e. about their children's learning – interests, dislikes etc.).

- Make time for two-way conversations with children, other practitioners and parents.
- Treat boys and girls the same, being aware that boys have different learning needs and may respond in different ways to girls.

(Adapted from Hofstede, 2001)

Masculinity–femininity:

- Do you create a warm, friendly, supportive work environment/climate which encourages children to be/become independent learners, knowing that you are approachable?
- How do you help children to succeed (i.e. do you encourage and develop a step-by-step approach to learning and praise children appropriately)?
- Do you give praise to weaker children in front of the group?
- Do you have awards for 'good' children?
- Do you socialise children to avoid aggression?
- Do you teach children to consider problems and work out solutions?

(Adapted from Hofstede, 2001: 306)

Long-term vs. short-term orientation:

- Encourage children to persevere (i.e. a step-by-step approach to problems and praise the successes en route, show them you do not give up, let them know that we all have to keep trying).
- Teach them how to tolerate people they might not like or get along with.
- Teach them how to include others.

Photo 18.2
Do you provide opportunities to hold a dialogue with children?

Pearson Education Ltd. Ian Wedgewood © Pearson Education Ltd. 2007

- Teach them that some things in life we have wait for (e.g. if you want to do well in a test/achieve something you keep trying and working – rewards lie in the effort).
- Help them to realise that we need to develop commitments to people to work and to situations.

(Adapted from Hofstede, 2001: 359)

REFLECT AND RELATE TO PRACTICE

For each statement or question listed within the dimensions, consider how you would address it in practice.

You only have to consider one way. You should choose one age group and consider each point from that point of view – i.e. 0–2, 3–5, 5–7 years old.

Cross-cultural issues

There are numerous theories about how people respond and react to each other at work. The different cultures of those who work in the same setting should be considered in developing internal structures. These differences are concerned with attributes such as character, situation, organisational climate, race, gender, tradition, and so on and suggest that people from different cultural backgrounds work in different ways. Research within the field of cross-cultural studies has increased our understanding of culture in practice. This section challenges the reader to consider why cultural differences between practitioners need to be considered both in theory and practice for teaching and learning to be effective in early years settings.

Culture is central to the way organisations work. While it is valuable in opening up understanding, and also in providing objective explanations for when misunderstandings actually occur, it cannot, nevertheless, provide a complete picture. In addition to Hofstede's dimensions, other relevant cross-cultural phenomena should be considered. These include:

- *Disconfirmed expectancies*: if people have a strong expectation, then any deviation from it is seen as greater than it really is (Helson, 1964). Brislin remarks that 'disconfirmed expectancies are certain in intercultural encounters' (1993: 44).
- *Fundamental attribution error*: this is the mistake of making judgements about the characters of others without taking situational factors into account (Ross, 1977). Actions of other people are judged through the value system of the perceiver, who may then form incorrect conclusions about the motive for the action – often thinking the worse of them.
- *Symbolism*: sometimes others do not understand the value and importance of the way people relate to the symbols inside their own culture; this can break down trust.

Cross-cultural studies now provide an increasingly rich body of research literature, which has helped to increase our understanding of the complex area of culture and how it can be addressed in the practices of an early years setting. However, it is not without its problems, particularly when applied to educational issues. Firstly, it is largely Western-centric (Trompenaars, 1993); the research tools are not appropriate in all cultures, which means suspect validity (Riordan and Vandenburg, 1994; Lonner, 1990). Secondly, it has tended to attach stereotypes to nation states (Hofstede, 1980; Trompenaars, 1993). Nevertheless, as long as it is remembered that cultural stereotypes only represent an average of many individuals in a country, and that there is danger in labelling individuals, or in believing that everyone of a certain nationality thinks and behaves in the same way, then stereotypes are useful in giving us, in the words of Brislin (1993), a 'shortcut to thinking', or a starting point.

DISCUSSION POINT

In her article, 'Quality in early childhood education and care: a cultural context', Miriam Rosenthal (2003: 112) considers the impact, on teaching and learning, of differing ideas of 'quality' in Early Childhood Education and Care (ECEC) which can be prevalent in multicultural educational communities. (Quality is a subjective term and as a result can lead to misunderstandings when trying to define it for practice. It relates to such areas as the extent to which children are provided with the opportunity for child-initiated activities, creative play and the extent to which practitioners interact with the child and the way they interact etc.) Consider the following excerpt from Rosenthal's article:

Quality ECEC is a major concern to anyone involved in designing, or providing, educational services and programs for young children. It is also a major concern to parents. The different stakeholders in multicultural societies . . . are likely to hold onto different cultural scripts and therefore, to differ in the educational goals and practices they value. It is therefore imperative that policy makers, early childhood professionals, and parents all articulate their valued educational goals and practices . . .

In cases where mutual agreement cannot be reached among the different stakeholders, one should consider the implications for children's development, and for society at large, of the conflicts that inevitably arise from discontinuity between the valued goals and practices of the education system and that of parents. For children to benefit from ECEC, such differences and disagreements should be openly discussed with the mutual intent of providing 'quality ECE' which meets most of the values of most of the stakeholders.

(Rosenthal, 2003: 12)

In light of the *Statutory Framework for the Early Years Foundation Stage: Setting the Standards for Learning Development and Care for children from birth to five* (EYFS) (DfES, 2007), to what extent do you agree with Rosenthal's view?

You should consider the extent to which this document gives clear guidance for practitioners developing 'high quality' provision and what you would consider to be important issues in providing a high quality education and care in early years settings.

Culture-free theory

One group of 'culture-free' theorists (those who propose the idea that an organisation's 'structure', i.e. staffing structure – who is the leader and who reports to whom, is not influenced by culture) argue that all organisations, regardless of where they are in the world, should be able to operate best with a single set of principles, as long as they have appropriate and similar conditions of structure (i.e. staffing structure – reflected in e.g. patterns of control, communication, co-ordination). It originates in contingency theory (Taylor, 1947; Fayol, 1949; Laurence and Lorsch, 1967) which searches for similarities between different organisations, and uses these to identify a number of ways in which universal principles of management can be applied. This theory would argue that settings are much the same everywhere, regardless of country, and that, as long as the same principles are applied, settings will run smoothly, and each person will be able to play her/his part in this.

However, this approach has declined in recent years as there is little linkage to the behaviour inside organisations and it does not give a great deal of practical help to managers trying to make sense of their worlds. Throughout the 1960s and 1970s there was little attention to the cross-cultural aspects of management, but Hofstede's research (1980) changed all this by looking at how national cultures affected the way organisations worked, thus initiating a new body of 'culture-bound' theory.

Connect & Extend

Look up the *International Journal of Early Years Education* for the last two years. Select articles which are related to practice in other countries. To what extent is practice influenced by the national culture? (Although 'culture-free' theory has been replaced by 'culture-bound' theory, you should consider the extent to which practice is influenced by national culture in light of 'culture-free' theory.)

From theory to practice: defining vision and mission

Most educational settings, whatever their particular constitution, have clear and unambiguous purposes, usually expressed as their vision or mission statement or as values or aims, many of which relate directly to the aims of the provider in providing a broad education suitable for babies and young children in the twenty-first century. The collaborative development of such statements can provide a firm foundation for co-operative practice within an international educational community. By defining vision and mission, this section considers how they can be developed in practice to reflect the culture of the setting.

Vision

The leader has responsibility for collaborating with the setting community in the generation of its **vision**. This emphasises a collegial approach to writing and achieving a vision; as each setting's ethos is distinctive, setting vision or mission statements will also be distinctive. A specific definition of vision within the context of settings would be the setting's aims. These are notably achievement orientated and, as such, should be shared by all members of the community. If a setting is to be successful, it has to be effective. A measure of a setting's effectiveness is the ability of the staff to work towards achieving the setting's vision, i.e. working towards a shared set of values and

Vision: precise goals that show where an organisation will be in the future.

beliefs. Fidler (2002: 105) suggests that staff could contribute by writing down their hope for the future of the setting: 'Bringing different ideas together', he further suggests, 'should produce a composite. Some components will be incompatible with others and discussion should help to resolve these' (ibid.). The vision statement should be succinct and should contain, within a few words, the philosophy underlying professional practice within the setting. Although literature emphasises the need for vision in organisations, vision is often an intangible, difficult and ambiguous concept. Fidler describes vision as:

> the creative 'double-loop' thinking of trying to envisage how things might be different in the future. It leaps the present and the short term. It looks 10–15 years ahead, sufficient time that things might change radically, and tries to vision the organization in a new and successful future . . . the vision is not just a projection forward of the present but it does bear some relation to the starting conditions.
>
> *(2002: 105)*

A vision will move an organisation forward from where it is now to where it would like to be. A precise goal is more credible than a vague dream. A vision should be realistic and attractive to all members of the organisation. As a condition, a vision should be more desirable in many important ways than that which currently exists.

Missions will provide a clear sense of direction and purpose. These are a means of creating operational plans: objectives or targets to be met by members of the setting community.

A vision must be clear and comprehensible to all: practitioners, teachers, parents, children, governors, visitors, etc. Setting vision statements should direct the setting's population towards a common purpose.

Identifying shared values is the starting point when generating a vision for the setting. Based on past and present values it might reflect what is good within the setting. A genuinely good setting with shared values and beliefs will be an effective setting.

As stated, a vision must be shared, but it is the responsibility of leaders to ensure that visions 'happen'. Knowledge and understanding of a setting's vision by staff is central to the success of the setting. A shared vision will provide a framework for practice. When shared, the vision can be debated and developed. Monitoring and evaluation of values and beliefs through the sharing process should be common practice in all settings.

Mission

Mission: to declare what a settings intended outcomes are for its children, their development and overall attainment.

A setting's **mission** statement will provide the framework in which a vision can become a reality. A mission statement is therefore operational. Grace (1998: 120) suggests that mission statements are of crucial importance in the context of developing an effective and inclusive educational setting. Mission statements set out what a setting's intended outcomes are for its children, their development and overall attainments – academic, social and personal. In practice, it is very easy for a setting to lose its overall direction because it is unsure about what kind of setting it is, and what it is trying to do. Figure 18.6 illustrates the relationship between vision, mission and aims, where

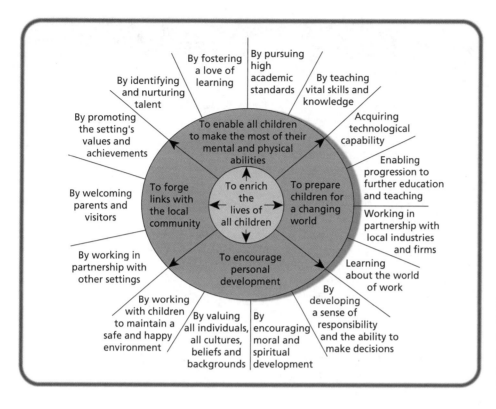

Figure 18.6
Setting vision and mission statements

Source: Blandford (1997)

the central core represents the vision, the second circle represents the aims of the setting and the outer circle represents the mission.

A mission statement (see Table 18.1) describes the way in which an organisation has chosen to conduct its activities. The extent to which practitioners participate in this process will be determined by:

- how much authority the leader has to make decisions
- how many staff each leader has to manage
- level of staff specialisation
- clear job descriptions for all staff
- clear lines of communication relating to the team.

Each of the following examples of mission statements and aims, taken at random from the websites of a sample of settings across the world, aspires to the development of confident learners, able to relate to others in the world. There is little here that most early years settings would not subscribe to:

- We foster independent inquiry, critical thinking, open-mindedness and service to others.
- The curriculum and learning strategies encourage the development of responsible, democratic citizens.
- We strive to embody the finest spirit of international co-operation.

Table 18.1 Example mission statement

As managers we are committed to:

- improving the quality and delivery of education and care
- ensuring that staff are briefed on the setting's objectives and are clear about their own limits of authority
- utilising to the maximum the skills of our staff
- encouraging staff to take decisions for themselves within the limits of their authority
- concentrating on achievement
- encouraging individuals to find solutions rather than putting forward problems
- fostering the building of teams to promote achievement
- increasing participation in Continuing Professional Development (CPD)
- encouraging a sense of belonging to staff, children and parents/carers
- being supportive to staff in their endeavours, allowing them an opportunity of putting forward their views and encouraging their initiative.

- We are committed to honesty and responsibility in all relationships, respecting the legitimate rights of individuals and stressing the importance of social awareness and sensitivity.
- We will seek to promote equal opportunity and social justice.

But the reality of meeting such aims is a different matter. In many of the management training and consultancy workshops which have been run, managers have identified a significant gap between rhetoric and practice.

DISCUSSION POINT

Where does this gap, referred to above, come from? What sort of learning environment is needed in order to promote values such as 'co-operation', 'international understanding', 'unarguably universal values', and 'responsible citizenship'?

Culture, ethos and practice: bringing it together

The examples discussed in this chapter have been partly explained by reference to cross-cultural social psychology research. In practice, cross-cultural misunderstandings can be overcome by employing the following:

- *Understand the possible cause(s) of the behaviour*: Leader practitioners need to find a way to discover the core values of the various nationalities represented in the workplace, and to understand how these interact, and whether, or to what extent, this contributes towards the misunderstanding in question. Explaining reasons for differences of behaviour in a mixed-culture team, however, is merely a start. If taken no further, it is easy to take a culturally relativistic stance and allow culture to become the reason why things cannot happen.
- *Provide relevant and culture-sensitive professional development experience*: The second step is to focus on professional development. This might take the form of sensitive cultural awareness-raising, or it might be more formal training for some people in the team to enable them to be heard, play a full role, or provide equal opportunity to others in the team. Leader practitioners in multicultural settings commissioning professional development experiences from outside consultants are therefore urged to make choices of training personnel, materials and ways of working that are appropriate to the context of their own educational setting's cultural mix (Shaw and Welton, 1995).
- *Develop a distinctive organisational culture for the setting*: The third step looks constructively ahead for the whole team, or preferably the whole setting. Some of the post-Hofstede research (e.g. Kanter and Corn, 1994; Cray and Mallory, 1998) indicates that developing a distinctive organisational culture is a powerful tool in helping people to work together *regardless* of their own cultural programming. Experience in many educational settings has shown that those which have *consciously* focused on developing their own distinctive culture, starting with agreed values and bringing together the policies, systems, structures, and behaviours of the community into a state of consonance, are the ones that provide the right environment for successful management of mixed-culture teams.

It is only through such awareness of our differences that we can reach understanding through a better quality of communication, and thus perhaps help to achieve some of the ideals mentioned in this chapter. Perhaps we can best conclude with the wisdom of Alex Rodger:

> the possibility of humane communities in a pluralistic context depends on establishing the conditions possible to foster communications which serve the goal of mutual understanding. That communication, in turn, can emerge only from the kind of comm-union between human beings which begins in the acceptance of kinship as a fact to be explored; develops through recognition of the other as both strange and familiar; and leads to the framing of language which can bridge the gulf of separation, incomprehension and antagonism.

(1996: 54)

DISCUSSION POINT

Consider the above statement by Rodger (1996). What is your view? Do you agree with him or would you view the situation in a different way?

SUMMARY

Ethos (p. 386)

To what extent is ethos in an early years setting influenced by the values and behaviours of practitioners?

Ethos can be defined as the 'atmosphere' which develops in a setting as the result of the social interaction (e.g. the way people show respect to others etc.) between the practitioners, children, parents and others involved in the day-to-day practices and processes (e.g. teaching, greeting people etc.).

Culture (p. 387)

Why is consonance between social environment, the formal management systems, policies and structures and the actions and behaviours of the people in the setting important?

Culture might be defined as the way in which all of us in this workplace agree to work together in order to provide the best service for the learners. It affects everything from the way decisions are made to the way children learn, and is in turn affected by these factors. Culture is influenced by the social environment, the formal management systems, policies and structures and the actions and behaviours of the people in the setting, as these determine ultimately how policy is implemented.

Developing culture: multicultural issues and practice (p. 391)

What factors would you consider in developing the 'culture' of an early years setting?

Settings do not consist of homogeneous groups of people with shared identities; settings are collections of individuals within a shared culture.

Developing the setting 'culture' requires thought and planning and is created by the people who work within the culture which is developed.

The influence of Hofstede (p. 395)

How can Hofstede's 'dimensions' be addressed in practice?

Hofstede (1991) derived from his data a way of categorising cultures into various dimensions, which provides a framework for exploring ways in which people interact with each other. The dimensions he defined as power distance, uncertainty avoidance, individualism, masculine vs. feminine and long- vs. short-term orientation.

Cross-cultural issues (p. 398)

How has the field of cross-cultural studies increased our understanding of culture in practice?

Research within the field of cross-cultural studies has increased our understanding of culture in practice. For teaching and learning to be effective in an early years setting, cultural differences, between practitioners in particular, need to be considered both in theory and practice.

From theory to practice: defining vision and mission (p. 401)

Why is there a gap between a setting's mission statement and what happens in practice?

A vision will move an organisation forward from where it is now to where it would like to be. A setting's mission statement, on the other hand, will provide the framework in which a vision can become a reality. A mission statement is operational.

Glossary

Culture: culture might be defined in terms of the values and beliefs held by individuals, which distinguish them from another group of individuals. Culture is made known through practices (words, greetings, dress, food, religious ceremonies etc.).

Ethos: the intangible atmosphere which develops in a setting developed from and through the values, attitudes, culture and policies promoted.

Improvement plans (IP): provides a framework for strategic planning in which staff can identify long- and short-term objectives to manage themselves effectively. An IP should relate to the setting's vision or mission, its

achievements, government policy and LA policies and initiatives.

Mission statements: set out what a setting's intended outcomes are for its children, their development and overall attainments – academic, social and personal.

Personalised learning: the adaptation of teaching the curriculum to meet the learning needs of the individual child.

Vision statements: precise goals which show where an organisation will be in the future. It moves an organisation forward from where it is now to where it would like to be.

Find out more

Hofstede, G. (2001) *Culture's Consequences*, **Thousand Oaks, CA: Sage.**
Hofstede describes his research in over 50 countries and shows how he developed his 'dimensions' as a means of considering national culture in more depth and as a means of making some form of comparison between cultures.

McLaughlin, T. (2005) The educative importance of ethos, *British Journal of Educational Studies*, **Vol. 53, No. 3: pp. 306–325.**

This journal article by the late Terrence McLaughlin of the Institute of Education provides an insight into ethos and its importance in educational settings.

Donnelly, C. (2000) In pursuit of school ethos, *British Journal of Educational Studies*, **Vol. 48, No. 2: pp. 134–154.**
This journal article considers how we might define ethos in practice.

References

Blandford, S. (1997) *Middle Management in Schools.* London: Pitman.

Blandford, S. (2006) *Middle Leadership in Schools: Harmonising Leadership and Learning.* Harlow: Pearson Education.

Blandford, S. and Shaw, M. (eds) (2001) *Managing International Schools.* London: Routledge.

Brislin, R. (1993) *Understanding Culture's Influence on Behaviour.* Harcourt Brace Jovanovich College.

Cray, D. and Mallory, G. (1998) *Making Sense of Managing Culture.* London: International Thompson Business Press.

Department for Education and Skills (DfES) (2007) *Statutory Framework for the Early Years Foundation Stage: Setting the Standards for Learning Development and Care for children from birth to five* (EYFS). Nottingham: DfES Publications.

Donnelly, C. (2000) In pursuit of school ethos, *British Journal of Educational Studies*, Vol. 48, No. 2: pp. 134–154.

Fayol, H. (1949) *General and Industrial Management.* London: Pitman.

Fidler, B. (2002) *Strategic Management for School Development.* London: Paul Chapman.

Goouch, K. and Powell, S. (2006) *Case Studies for Early Years Professional Standards 2.1–2.7*. Canterbury: Canterbury Christ Church University.

Grace, G. (1998) Realising the mission: Catholic approaches to school effectiveness, in Slee, R., Tomlinson, S. and Weiner, G. (eds) *School Effectiveness for Whom? Challenges to the school effectiveness and school improvement movements*. London: Falmer Press.

Handy, C. (1993) *Understanding Organisations*, 4th edn. Harmondsworth: Penguin.

Helson, H. (1964) *Adaptation Level Theory*. New York: Harper and Row.

Hofstede, G. (1980) *Culture's Consequences*. Thousand Oaks, CA: Sage.

Hofstede, G. (1991) *Cultures and Organisations*. New York: Harper Collins.

Hofstede, G. (2001) *Culture's Consequences*, 2nd edn. Thousand Oaks, CA: Sage.

Kanter, R.M. and Corn, R. (1994) Do cultural differences make a business difference? Contextual factors affecting cross-cultural relationships, *Journal of Management Development*, Vol. 13, No. 2: pp. 5–23.

Kluckhohn, C. (1951) The study of culture, in Lerner, D. and Lasswell, H. (eds) *The Policy Sciences*. Stanford, CA: Stanford University Press: pp. 86–101.

Laurence, P. and Lorsch, J. (1967) *Organisation and Environment*. Homewood, IL: Irwin.

Lonner, W. (1990) An over-view of cross-cultural testing and assessment, in Brislin, R. (ed.) *Applied Cross-Cultural Psychology*, Newbury Park, CA: Sage.

McLaughlin, T. (2005) The educative importance of ethos, *British Journal of Educational Studies*, Vol. 53, No. 3: pp. 306–325.

Peters, T. and Waterman, R. (2004) *In Search of Excellence: Lessons from America's Best-run Companies*. London: Profile Books.

Riordan, C. and Vandenburg, R. (1994) A Central Question in Cross-Cultural Research: do employees of different cultures interpret work-related measure in an equivalent manner?, *Journal of Management*, Vol. 20, No. 3: pp. 643–671.

Rodger, A. (1996) *Developing Moral Community in a Pluralist School Setting*. Aberdeen: Gordon Cook Foundation.

Rosenthal, M. (2003) Quality in early childhood education and care: a cultural context, *European Early Childhood Education Research Journal*, Vol. 11, No. 2.

Ross, I. (1977) The intuitive psychologist and his shortcomings: distortion in the attribution process, in Berkovitz, L. (ed.) *Advances in Experimental Social Psychology*, Vol. 10. New York: Academic Press: pp. 173–220.

Shaw, M. and Welton, J. (1986) *The Application of Education Management Models and Theories to the Processes of Education Policy Making and Management: a case of compound cross-cultural confusion*, conference paper at *Indigenous Perspectives of Education Management*, Kuala Lumpur.

Taylor, F.W. (1947) *Scientific Management*. London: Harper and Row.

Trompenaars, F. (1993) *Riding the Waves of Culture: Understanding Cultural Diversity in Business*. London: Economist Books.

By the end of this chapter you will be able to answer the following questions:

- What does leadership in practice mean in an early years setting?
- Why is leadership style important?
- What factors and human qualities contribute to effective leadership?
- How do you motivate your team?

This chapter will support your understanding of the following Standards *(see Appendix 1)*:
■ **Knowledge and understanding:** S06 ■ **Effective practice:** S24 ■ **Teamwork and collaboration:** S33, S34 and S35.

Introduction

What educational settings need is leadership based on shared values and beliefs, rather than rules and personalities.

(Adapted from Sergiovanni, 2007: 82)

The government's vision in England, for a less fragmented, more uniform provision of children's services, where early years practitioners work closely with professionals from social, health and educational services, calls for a more co-operative approach to management and leadership. Sergiovanni (2007) above highlights the essence of effective leadership. Leadership can be compared to being on a roller coaster, travelling at speed through many hoops, having to participate in many teaching and management activities from the 'top-down' and 'bottom-up'. During the journey a leader assimilates the view from every perspective: child, practitioner, parent and governor. This chapter will attempt to take the reader on a journey, progressing forward from a theoretical perspective of leadership in early years settings through to leadership in practice, examining some of the characteristics associated with effective leadership.

What is leadership?

Theories and practice

Leadership: the achievement of objectives through people, where leaders are those with power and influence.

Management: sustaining an existing code of practice, with limited authority to change the 'direction' of an organisation.

There are many definitions of **leadership** in educational and business literature. Blandford (2006: 4–10) defines leadership in terms of practice as the 'achievement of objectives through people', where 'leaders are those with power and influence'. This can be compared with management, where **managers** sustain an existing code of practice, with limited authority to change the 'direction' of an organisation. This is not to be confused with the management of people, where the role of the leader will also encompass the management of colleagues. The essence of good leadership hinges on the effective and appropriate management of people. By examining various definitions of leadership, this section will help the reader to build a theoretical picture of leadership in the early years.

It is widely acknowledged within the field of education that effective setting/school leaders contribute to the development of effective settings/schools. Fidler (2002), Professor of Education at Reading University who has written widely on educational management, suggests that:

Leadership is a complex area with many apparently contradictory requirements. Suggestions that particular approaches to leadership should be universal . . . should be resisted . . . Leadership will need to exhibit many actions in different styles on different occasions.

(2002: 32)

John Harvey-Jones (2003: 20), former ICI chairman, compared leaders to conductors of symphony orchestras. A conductor is responsible for interpreting the work of others (composer) through a large body of people (the orchestra) who are divided into teams (instrumental sections) with their own team leaders (principal players). The conductor directs and guides the orchestra in order to achieve and communicate musical excellence to a diverse and critical audience.

Similarly a setting leader is responsible for interpreting the work of others:

- local and national policies
- staff, parents and children who are divided into teams – according to task
- practitioners (from teaching and nursing backgrounds), non-teaching and support staff (including those from multidisciplinary teams – family support workers, health personnel – speech therapists, psychologists etc.)
- their own team leaders – in order to achieve and communicate excellence, through learning, to a diverse and informed audience – practitioners/teachers, parents and multi-agency team leaders.

Leaders/would-be leaders may wish to reflect on Bennis's (1959) view of leadership. Regarded as the founder of leadership studies as an academic area, Bennis, who has written widely on leadership and worked as adviser to the American government, highlights the difficulty in defining leadership, either in theoretical terms or for practice:

> Of all the hazy and confounding areas in social psychology, leadership theory undoubtedly contends for top nomination. . . . The lack of consensus in this whole area of leadership cannot be blamed on a reluctance by social scientists to engage in empirical research on projects related to these topics. . . . The problems involved in developing a coherent leadership theory are certainly not new. . . . As McGregor points out 'The eagerness with which new ideas in this field are received, and the extent to which many of them become fads, are indications of the dissatisfaction with the status quo in organizational theory'.
>
> *(1959: 259–301)*

Bennis, however, provided a definition of leadership within the framework of what he considered to be its constituent components:

> Leadership . . . involves three major components: (a) an agent who is typically called a leader; (b) a process of induction or the ability to manipulate rewards that will be termed power; and (c) the induced behaviour, which will be referred to here as influence.
>
> *(1959: 296)*

More recently, he highlighted the following critical issues for leaders contemporarily:

- One is the adaptive capacity, which I think is probably the sine qua non, absolutely the most essential and central aspect of leadership in this environment of complexity and turbo-change.
- The second critical ingredient is the capacity to engage followers in shared meaning – to align the stars around a common, meaningful goal.
- Third, leaders are really going to have to spend a long time – and it's a continual process – finding out who they themselves are: learning their

own voice, learning how they affect other people, learning a great deal about emotional intelligence.
• And finally, leaders will have to rely on a moral compass, a set of principles, a belief system, a set of convictions.

(Bennis, 2003: 335, cited by University of Western Ontario, 2008)

DISCUSSION POINT

At an interview for a leadership post in an educational setting, a candidate was asked, 'What is the difference between a manager and a leader?' Her response:

If the task of the team was to climb a mountain, a leader would climb to the top, throw a rope down and ask the team to join him/her. In contrast, a manager would consult his/her team at every stage of the climb which they would then complete together!

How would you respond to this question at an interview for a leadership post in an early years setting?

In essence, theorists define leaders as those with power and influence. How this applies to leaders in early years settings is described in the following sections.

The early years: distributed leadership

The centrality of effective leadership in education settings is widely acknowledged. The backdrop to leadership is the effectiveness of the organisation. Educationalists have found that effective leaders contribute to the development of effective organisations. While strong leadership is associated with good management and models of effective leadership are applied to educational settings, leadership has been given scant consideration within early years settings. Although recent government reforms have brought the concept of leadership to the forefront of change within the field of early years (primarily the introduction of new qualifications for early years leaders and the EYFS Standards), enabling practitioners to develop as leaders is vital for early years settings to develop as effective communities within the new multi-agency/inter-agency framework for the delivery of children's services. This section will consider how distributed leadership can be developed as an effective means of leading within early years settings.

Gillian Rodd (2006: 24), a lecturer at the University of Plymouth and known for her work on early years leadership, suggests that leadership is 'about working towards creating a community and providing a high quality service'. She also suggests that 'early childhood practitioners . . . display leadership' by developing and using their 'skills efficiently to administer a responsive service and to initiate change in a methodical way' (2006: 259). In practice, the way leaders lead, is dependent on numerous factors which influence individuals and affect the lives of the people with whom they come into contact.

Distributed leadership has become the most prevalent model in early years settings and can be defined in the following way:

> **Leaders and senior managers relocate their power, and are then freed to guide new developments. Those within the team are given ownership in some significant parts of their own working environment and are consequently empowered to act.**
>
> *(Knutton and Ireson, 1995: 61)*

The opportunity to participate in decision-making teams which impact on the effectiveness of an organisation is a relatively new phenomenon within education. This involves participation by team members and delegation from leaders. Participation can function in the following forms:

- Consultation: team members are invited to suggest ideas; decision-making remains the responsibility of the leader.
- Consent: team members, as a group, can veto any decision made by the leader.
- Consensus: team members are consulted, followed by whole team involvement in decision-making through majority vote.

A leader should be able to identify which participatory style is applicable to any specific task or situation. Democracy is fine if applicable; equally autocracy is acceptable and can work in the right circumstances. A leader will need to decide which style to adopt.

Delegation on the other hand follows different criteria. There are several factors which need to be considered in the delegation process:

- Quality of the result – will the outcome be good enough?
- The ability of the individual – how capable is the individual of completing the task?
- Relationship – will the individual be coached or left to the task? Either could cause problems.
- Time – have your staff the time to complete the task?
- Delegators should have positive aims, for example the Continuing Professional Development (CPD) of staff. Do not pass a job because it is unpleasant to do.
- The delegator should have a clear understanding of both the purpose and process of the task that is delegated.
- Do not abdicate all responsibility for a delegated task, but maintain a fine balance between interest, support and motivation on the one hand and interference or neglect on the other.
- Letting go can be difficult. But success has much to do with trust and depends on working things out in a realistic way.
- Clear and open communication is essential for effective delegation.

The following example of 'What happens in practice?' describes one leader's approach to leadership within a Sure Start Children's Centre.

Distributed leadership: a collegial approach, where team members share in the decision-making and take responsibility for certain tasks.

WHAT HAPPENS IN PRACTICE?

The initial aim of the Director at Sure Start Millmead was to *create* 'a multi-skilled, multi-agency, multi-disciplinary peripatetic team of workers able to respond to local needs in creative and innovative ways, able to evaluate services provided and change services and approaches as needed' (West and Carlson, 2007: 126). To achieve this aim the director proposed an 'open, non-hierarchical management style, founded on respect and a willingness to listen and learn', where views of parents and team members were valued. Time and money was invested in staff training and weekly meetings were chaired by different members of the team. Staff were encouraged to take on different roles within the centre and critique the cultures of established service providers. In addition, they were encouraged to be 'innovative' in their approach to work and to see themselves as active participants in building a 'new culture of professional practice'. Staff were relatively free to work under their own initiative within a 'no-blame culture'.

(West and Carlson, 2007: 143–149)

REFLECT AND RELATE TO PRACTICE

List the strategies used by the leader within this centre to implement a distributed model of leadership.

Consider the strategies implemented by the leader within this centre in developing a distributed model of leadership. Do you think they were effective? Would you have approached it differently? Why/why not?

Leadership style

Leaders carry out tasks or manage others to carry out tasks. How this is achieved is dependent on the leadership style adopted. This will be influenced by:

- the leader: his or her personality and preferred style
- the led: the needs, attitudes and skills of the subordinates or colleagues
- the task: the requirements and goals of the job to be done
- the contract: the setting/school, its values and beliefs, visions and missions.

(Knutton and Ireson, 1995: 61)

Early years leaders will decide on their own leadership style; some will appear charismatic, others less so. This is unimportant. Each individual's qualities will be identified according to their ability to get the job done. By examining some of the factors influencing leadership, this section will consider how particular styles of leadership develop in practice.

In their book *In Search of Excellence: Lessons from America's Best-Run Companies*, Tom Peters and Robert Waterman (2004) defined leadership as:

> being visible when things are going awry, and invisible when they are working well. It's building a loyal team at the top that speaks more or less with one voice. It's listening carefully much of the time. . . . It's being tough when necessary, and it's the occasional naked use of power – or the 'subtle accumulation of nuances, a hundred things done a little better' as Henry Kissinger once put it.

(2004: 82)

The following 'What happens in practice?' considers one of the roles of practitioners in the Reggio Emilia educational system in Italy, namely, the task of coming together to discuss both their work and that of the children. It provides a good example for reflecting on Tannenbaum and Schmidt's (1973) outline of the factors influencing leadership styles and how leaders might manage the situation.

Photo 19.1
An individual's leadership qualities will be identified by their ability to get the job done

Pearson Education Ltd. Jules Selmes © Pearson Education Ltd. 2004

WHAT HAPPENS IN PRACTICE?

Teachers work in close relationship to children, fellow teachers, parents and the community. They engage in a reflective self-discovery learning process alongside the children. Special time is set aside in the regular schedule for teachers, 'atelieristi' (art directors), and 'pedagogisti' (pedagogical co-ordinators) to come together and discuss their practice and the children's work. These honest, open exchanges often include confrontation and conflict over certain issues. However, the culture of respect and collaboration encourages these open dialogues as being necessary to the work of reflection and evolution. Suggestions are met with openness, just as they are offered in respect. . . . Reggio teachers embrace the potential for growth that is inherent in conflicts, and they negotiate through them respectfully and openly. This perspective allows teachers to learn from each other, just as conflicts in the classroom can be great opportunities for children to grow.

(Follari, 2007: 203–204)

REFLECT AND RELATE TO PRACTICE

In England practitioners and leaders also come together to discuss their practice and that of the children's work/progress. Consider the above example. List the ways that a collaborative approach to leadership has helped to lessen the impact of confrontation and conflict during these discussions.

☆ ☆ ☆

As a leader of an early years setting in England, what factors would you consider in the effective management of this type of meeting with your team/staff?

Selection of the 'best or preferred' style of leadership is critical to the success of the leader and team. A leader should not adopt a style which is unsustainable. 'Sincere insincerity' (i.e. adopting a style which is contrary to his/her character) is easily spotted; leaders need to be themselves and adapt as required.

Framework for practice

If to lead is to get things done, setting leaders get things done within a framework of practice determined by the early years setting as a community. This section will consider that although the basic organisational structure of settings is similar, each setting becomes an individual community through the day-to-day practices which are developed.

Harrison (1995: 8), formerly Professor of Education at Sheffield University, commented that 'managers live in a practical world'. As a community, each setting is self-centred, self-reliant and culturally 'different' from any other setting. As an organisation, each setting can work within existing structures or create new structures (i.e. leaders can change internal structures, e.g. introduce a model of distributed leadership). But for those who work within settings and as Greenfield and Ribbins (1993: 54), known for their work in the field of educational management and administration in Canada, stated, 'the self cannot escape organizations' (i.e. the ethos, systems in place and organisational structure of a setting will all impact on the people within it, who in turn influence and shape the organaisation, either directly or indirectly).

An early years setting will reflect its ethos (i.e. the way children are welcomed, the approach taken to teaching and learning, etc.). In contrast, the organisation of most of a setting will be similar to other settings (e.g. there will be a leader/leaders, teams and organised learning opportunities for children). Pugh and Hickson in *Writers on Organisations* (1989) collated a variety of definitions applied to the management of organisations, described by management gurus since the mid-1800s. Each focuses on the need to place individuals in the workplace within an identifiable structure. This applies to settings irrespective of cultural, social or community differences. There are generic responsibilities which apply to all settings/schools, from a small nursery, primary, secondary or special school to a large comprehensive school. It therefore follows that a framework for the organisation of settings can apply to all settings. Differentiation will occur in practice; in the 'real world' leaders will make choices as to how their settings will be organised. Each framework for practice can only function as a model interpreted by individuals as illustrated in the following example of 'What happens in practice?'.

WHAT HAPPENS IN PRACTICE?

School A is a primary school with 250 pupils on roll. In addition to the head, deputy head and appointed head of infants, all staff are given responsibility for one or, in certain cases, two subject areas.

The deputy head teacher sees teamwork as being very important to her role. She finds the job satisfying – 'being able to see the whole picture, the aims and being able to plan and work to achieve them'. The school provides a supportive environment for staff, where all staff are leaders, which gives people 'status and ownership' and staff are encouraged to make decisions. She considers the provision made by the school for CPD to be excellent, where training courses are available for middle managers (i.e. subject leaders, heads of lower school, etc.). She sees the new 'phenomenon of job shares' in primary schools as being difficult in practice.

REFLECT AND RELATE TO PRACTICE

What are the key factors in this school which contribute to and enable all staff to be 'leaders'? If you were a member of staff at this school, would these factors help you to be an effective leader? Why/why not? What other factors, if any, would you require to help you to be an effective leader in this school?

The setting as a whole

Early years settings are places where change is a constant. Rapid changes to the context and curriculum and the devolution of responsibilities have led to a shift in focus. By examining the changing focus of leadership in early years, this section will help you to reflect on what distributed leadership means in practice.

In an environment of change, a leader has to be adaptable. As illustrated in Table 19.1, the emphasis is on flexibility, sharing, collaboration and empowerment.

DISCUSSION POINT

In what ways do you think that the change in culture in early years settings, as indicated in Table 19.1, has contributed to the idea that every member of staff is a leader? Do you think it is a more positive culture in which to work? Why/why not? How does it contribute to improved teaching for learning?

You should consider a nursery setting for children of 6 months–2 years, a pre-school (3–5 year olds – within a primary school) and a primary school–reception class and Key Stage 1 (5–7 year olds).

Table 19.1 The changing culture of settings

From:	To:
fixed roles	flexible roles
individual responsibility	shared responsibility
autocratic	collaborative
control	release
power	empowerment

Source: Knutton and Ireson (1995) p. 61

It is worth reflecting on the following, which was highlighted by Ofsted (2008: 15) in their recent report as best practice in organisation, leadership and management in early years settings:

- children are at the heart of all that happens
- adults have a robust approach to keeping children safe
- providers further improve on already outstanding practice
- stimulating environments enable children to thrive safely
- records are used extremely well to support children.

In practice, leaders and their team are responsible for:

1 The day-to-day delivery of teaching, learning and the management of resources (planning and materials). Collaboration on clearly defined tasks, monitoring and evaluation (both of children's progress and any initiatives which are implemented).
2 Participation by representation in working groups set up by the senior leader to discuss specific tasks or directives from governing agencies or setting policy groups (e.g. the management of children with behavioural problems).

Divisions of responsibility within a setting are determined by the needs of the learners within the early years community. This is underpinned by government, LA and setting policies which will include:

- assessment and reporting procedures
- staff development
- curriculum
- learning and teaching styles
- support
- equal opportunities
- pastoral care.

A leader will be required to have knowledge and understanding of whole-setting issues as determined by the government, local authorities and governors. This will include the following broad areas (details of the legal requirements are available in EYFS, Section 3 – The Welfare Requirements; DfES, 2007):

- the provision of a safe learning environment which promotes children's well-being
- the employment of suitable people
- the support and training of staff
- the provision of suitable premises, equipment and environment (there is a legal requirement to carry out a risk assessment at least once a year)
- ensuring that each child is provided with a learning experience which is enjoyable and stimulating and meets their learning needs (in early years settings – 0–5 years – all children will be assigned to a **key person**)
- ensure that the necessary documentation is kept (children, staff and assessment, etc.)
- develop positive links with parents and external support agents.

Key person: the practitioner responsible for developing links with and forming a close relationship with a particular child and his/her family in an early years setting (0–5 years old).

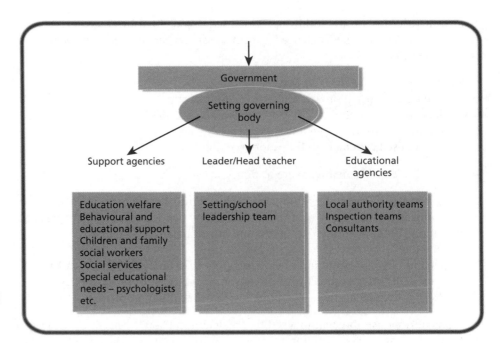

Figure 19.1
Setting/school
leadership –
agencies

Connect & Extend

Look up Section 3: The Welfare Requirements, of the EYFS (DfES, 2007; available from: **www.teachernet.gov.uk/publications**). Imagine that you are the leader of an early years setting for children aged 0–5 years, where there is one room for children less than 2 and one room for children 2 years and 5 years. Consider how you would put the welfare requirements in place. Consider the following: the learning space, resources, staff organisation, ratios, rotas, etc.

There will also be other agencies involved in the daily management of the setting, e.g. support groups, social services, education welfare and educational psychologists, inspection teams, and consultants. A leader should know who these agencies are and how frequently they visit, including those identified in Figure 19.1.

Leadership in practice

If the early years setting is to be effective, leaders need to adopt good practice. The National Commission on Education (NCE), established in 1991 as an independent government body to address educational requirements in light of social and economic changes, stated that effectiveness in educational settings involves:

> **leadership, ethos, high expectations of children and staff, positive teaching and learning styles, sound assessment procedures, recognition of children's participation in learning, parental involvement in the life of the school (or setting) and a programme of extracurricular activities.**
>
> *(NCE, 1996: 366)*

This is equally applicable to early years settings, where leaders will both lead and practise and will need to consider their practice commitment within the context of their leadership role. This is not merely an issue of time management, but also the compatibility of the roles. If a practitioner's values and beliefs are transferable to management practice, teaching and leadership may co-exist quite successfully. However, if leaders adopt values and beliefs which differ from their values and beliefs as a practitioner, this will be problematic. By considering the personal and managerial qualities needed by a leader, this section will help you to reflect on the characteristics needed for good leadership.

To know how to lead is an ongoing process. The development of the knowledge and understanding, skills and abilities required to lead others takes time. A leader is a reflective practitioner; a professional leader who evaluates his/her role. This is a two-way process; leaders knowing themselves and their team members, and the team knowing their leader. However, being a leader does not mean being 'all things to all people' (i.e. leaders cannot please all those who work within their team at all times). The issue for leaders, however, is to focus on the task 'in-hand', acknowledging that 'their team' is an important asset. Knowing what is required (i.e. the way leaders communicate with others, listen to the opinion of others and delegate responsibility, etc.) is the key in taking responsibility for:

- the implementation of setting/school-wide strategies, policies and aims
- being role models for staff
- the passing on of good practices.

An early years leader, with responsibility for teams which may include teaching and non-teaching staff, nursery nurses and other part-/full-time members of staff now connected with early years settings, will always have problems and dilemmas. Choices will need to be made and difficult people confronted. In a context where the teaching profession is reluctant to recognise failure, identifying colleagues as 'difficult' can itself be problematic. It is important to resolve difficulties as they arise. Courage, in measured doses, is required to deal with situations in a non-confrontational manner. How a leader approaches such situations often reflects their personal integrity (i.e. are they diplomatic in their approach, non-confrontational and keep the issue firmly in sight?). Personal integrity (honesty, reliability, trustworthiness, etc.) is very important, and Northouse underlined its centrality to leadership:

> **Leaders with integrity inspire confidence in others because they can be trusted to do what they say they are going to do. They are loyal, dependable, and not deceptive. Basically, integrity makes a leader believable and worthy of our trust.**
>
> *(2004: 20)*

Listening skills are critical in the management of others; leaders must listen and use information sensitively. Finally, persistence is a valuable tool. As a leader has many audiences in his/her role, it may be difficult to resolve dilemmas quickly. Persistence, without being overbearing, will produce outcomes; changes which will benefit both the leader and his/her team.

Effective team leadership will contribute much to the development of an effective team, able to create an effective learning environment. A leader will be concerned with the building blocks of teams. In essence, the way they communicate objectives and tasks and their ability to unite others in working towards 'shared' goals.

West Sussex Advisory and Inspection Service (1994) (an LA body established to help raise standards through partnerships with schools and family groups) provide a summary of the qualities required for effective leadership. Although based on a survey of middle leaders and their staff in schools during 1994, the human qualities so described are, as such, that they cross the barriers of time and place and are as applicable today to leaders across educational settings.

Personal qualities:

- Modelling professionalism, e.g. behaving with integrity, displaying consistency, being open and honest with colleagues, displaying firmness but fairness in their dealings with staff, hard working, committed, putting concern for students' well-being before personal advancement.
- Being well-organised and well-prepared.
- Being personable, approachable and accessible.
- Having a positive outlook and striving to act in a constructive manner, rather than being negative and overly critical.
- Manifesting confidence and calmness.
- Not standing on ceremony or taking advantage of their position; being prepared to help out or take their turn, if necessary.

Managerial qualities:

- Formulating a vision for the future development of their school based on personal philosophy, beliefs and values.
- Displaying the capacity to think and plan strategically.
- Displaying a consultative style of management, with the aim of building consensus and at the same time empowering others. Typically, determining overall direction and strategy, following wide consultation, and then handing over to staff to implement what has been agreed. Effectively delegating responsibility to other people, though following through and requiring accountability.
- Ensuring that effective whole-school structures are in place.
- Behaving forcefully yet not dictatorially. Having the ability to drive things along, yet at the same time displaying sensitivity to staff feelings, circumstances and well-being. Maintaining a good balance of pressure and support.
- Being prepared to embrace ultimate responsibility for the school and by manner and actions enabling staff to feel confident and secure.
- Displaying decisiveness when the situation demands.

- Paying attention to securing the support and commitment of colleagues and enjoying their trust. Actively shaping the ethos and culture of the school and fashioning a sense of community.
- Being adept at communicating, and being a good listener as well as keeping people informed.
- Being seen to act on information and views deriving from staff, so that consultation was seen to be a meaningful exercise.
- Emphasising the central importance of quality in the school's operations and encouraging colleagues to aim high, discouraging complacency.
- Ensuring that they keep abreast of new initiatives, though taking care not to be seen to be 'jumping on bandwagons'. Taking steps to prepare staff for future developments, thereby avoiding ad hoc decision-making and crisis management – though being sensitive to the risk of overwhelming colleagues with new practices.
- Revealing by their statements and actions that they are in touch with the main events in the everyday life of the school, and that they have their finger on the pulse of the school.
- Being proficient at motivating staff e.g., by providing encouragement or active support, by acknowledging particular endeavour.
- Being able to convey to colleagues that they have their concerns and well-being at heart, and behaving in such a way as to demonstrate this, e.g. facilitating their development as professionals.
- Protecting staff from political wrangling and backing them publicly in any dispute involving external agencies.

Source: West Sussex Advisory and Inspection Service (1994) cited in Blandford (2006), p. 22.

The local authority team also gathered evidence that determined ineffective leaders, and this is available on our **website**.

Earley and Evans (2003: 27), reporting on a government funded school leadership project, highlighted characteristics common to headteachers of very effectively led schools. These qualities are equally applicable in early years settings:

- problem solvers, 'solution driven' and highly visible during the school day
- develop strong senior management or leadership teams
- clear and high expectations of staff and students
- regard middle leaders as 'the experts', who enjoy professional efficacy as a result
- strong emphasis on continuing professional development
- effective mediators of change.

DISCUSSION POINT

In a group, discuss the qualities needed for and factors contributing to effective leadership. Plan a course in 'leadership in the early years'. It should cover the personal characteristics of an effective leader and general characteristics of effective leadership (to be delivered over a one-day programme) for staff (practitioners and would-be leaders) in an early years setting.

Leadership behaviour

In practice, the way leaders and their teams behave is dependent on numerous factors (including those intrinsic to the leader/team, e.g. personal qualities and extrinsic factors, e.g. relevant training) which influence individuals and impact on the lives of the people they contact. One important aspect of leadership is that of motivating those who work within your team. By examining various acknowledged models of motivation this section will consider how this might be effectively carried out in practice.

Motivation

Motivation: inspiring others to do/carry out and to want do/carry out what is required or needed.

Social model of leadership: people are motivated by social needs, friendship and acceptance.

Rational-economic model of leadership: people act to maximise their financial and material rewards, performing specialised tasks for high rewards.

Self-actualising model of leadership: people are self-motivated and self-controlled and integrate their goals with those of the organisation.

Motivation (i.e. inspiring others to do/carry out and to want to do/carry out what is required or needed) is central to good leadership. Effective leaders involve all practitioners and staff within their setting in influencing the quality of learning, teaching and achievement. Leaders should have knowledge and understanding of how to provide staff with meaningful work. Leaders should have little difficulty in identifying the teaching and learning elements which colleagues find satisfying and rewarding. Identification of motivational factors beyond the setting might be more challenging, involving managerial skills and abilities (e.g. are some practitioners motivated within the setting by outside interests – music, drama, family or money?). In brief, several models of 'motivation' exist which can be summarised as follows (from *Writers on Organisations*, Pugh and Hickson, 1989).

The social model (Mayo, 1933):

- People are motivated by social needs, friendship and acceptance; their basic sense of identity is formed through relationships with other people.
- People are responsive to peer group pressure.
- People are responsive to management if management meets their needs (belonging etc.).

The rational-economic model (Taylor, 1947):

- People act to maximise their financial and material rewards.
- People will perform specialised tasks for high rewards.

Self-actualising model (Maslow, 1943):

- Hierarchical needs – i.e. to progress to a higher position within their organisation.
- People work to develop skills.
- People are self-motivated and self-controlled.
- People will integrate their goals with those of the organisation.

Maslow (1943), the American psychologist renowned for his 'hierarchy of needs' theory, provides an introduction to the analysis of human behaviour. Maslow suggested that there are five levels of need that influence an individual's behaviour:

- physiological needs: food, drink and shelter
- safety needs: protection against danger, threat and deprivation

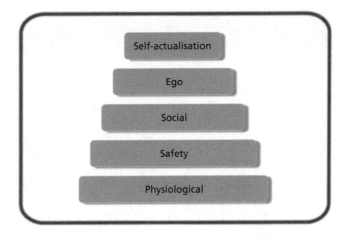

Figure 19.2
Maslow's
hierarchy
of needs

Source: Maslow
(1943)

- social needs: to associate, have relationships, affection, belonging
- ego needs: self-esteem, reputation, status
- self-actualisation: the need for realising one's own potential for continual self-development.

According to Maslow, the needs hierarchy means that the lower-order needs have to be satisfied before the other needs become paramount. In behavioural terms these determine the needs that motivate individuals (see Figure 19.2).

Essentially early years practitioners and leaders have needs, as Maslow (1943) stated: 'A musician must make music, an artist must paint, a poet must write, if he is to be ultimately happy. . . . This need we may call self-actualisation'. In theory, when these needs are satisfied the individual will be happy and motivated in their work.

REFLECT AND RELATE TO PRACTICE

What are the advantages and disadvantages of each of the models presented above? Why is it both relevant and important for leaders in an early years setting to understand what motivates their team? How would you motivate your team within an early years setting?

☆ ☆ ☆

Imagine you are a leader in an early years setting. A member of your team is demotivated. This person feels that they have a heavy workload – planning, teaching, observing, assessing and talking to parents. Not only are they tired, they also feel that they have little personal autonomy to decide what to implement and how to implement it. In addition, they feel that they have had little relevant continuing professional development. What would you consider and/or implement to enhance their motivation? You will find it helpful to refer to the models of motivational factors.

Table 19.2

Accountable to	Accountable for
Children	Attendance, activities, listening and learning
Parents	Reporting, consultation and safeguarding children, listening and learning
Colleagues	Teaching, management of staff and situations, listening and learning
Leadership teams	Participation and delegation, team effectiveness, listening and learning
Governors	Results – league tables, listening and learning
Government	Ofsted – league tables

Source: Blandford (2006) p. 15

Management accountability

Education reflects society and as society becomes increasingly more complex, education leaders encounter many new (and challenging) values and expectations. In early years, this is reflected in the day-to-day leadership and management of the setting, where leaders are becoming more accountable for the outcomes. By providing a brief overview of the areas within settings where leaders are accountable for what happens in practice, this section will consider **accountability** (taking responsibility for actions and results/outcomes) in practice. As their environment changes, practitioners and leaders of learning teams are increasingly accountable for their actions, as shown in Table 19.2.

Accountability: taking responsibility for actions and results/outcomes.

Leadership should understand and use accountability in a positive manner. In essence, this means not viewing criticism or shortfalls within a negative frame; to listen and learn is a skill. It should be seen as an opportunity for improvement; a time to reappraise what could be done better or how things can go from unacceptable/acceptable/good to excellent. There is little to be gained from viewing the tools of accountability with fear and anxiety.

How to lead and manage: bringing it together

The development of early years leaders underpins the government's drive to improve outcomes for all children. Effective leadership is an art which can be developed. Leaders/would-be leaders learn to lead and develop a style appropriate to their personal characteristics and adapted to the context in which they operate. In essence the skills required for effective leadership can be developed and enhanced by working within a framework for good practice. Before completing this journey through leadership from the theoretical to the practical it is worth reflecting on the following characteristics of good leadership:

- A good leader recognises and acts upon relevant information; listen and learn.
- A good leader develops a style of leadership appropriate to the individual and the task.
- An effective leader is forceful not dictatorial, decisive when necessary, driving things along, while remaining sensitive to team members, keeping abreast of initiatives and preparing the team for future developments. In addition he/she secures the commitment and trust of the team.
- A good leader recognises those tasks which can be delegated.
- A good leader motivates the team by identifying the areas which individuals find satisfying and rewarding, and provides individuals with meaningful work.
- Focus on staff development to enhance practice and to inform personal career progression.

DISCUSSION POINT

'There is no "one size fits all" model of leadership.'
  What does this statement mean to you?
  What factors and human qualities might contribute to effective leadership in an early years setting? How could you develop these factors and qualities (a) for/in yourself and (b) for your staff/team?

SUMMARY

What is leadership? (p. 410)

How would you define leadership?

There are many definitions of leadership. Theorists define leaders as those within an organisation with power and influence. In practice, however, leadership has many aspects (e.g. the personal characteristics of the people within the team, the situation 'in-hand' – where leadership approach can change on a day-to day basis) and no one model fits all situations.

The early years: distributed leadership (p. 412)

Why do you think distributed leadership is emerging as the preferred model in early years settings?

Distributed leadership is emerging as the preferred model within early years settings. It is characterised by shared decision-making and delegated responsibility.

Leadership style (p. 414)

Why is leadership style important?

How leaders do things, or get others to do things, will be dependent on their own leadership style. However, leadership styles will differ according to the task in hand, the character, views and attitudes of team members and most importantly acting in the best interests of each child.

Framework for practice (p. 416)

What issues would you consider when developing a framework for practice?

Each setting will develop as an individual community, different from any other community and influenced by the leaders and the practitioners who work within it. However, there are features, primarily organisational features, of leadership and leading communities, which will be common to all settings.

The setting as a whole (p. 418)

How has the leadership culture of early years settings changed?

A leader will be required to have knowledge and understanding of whole-setting issues as determined by the government, local authorities and governors. However, the culture of early years settings is changing, and leaders have to be adaptable; the emphasis is on flexibility, sharing, collaboration and empowerment.

Leadership in practice (p. 420)

To know how to lead is an ongoing process. A leader is a reflective practitioner; a professional leader who evaluates his/her role. This is a two-way process; leaders knowing themselves and their team members, and the team knowing their leader. However, being a leader does not mean being 'all things to all people' (i.e. leaders cannot please all those who work within their team at all times). The issue, however, is to focus on the task 'in hand', acknowledging that 'the team' is an important asset.

Leadership behaviour (p. 424)

How would you motivate your early years team?

Human motivation is central to the leadership of staff. There are several theories – *the social model* (Mayo, 1933), *the rational-economic model* (Taylor, 1947) and the *self-actualising model* (Maslow, 1943) – which focus on analysis of needs. In order to achieve goals with and through team members, a leader should have an understanding of what motivates his/her team.

Management accountability (p. 426)

What is management accountability?

Leaders are accountable to a number of people and agencies within their circle (children, parents, colleagues, leadership teams, governors and government). Accountability should be viewed as an opportunity for improvement; a time to reappraise what could be done better or how things can go from unacceptable/ acceptable/good to excellent.

Glossary

Accountability: taking responsibility for actions and results/outcomes.

Distributed leadership: a collegial approach, where team members share in the decision-making and take responsibility for certain tasks.

Key person: a member of staff assigned to a particular child who is responsible for welcoming him/her each day, observing the child on a formal basis and spending some time working with him/her to support his/her learning.

Leadership: the achievement of objectives through people, where leaders are those with power and influence.

Management: sustaining an existing code of practice, with limited authority to change the 'direction' of an organisation.

Motivation: inspiring others to do/carry out and to want do/carry out what is required or needed.

Rational-economic model of leadership (Taylor, 1947): people act to maximise their financial and material rewards, where people perform specialised tasks for high rewards.

Self-actualising model of leadership (Maslow, 1943): people are self-motivated and self-controlled and integrate their goals with those of the organisation.

Social model of leadership (Mayo, 1933): people are motivated by social needs, friendship and acceptance, where their basic sense of identity is formed through relationships with other people.

Find out more

Sadek, E. and Sadek, J. (2004) *Good Practice in Nursery Management*, **2nd edn, Cheltenham: Nelson Thornes.**
Chapter 1, The role of the Manager in Early Years Provision, provides a good insight into the central role of and the development of relationships with parents, children and support agencies – primarily through the manager.

Department for Education and Skills (DfES) (2003) *National standards for under 8's day care and childminding*, **Nottingham: DfES.**
By considering the 14 standards needed in the provision of full day care, this government document will help

you to further consider leadership in practice. Available from: **www.dcsf.gov.uk**.

Busher, H. (2006) *Understanding Educational Leadership: People, Power and Culture*, **Maidenhead: Open University.**
This book provides an overview of leadership in educational settings and provides a good insight into the role of collaborative practice. You will find it useful for supplementing your knowledge on the idea of distributed leadership and how you might develop it in practice.

References

Bennis, W. (1959) *Leadership Theory Administrative Behaviour: The Problem of Authority*, Administrative Science Centre, 22–23 April, University of Pittsburgh.

Bennis, W. (2003) Leading managers to adapt and grow, in Brown, T. and Heller, R. (eds) *Best Practice: Ideas and Insights From the World's Foremost Business Thinkers*. London: Bloomsbury.

Blandford, S. (2006) *Middle Leadership in Schools: Harmonising Leadership and Learning*. Harlow: Pearson.

Brown, T. and Heller, R. (eds) *Best Practice: Ideas and Insights From the World's Foremost Business Thinkers*. London: Bloomsbury.

Department for Education and Skills (DfES) (2007) *Statutory Framework for the Early Years Foundation Stage: Setting the Standards for Learning Development and Care for children from birth to five* (EYFS). Nottingham: DfES Publications.

Earley, P. and Evans, J. (2003) Leading and managing schools: a comparison between independent and state school leaders, *Management in Education*, Vol. 17, No. 1: pp. 24–28.

Fidler, B. (2002) *Strategic Management for School Development*. London: Paul Chapman.

Follari, L. (2007) *Foundations and best practices in early childhood education: histories, theories, and approaches to learning*. New Jersey: Pearson/Merrill Prentice Hall.

Greenfield, T. and Ribbins, P. (1993) *Greenfield on educational administration: Towards a humane science*. London: Routledge.

Harrison, B.T. (1995) Revaluing leadership and service in educational management, in Bell, J. and Harrison, B.T. (eds) *Vision and Values in Managing Education*. London: David Fulton.

Harvey-Jones, J. (2003) *Making it Happen: Reflections on Leadership*. London: Profile Books.

Knutton, S. and Ireson, G. (1995) Leading the team – managing staff development in the primary school, in Bell, J. and Harrison, B.T. (eds) *Vision and Values in Managing Education*. London: David Fulton.

Maslow, A.H. (1943) A Theory of Human Motivation, *Psychological Review*, Vol. 50, No. 4: pp. 370–396.

Mayo, E. (1933) *The Human Problems of an Individual Civilisation*. London: Macmillan.

National Commission on Education (NCE) (1996) *Success Against the Odds*. London: Routledge.

Northouse, P. (2004) *Leadership: Theory and Practice*. Thousand Oaks, CA: Sage.

Ofsted (2008) *Early Years Leading to Excellence*. London: Ofsted.

Peters, T. and Waterman, R. (2004) *In Search of Excellence: Lessons from America's Best-run companies*. London: Profile Books.

Pugh, D.S. and Hickson, D.J. (1989) *Writers on Organisations*, 4th edn. Harmondsworth: Penguin.

Rodd, J. (2006) *Leadership in Early Childhood*. Maidenhead: Open University Press.

Sergiovanni, T. (2007) *Rethinking Leadership: a collection of articles*. Thousand Oaks, CA: Sage.

Tannenbaum, R. and Schmidt, W.H. (1973) How to choose a leadership pattern, *Harvard Business Review*, Vol. 36, No. 2: pp. 95–101.

Taylor, F.W. (1947) *Scientific Management*. London: Harper and Row.

University of Western Ontario (2008) *Biography of Warren Bennis (1925–)*, available at: **http://www.lib.uwo.calprograms/generalbusiness/WarrenBennis.html**.

West, L. and Carison, A. (2007) *Claiming Space: An In-depth auto/biographical study of a local Sure Start project*. Centre for International Studies of Diversity.

West Sussex Advisory and Inspection Service (1994) *Head of Department as a Leader and Manager*. Sussex: West Sussex County Council.

By the end of this chapter you will be able to answer the following questions:

- What is meant by change in the early years sector?
- Why are leadership styles central to the effective implementation of change?
- How is change managed within a collaborative framework?
- What factors influence change?
- What strategies can be used to implement change effectively?
- What factors need to be considered when establishing an effective means of monitoring a specific change?

This chapter will support your understanding of the following Standards *(see Appendix 1):*
■ **Knowledge and understanding:** S03 ■ **Communicating and working in partnership with families and carers:** S29, S30, S31 and S32 ■ **Teamwork and collaboration:** S33 and S35
■ **Professional development:** S39.

Introduction

The childcare worker must become two tactically different workers – (1) with the children: conserving routines, developing systems and creating stability; and (2) with the organisation: introducing computers, accepting new forms of inspection, record keeping, training students, changing systems, changing their expenditure patterns and in, some cases, even changing their employers following take-overs.

(Sadek and Sadek, 2004: 65)

Since the introduction of the National Childcare Strategy (1998) (see Chapter 1), there has been an unprecedented rate of change in the provision of early years services. As Elizabeth and Jacqueline Sadek (2004), best known for their work nursery management in practice, highlight above, change puts great demands on practitioners. Although the changes have been largely positive, many practitioners within the field are still adjusting to new ways of working and new ways of thinking. This is to be expected and should be acknowledged by those leading change within early years settings; change is an important and complex process which can be unsettling, threatening and unpredictable but at the same time provides opportunity for creativity and learning. Effective early years leaders acknowledge the centrality of children's wellbeing, learning, development and achievement in implementing programmes of change within their setting. Change within educational settings has one overriding aim, that of improving outcomes for all children. Change should always have the best interests of the child as its focus and should be led and managed in a way which causes little or no disruption to the child's immediate learning environment. Sadek and Sadek (2004: 65) support this and emphasise that 'the children, their routines and the patterns of their lives, as far as the centre is concerned, should remain stable on a daily basis'. By addressing the reasons for change, factors influencing change, the implementation of change and the analysis, monitoring, evaluation and review of change, this chapter will consider how leadership approaches to change influence its effective implementation.

ACTIVITY

Before reading this chapter reflect on how Sadek and Sadek (2004) describe the impact of change on the role of the early years practitioner at the start. Do you think change has brought greater division in the role of the early years practitioner? Why/why not?

It is worth considering the impact of government policy on practice as outlined in Chapter 1 – you can review your thoughts at the end of this chapter.

Change in early years: what does it mean?

Change means different things to different people depending where they are placed in relationship to the change. Rita Cheminais (2006: 88), a senior adviser on Special Educational Needs (SEN) with Cheshire Local Authority, who has written widely on SEN and Inclusion, describes change as a 'process rather than a single event, where the aim is to improve practice, introduce new policies and functions, in addition to altering the "status quo"'. It provides an opportunity to say how we might work more effectively with the child as the focus; effective practice in early years settings is founded on the development of strong, trusting, interactive and supportive relationships with children. By examining some of the changes impacting on early years education, this section will consider what those working in the field can expect in practice.

This time of change provides the challenge and opportunity for early years settings to set their own agenda. Harris and Muijs (2005: 37) (Alma Harris, Professor of Education at Warwick University is renowned for her work on school leadership and Daniel Muijs of Exeter University is well known in the field of educational effectiveness – teaching, leadership, etc.) suggest that the 'success' of change is related to the extent to which an educational organisation builds 'capacity for change and development'. Although they define this clearly as that which 'is concerned with creating the conditions, opportunities and experiences for development and mutual learning', Michael Fullan (2005), Emeritus Professor of the Ontario Institute for Studies in Education of the University of Toronto and expert on organisational change, warns against accepting **capacity building** on a theoretical level alone. He emphatically states that 'it is not just workshops and professional development for all. It is the daily habit of "working together" . . . You need to learn it by doing it and having mechanisms for getting better at it on purpose' (2005: 69).

Given the scope of the change in education, the process will also include the wider local community. The network of support includes Local Authorities, private (e.g. local business sponsorship) and voluntary (local charities) sector organisations and other government bodies (e.g. Sure Start). In addition, settings can build on exisiting links with other local settings (e.g. to share expertise, resources, etc.). The government's vision for change across the educational system is far reaching and reflects a move away from education within the learning organisation to education within the professional learning **community of practice** (Wenger, 1998) (Etienne Wenger, the first to coin the phrase 'community of practice', is an internationally acknowledged expert on the subject and how institutions – schools, businesses etc. – can apply it in practice; see Chapter 12). In essence, communities of practice are characterised by social participation – the building of relationships (practitioner–child, child–child and parent–practitioner) through shared practice with common aims. Harris and Muijs (2005: 48), citing Thomas Sergiovanni (2000: 139), Professor of Education at Trinity University, San Antonio, USA and known for his work on leadership in schools, suggest that developing a 'community of practice' may be at the foundation of setting improvement. In his more recent work, Sergiovanni (2007: 117) suggests that in 'communities of practice', leadership is a 'practice' which operates at 'community' level, where 'knowledge is used and exchanged to achieve goals' and the 'roles or positions'

Capacity building: the provision of training or experience within a culture which encourages and promotes opportunity for learning and development.

Communities of practice: in essence, characterised by social participation – the building of relationships through shared practice with common aims.

of those involved is not so important. In essence, this implies a more collaborative approach to leadership, where ideas are shared and responsibilities are delegated; an approach which is beginning to emerge as the preferred model of leadership within early years settings (Rodd, 2006) (Jillian Rodd, an education and developmental psychologist at the University of Plymouth, UK, is also known for her work on young children's behaviour). In an early years 'community of practice', practitioners engaging with the change process can expect the following:

Personalised learning: the adaptation of teaching and the curriculum to meet the learning needs of the individual child.

Collegial approach: people working together as a team, sharing ideas, making decisions and deciding together how to implement the decisions made.

- teaching for learning within a **personalised learning** framework (i.e. a greater focus on teaching to the learning needs of the child, which is underpinned by the child's emotional well-being and development)
- **collegial approach** to decision-making (i.e. practitioners share ideas and together makes decisions which influence practice)
- staff have greater 'ownership' of their tasks and activities (i.e. effective leaders, through the more collaborative approach which is developing within early years communities of practice, delegate responsibility to practitioners)
- managing change is the norm for early years leaders/practitioners
- sharing of good practice with other early years practitioners (i.e. through monthly or bi-monthly meetings with practitioners in other local settings)
- enhanced Continuing Professional Development (CPD) (i.e. leader awareness of the importance of promoting and supporting practitioner personal professional development)
- an acceptable work/life balance (e.g. if a leader knows that a practitioner has a worrying problem at home, it might not be an appropriate time to give the individual extra responsibilities at work)
- staff more involved in policy and systems development (e.g. practitioners work together to develop setting policy)
- increasing partnership with parents/guardians (i.e. practitioners work together to consider and implement ways of involving parents and guardians in the education and care of their children).

Change of this type will impact upon the early years community as a whole. The positive outcomes might include raising achievement, improved partnerships with those involved (i.e. practitioners, children, parents and between professionals within the new multi-agency framework), increased interest and/or motivation of staff and children and improved learner social skills and behaviour.

DISCUSSION POINT

The new framework for practice, presented through government policy and summarised within this section, highlights the greater focus on the development of relationships. Why do you think this is important for early years practice? For each change mentioned within this section, consider if and how it relates to or encourages the development of relationships, either child–practitioner, practitioner–practitioner, practitioner–child, etc.

Leaders and change

Undoubtedly early years practitioners would agree that change of the type discussed in the previous section is to be encouraged and promoted. However, in practice, it is largely dependent on the personal qualities of the leader and his/her ability to develop a collegial approach to leadership, enabling his/her team members to accommodate change. This should be a collaborative process involving innovation, implementation and adoption. The real problem is how to manage change effectively. In practice, change within a setting is a mixture of and will be influenced by top-down, bottom-up and expert initiatives or factors. This section will define these initiatives and consider how they both initiate and influence change in practice.

Top-down

Someone in a position of authority introduces change. This scenario involves a clear statement by the decision-maker(s), followed by action and dissemination. In early years settings **top-down** initiatives will include the implementation of new: curriculum, health and safety procedures, recording and assessment procedures, procedures relating to the safeguarding and well-being of children, policy relating to multi-agency working, funding and change decided by the leader within the setting. Leadership, collaboration and a willingness to take (not make) decisions will make the difference between poor and excellent practice. A top-down model will allow changes to be made quickly, efficiently and with authority.

> **'Top-down' change:** change introduced by someone in a position of authority.

Bottom-up

A consequence of collaborative management is a **bottom-up** approach to the management of change. Within early years settings, change has the potential to be bottom-up and might be the result of a member of staff leaving, unrest between staff or parents asking for a particular change. This approach involves teams and will therefore concern leader practitioners when:

> **'Bottom-up' change:** change initiated by people, happenings or issues within the setting.

- there is a need to address a problem which remains unclear to those not involved
- a specific solution is required.

A disadvantage of this approach is that the need for consultation and agreement is time consuming to plan and implement. Many phases of the change within early years will require the involvement of all staff.

> **'Expert' change:** change brought about by someone with expertise within the field.

Expert

A leader may approach an expert if unsure how to tackle an issue. The **expert** could be a colleague or external agent. The expert approach may offer a quick and cost-effective means of bringing about change but could mean a loss of influence and control.

In practice, leadership within early years settings will be influenced by all these factors. Leaders, however, who take a broad view when managing issues which bring about change, can achieve the best possible outcomes within their 'community of practice'. When faced with specific changes they need to consider for each one:

- Who are the main players involved – staff, children, parents, external agents?
- Who will be responsible for making it happen?
- Who will manage the change process – early years leader practioner, colleagues, external agents?
- How will the change be evaluated – time-scale, questions?

The following example of 'What happens in practice?' considers a situation in a nursery school which could be a cause for change:

WHAT HAPPENS IN PRACTICE?

In a nursery attached to a primary school the staff were committed to the involvement of parents/careers. . . . Each year they had a successful Autumn Fayre, where money was raised for school funds. Each Thursday afternoon was 'open house' where parent/carers were welcome to pop in, for a few minutes or for the whole session, to their children's nursery. There was a rota when parents/careers volunteered to come to nursery to work alongside staff and children and there were always parents willing to accompany children on the various school trips which took place throughout the year . . . However, over the years it was clear that, although there was a group of dedicated parents/carers who were involved with the school, despite numerous initiatives, new parents/carers were simply not becoming involved in the life of the school.

Some years later it was discovered that the groups of parents/carers who were involved did all in their power to maintain their exclusivity and actually discouraged other parents/carers from becoming involved in the school. They fiercely guarded their relationship with the staff and ensured that no parents/carers from outside their group were allowed entry. The staff were oblivious to this state of affairs and as they became increasingly reliant on the group of involved parents/carers (because there were no alternatives) so the power and status of this group was enhanced. Thus the situation self-perpetuated.

(Keating, 2002: 24–25)

REFLECT AND RELATE TO PRACTICE

What issue in the above example of 'What happens in practice?' might prompt change in this nursery? Is this an example of top-down, bottom-up or expert change? Why? Considering the relationship with the parents, list the ways this nursery had involved the parents in their children's learning. Do you think the practitioners in this nursery had developed good relationships with the parents? Why/why not?

Consider those parents involved and those not involved.

 ☆ ☆ ☆

What would you do to change this situation/division which had arisen with the parents whose children attended this nursery?

You need to consider all the children within the nursery, that the parents who help might be needed, that practitioners undoubtedly had good relationships with the parents who were involved and other issues you consider to be relevant.

Analysis of change

As has been discussed in the previous section, change is a result of bottom-up, top-down and expert initiatives. However, within these areas there are various factors which will impact on the change process. This section will consider these factors, including staff resistance, and consider how analysis of change from the outset can bring about its effective implementation. Table 20.1 shows the possible factors which can bring about change.

When considering how to implement change brought about by one or more of the factors outlined in Table 20.1, leader practitioners will need to reflect on their own attitude towards change. This will influence their team. Generally people who have a sense of commitment and are in charge of their lives will see change as an opportunity. Those who are uncomfortable with their role will view change negatively. Every setting will have a combination of people who view change on a continuum from threat to opportunity! There may be individuals who will not be threatened by the change, but will feel threatened by the change process. Oldroyd and Hall (1990) identified factors within educational settings where staff response to change was poor; this is as applicable today as it was 18 years ago. These factors, highlighted below, should be taken into consideration by early years leaders when trying to implement effective change:

- morale is low
- change agents are not respected
- there is a track record of failed innovation
- risk-taking is discouraged
- leaders are inflexible in their attitudes
- there is little outside support . . .

. . . staff will be less motivated to support change strategies which:

Table 20.1 Factors influencing change

Factor	Result
Technical	Change in process or use of equipment, e.g. management procedures or computers
Social	Changes to beliefs and values, creation of a group, e.g. an issue-specific team
Power	Changes in political leadership at a macro and micro level, e.g. political party, head of setting
Financial	Change in funding mechanism, e.g. availability of resources
Personnel	Change in status, family or own, e.g. marriage, divorce, children
Physical	Change in setting site, e.g. condition of buildings, available facilities

- are unaccompanied by practical training and support . . .
- do not adapt to developing circumstances
- do not recognise local needs
- offer no sense of collective 'ownership'
- do not build a 'critical mass' for change.

Neither will they commit themselves to innovations which:

- are not seen as beneficial
- cannot be clearly understood
- are at odds with their professional beliefs
- are inadequately resourced.

People will resist change, especially if it is someone else's change that has been forced upon them. Resistance to change can be a major restraining force that can be overcome with understanding. Change may incur resistance due to self-interest, misunderstanding, different assessments of the situation, or, as stated, a low tolerance for change. Common responses to change are disagreement, excuses, rumour and/or 'political' behaviour. However, in many situations resistance to change can be minimised, if not eradicated. In any organisation, but most especially in educational settings, where the work endeavour is focused on the children, it is important to remember that practitioners/leader practitioners are all part of the same team and that good working relationships between people matter. The following provides a checklist for leader practitioners of issues and areas which should be carefully considered in theory and how they might be deployed in practice, prior to addressing change with colleagues; they can help to minimise resistance:

- The range of tasks and activities for the setting workforce should be determined by all staff.

- The setting workforce should be engaged according to setting needs and priorities.
- Training and resources are essential for effective change.
- All relevant government initiatives should be carefully considered – what do they mean in practice?
- LA initiatives/support can assist with the implementation of change.
- Professional development for managing the workforce is required.

Analysing the change process as discussed within this section (i.e. the change, the reason for change, how staff may respond and how it will be implemented) at the outset and during the process (you may need to re-evaluate the chosen strategy if there is resistance or it is simply not working) can have a big impact on bringing about the desired change.

Choosing a change strategy

Leader practitioners need to give careful consideration to the most effective and efficient way of bringing about the desired outcomes of change. In a 'community of practice' the development of positive relationships is of paramount importance. In what can be a hostile climate to change, leader practitioners need to ensure that change does not in any way, negatively impact on the children, the practitioners, the parents and other individuals or agencies involved within the setting. By examining the various strategies which can be employed to implement change, this section will consider how change can be implemented and managed in a way which both supports and enhances the development of positive relationships between those involved.

Sadek and Sadek (2004) offer the following mnemonic for the effective management of change:

CREAM:

- **C** – Communication systems and consultation systems must work effectively in the organization
- **R** – Responsibilities and duties of all staff must be understood by all personnel
- **E** – Effects must be monitored
- **A** – Aims and purposes of change – and the possible effects on the children – must be known and understood and considered seriously
- **M** – Morale must be maintained in the team (and consequently in the nursery).

(Sadek and Sadek, 2004: 66)

Action research: involves the identification of a practical problem/issue which is changed through individual or collaborative action, then researched.

In choosing a strategy for change their mnemonic can provide a framework for practice. Keep it in mind when considering the following strategies for implementing change:

- *Directed*: imposing change by management, top-down, hierarchical
- *Negotiated*: concedes everyone's wishes
- *Action-centred*: as a consequence of **action research** (see Implementing change section).

- In order to choose an effective change strategy the setting leader practitioner will need to:
  - identify the level of complexity and time needed (e.g. is it introducing a new curriculum or a more simple change in reporting procedure?)
  - identify any resistance from staff and analyse how to overcome it effectively
  - select the method of overcoming resistance (e.g. adopt a collegial approach to change)
  - take account of their own attitude towards the change (e.g. do you have a positive and persevering attitude to change?).
- The choice of strategy adopted will be dependent on:
  - the pace of change
  - level of resistance
  - level of status of the initiator
  - amount of information required
  - key players
  - time available.

Early years settings, as organisations, should not ignore these factors. A common mistake is to move too quickly and involve too few people. Forcing change will have too many negative side-effects. Equally, knowing and understanding change strategies will only go part-way to aiding/facilitating the change process. A leader can improve his/her chances of success by:

- analysis: current situation; problems; possible causes of problems
- evaluation: factors relevant to producing changes
- selection: change strategy
- monitoring: implementation.

As with all aspects of leadership, interpersonal skills (i.e. your ability to communicate effectively with others – how, when and with whom?) are critical to the successful and effective management of change.

Connect & Extend

Imagine you are given responsibility, within a team, to develop and implement the *Statutory Framework for the Early Years Foundation Stage: Setting the Standards for Learning Development and Care for children from birth to five* (EYFS) (DfES, 2007) as part of the 'pre-school' (3–5 year olds). How would you do this?

Consider how you would develop a collaborative approach, who would teach what, when and for how long, who would be responsible for resources, how children's progress would be monitored, how often observations would be carried out, who would do the planning for the curriculum, assessment and other issues you consider to be relevant. You will also find Rodger (2003) useful for this exercise (see references).

DISCUSSION POINT

You have just started working as a practitioner in a State funded nursery. A number of children have speech and language problems and/or behaviour problems. You notice that although some parents seem to be involved in their children's learning at the nursery, the majority are not. You do not know why and would like parents to be more involved. How would you bring about this change?

Plan from the outset to the desired outcome – a step-by-step approach to each stage works well. You also need to consider the reasons why parents might not be involved and refer to Standards S29, S30, S31 and S32.

Implementing change

Settings, as organisations, have the necessary structures (i.e. staffing – who reports to whom; administrative – record keeping, etc.) and tools (staff, support agencies, resources, government policy and training, etc.) to successfully implement change. This section will give a brief overview of how the tools, within the various structures, can be used to implement change.

Action research

Action research may provide an appropriate way forward for managing change in an educational setting. Action research involves the identification of a practical problem/issue which is changed through individual or collaborative action intervention, then researched. The problems may not be clearly defined and the change process may evolve through practice. As a mechanism for change, action research contains two key elements: collaboration and evaluation. By involvement, the team will try out a number of approaches to the problem and will learn from each; this will take time.

Training

Settings can achieve change through a programme of education and training. An education and communication programme can inform and provide a platform for analysis in which resistors can engage in debate surrounding the implementation of change. This approach will require a lot of time and effort if it is to be effective. Early years leader practitioners can (and should) play an active role in the planning of such programmes if they are to be relevant to practice.

Participation and involvement

Leaders should encourage participation in the development and implementation process. Through participation, resistors become informed and are able to contribute to the outcome of change. The participation process can be difficult and time consuming. When change is required immediately, it may not be possible!

Support

Another means of dealing with potential resistance to change is to be supportive through training, listening and providing time during busy periods. Support is most effective when fear and anxiety lie at the heart of resistance. Again, this can be time consuming and does not always produce positive results.

Negotiation

A leader practitioner will need to be a skilled negotiator. All but major resistance can be costly and is therefore best avoided; negotiation can be a relatively easy way to avoid major resistance. However, leaders must be sure of the parameters in which they are working to avoid a negative outcome.

Co-option

A form of manipulation is co-option, inviting resistors to join as change agents. Often the change will occur without the individual noticing. This will be difficult to maintain in the long term as people do not enjoy being manipulated.

Coercion

This is a risky process, as inevitably people will become resentful and the costs are high.

Successful approaches to change will often involve a combination of the above. Leaders will require the knowledge and understanding, skills and ability to approach change appropriately and effectively.

Photo 20.1
Should all staff members be involved in developing and implementing new strategies and processes?

Pearson Education Ltd. Ian Wedgewood © Pearson Education Ltd. 2007

DISCUSSION POINT

National Remodelling Team (NRT) Approach to Change (2003)

The National Remodelling Team (absorbed into the TDA in March 2006) promoted a change process, to help schools with remodelling, based on the techniques and experience gained in business and education. The following extract (NRT website **http://www.remodelling.org/**), adapted for the purposes of managing change in early years settings, outlines the NRT stages for the remodelling process as adapted from business models. Early years leader practitioners can use this outline to help identify and agree where change is necessary, facilitate a vision of the future which is shared across whole-setting communities and create plans for change in an atmosphere of serious consensus. It is important to remember that change can take a number of different forms, but always with the aim of producing unique outcomes.

The Mobilise Stage – Settings recognise the need for change. Representatives from the setting can seek guidance from the LA and/or attend any relevant training events organised. Key to the success of change in the early years is that the nature, scope and goals of the change process are effectively communicated to the whole-setting community.

The Discover Stage – Once the setting has been mobilised the change process begins to focus on uncovering the issues around workload and other setting priorities. The Discover stage involves identifying and acknowledging what works well within the setting as well as recognising issues and challenges which the change process should aim to address. This often involves holding workshops with staff members to discover why some elements of setting practice are more successful than others. Throughout the change process, it is important that there are good channels of communication within and between team members.

The Deepen Stage – When the team acquires a greater understanding of the scale and scope of the change issues, tools and techniques can be employed to help identify the root causes of issues and understand which staff members are most affected.

The Develop Stage – The team uses problem-solving techniques to develop strategies and solutions to address the issues identified at previous stages. Although learning from other settings can be of vital assistance, the change process envisaged by the government allows settings to develop plans which are 'made-to-measure', and which will be effective and sustainable.

▶

The Deliver Stage – When plans are confirmed and start to be implemented. It is essential that there is a continuing review process which ensures that as change happens it meets the original goals identified at earlier stages and moves the setting towards the shared vision of the future. There may be a need for solutions to be modified as they are put into practice.

REFLECT AND RELATE TO PRACTICE

Summarise what a leader practitioner would do at each stage in the change process.

☆ ☆ ☆

Government policy promotes the use of computers for teaching and learning in educational settings. Imagine, as a leader practitioner in a nursery setting, you have to introduce the use of computers for teaching, learning, administration, etc. Where possible you want your colleagues to use computers. You know there will be resistance amongst staff to this change. Using the stages proposed by the NRT approach to change, how would you implement this in practice?

Monitoring, evaluation and review

Once change has been implemented, it needs to be monitored, evaluated and reviewed; you will want to know if it is working and if not, why not and are things better than they were before the change was implemented? It is often difficult to test the outcome of change against the original objectives. There are often unintended outcomes, and defining criteria for success is problematic. If the objectives have been carefully constructed, evaluation should be possible. As change agents, leader practitioners will set objectives which can be measured after the change has been implemented. This section will address the centrality of monitoring, evaluation and review in the change process primarily at setting level, but through an example of practice will also give consideration to monitoring change in children's progress.

Monitoring: the means chosen to measure and compare the effect of a particular change against agreed objectives and outcomes.

Monitoring

Once a strategy has been implemented, appropriate staff will need to monitor its progress. If plans are not monitored, it will not be possible to determine whether their objectives have been achieved. **Monitoring** will also enable leaders to obtain the best results from the available resources. The process of monitoring enables all staff to work towards agreed objectives. Developing as an early years community of practice is not something that can be made to happen from outside or even by the commitment of a few dedicated individuals. It requires ownership by all staff. It also requires willingness on the part of settings to look at their own practice and to identify areas where they could develop. In contrast to monitoring, evaluation encompasses reviewing the status of a plan's objectives. Through the evaluation process, leader practitioners will determine the need to change objectives, priorities and/or practice.

Monitoring provides the basis for evaluating practice. Leader practitioners will be able to measure and compare their performance against agreed criteria by providing an insight into the strengths and weaknesses of continuing with a particular change. Most significantly, monitoring will provide a framework in which staff can reflect on their own practice, an outcome of which is enhanced job satisfaction. Siraj-Blatchford and Manni (2007: 17) (Iram Siraj-Blatchford, Professor of Early Childhood Education at the Institute of Education, London and President of the British Association of Early Childhood Education, is renowned for her work on quality provision – through teaching, learning and leadership – in the early years; Laura Manni was formerly a Research Associate at the Institute of Education, London) suggest that a 'routine and consistent system of monitoring, assessment and collaborative dialogue encourages reflective practice' in early years settings. Monitoring is an ongoing activity and is integral to teaching and learning. It should not be left to the end of the year.

Monitoring must be based on practice and outcomes, and related to agreed criteria/set targets. Furthermore it should provide a framework in which practitioners can reflect on their own practice and professional needs. Everard et al. (2004: 284) (best known for his book on *Effective School Management*, now in its 4th edition, which he wrote with Geoffrey Morris, a business consultant, and Ian Wilson, an educator) underline the need for 'yardsticks' by which to recognise when the objectives have been achieved and which can be used 'to set a ratchet to prevent backsliding'. Effective monitoring, which also includes 'managing the processes needed to take corrective action in case of a shortfall' (Everard et al., 2004: 285), enables leaders to obtain the best results from the available resources.

Everard et al. further advocate setting up, 'as part of the overall plan for change', some means of both 'gathering reliable information and analysing it . . . in order to measure if the change has been effective and has become truly assimilated' (2004: 285). Improving outcomes for children is at the centre of the government's vision for early years and as such will be reflected in the 'yardsticks' selected to monitor the established change. Monitoring is as such, that each change needs to be monitored in light of its objectives and desired outcome. *The Study Support Code of Practice* (Wilson et al., 2004: 30), employed by extended schools, underlines certain questions which schools should consider when developing tools/techniques to measure the effectiveness of a service/activity/facility. The questions below have been adapted from this and offer a good framework for monitoring specific changes in early years settings.

1 Which outcomes do you wish to measure? (i.e. changes in behaviour, or attainment etc.)
2 What baseline evidence will be needed? How can this be obtained? What new systems need to be established? Who will be responsible?

Photo 20.2
Monitoring plans: how do you know the objectives have been met? (See the following What happens in practice?)

Pearson Education Ltd. Ian Wedgewood © Pearson Education Ltd. 2007

3 What evidence is there of the 'quality' of this change at different times? How does this inform future development?
4 How are the purposes and the results of the evidence collected discussed and shared?
5 How reliable or valid is the evidence that is available?
6 How is the evidence used and how are results analysed to inform learning in the future?
7 How might the skills of staff in using evaluation be developed?
8 How are results used to inform whole-setting planning and development?

The following examples of 'What happens in practice?' ask you to consider monitoring at the level of the child; monitoring change in children's progress is a common day-to-day practice, not only in early years settings, but as you will be aware, across all educational settings:

WHAT HAPPENS IN PRACTICE?

A Mia, aged three, has been in the nursery class for two terms. She is regularly found in the book area where she likes to pretend she is the teacher telling a story. She uses picture cues and memory to retell her favourite stories, and does so in great detail. She recognizes much of the environmental print around the nursery and the letters in her own name.

B   Harry, aged four, has just entered the Reception class. He has not attended any pre-school provision and is an only child. His mother is anxious about him starting school and this is very evident when she leaves him in the morning. He, in turn, is tearful every morning and clings to his mother.

   When she has gone, he continues to need the constant support of an adult and refuses to choose any activity independently. His interactions with the other children are very limited but he will talk at great length to an adult he trusts.

(Egersdorff, 2002: 144)

REFLECT AND RELATE TO PRACTICE

You may want to consider Standards S03, S29, S30, S31 and S32.

A   What are Mia's talents? What might you do to help her develop this? Select one of the ways you have decided to help her develop this further. Imagine you have implemented change. How would you monitor her progress?
     You need to consider the aims/objectives and how you might measure them against the outcomes and how frequently.

B   What are Harry's problems? How would you help him to overcome them? Select one of the ways you have decided to help him overcome the problem. Imagine you have implemented this change. How would you monitor his progress?

☆ ☆ ☆

A   Consider Mia's talents. List all the things you would consider to help her develop her talents. How would you implement them? How would you monitor her progress? How would you know if the strategies you had chosen were effective? You will need to review and reflect upon what you read within this section.

B   Consider Harry's problems. List all the issues and ways you would use to help him overcome these problems. How would you implement them? How would you monitor his progress? How would you know if the strategies you had chosen were effective?

Evaluation

Evaluation can often proceed simultaneously with the change programme; this should not be left until the end. Hall and Oldroyd (1990b) suggest that 'Evaluation is a component of development planning and an essential prerequisite to preparing any subsequent plan'. Everard et al. (2004: 285) suggest that evaluation will highlight any 'unforeseen consequences of the change' which can subsequently be managed or 'made the subject of further change'. Evaluation is a collaborative exercise involving:

Evaluation: reviewing the status of a plan's objectives, enabling practitioners/ leader practitioners to determine the need to change objectives, priorities and/or practice.

- asking questions
- gathering information
- forming conclusions

in order to:

- make recommendations.

In contrast to monitoring, evaluation encompasses reviewing the status of a plan's objectives. Through the evaluation process, leader practitioners will determine the need to change objectives, priorities and/or practice. Hargreaves and Hopkins (1991) (Professor David Hargreaves, Fellow of Wolfson College, Cambridge, has written extensively on education, from planning to personalising learning; Professor David Hopkins, former government Chief Adviser on School Standards, has written widely on school improvement, leadership and personalised learning) stress the importance of evaluation in enhancing the professional judgement of practitioners. Evaluation can therefore lead to a change in practitioners' perception of their practice.

CHECKLIST: EVALUATION

1 Purposes, broad guidelines, aims or objectives for the subject under scrutiny which are:
   - clear
   - indicators of desired performance or outcomes.
2 Questions which are:
   - unambiguous
   - penetrating
   - useful.
3 Information which is:
   - accessible
   - related to questions
   - not too voluminous to handle.
4 Conclusions which consider:
   - conditions
   - effects
   - assumptions
   - alternatives.
5 Reports which are:
   - concise
   - focused on audience's need
   - likely to inform decision-making.
6 A good evaluation brief:
   - specifying much of the above.

(Hall and Oldroyd, 1990a)

The final stage in the evaluation process is to write the report. It is important to consider the purposes of the report as required. Essentially the following aspects of the evaluation process need to be considered:

- purpose – of the evaluation
- content – what is being evaluated?
- process – how?
- context – why has the need for evaluation arisen?
- outcomes – were they achieved?

Before disseminating the report, reflect on each process and ensure that only necessary and relevant information is presented. Ask the following questions:

1 Who monitors the change?
2 How is the monitoring carried out?
3 How are all staff kept informed?
4 How is the evaluation carried out?
5 Who prepares the final report?

Setting: self-evaluation review

Setting self-evaluation is central to the Ofsted inspection process. However, it provides an effective means of bringing about change and should be carried out by settings irrespective of the inspection process. By outlining the framework, endorsed by the government for setting self-evaluation, this section encourages the reader to consider how effective self-evaluation leads into effective planning.

Whereas monitoring is an ongoing process and a means of checking progress, evaluation is an overall check on whether objectives are achieved within the planned timetable. Setting self-evaluation should be a collaborative process. The desire to achieve success is motivating; evaluation should focus on identifying strengths and weaknesses. From these, the key priorities for change will be identified and a plan of action to bring about improvement can be established (DfES, 2005). Settings need to diagnose precisely what needs to be done to improve on any weaknesses (DfES, 2005). In practice, external and internal accountability are central to educational and management practice. Early years settings can use the following questions as a framework for effective self-review:

- Does the self-evaluation identify how best our setting serves its learners?
- How does our setting compare with the best settings, and the best comparable settings?
- Is the self-evaluation integral to our key management systems?
- Is our setting's evaluation based on a good range of telling evidence?
- Does our self-evaluation and planning involve key people in the setting and seek the views of parents, learners and external advisers and agencies?
- Does our self-evaluation lead to action to achieve the setting's longer term goals for development?

(DfES, 2005: 7–10)

Self-evaluation is central to Ofsted's inspection framework. Since September 2008, settings are required to complete the *Early Years Self Evaluation Form* (Ofsted, 2008a) prior to inspection (this document, along with *Early Years Self-Evaluation Form Guidance* (Ofsted, 2008b), is available at: **www.ofsted.gov.uk**). Its focus is on the extent to which settings are delivering the outcomes of Every Child Matters (be healthy, stay safe, enjoy and achieve, make a positive contribution and achieve economic well-being), through the early learning goals and educational programmes of the Early Years Foundation Stage (personal, social and emotional development; communication, language and literacy; problem-solving, reasoning and numeracy; knowledge and understanding of the world; physical development; and creative development). Job descriptions, which give all staff greater role definition, enable staff to evaluate their contribution to the early years community. Evaluation is a component of development planning and an essential prerequisite to preparing any subsequent plan. Evaluation is a collaborative exercise involving asking questions, gathering information and forming conclusions in order to make recommendations.

Leading change: bringing it together

Vision: an overall view of what you envisage for the early years setting in the long term.

All settings are different; there is no blueprint for managing successful change in early years setting. Knowing the direction of the setting as expressed in its **vision** will enable future practice and frame the wider workforce to participate with a shared sense of purpose. Developing a collaborative approach to the management of change in an early years setting can be demanding and may call for a new focus. Sergiovanni (2007) gives the following example which is at the foundation of sustainable leadership:

> Imagine a leader who you personally admire because of her or his ability to handle people well. But you do not agree with this person's goals. Compare this leader with another who you may not even like very much but whose ideas make a great deal of sense to you.
>
> Which of the two leaders would you be more willing to follow? . . . Action is much more likely to result when leaders and followers are connected to each other by a commitment to common ideas.
>
> *(2007: 3)*

DISCUSSION POINT

How would you answer the following questions? (What you have read in this chapter will provide a strong foundation for considering these questions, but you will also need to reflect on both theory and practice.)

- How do leaders influence followers to pursue a course of action?
- How do followers identify with leaders?

- How do leaders 'frame' meaning and mobilize followers?
- How do leaders define a 'meaningful' course of action?

(Fink, 2005: 99)

SUMMARY

Change in early years: what does it mean? (p. 433)

What changes can those working within the early years expect in practice?

There is a greater focus in educational settings on the idea of developing communities of practice, which are characterised by social participation. Change in the early years means adopting policy and practice which promotes collaborative working with children, colleagues, parents and other relevant professionals.

Leaders and change (p. 435)

Would you support a collaborative approach to the management of change?

Change is brought about through top-down, bottom-up and expert initiatives or factors. The extent to which the change is effectively implemented, managed and evaluated will depend on the personal qualities and ability of the leader practitioner.

Analysis of change (p. 437)

How can an analysis of change at the outset influence its implementation, management and success?

Analysing the change process from the outset can have a big impact on the achievement of the desired outcomes. Some staff may be resistant to change. A consideration of why there is resistance can help leader practitioners to approach the change process appropriately, efficiently and effectively; building and developing relationships is central to practice in the early years.

Choosing a change strategy (p. 439)

What factors influence the choice of strategy?

Strategies for change can be directed, negotiated or action-centred. It is important for leader practitioners to consider the pace of change, the level of resistance, the level of status of the initiator, the amount of information required, the key players and the time available when choosing the most appropriate strategy to implement change.

Implementing change (p. 441)

How do you involve staff in the change process?

Settings have the necessary structures and tools to implement change which can be done through one of or a combination of the following: action research, training, participation and involvement, support, negotiation, co-option and coercion.

SUMMARY *CONTINUED*

Monitoring, evaluation and review (p. 445)

Why are monitoring, evaluation and review an important part of the change process?

Effective monitoring (comparing objectives to outcomes), evaluation (considering if the objectives are effective) and review (is the change working?) will enable leaders to obtain the best results from the change.

Setting: self-evaluation review (p. 450)

How does setting self-evaluation relate to and impact upon children's learning and development?

Setting self-evaluation should be central to practice. Evaluation will highlight opportunities for change which can bring major improvements in practitioner learning, involvement and practice. This in turn will lead to improved outcomes for children.

Glossary

Action research: involves the identification of a practical problem/issue which is changed through individual or collaborative action, then researched. The problems may not be clearly defined and the change process may evolve through practice.

'Bottom-up' change: change initiated by people, happenings or issues within the setting.

Capacity building: the provision of training or experience within a culture which encourages and promotes opportunity for learning and development.

Collegial approach: people working together as a team, sharing ideas, making decisions and deciding together how to implement the decisions made.

Communities of practice: in essence, communities of practice are characterised by social participation – the building of relationships (practitioner–child, child–child and parent–practitioner, etc.) through shared practice with common aims.

Evaluation: encompasses reviewing the status of a plan's objectives. Through the evaluation process, practitioners/leader practitioners will determine the need to change objectives, priorities and/or practice.

'Expert' change: change brought about by someone with expertise within the field. It could be another member of staff or an external agent.

Monitoring: the means chosen to measure and compare the effect of a particular change against agreed objectives and outcomes.

Personalised learning: the adaptation of teaching and the curriculum to meet the learning needs of the individual child. It is based on the collaborative approach of the practitioner, child and his/her parents or carers, where practitioners are continuously collecting and evaluating evidence of learning, with a view, through discussion with the child, of engaging him/her in his/her learning to achieve the best possible outcomes for the child both emotionally and academically.

'Top-down' change: change introduced by someone in a position of authority.

Vision: an overall view of what you envisage for the early years setting in the long term, i.e. where you would want it to be in ten years' time. The vision is usually expressed in a statement which would be reflected in the setting's aims and organisational practice.

Find out more

It would be good for your professional development and practice to read the government document, *National Standards for Leaders of SureStart Children's Centres* (DfES, 2007).

Her Majesty's Inspectorate of Education (HMIE) (2007) *Leadership for Learning: The challenges of leading in a time of change*, Livingstone, Scotland: HMIE.
This is a Scottish government document which addresses the challenges facing leaders of change – it is very informative in that it gives a broader view of some of the challenges discussed within this chapter, which are also faced by leaders of change across educational settings.

Fullan, M. (2008) *The Six Secrets of Change: What the Best Leaders Do to Help their Organisations Survive and Thrive*, San Francisco, CA: Jossey-Bass.
Michael Fullan is acknowledged as a world expert on change within organisations – businesses, educational settings, etc. This book gives good practical advice not only on how to manage change in organisations, but on how to make it work for the benefit of the organisation. Business models of success are now widely employed in education and it is important to be aware of what is happening in the business world.

References

Cheminais, R. (2006) *Every Child Matters: A Practical Guide for Teachers*. London: David Fulton.

Department for Education and Skills (DfES) (2005) *A New Relationship with Schools: Improving Performance through School Self-Evaluation*. London: DfES Publications.

Department for Education and Skills (DfES) (2007) *Statutory Framework for the Early Years Foundation Stage: Setting the Standards for Learning Development and Care for children from birth to five* (EYFS). Nottingham: DfES Publications.

Egersdorff, S. (2002) Monitoring, assessment, recording, reporting and accountability: the challenges for the Foundation stage teacher, in Keating, I. (ed.) *Achieving QTS Teaching Foundation Stage*. Exeter: Learning Matters.

Everard, K.B., Morris, G. and Wilson, I. (2004) *Effective School Management*, 4th edn. London: Paul Chapman.

Fink, D. (2005) *Leadership for Mortals: Developing and sustaining leaders of learning*. London: Paul Chapman.

Fullan, M. (2005) *Leadership and sustainability: System Thinkers in action*. Thousand Oaks, CA: Corwin Press and Ontario Principals Council.

Hall, V. and Oldroyd, D. (1990a) *Management Self-development for Staff in Secondary Schools, Unit 1: Self-development for effective management*. Bristol: NDCEMP.

Hall, V. and Oldroyd, D. (1990b) *Management Self-development for Staff in Secondary Schools, Unit 2: Policy, Planning and Change* Bristol: NDCEMP.

Hargreaves, D.H. and Hopkins, D. (1991) School effectiveness, school improvement and development planning, in Preedy, M. (ed.) *Managing the Effective School*. London: Paul Chapman.

Harris, A. and Muijs, D. (2005) *Improving Schools Through Teacher Leadership*. Maidenhead: Open University Press.

Keating, I. (2002) Working with parents and other carers: enhancing learning opportunities, in Keating, I. (ed.) *Achieving QTS Teaching Foundation Stage*. Exeter, Learning Matters: pp. 18–30.

Ofsted (2008a) *Early Years Self Evaluation Form*. London: Ofsted; available at: **www.ofsted.gov.uk**.

Ofsted (2008b) *Early Years Self-Evaluation Form Guidance*. London: Ofsted; available at: **www.ofsted.gov.uk**.

Oldroyd, D. and Hall, V. (1990) *Management Self-Development for Staff in Secondary Schools*. Bristol: NDCEMP.

Preedy, M. (1991) *Managing the Effective School*. London: Paul Chapman.

Rodd, J. (2006) *Leadership in Early Childhood*. Maidenhead: Open University Press.

Rodger, R. (2003) *Planning on Appropriate Curriculum for the Under Fives: A Guide for Students, Teachers and Assistants*. London: David Fulton.

Sadek, E. and Sadek, J. (2004) *Good Practice in Nursery Management*, 2nd edn. Cheltenham: Nelson Thornes.

Sergiovanni, T. (2000) *The Lifeworld of Leadership*. London: Jossey-Bass.

Sergiovanni, T. (2007) *Rethinking Leadership: a collection of articles*. Thousand Oaks, CA: Sage.

Siraj-Blatchford, I. and Manni, L. (2007) *Effective Leadership in the Early Years Sector: the ELEYS study*. London: Institute of Education.

Wenger, E. (1998) *Communities of Practice: Learning, Meaning and Identity*. Cambridge: Cambridge University Press.

Wilson, D., Gammie, H. and Moore, J. (2004) *The Study Support Code of Practice: A Guide for Schools*. Nottingham: DfES Publications.

Appendix 1

Early Years Professional Standards	Standard	Content/Outcome	Evidence
Knowledge and Understanding	SO1 Early Years Foundation Stage	Understanding of EYPS	Practice
	SO2 Children's Development	Birth to thereafter	Practice and management
	SO3 Behaviour and Environment	Impact on development	Practice and management
	SO4 Statutory and non-Statutory	Implications for practice	Practice and management
	SO5 Legal requirements and policies	Framework for practice	Management
	SO6 Other professionals	Contributions to development	Practice and management
Effective Practice	SO7 High expectations	Achievement	Practice and management
	SO8 Safe and warm envornment	Children feel confident and secure	Practice and management
	SO9 Routine	Balanced and flexible programme	Practice and management
	SO10 Obseravtion and development	Planned progression	Practice and management
	SO11 Play	Children and adult-led activities	Practice and management
	SO12 Resources appropriate to age	Resources reflecting ages and abilities	Practice and management

Early Years Professional Standards	Standard	Content/Outcome	Evidence
	SO13 Personalised provision	Individual schedules	Management
	SO14 Personal response	Identify how to respond to children	Practice
	SO15 Language and Communication	Support development	Practice and management
	SO16 Shared thinking	Engage in thinking	Practice
	SO17 Promote positive behaviour	Develop childrens internal and external mechanisms	Practice
	SO18 Promote children's rights	Inclusive practices	Practice and management
	SO19 Safe environment	Promote well-being	Practice and management
	SO20 Recognise danger and harm	Act to protect children	Practice
	SO21 Assess, record and report	Use to develop children	Practice and management
	SO22 Feedback	Constructive and sensitive	Practice and management
	SO23 Personal circumstances	Identify and support when there are problems	Practice and management
	SO24 Quality	Be accountable for provision	Management
Relationships with Children	SO25 Constructive relationships	Fair, respectful and trusting with children	Practice
	SO26 Communicate	Age appropriate	Practice
	SO27 Listen and value	Pay attention to children	Practice
	SO28 Positive values, attitudes and behaviours	Demonstrate what is expected	Practice

Early Years Professional Standards	Standard	Content/Outcome	Evidence
Communicating and working in partnership with families and carers	SO29 Respect parents and carers	Recognise contribution	Practice and management
	SO30 Positive relationships with parents and carers	Trust – fairness and respecting	Practice and management
	SO31 Work in partnership	Settle and nurture children together	Practice and management
	SO32 Share information	Informal and formal opportunities	Practice and management
Teamwork and Collaboration	SO33 Collaborate and cooperate	Create a collaborative culture	Practice and management
	SO34 Work with collegaues	Share understandings about children	Practice
	SO35 Policies and practicies	Influence and shape practice	Practice and management
	SO36 Multi-professional practice	Shared practice and interventions	Practice and management
Professional development	SO37 Literacy, numeracy and ICT	Develop skills and use with children	Practice
	SO38 Self-management	Reflect on needs and identify response	Practice and management
	SO39 Innovate	Be creative and constructive	Practice

Based on Early Years Standards, The Department for Children, Schools and Families

Index

Page numbers in *italics* denotes glossary entry